How Social Science Got Better

How Social Science Got Better

Overcoming Bias with More Evidence, Diversity, and Self-Reflection

MATT GROSSMANN

OXFORD
UNIVERSITY PRESS

OXFORD
UNIVERSITY PRESS

Oxford University Press is a department of the University of Oxford. It furthers
the University's objective of excellence in research, scholarship, and education
by publishing worldwide. Oxford is a registered trade mark of Oxford University
Press in the UK and certain other countries.

Published in the United States of America by Oxford University Press
198 Madison Avenue, New York, NY 10016, United States of America.

Library of Congress Cataloging-in-Publication Data
Names: Grossmann, Matthew, author.
Title: How social science got better : overcoming bias with more evidence,
diversity, and self-reflection / Matt Grossmann, Michigan State University.
Description: New York, NY : Oxford University Press, [2021] |
Includes bibliographical references and index.
Identifiers: LCCN 2021017324 (print) | LCCN 2021017325 (ebook) |
ISBN 9780197518977 (hardback) | ISBN 9780197518991 (epub) |
ISBN 9780197519004
Subjects: LCSH: Social sciences—Research. | Social sciences—Methodology.
Classification: LCC H62 .G79 2021 (print) | LCC H62 (ebook) | DDC 300.72—dc23
LC record available at https://lccn.loc.gov/2021017324
LC ebook record available at https://lccn.loc.gov/2021017325

DOI: 10.1093/oso/9780197518977.001.0001

1 3 5 7 9 8 6 4 2

Printed by LSC communications, United States of America

In Memory of Steven J. Kautz

CONTENTS

PREFACE

Social science research is facing mounting criticism, as canonical studies fail to replicate, questionable research practices abound, and researcher political biases come under fire. Unpredicted high-profile events, from the election of Donald Trump to the Great Recession, undermine faith in social science knowledge just as research increasingly becomes fodder for polarized public debates.

Great news lies beneath the headlines. Far from being in crisis, social science is undergoing an unparalleled renaissance of ever-broader and deeper understanding and application—made possible by close attention to criticism of researcher biases and open public engagement. This book tells that story. In a sea of pessimism about academia and public knowledge, it promises an optimistic counternarrative. It documents and explains recent transformations, crediting both internal and public critics for strengthening social science.

Scholarly wars between scientists and their humanist critics, methodological disputes over statistical practice and qualitative research, and disciplinary battles over grand theories of human nature have all quietly died down as new generations of scholars have integrated the insights of all sides. Rather than deny that researcher biases affect results, scholars now closely analyze how our racial, gender, geographic, methodological, and political differences impact our research questions; how the incentives of academia influence our research practices; and how universal human desires to avoid uncomfortable truths and easily solve problems affect our conclusions. Ours is an unprecedented age of theoretical diversity, open and connected data, and interdisciplinary public scholarship. Contemporary social science provokes an informed revisiting of fundamental questions, enables a combination of diverse knowledge to tackle social challenges, and fuels the industries, social arrangements, and technologies of the future.

Ongoing critiques of the capacity of social science reflect the classic challenges raised by its philosophy, sociology, and history. Because humans are both the subject and object of study, social science is concentrated on currently relevant concerns, driven by our collective assumptions and aspirations, and affected by our many demographic, institutional, and ideological biases. Rather than an unconstrained search for truth, widely accepted answers often reflect idiosyncratic disciplinary histories, scholarly needs for self-justification and career advancement, and plans for immediate application. Scholars who traditionally raised these objections came from outside social science or from its most qualitative and interpretivist corners. Not anymore. Progress in multi-method research, openness to critique in the wake of prominent failures, and advances in science metrics and research availability have all brought these concerns to the center of social scientific debates, stimulating practical awareness and proliferating proposed reforms.

Recent revolutions in social science practice have made data and results more widely available, moved from esoteric theory to fine-tuned social regularities, spread methods of causal inference and generalization, and revisited orthodox findings to ensure reproducibility. Broader and more diverse teams sharing data and honing designs have replaced staid assumptions and elaborate constructions by siloed researchers. Reactions to each revolution have tempered overclaiming victors and pinpointed the contributions of new methods alongside perennial lessons. Social science has emerged less blinded by its biases but more aware of its limitations.

Given the advance of data and more efficient searches for information, progress is inevitable as long as new material is pursued with an acknowledgment of its incompleteness and awareness of our biases in interpretation. We can be made worse off by more knowledge only if we overhype its contribution so much that we lose track of what we still do not know. That does not mean we will fully answer the most important questions, but it does make us well positioned for at least incremental gains.

Further advance will require close attention to the perennial challenges of social science—from individual research practices to collective social and political constraints to the translation of knowledge through popularization and application. We must embrace the importance of these fundamental difficulties, not deny their importance. Myriad research biases, some arising from scholars' distinct social profiles and others endemic to human nature, affect our questions, methods, and conclusions. Although institutional reforms can be helpful, there is no easy way out of our inherently partial view of ourselves. More complete understanding requires researchers to consider knowledge across social science disciplines (as well as from adjacent natural sciences and humanities), both in the joint process of discovery and in research communication through public life. We can neither escape the motivations tied to our temporal, national, and institutional contexts nor assume a disembodied view from nowhere. The only road forward is understanding our biases to partially remediate and overcome them. Though unheralded thus far, social scientists are successfully following that path.

How Social Science Got Better offers an overview of these trends and strategies for addressing the biases of social science. It is aimed at scholars across the social sciences, outsiders with broad research interests, and general readers following social science controversies and wishing for insights on contemporary problems. Although the book mentions many methods and details some research literatures, it can serve neither as a guide to implementing statistical procedures nor as a compendium of research findings. It offers brief definitions, but fuller explanations are often relegated to footnotes and references. Readers unfamiliar with a term or a research topic can choose to follow up or just continue in hopes of later reaching more familiar examples. The key lessons should be accessible, beginning with the importance of self-evaluation of our perspective.

Miles's Law for Social Science

Rufus Miles, a federal administrator under three presidents, created the aphoristic "law" that states: "where you stand depends on where you sit."[1] After one of his subordinates changed jobs from the Bureau of the Budget to a programmatic agency, his views also shifted dramatically, moving from a vocal opponent of funding for that agency to its biggest proponent. Miles was unsurprised. Whether or not it was a conscious reevaluation, being surrounded by new people and information—and acquiring different motivations—had produced a 180-degree turn. One's aspirations, favored understandings, sense of importance, and core beliefs all can shift with one's institutional position. Fully characterizing someone's point of view, incorporating their evidence but acknowledging its biases, requires attention to their position.

The idea has since been generalized and widely applied. Human social views (and behavior) arise from the institutions in which people live and work, especially when those settings create incentives for particular beliefs, priorities, or justifications. Even in the budgetary context where it developed, that hardly means that known-to-be-biased views cannot be solicited. It certainly does not imply that no resources can be more efficiently allocated because all views are suspect. Instead, it suggests that awareness of likely biases (and the built-in incentives producing them) is a critical step in evaluating information and advice. Where institutions can correct or re-incentivize these biases, reforms are welcome. Yet there is no substitute for articulating and managing the biases, including those specific to particular individuals and those that arise within each domain of social life.

Humans can understand their own biases in part by taking other perspectives, whether or not they choose to correct for them. For example, I recognize that when I am a driver on my university campus, I am more likely to complain about rules violations and impoliteness by the walkers and the bikers; then as a walker, I complain more about the drivers and bikers threatening my safety; and then later as a biker, I am annoyed more by those on foot and in cars. We cannot always take on three different roles as in this illustration, but we can work to recognize that our perspective changes with our circumstances—and perhaps give the walkers, bikers, and drivers more benefit of the doubt. This view is usually called perspectivism; it analogizes differences in visual perspectives based on our physical position with variation in our go-to explanations based on our social position.

Like everyone else, I lack an unbiased view of social science and draw from my position. I am hopeful that my particular mix of biases and experiences can offer a useful perspective on the state of social science. As the author, I owe the reader an account of my particular biases and where they might lead me to focus. This preface will serve the role of a positionality statement (sometimes called a reflexivity statement) that outlines how my own social position may affect the research I undertake here. These statements are commonly used in qualitative research but could be more widely adopted. In addition to highlighting my personal characteristics and my setting, I focus on the large role of my discipline and research focus in defining my point of view.

A Political Science Take on Social Research

I write as a practitioner of social science who is attempting to apply the insights of its history, philosophy, and sociology to contemporary research practices. I am by no means an authority on these meta-scientific concerns, instead coming out of the long tradition of social scientists commenting on trends in their field— and seeing the need to return to fundamental questions about the goals and structures of academia and the social scientific enterprise.

My own discipline, political science, is a useful vantage point for the work because it relies on the other social science disciplines and combines their stronger priors on human nature. It studies politics and government, but is open to the important roles played by individual psychology, social institutions, economic markets, and human cultures. Each discipline has specific biases, but I see it as better to understand and attempt to correct for them through integration, rather than to lose the advantages of communities in critical conversation, including incentives for self-policing.[2]

Political science occupies a moderate position in the social sciences between emphasizing individual agency and social structure; we see a voter, for example, being affected by both her own beliefs and the party system she inhabits. The discipline recognizes humans responding to universal human impulses, mental predispositions, market incentives, and social structures. It is attentive to developments in psychology, sociology, and economics (drawing less from anthropology) and is both a basic science and tied to many applied fields. It also has long combined qualitative history, normative and empirical theory, policy-relevant analysis, and empirical hypothesis testing. It is united mainly by its dependent variables: what kinds of behavior (political) and institutions (government) to study. Like much of social science, it is also infected by the motivations of practice: the desire to do something to change the world, rather than merely understand it. Political scientists seek better governance and attend to current policy and social problems, but our motivations are diverse.

There is not even full agreement on the discipline's name. Reflecting the common nonchalant dismissal of the field's rigor, the "science" part is often put in scare quotes. At the Claremont Colleges, where I was an undergraduate, the major is known as "government" at the more conservative Claremont McKenna College, "politics" at Pomona and Scripps colleges, and "political studies" at the child-of-the-1960s Pitzer College. Political science was long taught to undergraduates primarily as civics, with some history, legal rules, and geography, while being taught to graduate students as a field made up of economic modeling and applied statistics. It is familiar with a variety of approaches and the often wide gaps between research, teaching, and practice.

Political science has never been more important to the human endeavor. But its applications are inherently politicized. The technologies that it enables are institutions, social strategies, and policies, rather than the physical tools that the public more readily accepts as innovations. Implementation of expert consensus in political systems may also conflict with other democratic values, so our goal cannot always be quick adoption of reforms suggested by our findings. We are (correctly) seen as offering a biased perspective based on incomplete evidence and particular points of view, but that does not make us unique as scholars. Astronomers know that they are studying universes from the vantage point of a particular planet surrounding an insignificant star. Anthropologists know that they are analyzing human history based on a few distinctive groups, incomplete physical remains, and analogies to distantly related species. Medical researchers conduct studies on mice and fruit flies as human models, without knowing how applicable they will be.

Political science has not generated the same public acclaim as the natural sciences. But that is not due to lack of popularity; the public often became aware of and interested in political science findings before other types of statistics, for example, from public opinion polling to government social indicators.[3] The rise of social science in the public mind was not about the acceptance of its objectivity, but due to the public's interest in self-understanding, especially the symbolic value of the "average" person and deviations from it.[4] As social statistics and social science explanations were immediately injected in public debates and political questions, they were also subject to public disputation and conflict.[5] Political science is not a failed or impossible project, even in the public mind, but it is definitely a politicized one from the beginning, with reaction to its latest products (such as presidential election forecasting models) part of the ambivalent public response to our increasingly information-driven age.[6]

In the last few decades, political science has advanced with a proliferation of data and methods and integration of diverse views. Political science conferences and journals have gone from reviewing the same election surveys and governing institution data, using many of the same concepts and tools (often borrowed from economics), to an endless variety in data sources, methods, theoretical views, and subjects. The data compilations, theoretical specificity, and causal identification strategies grow with each new round of graduate students and junior faculty.[7] Compared to a discipline like economics (where scholars agree more on questions, methods, and journals), political science remains more diverse and less oriented toward consensus. That can look messy, but also means political science has fewer collective blind spots that escape anyone's attention. But compared to sociology, political science has far more agreement on the topics of shared interest. That means different perspectives are often brought into conversation about the same historical events or even used to analyze the same agreed-upon data.

Political science was historically a compilation of many research traditions, with moral, applied, and scientific motivations.[8] Political science is dependent on all the other disciplines, but that does not mean it was last historically: it was often the first impulse in social science, as scientific tools were developed to administer early states, justify competing social aims, and optimize policy. Political science has ordered our subfields differently over time, but has consistently been interested in political ideas, comparisons across societies, and institutional development. There have been various shifts in intellectual effort—simplified as a (too-neat) historical trajectory from institutional analysis to behavioralism to rational choice theory—but we are well into a period with many different overlapping theoretical frameworks rather than one dominant paradigm.[9]

A majority of work published in top journals has long been empirical, with a smaller share oriented toward normative scholarship; the main trends in journals are the rise and decline of purely theoretical models and the long decline of scholarship framed as policy recommendations.[10] Empiricism has thus advanced over both theoretical construction and normative application. Most recently, major political science journals have begun to accept short (mostly empirical) articles more similar to those from the natural sciences, while several have added requirements for sharing data and replication materials. The dominant form of political science remains empirical research to assess theories of moderate scope, but we have never lost minority interests in normative philosophy, broad theoretical modeling, applied work, or qualitative history.

The globalization and expansion of political science have also increased topical diversity. Proliferating organized sections of political science associations have faced scorn but are now mostly celebrated as signs of diversity.[11] Many subfields within the discipline report feelings of marginalization or balkanization, but these complaints are often due to the disappearance of any shared disciplinary center (given increasing topical diversity). Theory, methods, and applications are now more interconnected, with multi-method research rising and more interdisciplinary reviews. The discipline now shows more attention to the relationship between theoretical schemes and empirical designs, to the validation and reliability of measures, to cross-sectional and time series variation at once, to replication, to causal inference, and to its relevance to contemporary concerns.

A recent relitigating of the debates over political science's relevance, concentrated in international relations and American foreign policy, was mostly met with derision.[12] The examples of the supposed Golden Era—with Henry Kissinger at the president's ear—had not changed since the same concerns were raised in the 1990s, but the complaints were now much further off the mark. Political science now speaks to popular, media, and policymaker audiences, with scholarly training opportunities, organizations and networks to serve as intermediaries, and many scholars prioritizing public engagement.

But we still lack a shared sense of our craft. A recent philosophy of social science book had entries for each discipline, but the political science chapter was called "Why Is There No Philosophy of Political Science?"[13] The discipline considers many philosophical ideas, the authors reasoned, but it does not have much interest in disciplinary history or the philosophy of its methods (despite having—or perhaps because it has—traditional philosophers). This choice might be born of a healthy skepticism of the discipline's potential and the many contested implications of our findings. Another analysis found that the philosophy of political science has always been vague because the subjects of research change over time and there is nothing that distinguishes political science other than what differentiates social science overall.[14]

The social sciences as a whole can thus learn from political science. A primary task of scholars, Max Weber thought, was to recognize inconvenient facts for their own political positions (advice he did not consistently follow).[15] Scholarship was organized into special disciplines in the service of self-clarification and the assumption of interrelated knowledge in each field; but views of our motives and the assumed connections among ideas were born of our historical context. One inclination was to try to divorce scholars from what they studied, emulating natural science. Another was to incorporate various standpoints, using critical reflection to "identify social desires, interests, and values that have shaped the agendas, contents, and results of the sciences."[16]

But political science has mostly followed a middle ground between skepticism and scientism, assuming that scholars are collectively on a biased search for truth. Much of the objectivity pretense in our methodological development is based on an earnest recognition that our biases creep into our research and that we seek and observe confirmation, making us reliant on the precision of claims as well as hard tests policed via community standards. We can be simultaneously committed to scientific virtues of clarity, empiricism, and reasoning; realist about our ability to achieve full explanations; and open to contingency and heterogeneity in views of the same data.[17] An effort to be objective, even if failed, can help the discipline collectively advance knowledge. Integrating micro-, meso-, and macro-level influences and short- and long-term causal mechanisms is also a strength of the discipline, as is its intent to reconcile these theories at different levels of analysis and time scales.

The many political scientists I interviewed for the book shared this view of the discipline's position.[18] Harvard political scientist Gary King, who oversees an interdisciplinary social science institute, told me that political science was the most intellectually diverse discipline. We have repeatedly "hedged our bets," he pointed out, integrating the latest theoretical and empirical approaches from other disciplines without fully committing to any of them. Columbia political scientist Andrew Gelman, who is also active in statistical debates throughout the social sciences, said political scientists were much more aware of disputes and tools in other social science fields. Both said we adopt reforms and trends more slowly than elsewhere, after deliberation.

My Vantage Point

I approach this book as a close observer and applier of disciplinary trends in progress, not as a committed reformer. My institution, Michigan State University, is a large land-grant state school in the Midwest. Political science has long been practiced here in a data-intensive and practical mode, but it has lately become more pluralist in interests and research strategies. I serve as director of a policy institute with a long applied history, aiding state government and all of the social science disciplines. I am more interdisciplinary in interests and views than most social scientists. I am a mid-career scholar, who has observed significant change in the two decades since I began graduate school. This book grew out of the generational change I observed. Over a short period, for example, colleagues who began as rational choice adherents with constrained views of the scope of the discipline became far more pluralist in their theories and wide-ranging in their research.

As I review recent trends in data availability, theoretical and methodological pluralism, and public engagement in the pages that follow, I do it from the perspective of one scholar observing change first in his own discipline. My optimism was first born of my positive view of trends in my discipline and across the social sciences at my university. My scholarship has long drawn from qualitative history as well as quantitative analysis, using theories from sociology, psychology, and economics. I am hardly making advances at the methodological frontier, but I am attentive to developments throughout the spectrum: from state-of-the-art methods of causal inference to generalizable global data to qualitative narratives. Part of my optimism is seeing progress in acknowledging and alleviating bias in all of these areas, even by those without ideal data.

I am also a very public scholar, having taken on roles in state and national politics and media. I am one of the most active promoters of social science research on podcasts, to reporters, and on Twitter. Others raise legitimate complaints about popularization (addressed in Chapter 10), but I have seen this as a tremendous boon to social science research and its application.

These are not my only biases that should be considered. I primarily study contemporary politics in my own country, the United States, and I am a well-off white man. Although I have tried to draw from diverse examples, I inevitably draw more from the unrepresentative topics I know best. This book reviews the biases in social science research that arise from our unrepresentative racial and gender makeup (in Chapter 4) and our American national focus (in Chapter 5). One of the inspirations for this book is watching how growing diversity in the social sciences is changing the questions we ask, the assumptions we make, and the interpretations of our results. Racial, gender, and global geographic diversity of researchers and research audiences have helped us understand where our theories and findings were more limited than we thought.

Scholars' political views have also gained research attention. Social scientists are overwhelmingly ideologically liberal and politically affiliated with parties to the left of center (see Chapter 8). But we are also economically and socially successful professionals reliant on government and philanthropy, giving us some conservatizing incentives to maintain existing institutions. I am personally now liberal in many ways, but I grew up in conservative politics and remain to the right of most social scientists in ideological predispositions (if not policy positions). I have studied and criticized the conservative movement's long-running attack on scholars as ideologues, but also joined efforts to increase political diversity and attentiveness to conservative critiques in academia.

I am thus no less biased than other human beings, including scholars, and my comments should be contextualized through my history, institutional and cultural position, and prior views. But I do have some atypical biases from those of other scholars and a willingness to delve deeply into the philosophy, history, and sociology of science to understand how they affect my understanding and our collective enterprise. Although our view of ourselves is forever incomplete, we understand more about how and why our focus narrows and how to discover and counteract our biases.

Rather than assume a disinterested posture or a disembodied view, I wanted the reader to know where I sit. But the trends and concerns I document here are widespread in the social sciences. They require engagement with diverse communities to evaluate and refine. That is the journey this book begins. There is danger in taking on too much, but it has to be weighed against the lack of integration in most of academic research. The opening I see is linking the innovation taking place among practicing social scientists with the big-picture interests of meta-scientific fields.

Although I do report the results of an original survey of social scientists, interviews, and institutional data, my primary goal is to synthesize and apply existing research findings. I draw from history, philosophy, and sociology of science, as well as Science and Technology Studies (STS) and higher education research, to understand the long-standing dilemmas of social science and to update social scientists on recent advances. But I apply these fundamental topics to recent research trends in five large disciplines: economics, political science, sociology, psychology, and anthropology. I cannot hope to be comprehensive in these reviews, of course, but I privilege breadth, including understanding the links between these core social sciences and other fields. I seek to be responsive to proposals for reform and change, in the scientific process and in academic institutions, but I do not presume that wholesale revision is forthcoming.

Like social science as a whole, this book requires a balance between universal and eternal interests and specific tools and trajectories. Philosophy of social science points us toward fundamental concerns but can get lost in difficult-to-apply ideal notions. History of social science reminds us of our initial aspirations and repeated blind spots but can be diverted from everyday progress by the largest controversies. Sociology of social science (and related STS) reveals how real-world research programs evolve in their surroundings but can privilege critique over understanding the slow development of partial and specific truths. Research on the American university system and the core social science disciplines provides the context for contemporary research but can divert us from the frontier of globalized and interdisciplinary research. The path trod here tries to combine their broad insights for researchers working to advance our understanding of human social life in particular arenas.

The COVID-19 pandemic has reminded us again of the importance of getting social science right. Studies of politics, administration, markets, cultures, social norms, and beliefs have all been important in understanding the spread and effects of the disease and in guiding policy and practice. Attention to social variables, such as partisanship and inequality, has been critical. Social science will remain important as we vaccinate the world and rebuild. Its subjects are critical, as are its methods of combining disparate data and incomplete theory on trends in progress. The pandemic did also stimulate studies of lower quality by those with limited expertise, but they also stimulated effective pushback. Critics often confuse dissensus on applications of social science knowledge for limited knowledge itself. But applications are often in policy or messaging, not technology, and thus require public and elite assent. Documenting polarization in pandemic responses is an advance, even if it does not lead policymakers to correct it. Social science is even useful for learning when knowledge is applied and when it is ignored (from masking advice to vaccine prioritization).

Improvements in social science and its applications likely require changes in scholarly behavior alongside improved understanding. I embrace reforms that increase the credibility of research and inference and improve the diversity of theoretical ideas and the sophistication of methodological tools available to social scientists. Not all changes yield fruit, but even incremental gains should be celebrated. Sometimes scholars learn that they only know a little more than previous generations (or that what they thought they knew turned out to describe only particular circumstances). By both recognizing the endemic challenges social scientists face and taking advantage of our newest tools of self-understanding and knowledge cumulation, social science can learn more and better inform collective decisions.

Plan of the Book

How Social Science Got Better pursues a broad look at social science advancement through the lens of efforts to recognize and address researcher biases. The structure moves from classic critiques of the possibility of social science to the particular institutions and disciplines where it currently operates, next to thinking through explanations for social life across time and place, and finally to considering how social science enters public consciousness and practical affairs. It does therefore sacrifice some depth for breadth in the service of synthesizing across the dominant concerns about social science. But I concentrate on the effects of trends in social science and academia on knowledge generation, rather than career outcomes or education. The intent is to study the scientific process, rather than navel-gazing about professional constraints.

Chapter 1 argues that understanding, investigating, and adapting to the biases inherent in social science research is the best path toward accumulating and advancing social science knowledge. It reviews many categories of bias facing social science, from those stemming from unrepresentative researcher demographics to those based on research practices and incentives. Each bias has implications for research practices, but none makes social science impossible. Scholars face inherent challenges larger than those of natural scientists, with more disagreement on the most important biases to address and the kinds of research necessary to do so. But there are important advances in scholars' self-understanding that can serve as the basis for our future progress.

Chapter 2 addresses the role of social science reform, focusing on research documenting problems of replication and proposed open science practices. The associated debates have drawn attention to the biases involved in research and to the misaligned professional incentives that perpetuate them. The reform efforts have made considerable progress quickly, in self-understanding and even in changing research practices. Where it has gone too far in emphasizing experimental methodologies for testing of causal hypotheses, reformers and critics alike have promoted procedures that reflect social science diversity and acknowledge the importance of self-conscious exploratory work. In the process, several social science revolutions have made shared progress more likely: middle-range empiricism has risen over grand theory; open and big data have stimulated new work while enabling cross-checking; new causal identification strategies have enabled observational work to speak to experimental concerns; and the rise of team science has forced us to reconcile theoretical perspectives and build on individual strengths.

Chapter 3 reviews the "science wars" and their surprisingly quiet resolution. Throughout the 1980s and 1990s, critics of science from humanities disciplines fought with scientists over the extent to which science is a social and biased process or a path to truth. Today, there are few absolute relativists or adherents of scientific purity and far more acknowledgment that science involves biased truth-seeking. Continuing (but less vicious) wars over Bayesian and frequentist statistics likewise ignore some key agreements: tests of scientific claims require clarifying assumptions and some way to account for confirmation bias, either by building it into the model or by establishing more severe tests for the sufficiency of evidence. This sedation was accompanied by shifts within social science disciplines. Debates over both simplistic models of human nature (especially over rational choice theory) and what constituted proper quantitative and qualitative methods died down as nearly everyone became theoretically and methodologically pluralist in practice. I herald this evolution, pointing to its benefits in the topics we cover, the ideas we consider, the evidence we generate, and how we evaluate and integrate our knowledge.

Chapter 4 assesses the most commonly cited distinct difficulty of social science compared to science in general: we are studying ourselves. Problems associated with focusing on our own species inside its social institutions have long animated philosophy of social science, but most thinkers have evolved toward a contemporary scientific realism on this point: there are biases, but they can be managed with close attention. Beyond perennial difficulties of self-knowledge, scholars tend to study their own time period, countries, and social groups, introducing additional biases while enabling research on how they affect our questions, methods, and interpretations. This often leads to accusations of "me-search," especially by underrepresented minorities. But many of the same considerations that drive those critiques and their responses apply to scholars studying their own countries and time periods, and to all of us studying our own species. I argue that the successful history of racial and gender studies (and the responses to them within traditional social science disciplines) shows that progress requires acknowledgment of biases and diversification of viewpoints.

Chapter 5 moves to the specific institution where social science is practiced: academia—especially in the United States. Social science is slowly internationalizing, with more cross-national collaboration. Yet the American university system still accounts for a large share of social science and is the primary home for debates about its future. Despite constant claims of crisis, US universities are a stable and competitive global industry. Social science is doing well within American universities and expanding globally, but often doing so by enlarging applied rather than basic fields. Most research takes place in the current academic context, requiring attention to the recent history and incentives of universities. Chapter 5 uses Cold War social science as a window into related biases and successful efforts to overcome them. It then considers how new academic challenges, such as the declining market for tenure-track faculty positions and increasing grant-chasing incentives, are liable to influence contemporary work.

Chapter 6 then reviews the effects of our disciplinary structure, including the constraints it places on research and the challenges of interdisciplinarity. The basic social science disciplines—political science, economics, sociology, psychology, and anthropology—each tend toward a particular view of human nature and have disciplinary prejudices regarding topics and methods. Interdisciplinary work has identified these differences and worked toward integration, especially in common applied fields, such as education and public policy. Chapter 6 reviews each discipline's historical inheritance and how it shapes contemporary practice. Rather than advocating a dismantling or reformulation of disciplines, I argue that strong and self-aware disciplines with scholarly exchange among them have advanced theory and empirical analysis.

Chapter 7 moves the discussion to human agency and social structure. I argue that explanations for human behavior often involve factors operating at multiple levels of analysis (from individuals to organizations to nations) across different time scales (immediate, developmental, and evolutionary). Continuing debates over methodological individualism within the social sciences ignore the growing consensus within philosophy of social science that influences on social life are present across individual and collective units, each with influential histories. Even if models of individual interaction offer useful templates, they do not imply that any social process started anew at any particular point in time or that individuals created social structures without also being influenced by prior groups and institutions. Using a comparison of traffic and weather, I argue that these difficulties are no worse for social than for natural science, once we welcome both simple patterns and complex multilevel processes. In both cases, lots of progress is made simply through observational generalization and many complaints involve our ability to change the world, not understand it.

Chapter 8 returns to the origins of social science to think through its relationships to other methods of generating social knowledge. Social science originated in the study of history and the desire to inform collective decisions, with often contentious efforts by budding social scientists to separate themselves in organization and status from historians and social reformers. Despite active distancing from this inheritance, social scientists are still limited by both the variation available from human history and the usefulness of our findings in policy. We are all searching for patterns across the times we can observe and subject to the goals of our societies (and our own unrepresentative political goals). Since the contemporary context affects our questions and interpretations, we can acknowledge our reformist impulses as well as learn from historians' approaches to counteracting presentism. I argue that we erred in thinking of our enterprise as fundamentally distinct: social scientists should accept our role in systematizing history and informing policy debate, rather than seeking to replace either.

Chapter 9 discusses the difficulties of conducting research with inevitable considerations for practice. The basic social sciences did not develop independently and later seek application; the practical motivations that animate scholarly chronologies in many subjects are inescapable. Historical investigations also show plenty of distasteful origins, including the consistent role of American social science in promoting eugenics. That matters not just for how we interpret the past, but also how we address the motivations driving us today. It is easier to see how the racist impulses of the past drove misinterpretations of evidence and poor design—but that epiphany enables a review of how our own motivations (new and perennial) continue to bias research. From finance to information technology, the rising industries of today are built on social science but tempted by triumphalism. Scholars are driven by proving our studies useful—in ways that can both uphold existing institutions and transform them. An acknowledgment of our evolving social, economic, and political goals can help address scholarly biases.

Chapter 10 addresses how social science makes its way into public debate, with worries about publicity-seeking scholarship but also potential benefits for engagement across disciplines and society. Social science debates are no longer, if they ever were, confined to universities and obscure journals; they are now central parts of popular media and political debate. Associated scholarly motivations for public influence drive research; then popular discussion of research findings feeds back into scholarship. I review the increasing role of media attention, popular nonfiction, and think tanks in academic debates and how they have changed the incentives and the practices of social scientists. Popularized scholarship not only (mis)informs the public and policymakers, but also shapes interdisciplinary debates. I argue that this enables integration by concentrating diverse minds on public concerns. I focus on the example of sociobiology studies, where scholars with very different views of human nature have put forward popular accounts, responded to one another, and created an ongoing space for advancing knowledge within and beyond social science.

Chapter 11 reviews my optimistic findings and addresses more pessimistic accounts. The explosion of data collection and availability, the expansion of academia and the spread of ideas, and innovations in theory and method all suggest bright days ahead for social science. Addressing human collective challenges such as climate change, poverty, and public health depends on the advance of social science. I revisit the benefits of accounting for human bias in advancing these efforts and for the further understanding of ourselves. I embrace reforms, but as pieces of a pluralist landscape rather than strictures. Descriptive inferences of generalized patterns, causal inference, and qualitative explorations will all remain important to the advance of social knowledge.

Social scientists have improved their abilities to credibly describe human social life, assess claims about human history and practice, and evaluate behavioral and policy prescriptions. They have developed more effective communities and procedures to debate and cumulate their findings from multiple viewpoints. Both gains have come despite inherent limits to understanding ourselves, fundamental uncertainties in matching theory and evidence, and incentives for dissensus and biased accounts. The steady progress does not enable the generalization of a small number of fundamental social laws or effective simplified models, but we should allow ourselves to learn that our difficulty is partially due to the state of the world. Even where we do build useful knowledge, we cannot expect society or government to automatically enact allied new procedures to solve social problems. But the limited ties between human knowledge and social action are also an aspect of the world we have discovered, rather than a failure of social science.

Like all research, this project has biases. In addition to standardized hypothesis generation and testing, I am open to ethnographic accounts purposely highlighting the perspectives of their subjects as well as popularized scholarship that steps beyond specific data to offer a broader point in public debate. In fact, I view books as an opportunity for scholars to describe what they see (and how they see it), with the goal of compensating for other perspectives that have already received more airtime. Academia in general and social science in particular have recently lost public esteem and come under criticism for failing to live up to their promise. This book is meant to correct the undue pessimism, emphasizing where advancement is happening and on the horizon.

Social Science Biases and Collective Knowledge

Dissertation books do not tend to merit fawning coverage in the *New York Times Book Review*, but Alice Goffman's *On The Run* was different: "Goffman's ability to understand her subjects' motivations are astonishing—and riveting. Indeed, it's a power of 'On the Run' that her insights and conclusions feel so honest to what she's seen and heard," the paper reported.[1] Goffman's book was a TED-Talkable portrait of an overpoliced neighborhood in Philadelphia, complete with racism, drama, and violence.[2]

Though many agreed it was riveting, there was more controversy over the degree to which it was honest and true to the views of her subjects. Law professor Steven Lubet led the (often vitriolic) attacks. In public screeds and eventually in a more measured book, Lubet called Goffman's research unethical, unreliable, and dangerous, later extending his critiques to ethnographic practice in general.[3] According to Lubet, Goffman simply had taken the word of her subjects, even where it was clearly embellished hearsay, and made extravagant claims extrapolated from an improvised survey. Many sociologists also critiqued the study, but some came to Goffman's defense. Some of Lubet's analogies to how evidence is considered in courtrooms and by journalists provoked thoughtful responses, though there were still some fundamental divides. Ethnographers often disclaimed the goal of objectivity, saying their efforts enlarged the otherwise neglected voices of the people they study (in this case, lower-class minority youth being pursued by police) and great efforts had to be expended to gain their trust, protect them, and promote their perspectives.

Social science does not need to decide between these two views. Each addresses an important bias: researchers often pursue a search for confirming evidence and are less likely to check on a good tale; they also do not hear enough from downtrodden voices and may be too accepting of equally self-serving explanations from powerful institutions. The good news is that social science is a broad community, where researchers can learn from many different types of projects with distinct and well-articulated procedures and rationales. As the debate evolved through several back-and-forth responses, it became less dramatic as core disagreements were better articulated.[4]

Lubet's central point about the need to appropriately characterize evidence is useful for advancing the field.[5] Lubet read the classics of ethnography and some recent splashy popular press titles, finding great examples alongside many problems: reliance on rumors without further investigation, little independent corroboration even when it was available, taking single interviews on faith, and obscuring of settings and times of events.[6] The key lesson from trials, he said, is that hearsay can establish people's state of mind, including their beliefs, rationalizations, and intentions, but not establish the truth. He acknowledges that some standpoints or perspectives may be underappreciated, but still seeks objectivity, given that many witnesses are mistaken or unreliable. Police do have their own motives, he says, but even criminal defense lawyers use the initial police report to find discrepancies before police have established a theory of the case. Like police, he says, ethnographers are influenced by their own theory of the case, giving preference to supporting facts and omitting others. Whenever a claim is checkable (such as death rates in specific neighborhoods), Lubet tries to do so, finding that the evidence often undermines the case.

Interviewing more people can help establish patterns. But ethnographies often include references to folklore as the beliefs held in common. Rampant anonymization leads to "pseudo-generalizability," he says, but makes it harder to judge representativeness. Many strategies used, like composite characters, were largely banned from journalism because they are misleading. Lubet began with some personal accusations, but his eventual case was that qualitative investigations should strive for accuracy, be clear about what behavior is typical, and acknowledge what was observed versus heard secondhand.

Social scientists can achieve these aims while representing more diverse views. W. E. B. Du Bois, the pioneer of ethnography in social science, applied these strict standards. He lived with study subjects, visiting homes and participating in social life, but also asked each person standardized questions and focused on details and systematic fact patterns.[7] There is value in perspective-taking and diversification of researcher perspectives, but social scientists must also account for their biases in the research process.

Although most methodological debates have softened, with researchers integrating across methods, ethnography has retained a stronger separation from other fields—while taking more incoming flak from other researchers. That is partially the fault of the critics: demands for methods improvement often do not account for the importance of other potential biases in social research, like those that arise from the demographics of the researcher and their subjects. As political scientist Mirya Holman told me, "There is a limited conversation about replication and limited participation. [Critics] do create impossible standards for some types of research." Critics often seek to apply their own standards—essentially maximizing the utility of qualitative research as quantitative research with less data—rather than trying to understand the goals of qualitative researchers.

These debates provide motivation for thinking through categories of biases facing researchers and how they might manifest in social research and infect public knowledge. In science, any systematic deviation from the search for truth constitutes a bias. This chapter outlines major categories of scholarly biases as well as their implications for research practices. It finds some underlying areas of consensus in seeking to address them. Social science relies on a continuation of attentive research of all kinds (even those that may not meet Lubet's standards). But it also gains from understanding the biases that scientific methods try to address. Researching and managing biases within the scientific community is the unheralded engine of progress.

Recognizing Bias in Social Knowledge Is the Key to Advancement

Social science is a collective enterprise to learn about and explain human beings' interactions and their joint development of social life. Compared to natural sciences, the classic problems of social science have been (1) that we are studying our species and ourselves, meaning we want to uphold our self-image and we can respond to the information we learn, and (2) that social practices are both aggregations of complex biological entities engaged in diverse interactions and consequences of the particular historical trajectories, cultures, and high-level social institutions that humans have collectively developed over time. Unlike non-human sciences, we are part of what we are studying and can change our behavior. We have also built social structures and cultures that influence individual and social development. Under these circumstances, social scientists are particularly vulnerable to anthropocentric, presentist, psychological, and cultural biases in the questions we ask, our research practices, and our interpretations of results. We inevitably see society from a human and contemporary perspective through a lens that is shaped by our cognitive process and cultural views. In conducting social science, we are helping to determine how we see ourselves and the world we want to create. That introduces corrupting motivations for research, such as a search for what we already believe or want to be true.

Social studies of science have taught us a lot about how the national, racial, gender, class, and political biases of scientists—and of scientific cultures—have influenced our historical and contemporary research.[8] We can acknowledge

demographic biases because the diversification of social scientists enables minority group scholars to uncover alternative interpretations and the cultural
roots of dominant understandings.[9] When it comes to human biases that we all
share, there is no possible "view from nowhere" and no analysis from another
species to add perspective. In making analogies between biases that affect social
scientists differently and those that affect fields collectively, I hope to both learn
from research on underrepresented perspectives and suggest that debiasing
requires a larger collective scholarly effort.

An inventory of likely human biases is both possible and necessary for understanding the progress and limitations of social science. This provides some
justification for social scientists to focus on our own species, our own time period, our own communities, and our own disciplines—but only if we are cognizant of the particularities of our many non-scientific motivations at each stage
of research and only if we take advantage of the scholarly community's ability to
self-correct and enlarge our particular views.

Social science is carried out in peculiar institutions and communities, which
need to justify their social role and promote their expansion. Social scientists
also internalize broader human aspirations for collective knowledge and identity. Far from representative of humanity, however, social scientists are outliers
in their social backgrounds, economic interests, and intellectual aspirations.
Long-standing critiques of social science point to these influences and the biases
that they generate. Social science in practice reflects these biases, sometimes
at the expense of following consistent impartial methods or scholars' claimed
motivations.

Yet there is no forced choice between acknowledging bias to dismiss social
science or pretending it can be free of bias. Biased perspectives can be valuable if
understood and mixed with other biases, especially in a community that collectively evaluates ideas, suggests revisions, and collects new evidence.[10] Abstract
human beliefs are built from social cues and cultural practices, which can guide
collective commitments.[11] Even where biases are endemic to the research enterprise, they can be mitigated if anticipated—especially by the scientific
community.

Deliberation within diverse groups helps improve collective understanding,
forecasting, and decision-making. Societies evolved to build on prior cultural
understanding, accumulating codified and layered knowledge, because humans
are uniquely better at social learning (though not general cognition) compared
to other species.[12] Theoretical models and empirical studies of problem solving
confirm the advantages of social diversity, open communication, and iterative and responsive knowledge generation over solitary thinking.[13] Although
humans are subject to myriad biases in individual thinking, they are surprisingly
good at spotting inconsistencies, logical errors, and unsupported conclusions by

others.[14] Innovations are slowly added to human cultures across generations if communities are large and interconnected.[15] Human brains evolved for learning within societies, with a tendency to draw from others' models of the world and interact within complex social arrangements; that sociality helps explain why our collective intelligence rises over time.[16]

Science has evolved as a community to take advantage of these features of human cognition, stabilizing effective values for supporting collective knowledge gains.[17] Although there is no clear method shared across the sciences, there is a necessary shared attitude of openness to evidence and public scrutiny, which allows communities to correct errors stemming from individual bias.[18] Science is a process designed to collectively remove researcher biases from the development of knowledge.[19]

Sociologist Robert Merton outlined key norms of science that emphasized divorcing knowledge from the particularities of individual researchers.[20] The collective ownership of intellectual property, he said, enables collaboration. The universal status of knowledge independent of individual characteristics means we share pursuits. The disinterestedness of researchers means we are aiming for common benefits over personal gains. And the "organized skepticism" of the community means we scrutinize claims. Researchers widely profess agreement with these norms of science and say they personally uphold them; and yet they widely doubt that the research community as a whole follows them.[21]

These scientific norms are aspirations. Science is still dependent on both individuals with biases and collective dynamics that may disrupt their achievement. Science does not automatically self-correct, but rectifying errors is possible (even in the face of bias) if the community is set up to learn from its mistakes.[22] Our social commitment to find and reduce biases, not any error-free methods, enables progress.

As cognitive scientists Hugo Mercier and Dan Sperber have recently argued, scientists "make do with same reason that all humans use, with its biases and limitations. But they also benefit from its strengths."[23] We are good at evaluating arguments, quickly gravitating to the most helpful theories from others. We use mental models and logic to evaluate ideas and reach actionable conclusions. As in vision, our minds are not always optimized to match idealized logic and we are quite good at justifying even wrong conclusions to ourselves. But as with optical illusions, we can recognize our errors with help in changing perspective.

Though we overrate our own cognitive abilities, we accord too low a value to our collective interactions to evaluate information. Groups can advance knowledge through argumentation, learning from prediction, and evaluating strengths and weaknesses.[24] Many arguments are improved with increased diversity of contributors. Individually, humans can use our reasoning skills in the service of rationalizations, but the same skills can be used to refine opinions within communities. Far from gullible, humans are often extraordinarily inquisitive and skeptical, repeatedly asking for the sourcing of information and alternative evidence.[25]

Scientists are neither solitary geniuses nor stubborn defenders of faith. Even older scientists are only a bit less likely to accept novel theories in the face of evidence.[26] Science is full of conversation. It idealizes discussions and disputes and institutionalizes correspondence among experts. Our reasoning works in the service of our intuitions, rather than counteracting it, but the same tools are useful for recognizing others' biases and interacting to advance knowledge.[27] Even children have the tools to think like scientists, but only if they make discoveries in a community of other learners with regular feedback.[28]

As a psychologist reminded me, the scientific process is built to respond to human biases, even if it often fails: "Research is done by humans, so every human foible applies to research. We don't get a different brain. The big difference is that the process of doing research . . . is highly constrained by the rules of the community. Is it unbiased? No human activity could be. . . . But it's the least biased human enterprise and it only gets better."

Within philosophy of science, scholars have increasingly recognized the importance of social epistemology: the idea that we learn about the world as communities, meaning the characteristics of community members and their interactions matter for what we are able to learn.[29] Feminist philosophy of science has taken the lead in recognizing the importance of social factors, taking advantage of historians and sociologists of science documenting changes in scientific concerns and practices when women researchers moved into new fields. These community-level factors matter for the success and blind spots of fields.

Scientific methods are, of course, promoted as tools to be implemented independent of the researcher. But that does not mean that methods are used, assessed, or policed impartially; instead, scientific norms, practices, and evaluations develop in communities based on their distribution of ideas and motivations and how they evaluate contributions in the development of scientific literatures.[30] Although there is agreement on the importance of diversity in interests and implicit models in driving fields to consider alternative hypotheses and interpretations, there is less consensus on how that agreement should map onto concerns about demographic and political representation within fields. Science works in communities that police norms of learning from evidence, but that requires diverse prior views and a shared willingness to fairly assess argument.

Interdisciplinary conversations raise both the benefits and the difficulties of epistemological diversity. It is quite useful to attack a problem with many models with different kinds of predictions and areas of focus, in order to evaluate how much each can explain (independent of the others) and to consider the lens of each theory on the same problem, but each field sets some hard questions to the side so as to make progress on its central concerns.[31] Nonetheless, prescriptions for scientific advance recommend a diversity of models even if they are theoretically irreconcilable, concerned with different levels of analysis, and differently focused on foundational theory or practical action.[32]

Social science is both a process of decontextualization through standardized methods, enabling inferences to be more independent of the researcher and their domains (matching Lubet's criticisms of ethnography), and a collective project to build knowledge within communities (aligning with ethnographers' aims). As a result, recognizing the likely biases of researchers and dwelling on their potential impact on the field's past knowledge, current practices, and potential directions represent a critical step in the process. Social science aims for collective knowledge but remains a social process with practices, cultures, and norms that vary across disciplines, geography, and time. The research community must regularly look into its distorted mirror to specify how its own collective dynamics incorporate and remedy the biases of field members.

Many known biases are accepted as part of social science research without undermining knowledge accumulation. Archeologists know that certain remains, such as teeth and rock, are preserved far better than cultural objects and practices.[33] Political scientists know that cities and imperial governments kept better written records for later investigation.[34] Survey researchers know that some attitudes are more easily shared than others and that people tend to over-report good behavior. Economists know that some costs and benefits are more easily counted. All of these biases are the subject of considerable discussion, with innovation in workarounds and estimation. Acknowledging a bias is often central to a field's advancement, not a permanent roadblock.[35]

An example from outside academia also shows progress despite bias. As more data moves online, traditional sports statistics have been interrogated and improved in a collective effort to apply scientific practices of measurement and assessment, most prominently in baseball sabermetrics, made famous by Michael Lewis's book *Moneyball*.[36] Nearly everyone in these debates has hometown favorites; statistics are often deployed in arguments over favorite players or teams. That reasonably makes fans skeptical of statistics that make their preferred team look bad, especially if deployed by fans of a rival team. But that process can also provoke useful critique and innovation, as each side responds to others' arguments. The known-to-be-biased perspectives do not take away from the improvement in measurement and prediction that new statistics can bring. They also remind us that the traditional claims of scouts and sports broadcasters also included home-team biases, often without clear specification and with less evidentiary support.

Social science started at a higher tier of analysis and has gone through a broader transformation than sports, but it still needs to remain wary of the difficulty of overcoming its biases, whether or not they take the form of a home-team bias. As physicist Richard Feynman wrote of science, "The first principle is that you must not fool yourself—and you are the easiest person to fool."[37] Science corrects these tendencies both through methods of minimizing bias and through communities that recognize and police the biases that remain.

Beyond articulating research biases and tracking improved efforts to acknowledge their implications and manage their consequences, this book accumulates trends in social science metrics, summarizes metascience findings, and interviews reformers and critics of social science practice, demonstrating how social science can best continue its progress. The main prescription is theoretical and methodological pluralism, built on social science realism. Scholars should understand how social science is practiced and how our biases change our questions and conclusions in order to build on diversity in scholarly perspectives, without necessarily upending our current structures, rejuggling our areas of focus, or forcing universal research practices across disciplines.

But researchers seeking to understand and overcome biases need to look beyond methodological objections to research practices. The long struggle to diversify social science offers a pointed example of new understanding. Bringing new racial and gender diversity to social science did not inevitably involve a statistical innovation, but it did commonly change the questions social science asked and the interpretations we gave—both those directly relevant to race and gender and those where we had (even unknowingly) incorporated gendered or racialized views into social knowledge. Cultural anthropology, for example, has a long history of learning how its assessments of deviations from normal behavior reflected the norms of the researchers' countries and social classes. Researcher biases are not confined to demographic unrepresentativeness; many of the same considerations apply to other sources of potential bias.

Progress to reduce biases does not require wholesale changes to the social science enterprise because there is already an under-heralded revolution underway. Researchers are more knowledgeable than ever about our areas of diversity and homogeneity and how our incentive structures affect our practices. They are not only institutionalizing reform efforts and formally seeking to promote diversity, but also studying how differences and changes affect practices and results. Social science is globalizing, taking on longer time scales, investigating more complex causal chains, and integrating qualitative and quantitative knowledge. Contemporary researchers are less dogmatic about disciplinary norms and scopes, more open to criticism from across the scholarly and public spectrum, and more attentive to threats to inference and validity. Although not always falling under the moniker of recognizing and reducing bias, social scientists are responding to long-standing critiques of biases in our aspirations, methods, and conclusions.

Rather than an exhortation to reformulate social science, this book is primarily a story of advancement already in motion. Social scientists are learning more about ever more topics over time, in part because knowledge is better transmitted across academia and between universities and practice. Innovations in methods of causal inference, more widely available subject pools, open and connected data, rising experimentation, coordinated multi-group studies, more flexible models, proliferating robustness checks, and broader research partnerships are all positive trends. Because each reform is framed as a critique of common scientific practice, however, the global improvement has been obscured. Acknowledging our biases, including how they relate to long-standing critiques of social science, is critical for further progress.

Social Science Is More Difficult but Hardly Impossible

There is no clear distinction between the social and natural sciences in the types of threats they face to inference, but there are large differences in the extent of their challenges. As philosopher Adrian Currie finds in his comparison of geology, paleontology, and archeology, each field made progress despite ambiguous signals from the known biases of what remains in the historical record.[38] In each case (whether aiming to understand rocks, animals, or specific humans), the available evidence comes from traces, which are degraded and cannot be manufactured, with researchers conducting controlled studies only of surrogates and combining that evidence with unrepresentative observational data. Experiments are impossible for some questions in many fields that are considered sciences; since they cannot manipulate history, scholars satisfice with model systems and observations. A trade-off between external validity and causal inference is common, with generalizable observational evidence often more useful but both necessary for advancement.

Social science is likewise not an outlier in the relationship between our theoretical models and empirical inquiry. In many fields, models are used to assess internal consistency, approximate broader theories, and investigate sensitivity to initial conditions, with incomplete empirical validation. No type of evidence is independent of other types: we have experiments (usually on models), observational associations, and particular example chronologies; all sciences theoretically model for tractability and explanation, connecting what they see to knowledge from familiar domains.

But there are real differences in scientific capacity based on what we are studying. As metascientists Daniele Fanelli and Wolfgang Glanzel demonstrate, there is a real hierarchy of science, from physical to biological to social science: "moving from simple and general phenomena (e.g. particle dynamics) to complex and particular (e.g. human behaviour), researchers lose the ability to reach theoretical and methodological consensus."[39] That is visible in many ways: social sciences have a lower number of authors per article, a longer length of article, more and older references in articles, a higher diversity of topics, longer titles, more first-person language, and a lower clustering of articles by topic. We also have more "theories" relative to "laws" in our introductory textbooks, fewer graphs, a lower early impact rate for young scholars, less peer scholar evaluation consensus, less concentration of citations, and a longer obsolescence rate in the literature. All of these factors are closely correlated, with disciplines falling on a spectrum—roughly where you would expect as far back as philosopher Auguste Comte's hierarchy of the sciences in the 1840s.

Social sciences are near the top of this hierarchy, with high complexity and dependence on other sciences, low consensus, and very slow outmodedness of past literature (with rare immediacy of new findings). Political science, for example, depends on nearly all other knowledge as it addresses the highest-level social entities, nation-states and international arrangements. But political and governmental aims have long been central to intellectual effort. The hierarchy of science is important for the difficulty of producing systematic knowledge, in other words, but it does not stand in for relative importance of topics or innate human interest.

Comte initially saw science as moving from inorganic to organic to social, with complexity and decreasing abstractness (as well as increasing dependence on other sciences) as you moved up the chain. The hierarchy of science has been associated with reductionism, the idea that explanations should be formed at the lowest level of analysis (and therefore that social science is reliant on natural science explanations). The hierarchy is a sign of the relative difficulty of reaching consensus via definitive evidence, but it does not need to imply reductionist views or practices. Philosophers and historians of science have concluded that progress can simultaneously be made at multiple levels of analysis. You do not have to finish biology before starting sociology, just as you do not need to finish physics before starting biology. Social science is more uncertain but does not need to be pursued after lower-level questions are answered. There is no first discipline; they are all interdependent.[40] Each is capable of progress, but their questions are not equally easy to answer. The social sciences and natural sciences are equally productive if you adjust for how the disciplines judge themselves differently, with more books and different journal databases.[41]

But the hierarchy has implications for research expectations. Social scientists work alone more often, combining large literatures in longer treatises, with less clustering of literature around universally agreed topic categories. Natural sciences concentrate journal articles in fewer journals with lots of short articles.[42] Across many indicators, social sciences have slower modification of codified knowledge with concrete language and general application, with social fields closer to the parts of the natural sciences with features more like them.[43] Subjective ratings of the hardness or "softness" of a science also match these indicators, as do educational measures such as the size of prerequisite chains in course sequences or even the fluency or ambiguity of professor lectures.[44] But social science actually uses fewer vocabulary words to describe more complex phenomena than natural science, meaning it has to give concepts multiple and ambiguous meanings.[45] However you look at it, social science makes it harder to codify consensus knowledge.

Natural scientists also succeed more in generalization. But that is based less on how they collect their samples than on the "expected heterogeneity of the class you are inferring across."[46] They can assume more generalizability, rather than demonstrate it. Many natural/social science distinctions entail this difference: if one set of rocks can be assumed to be more representative, a small subset can be used to draw more conclusions than from one set of human remains. But either may differ substantially across place and time; social science just has a tendency toward more particular variation and more meaningful differences from diverging historical trajectories.

Compared to models of natural systems, modeling people is more difficult because of human diversity, social influence, purposive action, learning, and agency.[47] Aggregation from the individual to the social is another key feature of social science, but there are analogies at lower levels of human life; cross-level interactions and emergence are difficult throughout the sciences. A long history of models of cooperative and competitive game theory and spatial competition, for example, showed that social science models can be useful in natural science research even if the same models are often too simple to account for human behavioral change.[48]

Although all sciences infuse value decisions into their research practices, social science also finds it more difficult than natural science to avoid values influencing scholar interpretation and methods because humans are the subjects.[49] Some natural science, of course, also works from assumptions about humans relationships to other animals. When biological researchers work from animal models or primate comparisons, they use triangulation across evidence types and prior findings, similar to social scientists.[50] Both natural and social sciences satisfice and develop and interpret natural and social models through stories that draw from our human social experiences.[51]

This has all made social science more politically controversial from the beginning, with early efforts to fund social sciences failing and funding streams less secure. Public legitimacy remains a problem. In 2006, Senator Kay Bailey Hutchison proposed cutting the entire social and behavioral sciences from the National Science Foundation; Tom Coburn tried to eliminate political science in 2009; Alan Wheat had also attacked political science support in the 1990s.[52] These efforts have usually questioned the authority of social science, rather than the importance of its questions. After all, social science generally addresses more topical questions, with less expensive methods. The objections are to how much progress can be made with a scientific approach to social questions and (more cynically) to the sensitivity of the results for funders, not to the quest to understand society.

Science survey researcher Ken Miller told me that the public is also warier of social than natural science, but the distinction is not clear-cut. The "science" the public views positively is mostly from real applied advances in medicine or technology; the "science" they view negatively is mostly personal advice, like conflicting evidence on the benefits or costs of coffee or wine. Similarly, the public rise of social science was not about the acceptance of its objectivity, but its importance in self-understanding; today's public skepticism of social science is related to ambivalence about public opinion polling or popular psychology wisdom. Americans have long valued both the expression of public opinion and calculation, from opinion polls to crowd size reports to sales figures, finding both instrumental and symbolic uses for these tabulations, but also long critiqued them.[53]

Social Scientists' Understanding of Our Place in the Sciences

There is considerable research on these challenges of social science. This book summarizes and applies analysis from metascience fields, research on science itself, to understand social scientists' quandary. I draw from research on the philosophy of science, the history of science, science and technology studies (and the related sociology of science), and higher education (which looks at the role of research within universities). All four of these fields have rich lessons to offer, but they are more focused on natural science than on social science. I draw from their social subfields, but their focus suggests that social science provides a more difficult layer to an already thorny set of problems in understanding and justifying science. Progress depends on understanding social investigations' higher level of difficulty despite our scientific aspirations.

To assess how social science researchers see their own fields, I conducted a survey of professors at major US research universities in five core social science disciplines: anthropology, economics, political science, psychology, and sociology.[54] These five disciplines are all long-standing and form the basis of contemporary social science methods and practice, though many applied fields that combine their interests have since developed. Though I conceive of the disciplines as a united social science, I consider the views and practices of each separately to match most scholars' self-understanding as members of their discipline.[55]

This book regularly reports the results of my survey, which was conducted by Michigan State University's Office for Survey Research (a unit of the Institute for Public Policy and Social Research that I direct) with the help of Karen Clark. We surveyed 8,863 tenure-track faculty members listed on their department's website (or obtained directly from the department chair) at sixty-seven public and private universities at the research level of the American Association of Universities (the top tier of research universities) about research trends in the social sciences.[56] We obtained a sample of 1,141 responses, which were representative by rank and university. Political scientists (21 percent) and sociologists (18 percent) were much more likely to respond than anthropologists (10 percent), economists (9 percent), or psychologists (9 percent), possibly due to my own fields and networks.[57] I report top-line results in the book, though I note where there are significant differences across field, demographics, university, and generation.[58] The most significant differences were by discipline.

The survey can illustrate how social scientists situate themselves within academia. They largely recognize both their disciplines' scientific aspirations and their lesser ability to meet them. We asked researchers how scientific they considered each social science discipline to be (on a scale of 1–5), along with comparison disciplines: biology, physics, education, philosophy, and history. Figure 1.1 reports the average results by discipline of the respondents. Every social science discipline considers itself less scientific than biology and physics but more scientific than education and history. Biology and physics were seen as at or near the maximum by most respondents, whereas the social sciences were mostly placed a little above the midpoint of the scale (and education and history were placed below it). Social scientists thus see themselves as engaged in science more than humanities or applied disciplines, but not to the degree of the natural sciences. They recognize the scientific hierarchy.

There are also some differences across social science disciplines. All disciplines unsurprisingly see themselves as more scientific than other disciplines see them and all but anthropology see themselves as more scientific than average. But not all disciplines see themselves as the most scientific among the social

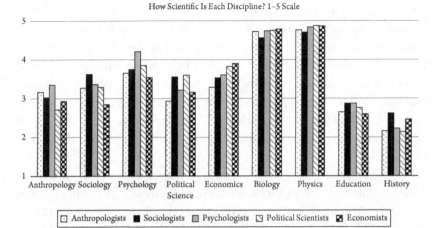

Figure 1.1 Social Scientists' Ratings of Whether Disciplines Are Scientific. Data from the author's 2020 survey of social scientists at major US research universities. n=1,141.

sciences: political scientists see psychology and economics as more scientific than their own discipline and anthropologists see psychology as more scientific. Averaging the five disciplines' responses, psychology is seen as the most scientific, followed by economics and then political science and sociology, with anthropology rated the least scientific (but still at the midpoint). Psychologists and economists have the most inflated views of themselves relative to how they view other social science disciplines; psychologists and sociologists have the most inflated views compared to how the other disciplines view them. Despite disciplinary rivalries and stereotypes, the social sciences largely see themselves in the same middle ground: no discipline thought of itself as more scientific than physics or biology and none thought of other fields as less scientific than history.

Social scientists also have relatively positive views of fields of knowledge that seek to investigate the scientific process itself. Figure 1.2 depicts their average rating on a 1–5 scale of the value of four metascience fields: philosophy of science, history of science, science and technology studies, and higher education. All four are rated above the midpoint on average, with science and technology studies rated the highest and history of science rated the lowest. Economists are the most negative about these fields, and anthropologists are the most positive. Every social science rated at least one metascience field above the middle point, even though the question specified its value to their own discipline.

Social scientists are cognizant that their disciplines are somewhat scientific and open to research on science itself. Most disciplines rated history and philosophy of science and higher education as valuable for their research even though they did not consider education, philosophy, and history themselves to

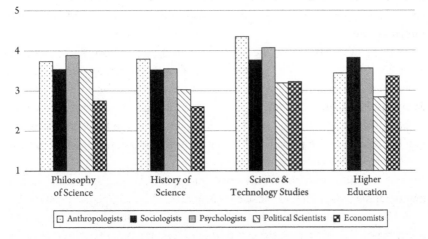

How Valuable Is Research in Each Field for Social Science, 1–5 Scale

□ Anthropologists ■ Sociologists ▨ Psychologists ◩ Political Scientists ▨ Economists

Figure 1.2 Social Scientists' Ratings of the Value of Each Field for Their Disciplines. Data from the author's 2020 survey of social scientists at major US research universities. n=1,141.

be particularly scientific. Social scientists' self-perceptions are consistent with the findings and demeanor of research I have found in these metascientific fields. The social sciences can draw substantially from scientific ideas, norms, and procedures, but need to be aware of the difficulties that make them harder to apply to social life. I return to this survey in later chapters to show that social scientists also understand many of their biases and believe their disciplines are seeking to address them.

Our Many Biases and Attempts to Ameliorate Them

The scale of the social science dilemma is immense: our research biases are likely to be large and multifaceted. We are humans, subject to all the same biases as non-scholars, but we are studying very complex high-level processes dependent on lots of lower-level factors we do not fully understand (from human health to brain science), with the manifestations we observe contingent on time and place in ways we cannot fully know. But we can overcome bias and limit its impact.

The good news is that categorizing and understanding human biases is part of the disciplinary expertise of the social sciences. Psychology has catalogued humans' many cognitive and social biases and their implications for science. Sociology, as the home of the sociology of knowledge and science, has investigated how our work routines and motivations affect the distinctions we make between ourselves and other knowledge seekers. Although we cannot achieve a God's-eye view, these projects help us understand and address biases humans share.

Drawing from research on the history, sociology, and philosophy of social science, Table 1.1 provides my categorization of common biases in social science research. I report potential consequences and strategies for amelioration for each bias. It is a simplification, as biases often interact or cut across categories. Although all categorizations are incomplete, outlining the kinds of biases that might affect researchers enables thinking through their different consequences and how well scholars can address them.

First, the lack of individual diversity among social scientists means we face demographic biases such as those based on race, class, and gender; geographic biases based on our disproportionate American or European location; and political biases due to our partisan and ideological attachments on social issues and goals. Social scientists' demographic and geographic diversity is improving, though our political diversity is not. Scientific practices can also bias research. Methodological biases such as those due a search for statistical significance to enable publication can drive results; disciplinary biases based on the clustering of like-minded scholars can constrain our questions and interpretations of answers; and institutional biases based on funding and doing research in universities can constrain our topics and our sharing of results. But we also face innate difficulties that are harder to overcome. We are all writing and arguing at the same time period; we all come with similar tendencies in human cognition; and we would all like to uncover knowledge that can be useful in the real world. In these cases, we can remind ourselves of biases and how they might affect our knowledge, but the community cannot escape them by adopting new practices or including new people.

Listing biases leaves out some sources of error in research, such as poorly executed research due to incapacity or made-up results due to fraud. Biases might enable these types of errors to go unrecorded (and reforms could still make them less likely to influence codified knowledge), but they are not the focus here. We can improve our errors in methods, but we also face systematic biases diverting our search for truth. And biases such as the search for confirming evidence or statistical significance are often central to the frauds and errors we do uncover.

Not all biases directly affect the quantitative results of individual research projects. Even the rare bias that only manifests in the questions we ask, rather than the answers we accept, can still divert science because we inevitably generalize beyond the cases and domains we study directly. When we do get around to researching previously understudied people, topics, or places, we then bring theoretical frameworks and conceptualizations from the areas we study most. Political scientists historically avoided studies of policing, for example, even

Table 1.1 **A Catalog of Social Science Biases**

		Threat	Strategy to Address	Capacity to Address	Primary Coverage
Individual Diversity	Demographic Biases	Limited topics and interpretations	Diversification and listening	Strong and increasing	Chapter 4
	Geographic Biases	Limited generalization	Globalization, cross-cultural comparison	Increasing; differs by discipline	Chapter 5
	Political Biases	Limited goals and interpretations	Empathetic recognition and sensitivity	Decreasing; recognition increasing	Chapter 8
Scientific Practice	Methodological Biases	Incorrect findings and interpretations	Reproducibility reforms; empiricism	Strong and increasing	Chapter 2
	Disciplinary Biases	Incomplete coverage; non-integration	Interdisciplinary research; team science	Strong and increasing	Chapter 6
	Institutional Biases	Limited goals and topics; translation	Reform of evaluation and rewards	Strong	Chapters 5 and 10
Innate Difficulties	Temporal Biases	Limited generalization	Long time horizons; historical data	Increasing, inherently limited	Chapter 7
	Cognitive Biases	Confirmation bias; non-cumulation	Reproducibility reforms; meta-science studies	Increasing, inherently limited	Chapter 3
	Application Biases	Limited goals and topics; translation	Learning from history; tracking basic science	Inherently limited	Chapter 9

though they constituted many people's main interaction with government. When overpoliced communities became central to American politics, the flowering of related research first had to confront the biases of prior work, tracking effects on traditional outcomes like voting.[59]

My aim is not to have value-free social science. Scientists do regularly appeal to epistemic values, like simplicity, precision, and accuracy; they also appeal to ethical, social, and cognitive values, which can have indirect roles in claims, methods, and interpretations that are appropriate.[60] But there should be a clear differentiation in the ways those values enter into research designs to assess our claims. And we should recognize the epistemic downsides from pursuing even socially redeeming goals. The existence of values is not a problem, but their role in research can be.

Including all types of potential biases does not mean that each is equivalently important or that we can focus only the greatest concern. Geneticist David Reich, for example, has waded into anthropological disputes over the spread of human populations across the world with new analyses based on ancient DNA. Given the fraught history of genetic explanations and racism, he expected to encounter concerns about stereotype confirmation bias and the impact of research claims on racial attitudes. But his larger research impediments turned out to be the need to justify his research on human history through its potential for practical medical advances (for grants), the unequal geographic distribution of scientists and samples (for an incomplete global view), and the mistakes of past researchers in making unkept promises to their human subjects (leading to little cooperation from Native Americans).[61] He knew to look out for racial and cognitive biases, but encountered geographic, institutional, and disciplinary biases as well. Focusing on one expected category of bias might inadvertently limit acknowledgment of others. We need to understand them all.

Demographic Biases

Studies of gender, racial, and class biases offer a useful starting point. Academics, like many professionals, are disproportionately white, rich, and male. The same types of studies that point to biases elsewhere attributable to this unrepresentativeness suggest similar problems in university work settings and in the content of studies. Like other professionals, researchers harbor and are affected by racial, gender, and class biases. Research investigating the effects of demographic biases has evolved to pinpoint systematically unstudied areas and unasked questions, biased methods, and incomplete answers (discussed in Chapter 4). Scholars have responded with an effort to unearth lost insights alongside an active diversification of academia. That has involved revisiting the historical context of disciplinary development and contingent understandings.[62]

These efforts have occasionally erroneously implied that only social minority viewpoints are valid, but they have successfully provoked a reassessment of knowledge and understudied questions. Combining inside and outside perspectives on social groups has provided the fullest picture. Racial minority researchers sometimes face pressure to study their own groups, where they are assumed to have distinct expertise. I emphasize the need to reconcile perspectives, rather than to institutionalize the incentives to study one's own social affiliations. But I still see the evolution of racial and gender studies as useful models for addressing other biases.

For example, early voting behavior studies—almost exclusively conducted by men—assumed that wives followed husbands or avoided voting. The evidence was flimsy, based primarily on women saying they were more likely to discuss politics with a family member. Evidence that men did this as well was dismissed. Scholars also assumed, largely without evidence, that husbands conceptualized politics on behalf of their wives. Other scholars later pinpointed how often men and women transitioned to their spouse's political views, confirming reciprocal influence, but (at least in the 1970s) wives did move further toward their husband's prior views on average.[63] Christina Wolbrecht and J. Kevin Corder review this history for what it says about our intellectual development and for clues to better understand changes in voting behavior over a century.[64]

Five political science journals also recently investigated gender bias in the publication process. They generally found that author gender did not influence publication decisions or journal reviews, even though women authors were underrepresented in the journals.[65] The evidence suggested instead that submissions from women were lower, especially on topics and methods common in the journals. The discipline's top two journals will now be edited by all-women teams, with the explicit mission of expanding the areas of coverage to include topics favored by women and minority authors and to promote a wider range of submissions.[66] The discipline thus investigated a potential bias in scholarship, closely analyzed evidence on gender effects in publication, and attempted to address the effects of bias based on that evidence.

Geographic Biases

With an open mind, academics can be nearly as forthright in acknowledging geographic biases in research. Because social scientists are disproportionately located in a few countries and areas within them, they have a different viewpoint and have access to different data sources than others might. Much of what we pretend are studies of human behavior or human institutions are actually confined to particular unrepresentative locales with peculiar circumstances. Social scientists are more interested in their own countries, which are not globally representative.[67] Psychologists have begun to outline some of these differences in thinking about whether their studies only apply to Western, Educated people from Industrialized, Rich, and Democratic (WEIRD) countries. Seventy percent of experimental participants have been US undergraduates, with 96 percent coming from northern Europe, North America, or Australia.[68] This suggests a need to examine how those contexts are different and an effort to improve global coverage, but hardly necessitates even geographic distribution around the globe by decree. The problem comes in assuming that data from the United States in recent years prove a general theory, not in knowingly using the best available data and acknowledging limitations. An "Americanist" subfield may be less problematic than a tendency to use overwhelmingly American data without considering a line of research a country-level case study. But either approach may inadvertently use the United States as a base case of comparison, rather than one country among many serving as the national contexts for human behavior. Geographic biases are also related to the potential for language bias. If English is the dominant language of science, its specific formulations, word associations, and etymologies might influence our understandings. Incorporating non-English speakers and evaluating translations might lead to discoveries or assumptions of unwarranted universality.

Political Biases

Political and ideological biases are also generating new attention. Traditionally, political critiques came from the left: scholars have incentives to uphold powerful institutions that include their employers and benefactors. Military considerations and the Soviet menace, for example, drove the questions, projects, and interpretations of Cold War social science (discussed in Chapter 5).[69] Despite changing national allies and enemies, concerns remain that government-funded research may reflect the strategic interests of the funders more than the goals of science.

Yet today, political critique often comes from the right: scholars are mostly on the left of the US political spectrum, the story goes, and unfairly impugn the ideas and people associated with the ideological right. One common example is the tendency to pathologize Donald Trump supporters, seeing them as aberrations from the normal state of enlightened liberalism. Denying the potential importance of objections from the left or the right is less productive than engaging the implications of each, as both are likely operating simultaneously and constraining theories, methods, and interpretations. Rather than assume that researchers are fair by virtue of being attacked by all sides, we can acknowledge where both our institutional moderation and our political liberalism guide us. Scholars can discover the role of political biases in historical chronologies as well as from contemporary comparisons of researcher and public values (discussed in Chapter 8).

Methodological Biases

Structural biases in the scientific process have provoked the most recent interest, especially with increasing awareness of the reproducibility crisis that began in medicine and psychology (discussed in Chapter 2). Studies have detailed how researchers misleadingly present statistics and how journals promote publication bias; mass replications have shown which findings are recoverable and revised views of effects and contingencies; and surveys have detailed the wide prevalence of questionable research practices in the full process of discovery.

Although the findings indicate large-scale problems, identifying them has not increased them. Instead, scholars are revising their views of past scholarship and designing better future studies. Finding that a result does not replicate, or does so only in limited domains, is itself an important finding. But we are not just correcting errors through the process and promising to be better researchers, we are also learning the mechanisms by which research provides misleading answers and where skepticism is most warranted. We have made the most progress when we discover how poor research practices follow misaligned incentives that are correctable, rather than merely result from sloppiness or fraud.

We are also making progress in quantitative research practice. Just seven years ago, critic Philip Schrodt articulated seven deadly sins of political science quantitative work.[70] But most seem to be improving. Rather than automatically include every variable in every model, more scholars are using multiple specifications to show how results change with each addition. Out-of-sample predictions are growing, as are acknowledgments that analyses may overfit. The number of datasets is expanding, as is their public sharing. Bayesian and frequentist assumptions, while hardly reconciled, are more regularly compared—with some articles even using both and showing differences. Non-linear models are increasingly pursued and compared with linear versions. The distinction between a statistical control and an experimental control is now well known, with rising concern about the difficulty of causal inference. Scholars still often use complex methods without articulating their assumptions, so perhaps they still prize technological sophistication for its own sake. But that may be evidence that scholars are trying to address the problems of past work.

Disciplinary Biases

A similar process has been at work in facing disciplinary biases, where more interdisciplinary research and new cross-disciplinary debates have enabled scholars to understand where they may be overemphasizing their own discipline's assumptions and can learn from others (discussed in Chapter 6). Disciplines continue their historical paths: psychology focuses on individuals over social context while sociology does the opposite. That is a reasonable way for scholars to select into a field based on their interests, as long as both recognize that their field's consensus reflects disciplinary bias, not unvarnished reality.

Interdisciplinary conversations with self-awareness are the path forward here. As psychologists and political scientists jointly investigate political partisanship, for example, they not only combine theoretical elements common in each discipline but also acknowledge past misperceptions or incomplete understandings. Cross-disciplinary debates such as those in behavioral economics have enabled understanding of where each discipline is overemphasizing their own assumptions or sticking with preferred models in the face of contrary evidence.

Institutional Biases

The vast majority of social science is conducted in universities, which incentivize research that is externally funded (usually by government) and can be sold to external actors as enabling progress. Like non-academics, social scientists are affected by fame and fortune generally as well as their more specific metrics of career success. That means projects and people that generate funding and external visibility gain over others. Because health research is funded at a higher level, social scientists may choose to test general theories in areas such as policymaking, social networks, or employment markets in this area, coloring the overall results. But universities have always faced multiple constituencies with different objectives and managed to muddle through (see Chapter 5).

Universities also prize famous scholars. And we have learned that popularized scholarship is unrepresentative, often trumpeting self-help strategies or convenient findings. Yet popular debate also allows communication across fields (discussed in Chapter 10). The trick is taking advantage of the wide public and interdisciplinary conversation that comes from publicity without building our knowledge on the least verified claims.

Temporal Biases

These biases are more easily understood and longer studied, but other biases scholars must address are not matters of demographics or scientific practice. The hardest biases to overcome are those that humans all share, but there are signs of progress there as well. For universal biases, researcher diversification is infeasible, but institutions and practices can still remediate their effects.

Scholars are all working in the same time period, for example, and seeking to address contemporary issues. Beyond the tendency to interpret information based on what is happening in our own historical period, social scientists focus disproportionately on recent and symbolically important periods. Longitudinal studies of research findings offer insights into when dominant concerns and interpretations are not eternal and why some periods are deserving of further study. Social scientists can also borrow from historians and area specialists, who are allies in furthering understanding of similar questions starting from different assumptions and methodologies. But the problem remains large: the gulf in ideas, culture, and behavior between demographically and geographically different researchers today likely pales in comparison to the differences between most humans alive today and those alive thousands of years ago. Even a few decades sometimes create widespread changes in attitudes or technologies that are difficult to similarly observe.

Political scientist Kevin Munger has looked at the lack of "temporal validity," especially in studies of social media where the results each year are dependent on the population of users and the constraints of each popular platform, but later expanded to other topics.[71] If you create a general theory of social media echo chambers based on Facebook use in the United States, it may not apply to behavior on another platform, in another context, or even a few years later as the service or behavior evolves. The point generalizes. Scholars often assume stability, building many models on data and observations from assumed-to-be invariant recent US and European contexts.

Cognitive Biases

Cognitive biases have long been recognized and applied to social science. Scholars have worried about difficulties in social experimentation, such as experimenter expectancy effects where subjects react to what they think the researcher is trying to find.[72] Because we are studying ourselves, we also tend to want to rationalize behavior in order to understand it. We judge simpler explanations more likely true, even if they are not best, and are too quick to apply lessons from storytelling.[73] We underestimate luck relative to talent in human endeavor, missing the effects of randomness.[74] We also search for explanations in physical changes, especially in the brain. The "cerebral mystique" sees a firm distinction between brain and body, erroneously separating both from their environmental influences.[75] A study of geologists found them susceptible to biases in optimism, hindsight, and framing in decision-making scenarios, reacting in similar ways to public samples regardless of years of scientific practice.[76] Social scientists suffer from motivated reasoning, beginning and stopping evidence collection and integration when it fits their prior views.[77]

Even though explanations for human behavior are complicated, we also have a tendency to believe that many social science research findings are "common sense" and obvious, even if we also would have thought the opposite finding equally obvious.[78] Paul Lazarsfeld intentionally misrepresented six findings from his book *The American Soldier* (making them the opposite of his true findings), showing that readers would claim that either the true findings or the opposite findings were intuitive common sense. Because social scientists deal with probabilistic and limited relationships involving humans, we can often readily come up with examples to match a theory we are told. That means we can also easily fit evidence from the past into our theories, even if we would not make those similar predictions from them.

Rather than developed for scientific methods, our cognition is optimized for reacting appropriately to risks and opportunities in the environments of ancestral humans.[79] Our perception systems make automatic inferences, often without our knowing how or why, and we can then justify them afterward. Humans are capable of exploiting and representing empirical regularities, but that leads to a rich "folk ontology" of stories that may not hold up to scrutiny.[80] Humans can uniquely publicly express their mental representations, including understanding numbers and mathematical values separately from the things being counted. We also have intuitions about arguments, such as their cogency, generality, and coherence, and can reason about our reasoning process.[81]

But that reasoning is mostly useful for social comparison and reputation management, rather than for working through our own thought process to reach decisions.[82] We seek to be socially recognized as providing good reasons for our behavior, using argumentation retrospectively for justification. But since we are more demanding of other people's explanations, we can take advantage of others' criticism, benefiting from the expansion of our interactions as society enlarges. As part of educational programs, humans can learn to better appreciate errors in thinking and statistical reasoning, but it does not come naturally.[83]

Application Biases

A related universal human bias is our desire to successfully use the knowledge we create. That means we often downplay causes of problems that are not easily altered and instead prefer explanations associated with obvious policy levers. Social scientists are interested in applying knowledge in areas of social life. That means we will be oriented toward findings that suggest solutions implementable by governments and other institutions. That is no great calamity, but it does introduce biases that can be tracked, and it suggests openness to research on problems without easy solutions.

Critical research in applied areas like criminology and education highlighting these limitations can productively feed back into basic research. Yet applied disciplines have also sometimes hung on to theories (such as ideas about categorical "learning styles") long after the original studies from basic disciplines are overturned. Social science must be willing to say when our findings do not entail ready-made solutions, but applied disciplines should also heed social scientists' calls for humility as well as action.

Recognition and Reform

The particular biases endemic to social science, that we are studying a social world in motion as we are inside of it (and trying to change it), have been recognized from the beginning.[84] Although sometimes generalized to a relativist critique of all social science knowledge, most current critics acknowledge that science overall is a biased search for truth, with social science having to look out for additional biases though not incapable of addressing them.[85] Scholars can ask themselves whether they are doing too much moral storytelling, consistent with social anxieties more than realistic dynamic processes.[86]

Yet the dominant proposed reforms have been to further systematize both theoretical models and empirical tests of them. Since we cannot look at data without theoretical guidance (acknowledged or not), we are asked to fully articulate and map out causal models and explicitly use them in empirical work.[87] But because theoretical construction is reliant on the reasonableness of our codified knowledge and assumed causal models, we will need to delve into the sociology of our science, the psychology of investigators, and the incentives of our community, rather than simply systematize for its own sake. Science is designed to address these biases, not simply to order our work, and it reconciles theory and evidence only as part of a community process of self-reflection (not just procedural standardization).[88]

Social science is hardly on a universal one-way street of continual progress. Yet looking back even on initially testy scholarly exchanges and overclaimed revolutions nonetheless demonstrates research gains. Initial innovations in areas like causal inference, network analysis, and behavioral genetics, for example, each brought zealots who were too dismissive of past work; they often popularized claims well beyond the evidence and ignored pitfalls. Some of the progress in each field involves toning down these initial aspirations, accepting limitations, and making connections to past work. But the advance years later in each field's methods, theoretical models, and applications is substantial. None turned out to be as revolutionary as claimed, but all added to knowledge.

Moves from overbroad theories to specific and supported empirical regularities with well-defined mechanisms are also visible in diverse substantive fields. Terrorism studies moved from generalized analyses of secondary sources on a few cases to more representative primary source data analyzed by more scholars, with recognition of the limits of incomplete information.[89] Debates over the employment effects of minimum wages moved from theory-driven confirmation to meta-analyses and natural experiments, enabling more precise estimation of heterogenous effects and theoretical revision. Investigation of religiosity went from vague concepts to understanding the different effects of service attendance, beliefs, social networks, and denominations. As fields recognize their early biases and flawed assumptions, they work to address them.

Overall, there is considerable progress. Data and tool availability alone, with both growing quickly, should increase our potential to advance knowledge. With more information and improved analysis, the only thing holding social scientists back would be declaring premature victory over the endemic challenges of studying human societies or failing to reflect on how our biases still enter into even better-estimated measures and relationships. But alongside new evidence has come reflexivity. We are biased operators, but those biases are increasingly noted. Confronting them does not undermine the gains in accumulated evidence and analysis. Pessimism seems to be the most common misconception of scholars and publics, with gradual improvements in knowledge and application much less noted than the crises that remain unsolved and the explanations that remain unknown.[90]

On the one hand, social science faces deep challenges: we are studying ourselves and can react to what we learn. Our ability to reach consensus is lower than for other sciences, and our initial biases in accumulating and evaluating evidence are greater. Scholars disagree about the most important biases to address, from those worried about reinforcing social prejudices to those concerned with researcher cognitive biases. But on the other hand, we are increasingly acknowledging all kinds of biases and starting to investigate them. Our difficulties stem more from the barriers to accumulating social knowledge and the lack of a God's-eye view than from errors in the implementation of our methods. But that hardly means we cannot improve with criticism and better research practices. Indeed, we are entering a flourishing era for social science reform.

2

Open Science Reform and Social Science Progress

"Your body language may shape who you are," blared a TED Talk viewed more than 50 million times, summarizing the research of psychologist Amy Cuddy.[1] Cuddy had found that "power poses" increase testosterone levels, making people powerful just by standing differently. That was catnip, not only for TED Talks but also for *Oprah* magazine, CNN, and trade publishers. But—like many studies since—it failed to replicate.

The original study included only forty-two participants and had them pose for only two minutes, claiming that power posing created physiological changes and increased risky gambles. Multiple meta-analyses of many replications failed to confirm these effects, and a coauthor of the original study said she no longer believed them. It was among the most public demonstrations of the discipline's new focus on replication.

The replication revolution came after analyses found that, by searching for statistical significance, researchers had many ways to report findings that were likely false; many psychologists admitted to engaging in related questionable research practices.[2] That meant that—even though failed replications should be a normal and routine part of science—the response to Cuddy was personal as well as professional, stimulating gendered online attacks. Cuddy defended her findings but left her tenure-track position at Harvard. Some researchers initially saw it as a "takedown" culture of jealous scholars using social media to attack well-known personalities, impugning their motives and reducing the public stature of the field.

Dozens of social psychology studies have since failed to replicate. Subsequent replicators have been less confrontational, and researchers have been more accepting of revisions. Several replications of multiple studies by many different teams failed to confirm some original relationships altogether and found nearly all effect sizes smaller than those originally reported.[3] Researchers and laypeople could predict replication success based on the evidence for the finding and the implausibility of the hypothesis tested.[4] If changing your pose to increase your power sounds too good to be true, it might be.

Talk of a replication "crisis" raised awareness of the stark challenges facing social science and the role of professional incentives and human cognitive biases in social research. The reform efforts and responses to critiques show the power of taking research biases seriously. But standardizing social science around the practices of experimental methodologists attempting to make universal causal inferences, including preregistration of strict protocols, cannot compensate for the diversity of current social science perspective and practice. Although reforms and methodological advances can address biases that emanate from publication incentives and research design, these strategies alone are not enough to grapple with the broader range of social science biases. This chapter outlines the role of scholarly reforms in achieving social science potential. It also outlines several recent revolutions in social science practice that can contribute to research progress in tandem with reproducibility reforms: the triumph of empiricism over grand theory, the rise of open and big data, the specification of causal identification strategies, and the rise of team science.

The Reproducibility Movement and Its Limitations

The central movement to address long-running social science problems goes by the name of "open science" or the reproducibility movement. It is particularly concerned with publication bias (the tendency for findings to be published only if they find statistically significant results), low statistical power (the design of studies without a large enough sample to assess relationships), p-value hacking (the use of many different formulations of data and tests to find a significant result), and Hypothesizing After Results are Known (HARKing, coming up with a theory that fits the data after seeing the results).[5] These problems are long-standing but only recently frontally addressed.

The new reformers are in it for the long haul: the anticipated pace of shifts in scientific practice is generational, rather than immediate.[6] Reformers have found that social scientists are still publishing findings that are disproportionately just below conventional statistical significance levels (with results just failing to meet this threshold missing from the published literature); randomized experiments and natural experiments are the most likely to avoid the problem, whereas even quasi-experimental efforts to determine causality studies suffer from it.[7] But even canonical experiments used in introductory psychology textbooks like the

"Robbers Cave" experiment (where boys on summer camp teams became war-like enemies) and the "obedience to authority" study (where participants "electrically shock" people for poor performance) have come under new scrutiny, as new materials suggest multiple tests (in the former case) and researcher influence (in the latter).

The contemporary reproducibility movement is usually dated to the publication of "Why Most Published Research Findings Are False" by John Ioannidis.[8] He showed that findings in the scientific literature could not be trusted, given low-powered studies and even modest p-hacking.[9] It had its most immediate impact in medicine, where the concerns had been growing. After clinical trial reforms, drug firms were moving fewer products to market. They looked back at the research studies that formed the basis of their translational work (from lab to drug trials) and found they could not replicate the initial studies.[10] The problems revealed publication biases, conflicts of interest, and low-yielding research programs. The National Institutes of Health moved to institute new reproducibility policies. Several research programs with seemingly firm support turned out to be based on misnomers; after years of trying to find the particular contexts where highly publicized factors mattered, broader analysis often showed no effects at all.[11]

Recent concerns revisit long-standing findings in the sociology of science. Sociologist Harry Collins had long argued that science had no algorithm for replicability: "since experimentation is a matter of skillful practice, it can never be clear whether a second experiment has been done sufficiently well to count as a check on the results of the first."[12] That means scientific findings are evaluated in social networks and institutions with many competing motivations, rather than regularly subject to the same process of review.

Yet the new critics thought that the recent practices of academia had further incentivized poor behavior. Competition for research funding, quantitative metrics to evaluate researchers, and decreased discretionary work created perverse incentives for quick, abundant, and problematic research.[13] Even systematic reviews across research areas, including meta-analyses, were liable to support predetermined conclusions, they found, because correcting the record is time-consuming and not compatible with career interests.[14]

The reform movement gained the most steam in social psychology, especially as famous studies could not be replicated. The Center for Open Science tested psychological findings in several "many labs" mass experiments, where lots of research teams attempted to replicate the same research, finding that many did not replicate and others showed smaller effects. The scrutiny has been widespread. Psychologist Jay Van Bavel told me, "I go through my introductory lectures and every year I cull a few studies that have not held up and have to add nuance to others." He has changed his mind on several landmark findings and increased his broader skepticism.

Surveys of social psychologists find that perceptions are pessimistic, but researchers want to avoid questionable research and adopt best practices.[15] New policies at journals and increasing researcher buy-in are leading to perceived improvements. Early surveys that showed widespread use of questionable research practices likely overstated the problems, as researchers misunderstood some questions or had reasonable explanations for their answers.[16] Researchers have since learned that many studies have too few participants to assess the claims they want to test. But the trends are mostly positive. From 2011 to 2016, social psychology studies got larger sample sizes, included more studies per article, and added transparency in measurement, though they also moved to online data collection that may trade off with generalizability.[17]

Both surveys and prediction markets (where bettors wager on the likely outcome of studies) can predict outcomes of large-scale replications reasonably well, though some of the predictive power comes from simply using the p-value of the initial study (studies closer to the threshold are less likely to hold up). Studies that imply easy fixes to social problems or easy manipulation of human behavior are also less likely to be replicated.[18]

In parallel, new research evaluating statistical significance tests found evidence consistent with widespread p-hacking, running many tests and specifications to find one that reaches statistical significance. Many nonrandomized studies also likely involved HARKing, including complex causal chains and interactions between variables that did not hold up to scrutiny.[19] In economics, the concerns became less about failed replication and more about specification search and multiple hypothesis tests; data availability was uncontroversial. Later studies toned down the concern somewhat, suggesting p-hacking was not distorting the majority of research in any discipline, was specific to particular subfields, and was not growing over time.[20] Published studies were actually growing longer, more complex, and richer in data. Scrutiny may go with improvement. Increasing retractions, after all, should be seen as a good sign of the integrity of the research process and the importance of community evaluation and enforcement of research standards.

Not everyone agrees there is evidence of a widespread crisis. We do not know what the true replication rate is or what an ideal replication rate would be.[21] Critics of the crisis narrative argue that, since the studies were not selected randomly for evaluation and no standard was established for an acceptable rate of replication, the "many labs" studies did not show what they purported to show.[22] There is little evidence that p-hacking, distortion in meta-analysis, or low statistical power are getting worse over time.[23] Social science biases seem to be larger than those of the natural sciences, but the problem types are similar throughout the sciences and are not getting larger.[24] Many failed replications were of single low-powered studies, rather than research findings from diverse evidence; the community evaluation that followed showed the value of openness and self-reflection.[25] In areas like personality psychology, there remains a long list of robust findings, including effects on longevity and educational, relationship, and career success.[26]

The reproducibility movement has been led by experimental methodologists in psychology seeking acceptance of new research standards. Even the randomized controlled trial is subject to potential result cherry-picking, data manipulations, and design changes following initial results—but its clearer theory testing and controlled design should make replicability easier to formalize. The common reforms ask for studies to be designed in advance, with key methodological choices explained prior to analyses, and fully disclosed (with data and materials available for replication).

The reforms are not meant to be limited to experiments, though some complexities arise in other cases. Researchers can develop a pre-analysis plan for an observational study (and preregister it if they want), but there tend to be many more design and data collection choices involved, some unanticipated difficulties and choices, and a tendency for existing related data to inform hypotheses. Even the movement to make data available and interpretable for replications of statistical analyses has proven not straightforward to implement. Authors often believe they are providing all of the materials for replication without actually doing so; extending the process to new data collection proves challenging. But even qualitative researchers have embraced transparency and reproducibility, not only as goals but instantiated in shared policies. There are now qualitative data repositories and attempts to develop common reporting standards. In political science, a three-year deliberative process brought hundreds of scholars together to debate practical guidance for designing and implementing qualitative research, though some came from nonscientific traditions and saw more risks to tempering research diversity.[27]

Reformers may have focused too much on the abuse of significance testing, ignoring the broader problem of application of models without attending to their assumptions and proper interpretations. Economist Aris Spanos says the focus has obscured more common misspecification and unwarranted description of results.[28] Statistical misspecification, poor implementation, and overbroad conclusions are more common problems than p-hacking supposes. Rather than actively trying to get a statistically significant result, many researchers use quantitative techniques that do not fit their theory or take account of their data. For most social science, post-analysis evaluation of sensitivity to assumptions (rerunning analyses afterward to see if a different choice would have led to different results) may be more feasible and appropriate.

Reformers often envision an objective ideal in research that can be compared against projects that test multiple outcomes, cherry-pick results, make flawed assumptions, or fail to publish all results.[29] But nearly all research projects evolve over time. The main challenges are in communication of results to enable oversight and in framing the findings to honestly report their limitations. Testing the claims of others (in a replication or a response) often involves the same series of potential biases, especially if initial claims and counterclaims are not fully specified.

A historical review of the rise of the common .05 standard for statistical significance suggests that the rise of datasets and informal copying drove statistical significance testing but editors and journal rules drove convergence on the .05 standard (and later the three-star system associated with .05, .01, and .001 p-values).[30] By 2007, negative published results were disappearing for most disciplines and in most countries, while positive statistically significant results had grown 22 percent since 1990.[31] Significance tests just below the threshold were more common in studies using non-experimental techniques to assess causality (such as instrumental variables or difference-in-difference designs, discussed later) rather than experiments.[32] These findings led many to argue against statistical significance thresholds or for making a stricter threshold.[33] As open science leader Robert Nozek told me, "The .05 standard debate is simultaneously essential and irrelevant. It is a substantial part of how we learn about problems. But the bad problem is still our dichotomous reasoning we can't get away from [rather than the threshold]."

The most difficult-to-implement and controversial reform is preregistration: submitting a plan describing tests and researcher decisions before executing a study (or a pre-analysis plan, posting similar information somewhere in advance). There has been lots of resistance, with opponents arguing it adds little while undermining the reputation of other research.[34] The main concern is that most decisions are unanticipated and imposing a straitjacket forces researchers to discard important findings. As one psychologist said, "I think the whole replication 'crisis' is overblown (which is not to say it's entirely wrong), and some of the cures seem worse than the problem. For example, pre-registering (in my experience) is making much worse science! People pre-register inappropriate analyses . . . and then they do them and find something probably wrong (usually a null result), and claim that it's a great study because it was pre-registered. It's become a political and PR tool, and very quickly ceased to be a benefit to the discipline."

Alex Coppock, a promoter within political science, told me these concerns are misplaced: "We want a pre-analysis plan even if you divert from it. Tell us how you learned. We know no one follows through completely. But [with the plan], you can tell which parts are exploratory. The problem was [repeatedly] estimating [different] interactions until you produced a story." But political scientist Tara Slough said some of the concerns are justified: "Pre-analysis plans do almost nothing to constrain researchers. Lots of things come up. You might want to suggest new mechanisms. It is still a valuable record of where you started and various permutations of [your] decisions . . . [but pre-analysis plans are] depressing reading lists of disembodied hypotheses, [often] 40 hypothesized relationships [and] not much better than what post-hoc theorizing looks like."

The largest proponents in economics explicitly recommend a moderate approach to pre-analysis plans, saying researchers do not need to list all potential analyses or stick strictly to their pre-specified plans.[35] Researchers can complete the plan as registered, but then write a more expansive research paper that includes more analyses, and still reap the benefits of planning.

Cyrus Samii, executive director of the Evidence in Government and Politics (EGAP) experimental research network, told me they have learned from early plans: "There is certainly more exploration that we thought; [they've given us more] reasons to be skeptical of past findings." He acknowledged people do not stick to them: "You often can't specify plans ex ante or it's not appropriate. [There is] real learning and calibration, but you need to know what you're learning from and commit to interpretations and methods." From seeing these plans in motion, he argues, we can learn about "self-deceit in p-hacking," where multiple tests or key decisions may be made without an account. "Lots of quantitative research for decades was demonstrating that you found an effect vs. a credible effect. Now you're forced to ask questions about 'what the goals is' and the mechanisms." Political scientist and statistician Andrew Gelman told me we have learned that "confirmatory research is very rare" overall. We are taught to frame research as confirmatory in PhD dissertations and it has become "the dominant paradigm," but social science is usually exploratory.

Despite the limitations, the broader research reform efforts have borne fruit. Political scientist Arthur Lupia summarized: "Compared to five years ago, we are having many new conversations about reproducibility. We are better at falsifying causal claims. The replication crisis in psychology was largely a media creation [but we've] asked more questions. . . . Other disciplines are now more aware of alternative specifications and weak causal claims. . . . We're in the early stages of learning. Over time, we will get honest corrections and awareness of models that don't hold up."

Gary King also assessed the efforts positively: "We've come very far. You used to ask for data and people would say it was moved or lost. Now the default is 'yes,' or they're embarrassed. . . . There is some replication, with different styles . . . [and we now understand that] all research involves qualitative and quantitative decisions." Andrew Gelman also judges most trends positively: "The rise of standards and recalculation of old analyses are both good; pre-analysis plans that are not a straitjacket. [They] just take a lot of work [but are] good to see." He said going through the process for his own research led him to learn that he did not anticipate some missing data challenges; he also reduced the authority of his past beliefs.

Political scientist Ken Kollman sees a revolutionary effect: "Open science has had a large effect on the profession and moved expectations, especially in the transparency of data analysis. We've shifted policies [and expanded] replications and extensions." Psychologist and reformer Chris Chambers also sees progress: "Lots has changed. Progress in [many] initiatives has already begun. [Many more] journals implemented guidelines [and accepted] registered reports. [What is] not moving as quickly is academic culture [because] senior academics are slow to change."

Nozek told me the main lessons have been about the scope of the problems: "We've learned that published and true are not synonyms. There is increased skepticism [even if] journals and institutions are slower to change. [We've made] most progress in finding what we don't know. . . . Experiments were the ideal case, with easy to run replications [but that is just] proof of concept." He acknowledges that scientific progress can happen via accident, rather than plan, but says we must make it clear when we are not doing confirmatory research.

A psychologist, however, says the reforms are largely responding to a manufactured crisis: "[The word] crisis is not accurate or helpful. . . . Cherry-picking 100 studies [to replicate] is pointless. It's based on a deep misunderstanding of what lab studies are meant to do. Lots of social science is parameter estimates, but psychology is just trying to do existence proofs that a causal mechanism can exist." Political scientist Christina Wobrecht says methods reforms cannot solve everything, but they have put important limits on our claims: "We've learned that small sample sizes create problems and that regression doesn't mean causality. But we can still use our old tools and multiple specifications [as long as we're aware of what we are doing]. It still takes triangulation and placebo tests."

Sociology has moved less quickly than economics, psychology, and political science. Jeremy Freese told me there's been "little institutional response in sociology to the reproducibility movement in journals. . . . The effort is to carve out space for qualitative sociology and not to [be perceived as] undermining it." But he says the discipline was receptive to the findings in psychology: "It should be hard. Small treatments shouldn't make large changes [in human behavior]. You can't work wonders with a fifteen-minute intervention. That's a profound point that non-reproducible science has reinforced." Sociologist Daniel Hirschman told me that some reforms are advancing; the archiving of working papers has been the "key step" in launching open science.

The impressions of young researchers are also positive about reforms, but they see more signs of inherent trade-offs. Political scientist Robert Kubinek told me, "there is a tension between the credibility revolution and open science: that you can and should trust experiments versus [the importance of] getting back to description and measurement, showing that even experiments can't be replicated and going back to theory to explain existing findings." He agrees that sharing data and code is an unalloyed positive and is "also a fan of preregistration and power analysis" but says there is a "real trade-off with tenure-track publishing and getting stuff out, especially the amount of effort required to anticipate everything in advance." He says we have learned that we are "mostly all doing exploratory research with theory very underspecified" but says the "Bayesian way out is to be clear about [our] priors and our reasons for changing them."

Political scientist Jessica Preece argues that researchers are learning to acknowledge the trade-offs: "Even in experiments, it's not easy to anticipate how research plays out and you can't stop and say it's an exploratory field experiment. When you deviate, just say it. You learn things along the way and accept it. The honesty about the long journey goes a long way." Political scientist Kevin Munger told me he expects generational change: "The Reproducibility movement is changing both norms and institutions, but especially the culture of younger scholars. The biggest contribution to knowledge is showing how many questions are tough to answer. The preregistration difficulties show that it is hard to do good social science."

One criticism of reformers has been that we are not learning anything new about the substantive topics of research. But psychologist Sanjay Srivastava told me we are "unlearning some things" and that is just as important, mentioning non-replicated studies of ego depletion (the using up of mental resources through self-control) and easy priming (using a small intervention to stimulate a later change in response on another topic) and not fully replicated studies of the growth mindset (beliefs that one can learn something helping them learn it). But he says there is a contradiction in the criticisms: "You can't have it both ways, telling us there are lots of unforeseeable decisions [in research so we are all exploratory] and that our past research is sacrosanct. . . . Researchers are real humans but they get defensive about it; openness and transparency help but ruthlessly policing [each other] is what makes it work." Most research is exploratory and should continue—but that also means we have confirmed less than we thought.

A prominent economist agrees that unlearning has been important, with other social sciences learning from psychologists' mistakes: "There were lots of weak effects put into leading textbooks. If they replicate, they're only one-third of the [initial] effect sizes. Economics is also guilty but less so because we are more unified around the same shared data." Scholars have now adopted a "more

Bayesian and honest approach," evaluating new evidence but not assuming vivid findings will hold. Indeed, economics research has held up better in replication, but mostly because it uses widely available public datasets rather than new experiments.

Two economists, Garret Christensen and Edward Miguel, have recently teamed up with sociologist Jeremy Freese to outline procedures for more reproducible social science.[36] They argue that p-hacking, publication bias, and HARKing are still widespread, but that social science methods are nonetheless quickly improving. They recommend data sharing and reporting standards, preregistration of analysis plans, accounting for multiple specifications and tests, and broader replication. They show the benefit of meta-analyses (statistical analyses of the distributions of estimates across multiple studies) with clear specifications. They highlight improved methods for searching for publication bias via p-value distributions (illustrating the ubiquity of just-under-the-threshold results unlikely to be meaningful) and finding biases via specification curves and related techniques (showing how results change across many different sets of researcher choices, such as inclusion of control variables and procedures for missing data).[37] But they acknowledge two key caveats: first, most tools were developed for experiments and considerable trade-offs go into making them useful for observational research; second, we do not know yet whether adoption of reforms leads to more reliable social science.

I also see signs of progress and limitations in the early results. Given that these are voluntary procedures embraced by researchers, all of the open science trends are positive for social science. They help researchers understand where biases can creep into the research process and they help other researchers check results, connect other projects, and offer adjustments and alternative interpretations. Even the debates surrounding reform implementation raise important considerations about research biases and what is gained and lost through procedural standardization.

Based on the biases I have identified and the benefits of scientific communities, a particularly promising innovation is the adversarial collaboration, in which scholars on different sides of a debate join forces to agree on a shared project to assess their differences with a critical series of tests. These collaborations can take many forms, but the key is to have scientists evaluate potential designs in advance; in the process, they might realize that their differences are in conceptualization or measurement rather than distinct hypotheses. Even the process of proposing adversarial collaborations, such as those to evaluate psychological and economic theories of decision-making in groups, have proven fruitful for differentiating where there is an empirical disagreement from where researchers are just using different languages or misperceiving the scope of their opponents' claims.[38] Where used, it has clarified important issues in psychology and economics, such as when people perceive that they are losing and how losses compare to gains.[39]

Across economics, political science, psychology, and sociology, individual scholars are increasingly adopting reproducibility reforms. By 2017, 73 percent of scholars reported posting data (compared to 15 percent in 2005); preregistration had risen to 20 percent of scholars from almost none.[40] Posting data was most widespread in economics and political science, whereas preregistration was most common in psychology (and experimental work across disciplines). Awareness and positive attitudes were growing across the disciplines, reaching the status of a norm in some fields, even among those who had yet to change their behavior.

The gains in some areas, however, do not mean that we can develop a one-size-fits-all set of research standards. As critics have noted, many scientific discoveries came accidentally or as spontaneous refinements rather than through strict protocols. Social science has advanced as much through induction from broad patterns as from testing deductively generated hypotheses. Unless it involves deceptive reporting or uses inappropriate statistical tests, reformulating hypotheses in the face of new data can be quite useful. Even in these cases, attention to each decision and its justification is of value. But there is danger that codifying procedures could further undermine the legitimacy of exploratory research.

Exploratory and descriptive work is often as useful as that aimed at causal inference. Social science can gain from research in history and area studies as well, so dismissing nonconforming research protocols is a mistake. The debate over whether qualitative and quantitative research should be held to shared standards has evolved to pinpoint potential improvements, cross-fertilization, and areas of continuing differences. An initially anti-quantitative movement of interpretivist scholars also stimulated new types of journals and scholarship, through careful engagement between those pursuing mainstream and alternative methods.[41] "Let a thousand flowers bloom" may sound like a cop-out in these debates, but in fact this precept has worked relatively well in practice—with new generations learning from scholars on both sides of disciplinary divides.

There is value in establishing reform institutions, because educating researchers about problems may not be enough to change behavior. As Chris Chambers told me, "Physics does not know about all the human biases [that psychology does] but still built in all sort of solutions to potential problems like [careful] methods, large teams, and low significance thresholds." Psychologists know about confirmation bias "but haven't been very good at applying our knowledge of its dangers." Genetic researchers also had to work hard to establish data-sharing incentives and agreement across fields, creating human biobanks but failing in studies of other species. Institutional change works better than education about the dangers of common social science practices, according to Gary King: "It does not usually work to tell people they are biased and ask them to correct their own bias"; you need a procedure to change incentives. But social scientists have improved research by evolving both their formal and informal institutions, often moving norms alongside rules—matching common patterns of social change outside science.[42]

Today's scientific reformers are attempting to use better research methods to account for human biases and improve objectivity. They have emphasized disclosure of research details, incentives for replication, and cross-study accumulation and comparison of research findings. This movement has improved science while also showing the depth of the problem; researchers are now in a much better position to address debates over methods and evidence, with more humility in facing the very large dimension problems of social science.

Although many science critics argue that objectivity is just a pretense of researchers for social advancement,[43] they fail to recognize that it is also often a recognition that our biases creep into our research—scholars are therefore reliant on the precision of our claims and tests and the community standards we create in order to reduce the influence of bias. Most critiques of social science practice were born of dissatisfaction with the dominant methods within our fields, including quantification.[44] Science studies critiques focused attention on topics that methodologists still ignore, such as how researchers reach consensus and attain status, how technology and funding shape questions and techniques, and how policy and public opinion considerations shape research.[45] But these broad critiques left open key methodological decisions critical to scientific practice, such as how to handle missing data, choice of procedures, and replication.

When reforms commence, it is hardly ever useful to side with those hanging on to old practices as evidence accumulates against key assumptions. But younger researchers usually draw from combinations of disciplinary sides, often when real research design innovations drive progress. As social science accumulates, the canonical model of independent theory construction with a key test is less important than building on past knowledge. It is now usually harder to make new theoretical ideas consistent with already known empirical regularities than to come up with a novel test. And that takes a lot of synthesizing, rather than merely new studies of the same idea.

Social Scientists' Views of Reproducibility Reform

Based on my survey of social science faculty at major US research universities, social science practitioners are aware of the problems the open science movement seeks to address, supportive of studies designed to investigate the concerns, and

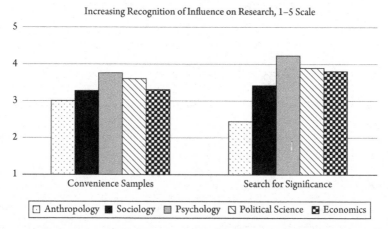

Figure 2.1　Social Scientists' Judgments of Discipline's Recognition of Influences on Research. Data from the author's 2020 survey of social scientists at major US research universities. n=1,141.

supportive of some reforms to alleviate biases in the research process. Figure 2.1 illustrates views of work to address potential biases in research. Researchers were asked the extent to which their discipline has increasingly recognized biases from unrepresentative convenience samples and from the search for statistical significance over the prior decade on a 1–5 scale from "not at all" to "a lot." All disciplines are reportedly showing a moderate increase in recognition of each bias, with psychology moving the most and anthropology moving the least. Opinion thus matches the trends in research.

Social scientists have mixed views about the extent of questionable research practices in their disciplines. Researchers were asked to agree or disagree with three statements: "P-hacking, repeated undisclosed tests to search for statistical significance, is widespread"; "Researchers search mainly for confirming evidence"; and "There is a replication crisis." Figure 2.2 portrays the net percentage in each discipline agreeing over disagreeing. In all disciplines except anthropology, researchers see widespread p-hacking and searches for confirming evidence. But only psychology has significantly more researchers seeing a "replication crisis" than not seeing it. That suggests that researchers understand the biases but do not necessarily see them as fatal. Anthropology's exceptionalism could be a product of their less-quantitative work; disagreement was especially strong in the socio-cultural subfield. Social scientists in quantitative fields may better understand the problems they face.

Figure 2.3 reviews researchers' opinion of studies designed to understand the influence of researcher biases on social science research. Respondents were asked the value (on a 1–5 scale from "not valuable at all" to "very valuable")

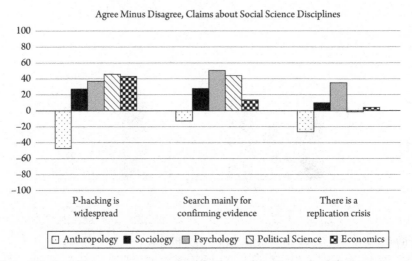

Figure 2.2 Social Scientists' Agreement with Claims about Reproducibility. Data from the author's 2020 survey of social scientists at major US research universities. n=1,141.

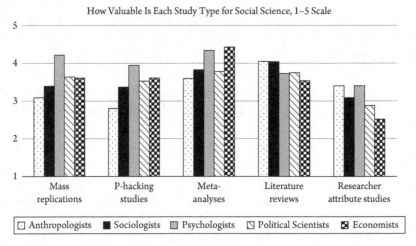

Figure 2.3 Social Scientists' Valuation of Meta-Science Research Studies. Data from the author's 2020 survey of social scientists at major US research universities. n=1,141.

of studies common in the open science reform movement: replications of previously published findings by many different teams, studies of p-hacking (searching for statistically significant results), and meta-analyses of research findings across studies. For a comparison, they were also asked to value qualitative reviews of findings in research literatures. Finally, they were asked to value studies of differences in research findings based on demographics of researchers (for example, to search for racial or gender bias).

The three types of reproducibility metascience studies were all seen as moderately to highly valuable, with anthropology the least enthused and psychology the most. Conventional literature reviews were also seen as valuable across disciplines. Social scientists still see room for qualitative synthesis alongside innovations, but economists stood out as preferring meta-analysis. Studies of the relationships between researcher demographics and findings were less popular, though still valued in anthropology and psychology. These kinds of studies are not yet seen as part of the reform movement, though they are also responsive to potential researcher bias. Overall, researchers both see increasing recognition of bias and value studies to analyze it, even if they do not see it as a crisis.

Figure 2.4 illustrates social scientists' opinions on reforms proposed by the open science and reproducibility movement. Reforms are again rated in value on a scale of 1–5. Public posting of replication data is rated highly valuable. There is also a reasonable consensus on disclosure of funding sources and conflicts of interest. Raising the threshold for significance testing above the .05 conventional level also draws reasonably high support, though preregistration of research designs remains less popular. Anthropology again stands out for its lack of support, with psychology and economics the most supportive. Overall, even respondents who said they do not see a replication crisis are still supportive of many reforms.

Given these results, it seems unlikely that academics will agree to near-universal preregistration or raising p-values (though journals may force the hand of their authors), but some reforms may gain widespread acceptance. The consensus on replication data should hearten open science reformers. They can also learn from the comparatively poor reputation of preregistration in some

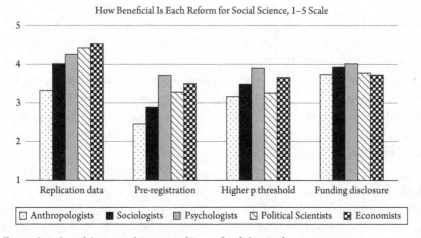

How Beneficial Is Each Reform for Social Science, 1–5 Scale

Anthropologists   Sociologists   Psychologists   Political Scientists   Economists

Figure 2.4 Social Scientists' Ratings of Reproducibility Reforms. Data from the author's 2020 survey of social scientists at major US research universities. n=1,141.

quarters, though there are still many social scientists willing to pursue it and others using it to learn how others' research develops. Even scholars uninterested in pre-analysis plans have learned to think more about which hypotheses were developed before seeing data as well as the costs of testing too many hypotheses without accounting for multiple testing. That means we may see changes in behavior and interpretation beyond formal registration. In total, the reform movement has achieved cross-discipline support. As one psychologist told me, "We've seen where there are some problems and started working on them. Sample sizes are increasing. People are becoming (I hope) more transparent, more honest. I think this is more about changing of norms than anything nefarious."

The Revolution in Credible Empirical Social Science

Reproducibility reforms are taking place in the context of several revolutions in social science practice, due to increased empirical data analysis and more serious efforts at causal inference with experimental and quasi-experimental research designs. Reforms were contemplated as researchers moved more toward theory testing, assessing rather than assuming prior knowledge of both the relationships among social factors and the global scope for theoretical claims. Scholars have also long repeated that correlation does not equal causation but still interpreted observational evidence in causal terms; they are now taking the difficulty of assessing causal claims more seriously.

The trends have been most pronounced in economics, which has become vastly more empirical. The transformation is visible in the titles of journal articles: many fewer now mention words related to theory and many more mention evidence, trends mirrored in the most cited articles in each decade.[46] "Theory" was the most frequently used word in the 1970s, with "model" closely behind; in the 1980s, "theory" falls to the third most used word; in the 1990s, to the fifth, with "model" falling to sixth and "evidence" appearing in the top ten. By the 2000s, "evidence" is the most used word; in the 2010s, one-fifth of the most-cited papers use it in their titles. Financial economics, which has grown dramatically since the 1970s, has also become steadily more empirical and complex.[47]

But economics started from a high point of theoretical focus. It had very formal models based upon rational choice decision-making and a related core graduate curriculum. As the theory consensus waned, work moved to applied topics and quasi-experimental methods. Model builder Scott Page called it a "huge move, it is now 80–90 percent empirical." He acknowledges it "could have been too far in favor of theory" in its heyday but still sees an important role for theory: "for productivity, you need balance and combination." A prominent economist told me it is a "total revolution. Starting in 1975, it was almost all theory; now it has flipped: all of most influential work is heavily empirically based; often connected to theory, but sometimes theory free." He sees it as a positive trend: "We've made more progress, all to the good, by forcing us to confront the facts and [leaving the] illusory world of theory." Economist Daniel Benjamin told me "economics is more based on reliable facts and causal effect estimates." That is "generally positive" but can lead to "using the best tools at the expense of the most important questions." Economist David Autor said, "Economics is now much more practical and relevant, less in the sway of ideology."

Political science has followed economics toward empiricism. Ken Kollman said, "The move in political science was based on pressure to match the empirical world. That means a loss of generality and narrowing scope for theory. [I see] no real recent deep breakthroughs [in theoretical modeling]." Empirical political scientists see little downside: "I don't see a loss from the decline of formal theory," said Robert Kubinek. "The move to middle-range theories has been positive if questions are not cherry-picked." Political scientist Neil Malhotra told me it is a natural progression from more evidence: "You used to have a lot of theories without many metrics. Now there are more tests. The pendulum swung too far in the other direction; we may now lack theory and economic training, but we're now [borrowing from] computer science. People respond more to empirics in [research] talks, even in formal theory rooms [because it gives them] something to respond to."

Sociology and psychology were always less enamored with formal theory but have also seen some changes. "The trend is somewhat econ specific," a prominent sociologist told me, "but grand theory has declined over the last twenty years [in sociology as well]. It is still embedded in teaching and grad programs, but people don't identify [as theorists]. The main journals are heavily empirical." But the heyday of grand theory is somewhat apocryphal, according to sociologist Daniel Hirschman: "The discipline was never dominated by grand theory. People say the 1960s and 70s that's what they were reading, but lots of researchers were doing middle-range sociology. Theory as a subject has declined for job openings but not for teaching."

Grand theorizing does tend to reappear, with social scientists after World War I seeking a scientific emblem on their disciplines, then after World War II seeking equal status with scientists for government support, and then in the 1970s reviving again with economic models.[48] But sociologist Duncan Watts says the impetus to agree on grand theory "didn't arrive until the mid-twentieth century" and was quickly critiqued as a product of the time and the biases of the leading scholars, such as Talcott Parsons.[49] Structuralist theories, neat historical periodizations, and theories of inevitable stages have all declined.[50] We have "found our telescope" with new tools, Watts says, but we still struggle to fit all the findings together to address big questions.[51] Sociologist Aaron Panofsky says, "Empiricism is rising with time and data, [as researchers move toward] applied social science [and are now] less ideological overall in theory." Within sociology, he cites the decline of structural functionalism and Marxism as similar to the decline of rational choice modeling in economics.

Psychology might be different, according to Jay Van Bavel: "It's not the same trend in psychology. There is some push to formalize theory in computational models, but also to connect more to other disciplines in behavioral economics and political psychology." But Chris Chambers says theory is less sacrosanct in psychology as well: "We know that theory sucks in many fields. It is vague and unfalsifiable. We are shifting the mindset to precision [and action]." The advance of applied empiricism is not making old social science standards superfluous, but it is changing the way we think about the relationship between theory and evidence.

The Causal Inference Revolution

In parallel, social science is well into the causal inference revolution. It started with randomized controlled trials (RCTs) in development economics. During the first wave in the 1970s, the proponents were administrative or research professionals within global government institutions, but the movement is now embraced by the private and voluntary sectors as well.[52] Researchers are now better positioned in the network of expertise, within social science and in the development and funding communities. The Poverty Action Lab at MIT had 33 projects by 4 professors when it started in 2003, but quickly expanded to 161 professors conducting 902 evaluations in 72 countries by 2017, with its founders winning the Nobel Prize in 2019. They are now evaluating shorter and smaller interventions and facing less resistance from government and more support from philanthropy. The rise was enabled by the empirical turn in economics, with increasing belief that applied projects could add to general knowledge.[53]

The rise of RCTs has stimulated some backlash for overclaiming their benefits. Isolating one variable does not change the need to think of other covariates, as an unbiased estimate of one impact sometimes lacks practical value if obtained from a trial sample.[54] That means researchers still have to build on prior know-ledge, as most studies to date have been proofs of concept, rather than full-scale interventions. Even if only testing a single intervention, researchers can still engage in multiple comparisons and make questionable measurement choices.[55] Experimentalists often assume that their results make for strong evidence of a broader claim with a long evidence chain. But the rigor of one analysis does not transfer to the full research endeavor, especially if scholars are interested in varied effects and extrapolating to a larger target population and a different context.[56]

As in any research design, there are trade-offs. RCTs reduce bias and error on average across many experiments. But that solves only one problem and is not guaranteed in any one study.[57] Many important factors in the world cannot be randomly assigned, meaning that we are often ignoring macro historical influences or national-level variables or are studying model systems rather than actually testing the influence of a real-world factor.

But increasing field experiments are part of a broader emphasis on the credibility of causal inferences, associated with a revolution in research designs in economics.[58] Early papers on death penalty deterrence based on simple time-series or cross-sectional analysis across states, even cited by the Supreme Court, came to be seen as poorly designed. The increase in panel data helped diversify methods to address time- and place-invariant factors and look for differences in change across units. Overall, references to "identification" (how causal inference is known in economics) went from 19 in Econlit (a research suppository) in the 1970s and 1980s to 742 in the 1990s and 2000s.[59]

The main proposed solutions, popularized by the book *Mostly Harmless Econometrics*, have been instrumental variables, fixed effects or difference-in-difference estimates in panel data, and regression discontinuity.[60] Each of these analyses asks a causal question and finds a related identification strategy for one key variable. They start from the experimental ideal but move beyond matching and regression as starting points for controlling for the impact of other confounding factors. Researchers also now look for more natural experiments where a cause is randomly assigned but not by the researchers; these studies can identify causal effects with more external validity (applying conclusions outside the context of a study, such as generalizing from a laboratory negotiation to consumer behavior).[61]

These innovations were associated with refinement of philosophical innovations in causal inference, especially the potential outcomes framework associated with Donald Rubin and (to a lesser extent) the Directed Acyclic Graphs (DAGs) associated with Judea Pearl.[62] Using the potential outcomes framework, researchers can estimate an average treatment effect across a group (at least through random assignment in an experiment) even though we cannot know the causal effect in a single case. A DAG specifies causal relationships and directions between variables and then estimates causal relationships given that model.

Neither specified how theories could be initially derived, but both offered potential solutions for testing. The potential outcomes framework is in broader use, as it draws from the manipulability of experiments and close analogues when applied to matching, instrumental variables, difference-in-differences, regression discontinuity, or synthetic control.[63] But each of the quasi-experimental methods has to meet core assumptions that are sometimes difficult to test. And causal inference is still usually based on a test of whether an effect is larger than zero, perhaps not much knowledge given that most plausible factors in social outcomes would have some effect if measured with enough precision.[64]

DAGs, essentially drawing a map of what factors affect others in what directions, allow a broader range of estimation strategies but require stronger assumptions about theory.[65] That means we can investigate causal relationships if we assume our theory is strong. But the approach is therefore reliant on the reasonableness of our codified knowledge and existing causal models. That puts us right back into investigating the sociology of science, the psychology of investigators, and the incentives of the scientific community to learn how causal models are developed and to correct for potential biases. Whenever Pearl applies his framework to real-world research, he implicitly (or explicitly in his history of smoking and cancer research) assesses the incentives of researchers, showing the effects of biases on the range of causal models evaluated.

For some young scholars, according to Alex Coppock, the potential outcomes model is now "deep-seated," including thinking about counterfactuals and choosing one of the prominent quasi-experimental designs. Researchers prioritize internal validity (establishing a trustworthy causal relationship) before seeking to assess the generalizability of a causal claim. Survey experimenters, suddenly able to secure samples from many online sources, seek to test all kinds of theories using model situations or conjoint experiments.[66]

But there remains dissent about the success of the causal inference revolution. Philosopher Nancy Cartwright argues that a "cause" means many things and different methods have different strengths and weaknesses in assessing them.[67] She raises the possibility of idiosyncratic systems, arguing that metaphysical assumptions about interventions and invariance (that a particular stimulus has a common effect) are driving methodological choices. These assumptions usually arise from what is needed to make the statistical procedures perform neatly, rather than core expectations.

Scholars are, in many ways, still left with the criteria articulated by statistician Austin Bradford Hill for causal evidence: the strength of the effect, its consistency, its specificity, the temporal order (whether the cause precedes the effect), the dose-response relationship (greater increases in the cause lead to greater increases in the effect), the plausibility of the mechanism, the coherence with other findings, the primacy of experimental evidence, the similarity to other associations, and the reversibility of the effect given the removal of the cause. One useful technique is still to divide data into a training set and a test set for later analysis to avoid overfitting.[68] New techniques of causal inference help but often still need to be combined with other observational data. Meanwhile, debates about the relative importance and potential trade-offs between internal and external validity are unfinished, especially as many key patterns are only observable in the wild.

In social science, we should assume our initial theories are likely to be far from the truth and only slowly converging on truth with accumulating evidence. Scholars are unlikely to be able to identify all of the relevant factors in advance, much less establish the likely directions of all causal relationships and their scope conditions (limiting the usefulness of DAGs and the generalizability of the potential outcomes framework). Although social sciences do search for general causal patterns, the world is complex; many processes are limited in time and by social context. There are social regularities and manipulable relationships, but the world was not designed to make all causal patterns discernable using our techniques.[69] Causal inference strategies have altered our focus, though some studies still make grand claims from global multi-factor observational research.[70]

Researchers claiming to be doing confirmatory causal research are now routinely asked for identification strategies. And critics should not assume that quasi-experimental innovations are being forwarded as a status claim by researchers driven to quantify. They are born of attempts to solve real problems with inferring causality from observational methods—even from a humility about how much their disciplines have been able to achieve even with abundant data. When research uses an arbitrary cutoff such as an entrance exam score to assess the effects of admission, it is to gain causal leverage (through regression discontinuity) rather than an aesthetic preference. Tara Slough told me that researchers are also aware of the downsides: "Some things are more easily manipulable or occur as if random, but [by focusing on them] we could have substitution away from more interesting mechanisms . . . experiments evolved positively but might not address questions of broad importance about power. . . . [It might be] harder to explain broad disparities and historical trends." Indeed, the long history of social psychology experiments suggests they often serve as existence proofs based on toy models that may not apply to the real-world situations that inspired them.[71]

Experimentalists tend to perceive little trade-off between internal and external validity, because they are conceiving of questions as narrowly about the existence of an effect from one cause. But as Kevin Munger told me, there is a trade-off in how research is conducted: "Reducing the scope of a research question from impossible to study to possible is reasonable, but it makes generalization more difficult and aggregating research findings [across studies] more important. A chain of causal reasoning is as weak as its weakest link." With experimental research, he says, "the external validity issue isn't [usually] sampling, but the connection to the real world. . . . We're in a high-dimensionality world with lots of factors and little research on transplantation of effects so we are often proving effects in model systems." Andrew Gelman agrees: "Most of the issue with experiments is not cross-cultural [adherence to laboratory manipulations] but other issues of realism. [We are doing] shallow studies compared to the [complexity of] real-world politics."

But Cyrus Samii says the trade-off is overblown: "People didn't know about effective sample sizes [that even in observational research, your analyses are often relying on a small number of cases with variation]. It is not a case of pure trade-offs. The premise that observational is more generalizable ignores that [studies] often [get their] power based on a couple of cases."

Rather than consider one gold standard of experiments, Kubinek says we should consider three silver standards, judging each by how much they reduce uncertainty around our causal knowledge; experiments, qualitative process training, and observational analysis could all play a role depending on the current state of research.[72] If we are studying voter turnout, the next in a long run of experiments may not provide much new knowledge; if we find a randomly assigned increase in democratization, that might have a lot more potential (because our prior research is observational). We thus cannot avoid assessing the limits of current research practices in a field and finding the biases most in need of amelioration via other methods and integration of scholarly perspectives.

The Rise of Big and Connected Data

The increasing emphasis on causal inference has (somewhat oddly) coincided with a revolution in "big data," large datasets often left from online behavior, texts, or administrative databases. The use of big data alongside applications of computer science now goes by the moniker of "data science," which combines statistics with machine learning techniques (applications from artificial intelligence using algorithms to draw conclusions from data). These researchers tend to inductively infer patterns from many different variables, such as an underlying ideological spectrum from the use of many different words in congressional speeches.

Some of the gains come from increased access to data alone. Economists now use individual tax returns, especially for the richest individuals, to better estimate inequality. Scandinavian researchers have access to detailed government data on individual health, family ties, and income stretching back from childhood. Political scientists have detailed voting records matched to individuals as they move. But when millions of cases are involved, researchers typically have to condense data (especially when it initially comes from text, audiovisual information, or websites) with techniques to classify cases or array them on simplified dimensions.

Although big datasets can sometimes be combined with experimental or quasi-experimental methods, they are most often used for descriptive inferences across large-scale populations or time periods. "The cutting edge is merging datasets of many types," Ken Kollman told me. But "there is a flat-out contradiction in the data science and causal inference revolutions: the massive availability of data and merging is the longer-term bet: that we can fill in missing pieces with data, not just a related model." A political science journal symposium showed that other scholars see the trends as potentially more aligned, with causal inference researchers seeing big data potentially useful for designing experiments or quasi-experimental studies and others seeing new opportunities for description that do not have to trade off with causal studies.[73] Researchers can now more easily collect data across time and place, starting from observed associations and building more complex models.

And data availability has grown enormously even in traditional areas like survey research and experiments. Political scientist Adam Berinsky told me, "It used to take forever to conduct experiments on large samples. Now it is trivial. . . . The ease of data collection has made self-replication easier. . . . You can see multiple realizations of what you are studying." He compared it to unreplicated studies of the past: "It's not that people were trying to get flaky results. They were doing their best given the norms and more importantly the resources of the time."

Data science is not a replacement for human-led consensus building in the scientific community. Handing over areas of scholarship to machine learning has not been successful, but focusing computational power on specific discrete tasks has been.[74] With practical applications in mind, data science also facilitates functional collaboration that is not weighed down by jargon-laden theoretical argument.[75] Political scientist Kevin Munger told me big data approaches are "reinvigorating descriptive inference" while experiments are improving causal inference without displacing other research. "The returns are up to investigating social phenomena. . . . The diversification of duties could be good."

In addition to individual-level data, scholars are also now better able to collect aggregate data on geographic or group-level attributes. Geographic Information Systems have quickly advanced to collect, map, and analyze physical and social characteristics of places such as neighborhoods and political districts. Replication data and inter-operable software now allow quickly merging and aggregating many data sources so that analyses of individuals can account for their social context, such as studies of policy views now including people's surrounding demographics. And scholars can now combine limited local data to reach better aggregate estimates of geographic variation using a technique called multilevel regression with post-stratification, which combines survey responses with census data to provide credible localized data.

In addition to proliferating contextual data, new large datasets often include relational data on connections between cases (such as social network data with friendship ties and browsing patterns between websites) in addition to many attributes of each case. Researchers know a lot more about you and about your connections with others. Models that incorporate the spread of behavior and social ties are often more realistic, but also more complicated to estimate, with additional assumptions about causal direction. Political scientist Mirya Holman said she expects researchers to find the most lucrative approaches over time: "Network models were so hot before they settled in. We are still using them, but where they are most appropriate. Text analysis is still rising but we will figure out when it is most useful." A sociologist was quite hopeful: "The state of the art of quantitative analysis continues to improve. In addition, new methods like social network analysis and big data and computational methods are improving and widening their influence."

With new approaches and more data, social scientists fear being overwhelmed or not keeping up. The main solution has been the rise of team science: increasing coauthorship and codevelopment of projects across researchers. Coauthored articles are quickly rising, as is the number of coauthors. And there is evidence that teams produce more scholarly impact and commercial use.[76] Team science is also coinciding with increasing researcher diversification, interdisciplinarity, and internationalization (discussed in Chapters 5 and 6).

Team science has advanced quickly in some fields, where mass collaboration has focused researchers on the same problems; having a group with both focused experts and those with more varied interests helps make connections between ideas.[77] Large mapping initiatives to identify the parts of the ocean, the brain, and the earth's climate have advanced, while smaller projects also generate online feedback and collaboration. Scott Page told me he has found that scale and diversity generally help research progress, but diverse teams can become too big; new ideas often come from small groups linking disciplines and their different assumptions. Bigger data has come with larger teams, but the critical work is still integrating diverse perspectives in the research community.

Credible Social Science, with Remaining Pluralism

Methodological advance has long been combined with fears of declining research diversity. Across the social sciences, quantification was associated with the Americanization of social research: the techniques slowly globalized, but also brought a negative reaction from traditional qualitative and philosophical corners within and outside social science.[78] Methodological advances were often met with the criticisms that scholars were prioritizing methods over problem-driven research and were focusing on smaller questions rather than answering the most important questions.[79]

This is to some extent a false dichotomy. Scientists across fields are opportunistic "methodological omnivores" who create local models, debate consistency, assess the extent of regularities, and distinguish associations and causal structures; they do so slowly when evidentiary opportunities arise, rather than as part of a grand plan.[80] They have always faced pressures to direct resources to addressing questions where there is some chance of answering them, but also to address questions of greater importance. Nonetheless, research agendas often begin with empirically grounded speculation and storytelling. Science learns as much from the evolution of new questions and interpretations as from definitive answers.[81] Social scientists recognize this: realist positions are now the default, with debates among philosophically purist views disfavored.[82]

Models of scientific discovery find that reproducibility alone does not help build research knowledge as much as communities trying different strategies and methods, facilitating exploration of potential explanations.[83] Communities need both constructors of new theories and simplifiers of seemingly diverse ideas.[84] The scientific community makes a division of cognitive labor possible, where most are ignorant about most aspects of a problem, but the community filters and narrows potentially important factors.[85] In the process, attempts to generalize middle-range theories limit the scope of explanations, leaving only a small number of globally important factors.[86]

That requires a working and interactive scientific community. Social scientists are wary of being judged on the number and technical sophistication of their articles (perhaps linked to misaligned incentives and irreproducibility). Major journals are now receiving far more submissions, and graduate students are increasingly expected to publish. But these trends partially reflect large increases in the number of active researchers. Published research still gets noticed; claims that most research is uncited are based on incorrect zombie statistics.[87] Even though academic status is still tied to top-journal research, the trend is toward more journals publishing more papers. Top-cited articles are increasingly published in nonelite journals as scholars can find the most relevant articles in online databases, regardless of where they were published.[88]

The Robert Merton vision of "middle-range" theory and questions has had a resurgence, with more integration of theory and empirical analysis, multiple testing, and slow generalization.[89] These developments fit with the advice from forecasting tournaments of world political and economic events: even if the goal is prediction alone, it is better to draw from many theories, multiple models, and probabilistic thinking—and even better to integrate multiple views in teams.[90] These ingenious mass experiments have convinced governments that lone subject-matter experts are less effective than somewhat-informed groups that know how to aggregate and reconcile competing evidence. Social scientists, who seek to understand as well as predict, are improving techniques without losing diversity of perspectives.

Reforms of questionable research practices are certainly part of the advance of social science. Scholars have been mostly accepting of the reforms, such as sharing data and investigating the search for confirming evidence and publication bias. Where many scholars have been skeptical of some of the new expectations, such as preregistration, open science advocates have in turn clarified that the new procedures are not meant to be straitjackets but guides to just how much of our research ends up being exploratory. That realization alone is worth the price of scholarly conflict and some negative publicity. Social scientists are in wide agreement that new data and better tools have become available to them, even if they do not see them all as revolutionary. Social science can be reformed, quickly and persuasively, but the process of discussing and implementing reform also broadens our perspective on what we are doing and moves the critics and proponents of social science toward more consensus on the challenges ahead of us.

3

The Quiet Resolution of the Science Wars

Bruno Latour, a leader of skeptical studies of science, issued a mea culpa in 2004.[1] Studying the scientific process as a social system with no independent authority had backfired, he acknowledged, giving license to climate change deniers and creationists rather than improving scientific practice. The leader of critiques now argued there was too much critique, undermining public faith. Arguments emphasizing uncertainty in science as well as social influence on research weakened scientific claims, without adding to the store of knowledge. Universal critiques should be replaced with more specific and limited objections to allow science to respond, he now said.

And that was all well before the election of Donald Trump in 2016 and the fears it prompted about moving into a "post-truth" society with the spread of "fake news." Democratic Party nominee Hillary Clinton used "I believe in science" as an applause line that year. After his election, Trump was greeted with a "March for Science" protest series, demonstrating scholars' politicization around the truth claims of science: "I can't believe I'm protesting for reality" and "Without science, it's all fiction," read the signs.[2] Joe Biden, after defeating Trump, inaugurated his administration promising to "defend the truth." Liberal skepticism of scientific authority and claims of technological progress had given way to fears of unbridled populism when scientific experts are ignored.

Although the "science wars" of the 1980s and 1990s were mostly seen as a fight between a triumphalist natural science and the skeptical humanities, some of the practitioners were trained in social science theory and methods. The interdisciplinary wars coincided with fights within some social science disciplines between ascendant mathematical and scientific approaches and traditional historical methods. Part of the war's end was a realization that the argument was largely over straw men. Social science was quicker to realize what could be gained from studying scientific organizations and patterns of behavior like other social institutions and practices, but also what could be lost down a rabbit hole of critique, with unanswerable questions and untestable ideas.

Alongside the end of the public wars over science, social science saw a rise of pluralism in theory and methods with a recognition of their strengths and limitations. Social scientists also became prominent allies of natural scientists in understanding how scientific findings in areas like climate change and vaccination are best communicated. And along the way, many scientists and humanists learned to tone down their irreconcilable fights over fundamental truths while partnering to improve scientific practice and restrain overbroad claims.

Today, metascientific studies have reinterested scientists in the same concerns that drove social studies of science. New research shares the initial skepticism but uses contemporary quantitative approaches to research the scientific process, adding an applied aim to reform scientific practice. The findings of the new and old studies show flaws in theory generation, hypothesis testing, generalization, peer review, and public dissemination, but scholars are now reticent to undermine scientific authority. As defects are more widely understood but potential advances are abundant, few are motivated to reduce science's imprint but still fewer adopt a posture of avoiding tough questions. In parallel, disciplines have tempered their long-standing methodological divides and embraced pluralism. By becoming more practical as well as reticent to make global claims based on single methods, social science has gained an important role in understanding and improving the place of science in universities and in society.

Social Science and the Evolution of the Science Studies Conflict

Robert Merton's 1957 presidential address to the American Sociological Association focused on the need to study science like other social institutions and value systems.[3] And many took up his call, with sociology of knowledge becoming a separate field within the discipline and social studies of science becoming its own quasi-independent field. Natural scientists were initially dismissive, but became less self-confident and more willing to listen.[4]

Philosophy of science always played a foundational role in these research areas, but its traditional bedrocks were unable to account for changes in the process of discovery or to answer common critiques. The focus on empirical disconfirmation made Karl Popper a default influence for many practitioners, but philosophers mostly moved on after finding his views incomplete. Thomas Kuhn's theory of scientific revolutions was also taken up widely in social science, even though it focused entirely on natural science.[5] Even when citing philosophers, social scientists were mainly applying those with the most socio-logical conceptualizations of the scientific process.

Meanwhile, history of science was also evolving to critique how science had risen in social esteem and to document how science reflected the social and po-litical concerns of each period.[6] Science could not be demarcated on methodo-logical grounds alone and had to be understood in its social context.[7] The 1960s brought claims that science was co-opted by the state and the military alongside concerns about assumed natural laws being used for social engineering. This new focus led to reinterpretations of scientific history, as scholars used social justice lenses to challenge a narrative of progress. This was followed by broader critical claims that all forms of reasoning from different perspectives were equally valid (or close to it), that all communities selectively attend to parts of the whole, and that all knowledge was provisional and reflective of its time.

Science studies likewise moved from an initial fan club of science to a more critical focus on science as a social construct, with debates about whether sci-ence had any special claims to knowledge. Although initially accepting scientists' claims that technology was proof of the utility of scientific claims, sociologists of science discovered that most claims to knowledge were not instantiated in tech-nology and many innovations did not descend from basic science to application.

Cornell University held the first Social Studies of Science gathering in 1976, formalizing the critical community. Latour's *Laboratory Life*, a social chronicle in the lab of a Nobel Prize winner, was published in 1979. By the 1980s, social critics were making larger splashes, and other scholars (hardly just scientists) were becoming more displeased. Although the "science wars" were not named until 1996, they were ongoing in scholarly conflict well before that. Alan Bloom critiqued what he saw as a creeping relativism across universities in *The Closing of the American Mind* in 1987. But the landmark was *Higher Superstition* by Paul Gross and Norman Levitt in 1994, which posited that postmodern theory had infected academia, moving from the humanities to social studies of science, and that only a resuscitation of scientific rigor could help universities regain their so-cial role.[8] This became a default argument in debates over higher education and humanities decline.

What is remembered most vividly is the Sokal hoax, the publication of phys-icist Alan Sokal's meaningless drivel about quantum gravity being a social con-struct as an article in the theory journal *Social Text* in 1996. He revealed shortly after that his article submission was an elaborate ruse to demonstrate the ab-surdity of science studies, becoming the center of a public conflict on the limits of social theory in science. Although only part of a wider debate on claims to authoritative expertise, scientists and commentators saw the papers he was parodying as emblematic of the excesses of science criticism.

By that point, science and technology studies (STS) had become dominated by theoretically grounded and jargon-heavy case studies, which are particularly subject to confirmation bias and to obscuring central claims and evidence from those outside the field. While highlighting severe examples of overclaiming, opponents of science studies saw themselves as upholders of "science and reason," raising the specter of a broader academic left.[9] Science studies scholars became less welcome in scientific labs and increasingly identified as relativists. As conservative critics of science—particularly in the intelligent design movement and the climate change denial community—gained notoriety, the science studies community sought to reframe their critique.

Self-styled science defenders then targeted the federal funding for science and technology studies while they accused science critics of threatening public support for science, increasing the stakes. Only a small fraction of scientists and science studies scholars were directly involved in the public "science wars," and much of the scientists' ire was directed more at postmodern philosophy than actual case studies of science.[10] Nevertheless, social studies of science were demeaned as a project of deconstruction and broadly dismissed. Mainstream social science, neither taken by postmodern theory nor willing to take natural science claims for granted, was largely left out of these debates (though its interpretivist corners were also critiqued as relativistic). Sociology of knowledge and science seemed to stagnate as separate fields by the twenty-first century, with related studies increasingly treated as more generic examples of sociology.[11]

Social studies of science serve as an important prehistory to recent critics of hypothesis testing—with similar constructive concerns. Harry Collins argued persuasively that critique should not mean deconstruction: "We understand the fallibility and interests of financial advisors, lawyers, politicians, art and literary critics, doctors, builders, car mechanics, and travel agents without concluding that they are not more expert in their areas than we ourselves. Neither anarchy nor nihilism follows from the recognition of the human basis of expertise; instead comes the recognition that there is no magical escape from the pangs of uncertainty that underlie our decisions."[12] Scientists tracking their own behavior had long been interested in ethics and improving practice, and social studies of science drew from this history to understand science in its own terms.[13]

The primary theoretical view advanced in science studies was perspectivism: the idea that scientists cannot assume a view from nowhere; they are affected by their backgrounds and assumptions like other observers. Feminist Sandra Harding, who helped inspire this scholarship, articulated the view as consistent with science: "we share the valuing of knowledge of how worlds actually work—their regularities and underlying causal tendencies . . . [but] the 'harmony' desired must always be partial, tentative, and fragile, and must be created through negotiation and compromise."[14]

Yet what science critics see as a disingenuous pretense of objectivity in science is, in many cases, a recognition of shortcomings: because biases influence research, scientists are reliant on the precision of claims as well as tests that meet community standards. Likewise, defensive scientists sometimes see the empirical claim that scientific consensus is reached through social construction as a philosophical nihilism that assumes no truth is possible. Instead, scientists could see science critiques as responsive to their own concerns about the scientific process, though more skeptical that perfecting the methods will solve the problems. Scientists need to be analyzed as fallible social and partially self-interested actors, despite our normative hopes for their project.[15]

By the time of Latour's mea culpa, science critics had realized that a focus on critique had been counterproductive, that progress through the gathering of multiple views and the perfection of methods was complementary, and that they should aim to be additive rather than tearing down knowledge.[16] As one review summarized, "After a while, views on both sides mellowed, and at least some people from both camps settled for acceptable compromises. Conciliatory positions emerged, more credible than many of the radical caricatures."[17]

Scientists recognize their own moral structure, even if they did not fully explain it as part of their methods. They prize curiosity and virtues such as creativity.[18] They recognize aspirational values, even if they do not live up to them. Because they acknowledge personal biases, they try to perfect scientific methods as "systematic procedures of bias reduction."[19] They see themselves as disciplined by method and their humility about evidence. When accused of having no independent claim to knowledge, scientists see critics as relativists with no shared goals. Those taking their side, like Robert Pennock, see the science wars as "not having ended with a surrender, a settlement, or even a bang, but with a belly laugh," referring to the Sokal hoax.[20]

But those who have tracked developments in social science, including philosopher Heather Douglas, see more of a truce with enlarged understanding.[21] It is hard to find anyone defending the strongest constructivist claims attributed to science critics; the fights were more about claims to authority than the dynamics of knowledge production. Critics still want to dismiss junk science, use (even uncertain and error-prone) science in courts and policymaking, and avoid the politicization of science by industry or religion. Scientists can recognize that they bring values to their enterprise and yet keep them out of their direct assessments of evidence, seeking to imagine what evidence could counter their own views and gather it. One sociologist said they were optimistic about "the extinction of old and tired debates and arguments originating out of the turmoil of the 60s and new young scholars who just don't care about those debates and are doing novel work."

Social scientists have been less likely to misread the science wars because they see similar arguments over culture, economics, politics, and religion. They understand that something with a tangible basis, like a legislature or a church, can still be influenced by shared beliefs without undermining its reality. They also know the difference between the philosophical claim that there is no path to the truth and the sociological claim that the truth of a statement may not be the explanation for why people accept it. For example, we have to explain why behavioral economics won an internal conflict in the economics discipline, rather than assume it was an inevitable result of its stronger truth claim. Social scientists can evaluate the epistemic claims about how knowledge advances without assuming the dead-end ontological view that no knowledge is possible.

The Rise and Influence of Metascience

Metascience denotes the use of large-scale scientific studies to understand the scientific process. Symbolized by a 2019 symposium at Stanford University, it marks the coming together of researchers concerned with reproducibility and statistical inference, mostly using large-scale quantitative datasets across disciplines. Although it draws some from social studies of science, the overlapping of the schedule for the metascience symposium and the annual conference of the Society for Social Studies of Science (the main STS conference) suggests there is not a lot of perceived overlap (or respect).

Many of the recently touted metascience findings also have a long history within methodological research. Scholars have long known that the (commonly used) .05 standard for statistical significance tests is arbitrary and bias-inducing and that most studies lack the statistical power to find small effects, but large-scale studies have brought these findings further to the fore.[22] Metascience has generated immediate attention among social and natural science practitioners, including calls for reform, while STS has had limited recent influence on how scientists act.[23] Although metascience is designed to be more constructive than science studies, it is still fundamentally a new version of sociology of science. It will still need to extrapolate across time periods with changing data, compare patterns across disparate geographic and disciplinary areas, and account for affecting the behavior it is trying to study even with its imperfect metrics.

Although self-consciously revolutionary, metascience may represent more of an updated critique. As political scientist Arthur Lupia told me, "Young academics like to think they are revolutionaries where everything is new, even when there's probably some re-learning [of older ideas] but the breadth and rigor of conversations in metascience has improved. Many more are buying in and discussing principles together." Although "there have been methods nags for all time," reformer Alex Coppock told me, new findings have shown that most studies are underpowered (or reliant on a few unrepresentative cases to prove relationships), leading to real changes in practice such as larger sample sizes and quasi-experimental approaches.

According to open science advocate Robert Nozek, there are many relationships between traditional science studies and metascience, but the new community is made possible by a large interdisciplinary group of practitioners with shared interests in both large-scale research and reform. Reformer Andrew Gelman agreed: "Maybe metascience is just sociology of science, but it has a different audience and gets more attention from practitioners by involving them." Sociologist Daniel Hirschman told me that the fields are "parallel but separate," with more objective ways to measure scientific trends not replacing traditional narratives of field development. Psychologist Sanjay Srivastava said he "would like to hear more from sociology of science . . . but quantitative metascience benefits from more contact with applied and translational work." Since both fields are "self-examining," they might be able to "see each other's blind spots."

Sociologist Aaron Panofsky, however, sees some overzealous patterns repeating. "The problems with preregistration are completely unsurprising from a science studies perspective. People fool themselves into accepting a model of science that doesn't fit reality. We've [long] known [that] we're not doing what we thought we were doing and [yet we] predict that doubling down to reduce researcher degrees of freedom [will work]." This skepticism of methodological solutions to endemic problems of social science is justified but it does not undermine the value of highlighting problems and offering tools to address them. And some simple procedures like providing data and more fully describing protocols for others to confirm results have been successful. By empirically examining scientific results in a way that scientists understand and can address, metascience has quickly gained a broader practitioner audience. But the loss of critical perspective and the assumption that technological fixes are the answer suggests the older style of critique still has value.

Metascience also draws from the rise of scientometrics, the analysis of citation histories in field development, that is now conducted via big data text and network analysis techniques. These studies have a longer history that quantifies how disciplines evolve and interact. Panofsky said that STS was "more qualitative and caught flat-footed with interlopers [before]" and may be doing so again. In addition to rediscovering old findings with more data, metascience is also discovering new patterns and using new tools with a "reformist disposition." Metascience arose out of the wreckage of the science wars, refining critics' points without the deconstructionist edge. The community acknowledges that they are to some extent re-creating the wheel, but consciously has a different purpose and new methods.

The Broader Decline of Methods Dichotomies

The welcoming of metascience research coincides with a decline in seemingly irreconcilable debates over core assumptions about how to do social science research. As the public science wars receded, so did the within-discipline conflicts over what constitutes science.

Debates over the normative or empirical role of social science, the relative importance of theory and data, qualitative vs. quantitative approaches, human rationality, and American uniqueness are all more than a century old.[24] But there is increasing agreement on the difficulty of reaching causal conclusions or representative findings and more consensus around the most common inferential errors.[25] Social scientists cannot expect to develop and test models to explain all history that apply to all people and situations; simplification and boundary conditions are important for theories to develop and to enable assessment. But early attempts to require necessities for explanation, outline all relevant premises, add all conditions, and unify across theories were bound to fail and have been replaced by middle-range theories and a strong focus on stylized empirical facts.[26] Requiring fully specified, testable, and falsifiable theories has not been a good guide to evaluating candidates for social explanations or differentiating among them, even though the impetus to find difficult tests before confirming theories has been quite valuable.[27]

Among the longest-running errors of researchers has been the desire to divide factors into two large boxes to subsume all other variation.[28] Philosopher Brian Fay warns that social scientists should beware of false choice dichotomies and instead acknowledge their perspectives and preferred tools while engaging with criticism.[29] Close reviews of dichotomous debates highlight the predominance of binary reasoning, with each side portraying the other as straw men, but also find researchers slowly becoming more pluralist and pragmatic about how to collectively move forward.[30]

The Views of Researchers

Agreement on pluralism does not mean that research lacks methodological direction. Researchers can recognize trends in research practices but remain supportive of continuing diverse approaches with less conflict. To illustrate, my survey asked social scientists to assess the research trends in their discipline. Figure 3.1 reports average ratings of the direction of research. Professors were asked to rate to what extent research was moving in one direction or another on a scale from −2 to +2. The end points of the scales reported below were

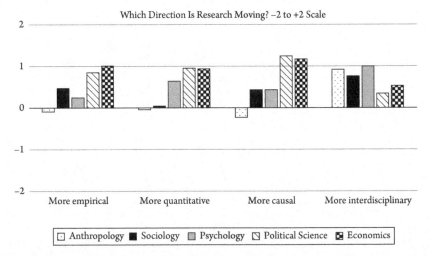

Figure 3.1 Directions of Social Science Research Trends. Data from the author's 2020 survey of social scientists at major US research universities. n=1,141.

"theoretical model building" vs. "empirical testing"; "use of qualitative data" vs. "use of quantitative data"; "descriptive analysis" vs. "assessment of causality"; and "single discipline research" vs. "interdisciplinary research." This replicates popular dichotomized divides but allows researchers to perceive more limited trends.

Social science research is perceived to be more empirical (and less theoretical), more quantitative (and less qualitative), and more causal (and less descriptive) in every discipline except anthropology (though sociology is reportedly not moving on the quantitative dimension). Younger and quantitative scholars across disciplines were more likely to perceive these trends. Cultural anthropologists were the only major subfield in any discipline to perceive research as becoming more theoretical, qualitative, and descriptive. Agreement on the trends is strongest in economics and political science—but note that no discipline sees them as overwhelming. All disciplines also see research as becoming more interdisciplinary in recent years, with the strongest changes perceived in psychology and anthropology. Scholars thus perceive the trends reviewed in Chapter 2: disciplines are moving toward empirical, quantitative, and causal research, while learning from each other.

Figure 3.2 reports social scientists' views on whether types of research are becoming more or less common. There is wide agreement across all five disciplines on the increasing use of "big data" approaches, such as using text and online data, and the use of relational data and network analysis; big data trends seem to be strong in all disciplines other than anthropology. Two methods of causal

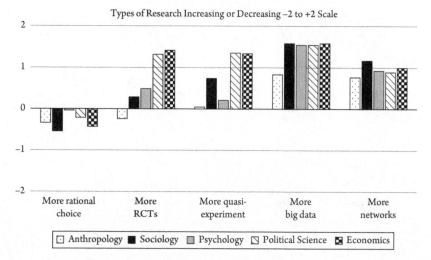

Figure 3.2 Trajectories of Social Science Research Types. Data from the author's 2020 survey of social scientists at major US research universities. n=1,141.

inference, randomized controlled trials and quasi-experiments, are reportedly increasing in most disciplines—especially economics and political science. Acknowledgment of the growth of new causal analyses is thus more widespread than perceptions of a march toward causal empiricism generally. Scholars can accept the advance of new data and methods without necessarily seeing them as jiggering the balance of social science goals. Big data approaches may be gaining adherents in the areas of social science where they are most helpful even if they do not reorient full disciplines. Scholars confirm that the use of rational choice models, on the other hand, is declining across the social sciences (except in psychology, where it never had much purchase).

But have these trends in research produced or alleviated scholarly conflicts? I also asked researchers whether debate had intensified or lessened in three hot-button controversies: the use of qualitative vs. quantitative research; the historical vs. contemporary focus of research; and "nature vs. nurture" in determinants of human behavior. Figure 3.3 presents the percentage reporting more conflict minus the percentage reporting less conflict in each discipline. Most social scientists perceived declining conflict in each of these debates over the past decade, though the modal answer was no change. Anthropological exceptionalism was again apparent, but here it was not restricted to the cultural subfield: anthropologists perceive more conflict on type of research and time period but less on nature vs. nurture (where they perceive the largest decline). Overall, the end of the public science wars has coincided with a dampening of dichotomous conflict within disciplines, despite trends in research mostly favoring quantitative empiricism.

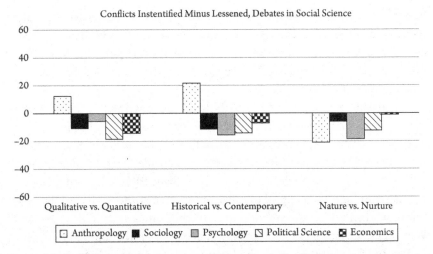

Figure 3.3 Social Scientists' Assessments of Disciplinary Conflicts. Data from the author's 2020 survey of social scientists at major US research universities. n=1,141.

Perpetual social science conflicts endure, though to a lesser extent. The trends toward empiricism, quantification, and causal inference all have their critics, though the movements do not seem to have made conflicts worse than before. Social science disciplines are in consensus that new types of data are rising, alongside better causal inference strategies in many disciplines. Several scholars also commented on the survey that both qualitative and quantitative standards had improved, and that they saw current scholarship drawing from the best of both worlds.

What Is at Stake in Conflict over Quantitative Research?

Critiques of social scientific knowledge have long focused on its most quantitative areas, drawing from a history that links quantification with its overbroad authoritative claims. Across disciplines, social science saw increasing quantification after World War II, but each discipline also saw a reaction to quantitative overreach.[31] All social sciences mathematized over time, with increasing statistics use, more importation from math and natural science, and indigenously developed methodological innovation in measurement, theory, and research design.[32] The trends were visible early in increasing uses of percentages and equations in manuscripts.[33]

The science studies research that began the science wars has been highly critical of quantification, seeing it as performative expertise motivated to gain social and political status.[34] Many of these analyses still end up using statistics where possible to substantiate basic claims, but most are structured as histories or qualitative reviews. Quantification, like scientific methods generally, is often seen as providing only the illusion of precision and objectivity. Indeed, social science abstracts that include meaningless mathematics are judged to be of higher quality; this "nonsense math effect" suggests we may give too much credence to quantification for its own sake.[35]

Skepticism about the urge to quantify has been a long-running theme because there are many examples worthy of critique apparent from the beginning of social science history. When William Petty attempted to extrapolate the value of Ireland's population using wealth and other obtainable weights and measures, it set the stage for Jonathan Swift's famous satire. Swift critiqued the false modesty of quantifiers and their appeal to calculation as the arbiter of truth. The quantification of social life was political from the beginning, according to historian William Deringer.[36] Each side of political debates over the unification of Great Britain and the assumption of debt, for example, appealed to "honest numbers" and innovated in the analysis of social statistics to make their point, elevating new elites with numerical competence.

The early mathematics of social life (often applied from models of gambling advice) mixed moral expectations and (often prejudiced) common sense to "calculate" values that could not be determined.[37] Nineteenth-century astronomer Adolphe Quetelet readily applied mathematical regularities to assess crime rates, disease, court cases, and death, generating aggregate national and local data from extrapolations. He reported numerous seasonal, life cycle, and national variations, all with little assessment of error or account of the degree of deviation from random patterns. Rather than see the move from natural patterns to social life as a difficult exercise, he used it as an excuse for the lack of fit between his data and the general laws of social life that he proffered.

Tracking subsequent developments, philosopher Ian Hacking argues that social determinism (structured by religion) was gradually replaced by a conception of the normal person and the dispersion of others from that norm. Following the development of annualized counting of births, deaths, and other church and state figures, social scientists decided that the world—although not deterministic—was still regular, enabling the development of statistics, the expansion of government and private data collection, and the rise of social engineering.[38]

Social and political evidence gathering became more structured over time, as oratory and painting were replaced by elections, crowd counting, letter campaigns, and surveys.[39] Public opinion become a commodity that could be quantified and used in political debate. The more the numbers were disputed, the more they became primary objects of political controversy. Quantified facts were also critical for states: helpful in measuring the reach of empires, managing interests, collecting taxes, administering censuses and fiscal reports, enslaving people, and accounting for labor and debts.[40]

As historian Theodore Porter argued, numbers enabled the expansion of so-cial science to new topics, often mixed with moral disdain and reformism: "the moral distance encouraged by a quantitative method of investigation made the work much easier. It is not by accident that numbers have been the preferred vehicle for investigating factory workers, prostitutes, cholera victims, the insane, and the unemployed."[41] Quantitative social science thus reflected the moral concerns of each time period, with precise numbers often hiding social biases inherent in data gathering and analysis.

Within the social sciences, economists took the lead in calculating the state of society, later drawing from computation to formalize their theories and methods.[42] Other social scientists followed. Eventually, methodological rigor became part of a compact for public support for social science with limited gov-ernment interference; standardized measures like crime rates and economic production then became policy ends in themselves. But these measures still hide assumptions and imply erroneous authoritative precision.

The history of social science reviewed by science critics should thus temper claims that quantification can minimize biases in social research. But they do not undermine the gains that social scientists can make from quantification. And they suffer from lack of comparison with other less-quantitative social pronouncements that also guide popular opinion and policy. Critical studies of social science can lose sight of biased views that quantification aims to correct.

To put it simply, if we want to assess how widespread or long-standing a phenomenon is, we need more data; if want to see how consistent a pattern or relationship is, we need more data; if want to see if something is increasing or decreasing, we need more data. Human counting, sorting, and tracking—and numeric representations of abstract concepts—helped expand culture and ad-vance social life.[43] Mathematics has been a powerful system of reason that has enabled technological advance by breaking down problems and synthesizing results; social science needs it more often because its common problems have more variables and nonlinearity.[44] Mathematical guidance is useful for theory, empirical analysis, and practical work; even if you know the history of its misuse, it is often the best route to clarify and assess arguments.[45]

Although the results of rising quantitative empiricism were often critiqued as method-driven, rather than problem-driven, even critics agreed that theory-laded observation of a small subset of cases had to be combined with the broadest metrics available.[46] In more recent years, both the "perestroika" movement in political science and similar conflicts over journal editorial control in sociology featured qualitative and interpretive scholars critiquing the quantitative main-stream. But the effects of these movements were pragmatic, with funding slightly broadened, diversity of techniques honored, and journals reformed.[47]

Critics of quantitative empiricism can usefully point out overgeneralization and overclaiming, but they often end up acquiescing to the terms used in quantitative work. Scholars should understand contingency, variation, and uncertainty, both say.[48] Different methods provide different kinds of data, such as more variables on fewer cases or more cases with only a few well-specified and comparable sources of variation.[49] Both sides agree that social science needs studies of particular instances known as important and broader consistent patterns in order to articulate scope conditions on theories. Phenomena are usually multi-causal and interactive, as qualitative scholars point out, but that means even more data are needed to assess relationships. Although qualitative case studies often come with elaborate theories, the more complicated the causal process envisioned, the larger the dataset needed to assess it.

That hardly means there is no qualitative niche. As sociologist Mario Small pointed out, many policy problems, public commentary, and research areas have limited "qualitative literacy."[50] Observers lack the ability to investigate what and how others are feeling, without feeling the same. They notice heterogeneity in their own field but see other areas as homogenous. They are not suspicious enough of their observations conforming to stereotype. Researchers think of "Trump voters" or "poor neighborhoods" too monolithically. They would be better equipped to understand what they study, Small says, if they treated interviews or case observation as a different tool rather than a limited version of a survey or mass observation. Qualitative researchers also more often acknowledge their positionality in the research process and their mixed research and practical goals.

An analysis of sociology journal articles shows that division between qualitative and quantitative research remains, with large splits by topic area and a small increase in quantitative research in general-interest journals.[51] But sociologist Daniel Hirschman told me that quantitative-versus-qualitative battles no longer capture the real fault lines in social science, with the consensus calling for mixed methods. Political scientist Jessica Preece said quantitative researchers largely won by the 1990s, but there has since been a swing back to mixed methods. The key critiques of quantitative work, that causal inference is assumed rather than proven and that conclusions fail to apply universally, also apply to most qualitative work, she says. But each can complement the other.

A prominent sociologist told me we have reached an equilibrium, with some ignoring those using other methods but few not seeing some value in both. Political scientist Mirya Holman agreed: "The big quant vs. qual wars are over because few people are saying there's no value to one; there's now multiple methods expectations, with graduate programs adopting that focus and single-approach scholars in decline. Pluralism is required by our trainees." Another political scientist agreed: "While in training, there was a palpable divide between quals/quants. I don't see that anymore, so less imperialism or insecurity on both sides. Lots more folks fluent in both idioms."

Experiments and Their Limits

It looked possible for a while that the fight over methods would move to experiments vs. observational research (discussed in Chapter 2), but that battle has also died down somewhat. As political scientist Gary King told me, experiments are "great for causal inference" but that's "only one thing you might want." Theories instead might have observable implications that are descriptive or about the generalization of relationships. Experiments are often used to assess similar processes rather than test the same intervention studied observationally. There is now less a clear experimental subfield than a common set of experimental, quasi-experimental, and observational tools used across subfields, with methodological innovations "near the data" to solve specific problems, King said.

Debates over the centrality of randomized experiments also have a long history. Four related disciplines invented randomized controlled trials in the 1920s separately: agriculture, clinical medicine, educational psychology, and social policy (within political science).[52] Although they lost favor in each of them before regaining interest, the same concerns they solved (the need to identify causal relationships) and retained (the need to understand broad patterns that were not subject to interventions) remained largely constant. They have been regularly touted as the solution to make social life amenable to science, then regularly critiqued as insufficient for answering key questions.

Economists led the way to the resurgence of field experiments in international development, but many lessons learned from those experiments either did not turn out to be widely applicable or were the product of limiting the questions asked to more specific policy debates.[53] Randomized controlled trials also gained in criminology, education, and social welfare, leading some to argue that they were the only reasonable tool for assessing policy.[54] But even proponents acknowledged the need for many repeated experiments in different contexts as they encountered common problems scaling up from tested programs. And that might be the best-use case: policy analysis often fits with a potential experimental design because it evaluates a single specific implementable proposal. But the experimental context is still often different from where a policy will be applied, necessitating observational research and replication as well.[55] And many social scientists are not studying potential interventions.

Critiques of the experimental turn in lab and survey research have raised similar concerns. Most experiments do not explore or model the space of possible stimuli they use to invoke responses or the settings where the responses occur anywhere near enough to support generalized theoretical claims.[56] Differences in stimuli and setting may account for some replication failures in psychology; the focus on the validity of statistical tests can distract from both construct and external validity concerns.[57] Fixes to improve internal validity can also involve trade-offs, such as when researchers move to less realistic online survey settings to increase statistical power. The resolution is that many social science ideas are unlikely to be ready for hypothesis testing because of difficulty measuring concepts, identifying boundary conditions, and assessing ranges of potential effects.[58]

Diversity of Statistical Approaches

Social scientists also used to battle over statistical approaches like Bayesian or frequentist inference, different ways of using probability theory to define statistical estimates and tests. But many scholars now use or cite methodological tools from both families without consequence. Controversy over statistical tests and decision rules has tended to cross over between approaches, with most attention on outlining alternative hypotheses, the replicability of analyses, and the practical availability of tests.[59] Most statisticians and social scientists now take an ecumenical approach, agreeing that common problems are due to poor implementation.[60]

Bayesian Judea Pearl has now focused on building causal models over statistical approaches, sharing the frequentist focus on understanding generalization, mechanisms, selection bias, mediation, causal direction, and confounding.[61] Frequentist Deborah Mayo has focused on the need for "severe tests" of theories, regardless of the statistical approach used, arguing that the main problem is that confirmation is too easy.[62] The shared focus is now on building theories to face multiple difficult assessments. Frequentist approaches want to make this possible by requiring low rates of error, whereas Bayesian approaches address it by quantifying and manipulating what researchers should believe. But researchers can use Bayesian machinery without committing to it as the only possible form of reasoning.[63] Which tools to use is often less of a philosopher's question than an engineer's: researchers use whatever they need and cross-check results.

But there is still progress on consensus interpretations. The American Statistical Association has agreed on a set of principles regarding p-values. It included several reminders of what significance tests cannot tell us: "P-values do not measure the probability that the studied hypothesis is true, or the probability that the data were produced by random chance alone," they do not "measure the size of an effect or the importance of a result," and they do not, by themselves, "provide a good measure of evidence regarding a model or hypothesis."[64] Scholars are thus in agreement on more caution and the necessity of combining different types of evidence.

Similarly, debates over linear models and alternatives are no longer very contentious. The linear model is a basic idea for theoretical development, but so are concepts like exponential growth or a half-life. Both theoretical models and empirical assessments select distributional assumptions and relationship shapes based on topic and context, with normal distributions playing key assumed roles in some areas and power law distributions common in others.[65] And the shape of relationships may not make as much difference as we thought: robustness checks to run the same models with logit or probit instead of ordinary least squares regression rarely show large differences.

Researchers are also no longer limited to analyzing attributes of cases. Network models and spatial geographic models, both based on relationships among cases, have gained steam but not replaced traditional analysis.[66] Most relational data models also consider traditional attributes of cases, and more traditional data analyses can now incorporate contextual data that proxies for social relationships. Overall, more researchers are considering individuals in their surroundings. Debates have moved to the specific mechanisms linking cases and contexts in particular domains.

Answering the Interpretivist Holdouts

Although the central tendencies of social science have moved on to empirical and largely quantitative social science while leaving room for qualitative and exploratory work, a minority of social scientists still sees much of contemporary social science research as illegitimate and seeks to replace it with an interpretive approach. But the latest versions of these proposals voice some acceptance of multiple methods and improved techniques. Beneath the dismissals, I see signs of openness—especially given recent social science innovations and remaining pluralism.

Political scientists Mark Bevir and Jason Blakely argue that social scientists must choose between interpreting the "holistic matrix of meanings" in social life or pure naturalism (the reduction of social practices to the laws of natural science).[67] This leads them to privilege social science explanations that rely on humans socially constructing the meaning of their behavior over long-term historical processes (I take this to be selecting theories that assume strong social agency on moral grounds). This leaves out some useful categories of naturalistic explanation: lead poisoning does have social consequences by changing brain development; mosquito-borne illnesses do affect the course of war and peace; iodized salt did change health outcomes. But it also leaves out other categories of influence that are not naturalistic: random factors such as lottery winnings or the precise timing of recessions can influence social life; individual idiosyncratic decisions of leaders like judges and presidents can also have large consequences; and social actors may concoct impactful institutions like administrative requirements without consciously meaning to construct their effects. Social science should not be committed to naturalism or social construction as the only alternatives.

Most social scientists seek to choose among theories on the basis of consistency with evidence, rather than strong ontological assumptions. They see important differences with natural science, but no reason not to learn from the factors that natural science considers or the methods they use. But even Bevir and Blakely pronounce themselves agnostic about quantitative or qualitative methods and choosing among most types of data analysis. Their concern is mostly with interpreting results. In fact, the most objectionable global claims they cite (such as theories of "contentious politics" and "the clash of civilizations") are insufficiently evidenced, rather than definitively proven with contemporary techniques. And their objections to the broadest global claims are shared by many empirical social scientists, who are better able to assess and refute them.[68]

Blakely (2020) followed up with an oddly juxtaposed pair of claims: that it is near impossible to study social life scientifically because of the complexity of human behavior and that academic ideas from social science drove social change more than many other factors. In his telling, social science ideas are often malevolent, serving as the roots of economistic and conservative trends in popular thinking. But these are very broad empirical claims just as vulnerable to critique as other social science theories. They place large causal power with academic ideas, even if they are secondary to interests or emotions in human behavior or used as post-hoc justifications rather than driving decisions. Scientific ideas can certainly be influential, but so can ideas from historians or humanists, and we can hardly assume that ideas are the most important causal forces in world events. That we are part of what we study is a core problem of social science, but not because human nature is so easy to change with academic ideas. The problem, affecting humanists as much as social scientists, is that we are so affected by what we want to be true, aligning our interpretation of evidence to fit our goals and opinions. As historian Andrew Jewett argues, critics of science have long overclaimed its cultural dominance while ignoring social scientists' acceptance of the limits of their knowledge.[69]

A less philosophical version of the interpretivist critique is advanced by critics of conventional economics such as John Kay and Mervyn King, who argue that statistical analysis is unhelpful because causal patterns can change over time and economic models are not useful because they have to choose parameters without complete evidence.[70] They instead recommend developing narratives to answer the general question, "what is going on here?" and guiding decision makers with the identification of key factors. This approach puts a lot of odd faith in common-sense views of social situations (which also embed causal assumptions) and discounts humans' often-complex interactions. Most social scientists do not assume the straw-man economistic assumptions they critique but also see some relatively stable causal relationships in human life. Thankfully, Kay and King also hedge their bets: they remain open to a variety of data collection and analysis techniques. They seem mainly to oppose economists' overclaiming from models in policy debates. That complaint is again shared by many social scientists, who are working to correct and test their claims—and are even winning converts in economics. The remaining holdouts would be better off celebrating the reforms and trends in progress, rather than calling for rebuilding from scratch.

End of the Rational Choice Wars

The rise of the "rational actor model," the use of rational-choice and game-theoretic models of human behavior based on economistic assumptions about the relationship between preferences and decisions, was among the most important social science trends of the twentieth century.[71] It was tied to both the rise of economics and the use of related decision tools in government contracts, but was disputed from the beginning by many scholars, especially those in public administration and psychology.[72] It reached its apogee in Gary Becker's extension of economic theory to understand marriage and family life and democracy (celebrated in economics but widely panned across other social sciences).[73]

The benefit of the approach was its tractability in formal modeling. It was a full specification of preferences, beliefs, and situations, with canonical assumptions that could be debated. It also captured human interactions based on interdependencies, enabling analysis of unintended consequences or externalities in public policy as well as strategic interaction in human behavior.[74] Many of the arguments took the form of "even if" statements showing the difficulty of collective rationality: collective bodies may not reach decisions reasonably, for instance, even if all individuals are behaving rationally.

The models were mostly seen as idealized representations, with pragmatic usage by empiricists understanding particular situations. When challenged, they were mainly defended as offering unrealistic assumptions to highlight core mechanisms and enable predictions.[75] But economics, both in its microeconomic concern with strategic interaction and its macroeconomic interest in social welfare calculations, indeed took a strong mathematical turn, becoming less interested in testing core assumptions than in building elaborate models.[76]

Defenders attacked non-rational-choice theories as not offering explanations at all, since they lacked appropriate microfoundations in individual behavior; they also saw their project as the main option for properly specifying the relationships between axioms and predictions.[77] Rational choice theory rose as behavioralism fell in the social sciences, so proponents argued that atheoretical data analysis would resurge if theories were not fully specified.

Older debates within psychology and philosophy joined these method disputes to produce "rationality wars," with modeling assumptions being seen as sides in an intractable conflict over human nature.[78] Philosophical defenders also tied rational choice theory to individualism generally, arguing that sociological accounts of group actions, beliefs, or desires were improperly moving individual concepts to collective behavior.[79]

One of the useful outcomes of these debates was noticing the predominance of rationalization—lots of human behavior could be seen as rational after the fact, even if it had an instinctual basis; voicing reasons for actions (even if they are not the true reasons) is important in human communication and debate. We are driven to self-justify our actions and convince others of them, with simple models of rational behavior useful for both.[80]

Economics retains many debates about whether to start with models, which still form the basis of undergraduate and graduate curricula, but rising stars like Raj Chetty have helped reorient the discipline that was previously most focused on rational choice models toward empiricism.[81] New theoretical advance is more closely tied to problem solving and less imperialistic. Economist David Autor told me scholars are "not committed to grand unified theory. They now want to let the data speak and are open to alternatives. They recognize many deviations from core assumptions. . . . There was a time when things that came out of data that were inconsistent with theory were rejected. You don't get that anymore. Evidence is taken seriously and feeds into theory."

The behavioral economics revolution, which began before moves toward empiricism with seminal work by Richard Thaler, Daniel Kahneman, and Amos Tversky, helped to revise the discipline's assumptions. But economist Daniel Benjamin told me rising empiricism also helped these trends along: "It made it easier to compare rational and behavioral models with data, and behavioral models generally came out well. . . . The mainstream of the economics community moved to a pluralist view of accepting [that] both perspectives have their place [in specific applied topics]."

The financial crisis leading to the Great Recession also helped stimulate a re-evaluation of curricula and model-dependence. But rather than replace one paradigm with another simplistic version, social scientists acknowledged that many ideas about both individual and collective behavior were often unrealistic with limited application.[82] Scholars now took the models as exemplars of the difficulty of predicting social behavior—even if you assumed easy-to-model individual behavior—rather than a sign that one set of assumptions had to be replaced with another.[83] Since individual behavior is multifaceted and changeable, that only makes collective behavior more uncertain.

Among the modelers, the notion of "many-model thinking," the application of many logical frames with distinct causal forces to the same problem in order to simplify and compare ideas, gained ground.[84] As political scientist Scott Page articulates, rational choice models are most useful where learning is regular, there are large stakes, the situation is stable, the information is consistent, and benchmarking is necessary. Other purpose-built models work better in other situations.

Meanwhile, psychology has become intrigued with affect and emotion as underlying drivers of human behavior—but there remain disputes about the number and application of human emotions and how cross-cultural and long-standing these concepts should be applied.[85] Regardless, irrationalities no longer stand out. Even the human body has many odd features with poor designs, making it unsurprising that the human mind would also have features unexplained by evolutionary imperatives.[86] In fact, chimps often play economic games more "rationally" than human participants because they lack human learned behavior and the unique human responses to social pressures that override self-interest motives.[87]

Promoters of rational choice theory now accept limitations and just note their contributions. As political scientist Arthur Lupia told me, "Formal modeling is just a mathematical language allowing us to be precise. It is sometimes helpful but still complementary and not going away. Like other methodological innovations, the initial hype dies down but obscures real change in the best areas." Ken Kollman said rational choice perspectives have "seeped into" all kinds of social science areas; "people are using the terms and ideas" but "the rise of behavioral economics has pointed out its systematic limits."

Political scientist Tara Slough told me, "Theory is not as divisive for young people. There's no broad rational choice conflict anymore." If young people can draw from the analogies and ideal typical situations of rational choice theory without counting on it as the necessary way to formalize theory, all sides can benefit. A behavioral economist told me, "The age of the big theory wars has ended; [it went from] 1980–2000, with enormous animus at behavioral economists, [saying they were] ruining economics; now we're all behavioralists." Political scientist Gary King assessed a new pragmatism: "No one is saying everyone is rational anymore [but we're still] making models. . . . It's never going away [but we're now focused on] what works [for a specific problem], not the philosophical debate."

Philosophy of Science Moves to Social Science Approaches

The decline of dichotomous conflicts over research practices also reflects advances in the philosophy of social science. When social scientists learn or deploy philosophy of science, it is often to the classics. Annoying practicing philosophers of science, scholars repeatedly cite Karl Popper rather than keep up on an evolving field. Modern analyses of HARKing and p-hacking are, of course, related to the need for falsifiability; the open science reform movement is implementing some procedures Popper suggested.[88] But the calls for methodological unity based on falsification have declined in philosophy as close studies of scientific practice failed to match theory and even canonical examples did not seem to fit.[89] Fetishism surrounding particular methods is waning, with scientists seen as working their way up from evidence, applications, and models.[90]

Social epistemology now takes socio-political systems as central to its understanding of how expert communities reach consensus on knowledge.[91] Scientists rely on social markers of inclusion and expertise to evaluate claims as they inevitably cumulate well beyond their specific observations. They also evaluate disputes between peers, both over specific evidence and about wider questions of how investigations should proceed, following the incentives and norms in scientific institutions.

Philosophy of social science has long been linked to social science practice. Researchers still study the differentiating factors between social and natural science, whether to pursue law-like regularities, and the divide between holism and individualism.[92] But as social scientists evolved, so did philosophy, with active debates on causal inference, rational choice theory, qualitative approaches, and evidence-based policy. As in the practice of social science, there remains less consensus than in natural science about the philosophical underpinnings of social science research and its methodological approaches.[93]

Philosophy of social science is also more closely integrated with sociology of science. Philosophy of science citations outside the field go more to social science than natural science.[94] Analyses of the evolution of intellectual schools and scholarly networks within science studies have been integrated in philosophy.[95] Ideas about social movements and marginalized perspectives also instigated useful conflict over objectivity and stimulated philosophical revision.[96] Consideration of social and cultural epistemology is moving philosophy more toward sociology while attention to interpersonal testimony and belief formation is making it more conversant with psychology. Epistemology has moved from long-running debates over rationalism, empiricism, and idealism (which tend to assume access to knowledge internal to the thinker) to externalist ideas about evaluating methods and evidence in communities. Science is dependent not on value-free individual application, but on remaining diverse, non-defensive, and self-critical.[97]

Philosopher Angela Potochnik cites an "increasing recognition of the myriad ways in which human expectations, concerns, and limitations influence scientific practice" within philosophy.[98] Science has no single method; it combines the aims of practice, understanding, explanation, prediction, and generalization. Because universal laws are infrequent and hold only approximately (and because causal complexity is rampant), there is pervasive idealization.

As in science studies, philosophy sought first to explain and reinforce scientific successes, then moved to social constructivism, and then to develop useable and particularized accounts of scientific advance.[99] The idea of value-free science was replaced by the understanding that scientists have epistemic values like simplicity and generalizability as well as moral values that can be useful in deciding what to study.[100] Philosopher Heather Douglas argues that we should accept a "pervasive role for values" but we still "need reliable claims" when doing incomplete induction.[101]

Philosopher Adrian Curie argues that philosophy of science has been hobbled by its focus on physics and biology, because it has learned from their fixations rather than all fields. "Philosophy of science would have looked very different if it took paleontology or archeology as its representative case," Curie argues, where middle-range theories predominate and researchers cannot assume generalizability across time and space.[102] Most sciences seek to unify their traces of evidence, slowly testing for coherency and consilience by creating localized models and finding the extent of regularities.[103] They are sometimes methodologically driven, but only because there are practical reasons to spend resources on questions scientists have some chance of answering. Scientists create hypotheses that go beyond current evidence, but they spend most of their time trying to integrate what is already known and take small steps forward; it looks less like deductive models and more like "empirically grounded speculation" that is context-sensitive.

The cookbook scientific method, as taught in children's textbooks, is more a product of John Dewey's popularization (designed to raise the status of American social reformers) than a set of codified procedures in wide scientific use.[104] Philosopher Lee McIntyre finds no agreement on a demarcation of the boundaries of science or a shared scientific method.[105] Most new theories re-explain existing knowledge that is inconsistent with other theories, rather than making new predictions. The scientific community induces self-correction through an open attitude toward evidence and accumulating through induction with a regular comparison of competing theories. Working toward objectivity is a community practice based on group scrutiny; the group has to share scientific attitudes to correct for human biases through public exchange and commitments to change views based on evidence. Social science, McIntyre says, has to take extra steps to preserve collective objectivity because it retains normative aspirations that bias its self-conceptualization.

These philosophical assumptions are much more reasonably applied to social science. The dominant move has been toward a plurality of acceptable methods, an anti-reductionist acceptance of simultaneous work at different scopes and levels of analysis, and an emphasis on the virtues of clarity and heterogeneity in addressing the danger of confirmation bias.[106]

Pluralism of the New Generation

The social sciences move forward through accumulation and integration of varied evidence. Although social scientists seek broad law-like generalizations wherever possible, they know them to be rare or trite.[107] They almost always have to integrate and weigh evidence at different levels of aggregation and scale, acknowledging uncertainty. A prominent political scientist told me that the best young scholars combine interests from advisors with different preferences for systematization and quantification, with a problem orientation and less methods fetishism.

In the last generation, social scientists have indeed become more theoretically and methodologically pluralist. Few scholars now stick by the view that everyone behaves according to the dictates of rational choice and game theory, but few scholars also entirely discount the potential gains from a simplified model. Few researchers view historical qualitative research as irrelevant, but fewer also see no reason to ever quantify. Many-model thinking has gained steam, using several diverse logical frames can evaluate potential causal forces. Although all models are wrong, multiple models can simplify and formalize, allowing users to better reason, explain, predict, explore, and communicate.[108] But the initial "model mania" of the 1990s died down as evidence accumulated.[109]

Collectively analyzing society from different perspectives does not match the canonical model of a hypothesis-testing academic paper, but it does match the oldest notions of building community knowledge, working from specific data to information, then enlarged to knowledge, and then to wisdom.[110] That means scholars must privilege meta thinkers as well as specialized expertise. One-trick expert knowledge, even with intense area focus, only improves decisions in narrow domains.[111] The best scientists often have artistic sensibilities and generalized interests, rather than monomaniacal obsessions. Forecasting tournaments also consistently show the benefits of drawing from many theories and models, forming probabilistic and contingent judgments, and making frequent small adjustment in response to new evidence.[112]

Both the enlargement of the scholarly community and the invention of new tools of analysis are pushing us toward theories more constrained by evidence. Detailed studies of particular contexts are replacing grand narratives of human development.[113] Fields as diverse as quantitative behavioral genetics, molecular genetics, developmental psychology, neurophysiology, and ecology, for example, have all addressed similar questions about human nature, starting from different goals and questions; but the pluralist approach of integrating findings from each field is winning out, mapping particular gene-environment interactions and simultaneously progressing on both broad societal patterns and within-brain individual mechanisms.[114]

Knowledge has a network structure across levels of analysis, rather than a core fundamental discipline that has to be finished before others can begin.[115] Many historical scientific advances came from advances in record keeping and information sharing for developing consensus, rather than from one-off discoveries.[116] Middle-range approaches within disciplines combine with interdisciplinary conversations to integrate theory and empirics.[117] But for that to be successful, scholars must also incorporate meta-level insights about how knowledge is created in the scientific community. Just accumulating studies within disciplines and haphazardly comparing them will be less effective than accounting for which areas are generating research and which factors remain unaddressed, reflecting on how scientists are attending to each other's work.[118]

Social science disciplines have moved from bemoaning fragmentation to celebrating diversity of topics and goals. That's visible in proliferating sections of scholarly associations and in the transformation of "state-of-the-discipline" books from venues for framework wars to volumes applying disciplinary lessons to contemporary issues.[119] The winner has been mostly interconnected theory, research, and practice, with empirical multi-method research and regular reviews of cumulative findings driven by substantive application.[120] Historically, this process has led to the decline of internal divisions in scholarly networks, with long-running field disputes dissipating through efforts to find consensus in applied work.[121]

According to an international survey of political scientists, methodological pluralism also remains (with little variation across world region). Historical methods and policy analysis are in decline in new cohorts (with econometrics and big data rising), but stability and diversity continue. The most widely shared goal across methodological views is advancing scholarly knowledge.[122]

Scholars I spoke with agreed that social scientists were becoming more open to a variety of approaches. "The field is dominated by pluralism. Everyone will say [different theories and methods are] great for different questions," sociologist

Daniel Hirschman told me. "Graduate students are committed and passionate, but see rising rigor [across methods] as tools to make research better." A prominent economist said, "Most young people are taking from multiple fields and tools . . . . The pluralists are leaders in the field."

Pluralism has also come with epistemic humility. A prominent sociologist said scholars have "tamped down claims about causality and generalizability" and accepted the necessity of slow theory building and testing. Political psychologist Amanda Friesen cited the rise of meta-analysis and replication, borrowing methods across fields: "New cohorts are more interested in good science than legacy building with major claims." As biologist Stuart Firestein says, "No datum is safe from the next generation of scientists with the next generation of tools."[123]

My survey of social scientists also asked researchers to agree or disagree that "New generations of scholars are more varied in their theoretical orientations" and that "New generations of scholars are more varied in their methodologies." Figure 3.4 reports the percentage agreeing minus the percentage disagreeing in each discipline. All disciplines agreed that the new generation was more methodologically pluralist, with the largest agreement in anthropology, sociology, and psychology. Scholars in all disciplines except political science agreed (more than they disagreed) that new generations were more theoretically pluralist; anthropology had the largest agreement. Surprisingly, these views were each near-equally prominent across assistant, associate, and (full) professors. Scholars of all ranks see a generational shift in the works.

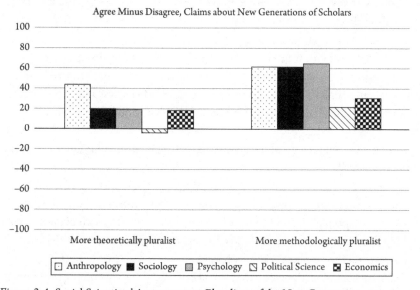

Figure 3.4 Social Scientists' Agreement on Pluralism of the New Generation. Data from the author's 2020 survey of social scientists at major US research universities. n=1,141.

The social sciences are changing, and new generations of scholars are taking the lead: they are becoming more empirical (especially as opposed to strict adherence to economistic models), as well as more quantitative and oriented toward causal inference (without losing their qualitative and descriptive roles). Scholars have access to more tools and more theories to apply to social life—and they are using them in diverse ways. There are still some who see the enterprise as hopeless (or at least overexposed). But new generations of social scientists have responded to critiques of their abilities with new approaches and less adherence to a few grand theories.

Critiques of scientific authority and claims will always help tamp down extravagant claims and point out historical contingencies, but science advances through continued measurement, testing, and analysis. The limits of the "science wars" help us frame the gains from self-reflection but also the dangers of dichotomous debates with misunderstood sides. Critiques of existing knowledge that are framed as additional tools for contributing to (inevitably partial) understandings add more than those from a posture of taking down science. Approaching critics as sharing concerns about how biases creep into research, rather than relativists seeking to burn it all down, likewise can help science advance. Like the old fears that scientific practice was mere political theater, newer critiques of social science wizardry are overblown. Better measurement and identification are major improvements that can counteract overclaiming, not obscurant mathematics. As conflicts over broad theoretical frameworks dissipate and model builders face evidence within diverse communities, social science is progressing even in our most fraught and personal investigations.

4

Me-Search All the Way Down

In 2018, three scholars wrote twenty fake academic papers to parody what they called "grievance studies," eventually publishing several in peer-reviewed journals. They studied (mostly gender-related) topics designed to both poke fun and provoke backlash, such as "rape culture" in dog parks, "fat bodybuilding," transphobia in sex toys, objectification at the Hooters restaurant, and pornography's effect on implicit bias. Although the stunt was immediately compared to the Sokal hoax and celebrated by opponents of identity politics in academia, it was not universally seen as indicting the fields it pilloried.

Some of the papers were vague opinionated essays targeted at low-tier humanities theory journals, but others were ostensibly social science research. In contrast to the Sokal hoax, these were empirical studies that involved old-fashioned fraudulent data alongside the bogus theorizing—and the papers with made-up empirics had a higher success rate. The dog park rape article, which was selected by journal editors for highlighting, supposedly involved hundreds of hours of observation with detailed coding.

Although the hoaxers did not have a control group of non-identity research, they said their stunt gives reason to doubt the integrity of scholarship that begins from ideological predispositions. It is fair to suggest that otherwise-equivalent papers that began from anti-feminist hypotheses would have faced harsher peer review, but the broader indictment may not be warranted. Not only did they fail to get their research accepted in mainstream sociology journals, but they got a hearing in social science mainly based on fake data. Reviewers dutifully tried to help improve the paper's methods and presentation, in many cases giving far too much benefit of the doubt. But data frauds and insufficient pushback on shared hypotheses afflict many fields.

The results of the hoax may not have been as advertised. In fact, one review of the project found that (1) higher-impact journals were more likely to reject the papers; (2) they were accepted more when supposedly based on empirical data; (3) peer reviews improved the claims and interpretations based on these (fake) data; (4) papers following reviewer advice, including some reasonable interpretations, were more successful; and (5) the community uncovered the fraud before the project concluded.[1] That is quite the evidence for effective social science coming from a supposed takedown.

The attempt to replicate the Sokal hoax may say more about the increasingly rigorous empirical transformation of these fields. Social science, even in its oddest corners, still now usually requires systematic data and interpretation. Authors can still add rhetorical flourishes if they advance trendy academic causes, but peer review in social science is usually about the underlying data and its connections to authors' specific claims.

Studies of race and gender, of course, have been home for decades to critiques of both academia run amok and scholarly bias and insensitivity. The publication of *The Bell Curve* in 1994 touched off a firestorm of criticism with its claims that genetics might be partially responsible for racial group differences in IQ scores, itself a repurposing of theories and data that had roiled behavioral genetics for decades. But even author Charles Murray and his perennial critics have updated their ways. Murray's latest book, *Human Diversity*, dives back into the same territory but is more careful to stay awash in technical details and citations before marking his (largely unchanged) speculations. The new book provoked a less prominent backlash focused on critiques from authors who say their specific findings were improperly cited. Rather than attack vague claims about social construction, Murray now feels the need to address considerable evidence of environmental influences and finds more common ground with social scientists on gene-environment interactions in gender roles. In contrast to what you might expect from reading complaints from Murray or the new hoaxers, their social science critics also now stick more to the details of claims and evidence, often successfully challenging unwarranted conclusions.

There will always be a market for salacious headline-grabbing, but that should not be taken to mean that nothing has changed in social science. Instead, social research is advancing by accounting for its starting assumptions along with its potential to reflect society's racial and gender biases. Even controversial research is progressing by taking bias seriously. And in that project, studies of identity have long taken the leading role.

Problems of Studying Ourselves

Social science is differentiated by humans' ability to respond to the information we collect as we study ourselves. As the object and subject of our study, we are also open to more biases—both as we study humanity as a whole with our aspirations and self-image and more specifically based on the particular people we choose to study and those conducting the studies.

But the lack of a "God's-eye view" is a problem throughout science. We study our galaxy, our star, and our planet most and we study our species and geographic locations most. Social science gains the notoriety for "me-search," the tendency for scholars to study human groups that they belong to or people like themselves, but scholars are all doing me-search of a kind. Attention to social group biases in human research can help us understand not only the disproportionate influence of majority and well-off groups in research but also the biases that come from social science as an occupational and status category and as a particular field of governance and education.

Although scholars are abstract thinkers, their abstractions are still rooted in concrete realities. We make errors, for example, in interpreting maps, drawing models, describing relationships, and assuming the linearity and direction of trends all because our spatial reasoning is tied to where we are in the world and how our language describes the past and future.[2]

Whether or not scholars are interested in examining interventions in the social world, their hopes for changing human behavior and their beliefs about ideal behavior—which often stem from the norms of their social groups—also influence their studies.[3] Even when scholars claim to build universal theories of social systems or behavior, their assumptions tend to reflect the societies and time periods in which they are embedded; this realization is often key to overcoming grand theorizing as scholars encountering diversity recognize that knowledge is more unsettled and humanity is more poorly understood than previously thought.[4] The catch-22 is that social scientists are told both that regularities of human behavior are obvious and that human behavior is too fundamentally varied to be predictable. Social science looks at the underlying conditions that make the seemingly obvious patterns possible and finds the circumstances under which human behavior can change or cultural patterns differ.

Acknowledging the specificity of our backgrounds and assumptions goes against science's tendency to decontextualize ideas. We want generalizable knowledge but have specific foci and bring top-of-the-mind examples to our studies. Academia advances through a pendulum of fractionalization and synthesis, as broad framework wars give way to clusters of interests with more specific theoretical formulations that borrow from more than one tradition.[5] But scholars are also humans narrating and self-justifying our own lives, meaning we are hesitant to give up on folk ideas.[6] The long study of consciousness has illustrated the problems of combining our self-justifying human views with the empirical study of thought. It is also hampered by our inability to directly observe other humans' (and possibly other animals') conscious thoughts.[7] Understanding how we reach conclusions given this context is itself a social science question; we combine internal reflection, observation of the world, and assumptions that others think like ourselves.[8]

The good news is that social scientists are more aware of the implications of our values on research than are natural scientists, even those who use metaphors with important human connotations.[9] The realization of value-driven research has driven some researchers toward full-throated interpretivism, which mainstreams the perspective of the scholar above empirical observation.[10] It is true that our interests, goals, and views are formed within communities and it is difficult to translate across them.[11] Awareness of one's presuppositions is important—but giving in and letting them drive conclusions is another matter. We should recognize our partial views without succumbing to merely celebrating them.

This dilemma is part of the human condition. We are storytellers, invoking fables with lessons that reason backward from effects to assumed causes.[12] Social scientists reasonably seek to explain the fast growth in layered complexity and diversity in human societies—humans are really quite different from other species.[13] But we anthropomorphize both institutions and non-human animals and base hard lines of human distinction on invoking our higher normative status.

The proposal to see the current period of earth as the "Anthropocene," for example, is both a recognition of human fealty and a species-wide claim to importance and dominance. Our scientific knowledge is in part both what made humans distinct and what enabled our destructive environmental impact.[14] We are unique, but that should chasten our theorizing rather than foreground our opinions. The anthropic principle, the idea that theories of the universe must be consistent with human existence, similarly has physicists arguing about whether the universe is fine-tuned for intelligent life or we are simply present in the one part of it that allows it.[15]

Our cognitive landscape may be as limited as our physical one, but acknowledging that should stimulate creative investigations instead of justify treating science as one of several good-as-any-other voices.[16] Social science critics that attack pretenses of objectivity can help us see how our desires to systematize may have deep roots in human life-and-death concerns, but they are also beginning from a biased particular perspective.[17] In fact, many humanist critics would benefit from some quantification of how far the patterns they identify extend, even some systematization of their data collection and analysis. Social scientists did gain a public role, even with widespread skepticism, by being willing to systematize.[18] But that involved putting our assumptions to more tests, sharing our expectations in a community, and giving ourselves the chance to be proven wrong.

Intellectual Humility

The philosophical virtue of being able to understand what we know and do not know goes by the name of "intellectual humility." A popular understanding characterizes it as the ability to own one's limitations and attend to one's strengths.[19] Another sees it as lacking a concern for social status in the consideration of evidence.[20] Both views recommend individual strategies like systematic thinking, critical scrutiny, and elevating curiosity for knowledge over lust for power. But both also conceive of belief formation in communities, which requires active perspective taking, a willingness to revise beliefs, and an openness to reliance on others. The virtue is desirable because it leads to true beliefs by individuals and helps communities reach consensus knowledge.

Psychologists have attempted to measure intellectual humility. The comprehensive intellectual humility scale includes several subscales, measured via self-assessment: openness to revising viewpoints, intellectual overconfidence (reverse-coded so that higher is worse), respect for others' viewpoints, and independence of intellect and ego.[21] Another focuses on low concern for intellectual status, perspective taking, and intellectual defensiveness (reverse-coded).[22] These self-reported measures are improved with ratings from others to see if one's impressions match those from friends and family, but individuals are willing to admit some of their own weaknesses.

This virtue of intellectual humility should be even more important in social science (when we are studying ourselves) because we have strong priors and psychological needs for self-affirmation. Social scientists may depend on more intellectual humility because they are interacting with those they study and communicating to reach consensus within the human community. The fact that philosophers have come to the conclusion that it requires understanding individual limitations and learning from others lends credence to my goals of improving social science through understanding biases and improving community standards. Although psychologists are only beginning to measure intellectual humility and assess its consequences, their efforts show that philosophical ideas can be usefully instantiated within social science. Their efforts thus far highlight the importance of being prepared to accept a variety of evidence in a community collectively searching for knowledge.

Social Science Realism, Even from Critics

Philosophy and history of science—and especially science and technology studies—operate from a position of critique, often chastising scientists for overly bold claims. But most also assume that scientists are doing important and differentiated work and they seek to understand it in positive terms. The inclination is still a comparison with other forms of knowledge, limiting scientific methods to variations on human perception, reason, memory, and testimony, with justifications similarly done in local communities.[23] But even when the boundaries of science are hard to draw, most scholars of science seek to understand what is special about it; when social science comes up, it is often from an inferior position, with an assumed position between science and non-science.[24]

Social science critics draw from a wider history of social critique attentive to how power relationships guide knowledge generation. The most cited critic is philosopher Michel Foucault. Although his followers usually see him as akin to an interpretivist eschewing broad metanarratives, he functioned at the time more as a historian of social knowledge and related practice. Articulating his own method in *The Archeology of Knowledge*, he formulated his own chronologies of intellectual history while being skeptical of received neat historical stories.[25] He argued persuasively that you should attend to the motivations of writers and participants in social life, describing the contradictions in accepted views and the needs for status and repeatability that bred them. But to a modern eye, he uses social science theory and methods to make the case, building his specific critiques of psychiatry, criminal justice, and sexuality from concrete research, advocating a skeptical but painstaking review of past documents to track the politicization of knowledge development. In *The Order of Things*, Foucault applies his method to the human sciences, training his eyes on linguistics, biology, and economics.[26] These disciplines' claims to timelessness and inevitability, he says, hide the historical contingencies that gave rise to them. His periodization is still rather crude, however, dividing intellectual history into the renaissance, classical, and modern periods. He remained skeptical of claims to comprehensiveness, formulated in projects like encyclopedias, but his own project attempted to track how humans see ourselves through a simple chronology.

Foucault's main concern was that intellectuals are agents of the powerful of their time periods; their biases do not just cloud their view but also justify the power structures of their time.[27] His role, he said, was to shine light on this process, disclosing relationships between ideas and power. Although this does fit well with some contemporary deconstruction projects, it is also consistent with a social science that is more cognizant of its historical context and contemporary constraints. In fact, Foucault was largely generalizing from his experience with psychology, finding answers in its history and sociology.[28] He gained fame from his more specific studies of madness, crime, and sexuality, where he applied his general concerns about social scientific ideas to the institutional practices in these fields. These examples showed that attention to the political context of social science history could enable scholars to understand contemporary knowledge biases.

Pierre Bourdieu, another French philosopher commonly cited in critical tomes on social science topics, was self-consciously a sociologist of science seeking to understand how intellectuals gain autonomy to pursue knowledge despite the necessity of working for social, corporate, and government interests.[29] He also mapped social science disciplines, arguing for more reflection on their scope and the foundational role of their instigating ideas. He used theory alongside qualitative and quantitative data to make his case, settling on now-common sociological concerns like social class and forms of capital. He asked social scientists to be reflexive, constantly studying their own learning process and fields and being skeptical about the objective basis of their intellectual role. Bourdieu and Foucault can both serve as precedents for self-aware social science as much as for the critical traditions they stimulated.

Critics focus on skepticism of historical progress based on increasing knowledge—and here there is a real difference. The assumption that we gain and use knowledge over time has been important for both scientific advancement and the position of science within society.[30] But we should not conflate knowledge advance with an inevitable improvement in social welfare; findings of increasing inequality in outcomes or failures to solve problems do not undermine the premise of knowledge growth. We can gain knowledge of human environmental degradation or the role of information technology in economic development without producing better collective goods, for example, if social policies and technologies dependent on our increasing knowledge are still applied inequitably or incompletely by the powerful and well-resourced. Admitting that knowledge has grown overall does not entail agreeing that any new consensus idea is better than those of the past or that we are successfully applying most of what we have learned. The progress of knowledge can be both overstated in the service of authority and still trivially evident: we have more and better data on more aspects of society, allowing knowledge to cumulate.

Standpoint epistemologists nonetheless offer a useful intervention in these debates. Philosopher Sandra Harding argues that "strong objectivity" should not mean ignoring the social backgrounds of researchers.[31] Instead it should entail "strong reflexivity" or critical reflection to "identify social desires, interests, and values that have shaped the agendas, contents, and results of the sciences."[32] Understanding these potential influences on research and mitigating the dominance of the inclinations of the powerful can be a route to uncovering a more robust truth, she says, rather than a dismissal of our potential to achieve it.

The anthropologist and political scientist James C. Scott has been an exemplar of integrating these ideas into the foundations of social science. He argues that many social "advances" are pursued by state planners and upper classes for their own power and efficiency, such as modernist urban planning, zoning, and family naming practices.[33] Because state-building depended on the belief in the linear progress of science application, he says, social scientists find it hard to view city-centered development objectively. Political scientist David Stasavage further argues that much of our knowledge about the development of democratic government is mistakenly linear and progressive, focused on the Greek and Roman roots we want to see as our inheritance.[34]

More generally, scholars have changed the historical stories we tell to fit a developmental trajectory with each current period at its apex, which might today entail the promotion of academic expertise.[35] As a result, it is not mere navel-gazing to focus on the incentives and constraints of academia; scholars need to understand our own role in the processes we study. The tendency to apply scientific concepts to social life (especially evolution) has been a long-standing target of critics, reasonably based on our flawed history of translating from natural to social science. As Historian Richard Olson argues, "Every major tradition of natural science . . . spawned efforts to extend scientific ideas, methods, practices, and attitudes to matters of human social and political concern. That is, they spawned scientisms."[36] But scholars can recognize when natural science concepts apply poorly in social life without necessitating an abandonment of systematic investigation.

Some argue that accounting for the standpoint of researchers is a biased American form of investigation: as the French focus on systems and structures, Americans pursue self-knowledge, imagined communities, and themes of identity.[37] We focus on direct experience for our inferences, believing strongly in the power of personal testimony.[38] But the problem may come less from Americans' tendency for me-search than from social scientists' assumptions of representativeness. Social science popularizers Robert and Helen Lynd, the authors of the *Middletown* studies of 1929 and 1937 that brought sociology to the popular imagination, created a reality-television-style depiction of American lives based on a supposedly representative place (Muncie, Indiana) despite believing themselves above their co-national subjects and taking their social prejudices with them.

Whether we are studying our own groups or others, humans instinctively sort people based on likeness to themselves.[39] The tendency to view the world from your own social group's perspective has long provoked philosophy that argues that truth is either relative to the observer or at least limited by times and places, becoming seemingly universal only when intellectuals synthesize a shared ideology.[40] During the science wars, this was a common rhetorical move of nonscientists, seeing science as a dominating culture that could be replaced by a multicultural approach.[41] It is thus unsurprising that calls for multi-perspective research are sometimes treated as attacks on the goal of objectivity. But today, the move to promote researchers from different standpoints can coexist with a shared search for truth and an acknowledgment of our difficulties.

Epistemic Injustice

Philosopher Miranda Fricker incorporated concerns about the importance of diverse viewpoints further into philosophy with her concept of epistemic injustice.[42] Because learning takes place in social communities with power differentials and group identities, our collective generation of knowledge depends on how we treat other people's perspectives. Testimonial injustice means giving too little (or too much) credit to the word of others based on their identities or powers; while not easy to eliminate, it is straightforward to address. Hermeneutical injustice is more structural, she says: because of the history of biases in a community, people have access to different interpretive resources to understand their collective situation. Social movements by the disadvantaged are necessary not just to address direct discrimination, but to internally develop new theories and tools for social understanding that can then be elevated for use in wider knowledge production.

Within the sciences, communities develop different epistemic cultures based on their histories and common tools and the social characteristics differentiating their group.[43] Social epistemology has thus become concerned not only with choices about what to believe and how to search for evidence, but also about the arrangements that improve collective learning.[44] In some cases, that might suggest borrowing from practices in more diverse non-scientific communities like Wikipedia or courtrooms. Since we cannot directly observe or examine all evidence, a lot of knowledge development—even in the sciences—involves relying on testimony from experts or adjudicating between equally qualified peers. That means scholars have to be especially concerned not only with equal treatment but with surfacing less-accepted views.

Observing from the Contemporary Human Lens

Scientists, as contemporary human observers, are viewing their subjects from a particular perspective. As philosopher of science Adrian Currie argues, we face some lucky circumstances (e.g., lots of preserved history and technologies to date events) and some not so lucky for global knowledge (e.g., researchers unevenly distributed around the globe).[45] We are always focusing and generalizing, both doing case studies of a particular place and time period and analyzing patterns across similar but non-identical cases. But our sense of self is strong enough to evaluate our own role as an observer. Proprioception, the ability to sense our own position and movement, is a basic human facility, and we have an analogous broader self-perception.

Some philosophers take this to an extreme, reasoning entirely from our place in the universe. You can use "self-locating information," for example, to predict that human doomsday is imminent because most of the human population has lived very recently despite 200,000 years of human life.[46] Using weak Bayesian assumptions and seeing oneself as "self-sampled" from all humans (reasoning that you are part of a random sample from a reference class, such as humans) can lead you further off the deep end, even toward thinking of humanity as part of a computer simulation. Investigating the observer is crucial to this line of thought, but it relies on a single observer doing thought experiments rather than sociology of science about how communities investigate together.

The Drake equation is a fun way of illustrating the too limited place of social science in these discussions. It is designed to understand the likelihood that we will find intelligent life in the universe. It requires estimation of several quantities: how many stars with planets are in the galaxy, how many planets are in each solar system and which have capacity for life, how many living species would be intelligent and how long they would last, and how many would produce broadcast signals that could reach us. Oddly, there is little recognition that the social questions here are at least as difficult as (if not more than) those about astronomy and biology. We do not even know the range of possibilities for what intelligent life would look like and are liable to reason far too much from our own aspirations and experiences. We do not know how others would think about space or time, much less whether they would produce radio waves to try to reach us. Social science uncertainties are central to what we can know about our place in the world.

The desire to separate humans from other animals, which also has a long fraught history of bias, has nonetheless progressed with social science knowledge. We used to define human difference based on tools, then by knowledge, then by arts, and now mainly by our social life.[47] We tend to think of differences in kinds across the species line, but differences in degree can add up—especially when magnified by social influence. But we interpret other species' behavior through our own lens, making it harder to recognize what attributes are analogous and making us look harder at our closest relatives. A long list of human uniqueness claims has turned out to be flawed, but scholars have settled on the accumulation of shared and learned knowledge for iterative improvement as central to human societal growth.[48]

Closer to home, sociologist Dan Hirschman has examined the distinct lives that contemporary academics live. In contrast to most Americans, professors live farther away from family, concentrated in college towns, and have lived in several similar locations; we have had less labor mobility and have worked in professional and knowledge economy occupations.[49] Scientists also may have distinct personality traits: more curious and idealistic but less agreeable compared to other professions.[50] Scholars are also less religious, meaning that studies of religious identities (though perhaps just as important to human life) are less prominent than studies of racial and gender identity and less often pursued from an internal perspective.[51]

These examples all show some value in thinking about the perspective we bring to research, but they amount mostly to listing potential biases. It would be nice if we could simply conduct philosophical thought experiments about all of these biases. But improving social science will require delving into the actual behavior of social scientists and its impact. And that project has been concentrated in studies of racial and gender identity.

Race and Gender: The Frontline of Bias Research

Within philosophy and sociology of science, calls for emphasizing the social character of research and the values driving research came from feminist standpoint theory.[52] Feminism highlights inadvertent universalist claims and the influence of cultural notions on research.[53] The aversion to claims of scientific certainty and calls for accommodation of alternative views were also pronounced in critiques brought in cultural studies of disadvantaged groups.[54] The attack on the "value-free ideal" of science was led by feminists and minorities.[55]

Today, these critiques have blossomed into an interdisciplinary theory articulating the intersection of multiple categories of domination, hidden by conventions of colorblindness.[56] Scholars challenge invocations of human nature or commonsense values as reflecting interests and ideas of dominant groups. In the process, they have successfully questioned disciplinary canons and mainstreamed critiques of racial and gender exclusion.

Within social science, these critiques were sometimes dismissed as political perspectives, rather than epistemological ones, but ideas about cultural bias in knowledge have made enough of an imprint to provoke studying the diversity of each discipline's scholars.[57] A "Chicago school" emerging in sociology, political science, and economics (though not unified across disciplines) was seen as agenda-setting and male-dominated, ignoring the growth of women and separating women's concerns into practical social services, human relations, urban reform, and social work.[58] Attention to the history has provoked both research into its consequences and efforts to diversify scholarship.

In political science, for example, nearly all landmark voting behavior scholars assumed that husbands directed women's voting or that women lacked political interests, despite scant evidence (as reviewed in Chapter 1).[59] Political scientist Christina Wolbrecht told me that the field studied power but excluded those with less of it, biasing what scholars saw and how they explained events. Wolbrecht has been active in an important group effort to expand gender diversity in public engagement called Women Also Know Stuff (at womenalsoknowstuff.com) that highlights women political scientists. It arose to help reporters find women researchers but has become an important home for considering gender biases in academia and public life—and spawned similar efforts in other disciplines and on behalf of other disadvantaged groups.

Research has shown that gender biases show up in myriad interesting ways. There is a strong male bias in fossil collections across the animal world, for example, with differences by collection and species that confound comparisons.[60] Even where scholars are trying to build representative collections, they end up with male-biased averages and erroneous site-specific conclusions based on comparisons of gender-distinct collections. Heterosexual behavior of the most stereotypical form is also studied most often in social research, long biasing studies of dating and family life.[61]

Women brought different research questions to the fields they entered. Sustainability gained importance over maximization in agricultural studies, distributional outcomes became more important in cost-benefit calculations, new artifacts were categorized as tools, and divorce research evolved to include impacts on adults.[62] An anthropology survey found gender differences on 21 out of 38 survey items tracking research interests and methodological approaches.[63] Gender diversity brought more research on stereotypes, barriers, and prejudices, including new journals and association sections dedicated to gender studies.[64]

Research on gender differences in research strategies found not just topical and interpretive differences but also workflow variation that held women back in academic life. In sociology and linguistics, for example, women specialize less than men and lose the associated productivity increase; they also lose more production from marriage and children.[65] Attention to these issues differs by discipline, in part based on their diversity. Psychology came close to achieving gender parity, and anthropology and sociology became majority women; political science is still majority men and economics is overwhelmingly so.[66] Economist David Autor told me his discipline has "been shaped by how macho it's been, arrogant and aggressive," but the discipline is increasingly recognizing how that holds back diversification and research gains.

Critiques of white male dominance had broad effects, even expanding federal medical research funding in the direction of social science concerns with inequality, social disparities, and stereotypes.[67] Despite controversies about biological and cultural sources of sex differences, women took the lead in critiquing a universal human model in research, working through Congress, advocacy groups, and agencies to change policy and priorities.[68] The receipts included new group-specific research as well as inclusion policies in panel reviews.

Concern with identity and group differences dominated university politics in the 1980s and 1990s, with new required diversity courses and initiatives.[69] Some of the change was driven by students. Women went from 42 percent of students in 1970 to 57 percent in 2010, and underrepresented minorities rose from 14 percent in 1980 to 32 percent in 2015.[70] Campus social movements demanded new institutions, expanding general education to incorporate minority groups and increasing diversity of funding, public panels, research institutes, and staff. A review of university strategic plans found that the only theme shared by every single research university was a commitment to diversity.[71]

Across American universities, student movements helped propel the organization of Black studies departments and the hiring of new Black faculty. Other minority groups used these new departments and programs as models for other new ethnic studies programs. In part through joint appointments, these efforts eventually culminated in ethnic studies footholds within traditional social science and humanities departments. But sociologist Fabio Rojas finds that many programs were scaled back or did not survive and most of the others remain small. Rather than organize to help the community, he finds that "black studies succeeded when it was organized as a more traditional academic enterprise."[72] That meant hiring scholars trained in traditional disciplines and methods and a community canonizing major texts, focused at elite research universities with doctoral programs and joint appointments.

The rise of Black and Hispanic academics and research areas to study each racial and ethnic group within each social science discipline is advancing research on previously specialized concerns. Research on overpolicing in race-class subjugated communities and the legacies of lynching, for example, have moved to the center of social science after long dismissals.[73] The importance of slavery also gained a more prominent place in social science, with researchers identifying long-term effects throughout social life.[74] Attention to race broadened social science explanation to unseen, longer-term, and broader-scale causes for inequities.[75]

Psychology has also seen an increase in racial discussion in developmental and social psychology, though race remains a rare topic in psychology journal articles, especially those published under (still disproportionately) white editors.[76] Economics has recently faced criticism for the way that major journals controlled by editors at top universities have been dismissive of racial minorities and related political and academic concerns.[77] Although the discipline is (not coincidentally) behind in both racial representation and racial research, responding to critiques of representation is likely to expand the scope of research as it has in other fields.

Initial skeptics of new fields like Black politics embraced the gains as the fields codified their knowledge and research standards.[78] Any perusal of contemporary social science journals on race or gender confirms that they are closely tied to the broader trends toward more credible empirical evidence in their disciplines. And their inclusion in general-interest journals advances social science theory and methods beyond their specific applications. These research areas are hardly the domains of postmodern self-congratulation that identity politics critics imagine. In fact, they are willing to take on controversial topics—even putting old heavily critiqued methods to better use. A recent study, for example, found that darker-skinned whites—measured via a light-reflectance spectrophotometer—identify more strongly with their white racial identity and are more likely to hold conservative political views on racialized issues.[79] The gain was from taking critics seriously, measuring identity and perception as well as skin color to understand the effects of each.

Initially, race and gender subfields within social science disciplines were separated and marginalized, but they are now playing a broader role. Political scientist Jessica Preece told me the initial mobilization of a separate community helped build a field of growing stature, but now gender-related matters are also incorporated into many subfields. Political scientist Mirya Holman argued that "there's an essential trade-off between creating spaces to professionalize rising underrepresented groups and making inroads across all fields." Some political science topics, such as race and gender, interest groups, health care, social movements, and government spending, are more often studied by women, with some generating more attention as gender diversity rises; other topics, such as voting and war, are still dominated by men and might gain from more women.[80]

Social scientists now understand that diversification of disciplines helps respond to potential bias and change our perspectives. Political scientist Scott Page told me, "Identity affects everything we study or do . . . . If you make a room more diverse, people think differently; it is a filter on what everyone said." Political scientist Ken Kollman told me that "changing demographics means the breadth of topics has expanded and methods changed." Psychologist Robert Nozek commented, "Viewpoint diversity makes confirmation bias easier to identify." An economist said they were optimistic about "the recent discussion within the profession about the continued under-representation of women, and other racial and ethnic groups, and a willingness to see that this absence affects and colors the questions the profession asks as well as the answers it gets."

Philosopher of science Kristen Intemann has articulated seven ways diversity enhances social research.[81] Diverse groups help generate new research questions. They identify more limitations with existing models and propose more new models. They propose a greater range of alternative hypotheses and interpretations of results. If they match the people they study, they can access more accurate and complete data from their human subjects. They can find new lines of evidence and think of new data sources. More diverse groups are more attentive to "loaded" language that is used in scholarly descriptions and can convey unintended evaluation. They can identify and weigh more potential risks in research findings. That leads Intemann to highlight the role of diversity in the content and impact of research and to place particular weight on diversity in research on human social life.

Sociologist of science Aaron Panofsky told me he sees some potential trade-offs in practice. Fields of underrepresented groups may start off with a politically left-wing and ontologically constructivist orientation, with a strong belief in the nurturing power of human institutions to change inequalities. That same orientation has come under attack in the reproducibility movement, he said, giving the example of "stereotype threat" research that has not fully replicated.

Standpoint theory can be taken too far when it limits research, rather than expands it. Social identity diversity provides potential access to different information or perspectives, especially when a researcher is studying the viewpoint of normally otherized subjects. But that does not necessarily mean that the theories or methods favored by dominant groups are wrong or that truth is revealed rather than discovered. Critics, especially from humanities disciplines, have sometimes reverted back to generic critiques, rather than empirically mapping the values of society, researchers, and projects on to their results and proposing alternative theories and evidence.[82]

Some versions of identity-based research can initially rely on assumptions that are too strong, but science has a way of exposing and reworking them. The emphasis on intersectionality is a good example. Even as a banal point, the idea that identity categories like race, sex, and class overlap has been fruitful for research on potential interactions. If researchers divide each category into exploiter and exploited and assume that disadvantaged identities will compound, their ideas may not be confirmed. But the scholarly history of examining intersections has been more nuanced. Research on the disproportionate impacts of the criminal justice and education systems on Black men considers the importance of that intersectional identity as a disadvantage, for example, even though women face more social disadvantages overall. It would be a shame if minority researchers only forwarded hypotheses about compounding unfairness in the service of affirming their identities, but that is an unjustified fear.

The experience of diversification across scientific disciplines suggests any trade-off may be well worth it. Women and racial minorities produce higher rates of scientific novelty, according to an analysis of research text from US doctoral recipients since 1980.[83] The problem is that their contributions are taken up by other scholars at lower rates than majority group members, resulting in fewer academic positions. New ideas always have to be tested and integrated into existing knowledge, but we still appear to be erring on the side of closing off fields to new perspectives.

Peer-review panels in social science request originality but have difficulty evaluating diverse methods.[84] Federal grant gatekeepers want to impress one another and avoid conflict, meaning preexisting networks and dominant ideas about significance and impact drive decisions.[85] Criteria like clarity, quality, originality, social significance, methodological rigor, and feasibility are all subjective. Panelists seek institutional, disciplinary, and topic diversity but also use race and gender as default signals. They seek conformity in scientific ideas despite researcher diversity, sometimes unwilling to see the methods and topics as reflective of the dominant groups. But objectivity is stronger when statements are evaluated by their severest critics, including the perspectives of those being studied.[86]

We should seek multiple lines of independently collected data within a diverse group of researchers and evaluators, checking for consistency in claims and evidence. There may be epistemic advantages to thinking from a position of subordination, but they become most useful within diverse social groups that acknowledge multiple goals and values and look for divisions of cognitive labor.[87] Dominant group philosophical perspectives are also advanced by thinking through their ties to national communities, such as philosopher Richard Rorty's argument for drawing from multiple American traditions incorporating instrumental creativity, mistrust of binding principles, and pragmatic social action.[88]

The identity-based activism born of increased representation for demographic minorities in scholarly communities has provoked a reaction from conservatives and some liberals. Judging views based on the identity of the speaker is wrongheaded, opponents say, and has chilled speech due to fear of seeming unsympathetic to minority concerns.[89] The debate can sometimes seem unbridgeable, especially when paired with nature/nurture debates on issues like sex differences, where any attention to biological determinants of human behavior is seen by one side as offensively aligned with bigotry and another side as the essence of free speech and academic inquiry. But increasing pushback to traditional claims can seem like silencing, even when all views continue to be represented and evaluated.

Take the controversy over Harvard president (at the time) Lawrence Summers's demotion due to his contention that innate differences in mathematical ability may explain women's underrepresentation in science. Putting aside the (important but distinct) debate about when and why academic leaders should be pressured to step aside, the effects on the actual academic debate were modest and likely positive. Plenty of research on the biology of sex differences, including the pinpointing of mental rotation skills, has continued alongside research on gender pipelines in scientific research. The additional efforts to find, motivate, and promote women scientists can be valuable however the academic debate turns out. The public political debate likewise brought attention to, rather than chilled, academic research that continues to refine reasons for women's underrepresentation in science.

Social Scientists' Increasing Recognition of Biases

Scholars uncovering racial and gender biases in academic research point to the underrepresentation of minority and women researchers. Indeed, the social sciences have long been dominated by white men—and that is hardly a phenomenon of the past. Social scientists at American research universities remain unrepresentative of the American public by race, ethnicity, and gender. My survey asked researchers to self-identify as men or women and based on their racial and ethnic group (using the two-question format of the US Census). Figure 4.1 reports a summary distribution of social scientists' race and gender. The average social science discipline is composed of 55 percent non-Hispanic white men, 30 percent white women, 9 percent minority men, and only 5 percent minority women.

If it were representative of the US population, the split would be 30 percent white men, 30 percent white women, 20 percent minority men, and 20 percent minority women (though the racial distribution of US residents of similar ages as faculty would be less diverse). No discipline underrepresents white men or overrepresents racial and ethnic minorities (at least at top US research

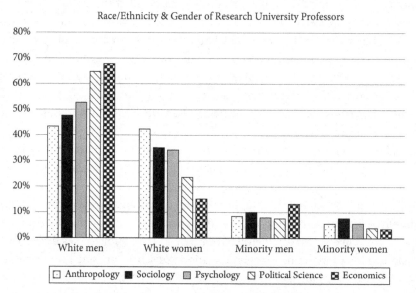

Figure 4.1 Distribution of Faculty Race/Ethnicity and Gender. Data from the author's 2020 survey of social scientists at major US research universities. n=1,141.

universities). Anthropology, sociology, and psychology have more white women, but no discipline has high levels of racial and ethnic diversity.

One sociologist described why this should be cause for alarm, citing "the complacency that seems to leave most US sociologists utterly indifferent to the highly skewed racial makeup of the profession. For people who routinely study racial, gender, and class inequalities, they seem strangely unaware of—and unwilling to consider—how such inequalities structure their own profession and the knowledge that it produces."

But I am not so sure they remain unaware. In fact, social scientists widely believe the gender and racial composition of their disciplines affects the content of their research, though they also see other influences. Figure 4.2 illustrates their assessments. Researchers were asked to what extent they believe each factor influences the content of research on a 1–5 scale. Here I compare their responses for "Racial and ethnic composition of researchers," "Gender distribution of researchers," "Funding available from government agencies," "Nationalities of researchers," and "Topical interests of the public and media." The average discipline rated the influence of researcher ethnicities at 3.5, genders at 3.4, and nationalities at 3.2, suggesting that they do see influence of researcher demographics in their discipline's research. But public and media interests were rated at a 3.6 while government funding was rated at a 3.9, so social scientists see other influences potentially biasing researcher output as well. Most respondents saw important influences across the board.

All disciplines rate government funding as the largest influence, except economics (which rates public and media interest the highest). Economics also

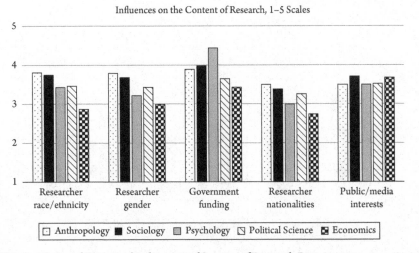

Figure 4.2 Social Scientists' Judgments of Sources of Research Bias. Data from the author's 2020 survey of social scientists at major US research universities. n=1,141.

stands out in rating researcher demographics as less important than other disciplines rate them (perhaps due to its relative lack of diversity). These influences are usually not compared, but social scientists I spoke with provided similar examples when asked about each type: both researcher demographics and patron interests could affect the topics studied and the questions asked as well as the interpretations of results. Funding to address specific diseases may lead to explanations for social outcomes based more on health than economic disadvantage, for example, just as unrepresentative researcher profiles may lead to victim blaming in criminal justice research.

I also asked researchers whether their disciplines were increasingly noticing the potential for biases in research. The question was, "In the last ten years, how much more, if at all, have researchers increasingly recognized the following potential biases" in their discipline's research? Figure 4.3 reports the average answers by discipline for biases based on race and gender, nationality and geography, or temporal focus, with the answer choices ranging from 1 (not at all) to 5 (a lot). The average discipline said they were increasingly recognizing racial and gender biases (3.5) more than those based on nationality (2.9) or temporal focus (2.9).

Anthropology saw the most perceived recognition of all three biases, while economics saw the least. The increasing recognition of racial and gender biases was similar to the reported recognition of searching for statistical significance and convenience samples (reported in Chapter 2). Social scientists thus both personally see the potential for racial and gender biases in the content of their research and believe their disciplines recognize these biases; like methodological

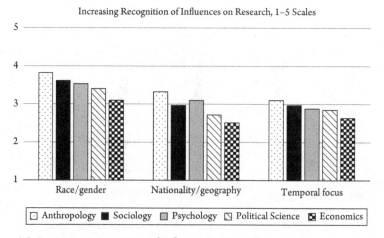

Figure 4.3 Increasing Recognition of Influences in Disciplines. Data from the author's 2020 survey of social scientists at major US research universities. n=1,141.

weaknesses, the unrepresentative composition of researchers is now seen as biasing social science.

Few see diversification as a panacea, but many see it as a necessary first step. As Andre Perry of the Brookings Institution puts it, "Truly rigorous research actively addresses our biases, particularly around racial prejudice. Think tanks and universities must see diversifying the stable of researchers as a proactive solution to hedge against bias and to add value to Black communities. While there is no guarantee that Black, Latino, Asian, or Indigenous researchers will challenge the orthodoxy they were trained in, they are more likely to have insights into how the methods and findings may or may not serve the community the person lives in or is from."[90] Indeed, diversification can both critique and improve methods, and minority scholars are often better able to identify problems that affect entire literatures, rather than individual studies.[91]

If scholars recognize racial bias, they can also recognize other biases based on such researcher characteristics as American national identity, occupational sector, social class, non-religious practice, and heterosexual preference without equating their impact on the content of research. Each unrepresentative demographic trait is likely to influence the scholarly community, even if they do not deserve the same emphasis as America's long history of racial oppression. In each case, scholars can learn from minority identities. That is true even in areas without a clear social hierarchy such as religion, where scholars' less frequent church attendance and Christian identification compared to the US population likely change their questions and interpretations of US evidence (and where their very low Muslim and Hindu representation compared to the world's population likely affects their global view).

Systematizing Data by Learning from Outsiders

Although critiques of the social and political biases of social science today often come from its less scientistic corners, the historical story shows that social outsiders often led the systematization of social science in order to avoid biases. From Florence Nightingale to W. E. B. Du Bois, early women and minority scholars often critiqued the mainstream for relying on biased interpretation when wider and more systematic data collection was better attuned to assessing assumptions and refining views.

Nightingale was an innovator in data visualization and measurement for improving public policy. She conceptualized soldiers dying in war as a technocratic problem; she sought to clean data of errors and reconcile various sources, making suggestions for record keeping and institutionalizing statistical analysis. Her contribution was showing that war deaths were a product of poor hospital administration rather than actual battle injury, which led not only to social reforms but to the founding of modern nursing (an astonishing feat, given the constraints on women in public life). Nightingale's data enabled her to gain a hearing, even taking advantage of women's assumed advantage in aesthetics to become known for data visualization. She then turned data into an object to provoke social change, arguing that we could "expunge the wedges" in her diagrams of hospital deaths due to error, removing the gruesome details to attribute institutional responsibility.[92] She took the further opportunity to suggest more statistics collection and new bureaus for social research.

Du Bois founded the modern practice of broad-scale community studies, complete with geographic analysis, surveys, statistics, interviews, and policy evaluations. Even though he was critiquing poor scholarship that saw African Americans as inherently inferior, he was unbelievably attentive to his own potential research biases in order to demonstrate his methods. He began his Philadelphia study admitting bias and saying researchers "must ever tremble lest some personal bias, some moral confliction or some unconscious trend of thought due to previous training, has to a degree distorted the picture in his view."[93] A researcher's convictions will always disturb scientific research to some extent, he said, but social problems still demand systematic study reliable enough for stimulating future scientific work and practical reform. He began by tracking the condition of 40,000 people over fifteen months, complete with schedules and questionnaires and copious qualitative examples from interviews and observation. It had to be reliable enough to use in further study and convince both white White and Black audiences.

As sociologist Aldon Morris details, "In contrast to white social scientists, Du Bois insisted that the newly emerging social sciences be built on careful, empirical research focused on human action in order to pass the test as genuine science."[94] As Morris discovered, "Because he believed that an authentic social science was possible and that inferior and superior races did not exist, Du Bois was the first social scientist to establish a sociological laboratory where systematic empirical research was conducted to determine the scientific causes of racial inequality."[95] His aim was critical and empirical social science. He thought that the search for truth had to be the sole aim of science, with social reform enhanced by that truth rather than a separate object of investigation. He had learned from study in German universities that "sociological generalizations were to be based on empirical findings rather than on a priori systems of invented 'natural laws.'"

Jane Addams and her compatriots followed similar methods and strictures in producing the Hull House Maps and Papers and related community studies.[96] In order to stimulate community action on social problems, they sought to closely examine their manifestations and variations across geographic areas and social groups. They made cautious generalizations and causal inferences compared to their more academically established male colleagues. Women-run studies and activism on behalf of immigrants and the working class innovated in quantitative sociology and social surveys.[97] The work of all of these outsider scholars in developing social science methods and theories has been obscured by racism and sexism, but recent historical reviews have shown their long-standing impact— not only on addressing the problems of downtrodden social groups but also on transforming their fields into empiricist and systematic investigations.[98]

These scholars were not interpretivists. They were attacking the racist and sexist interpretivists of their day and arguing for more evidence. They were debunking incorrect assumptions when the numbers did not match up, arguing for investigations of selection bias in observing events such as burials and sickness. This realization has had an important effect on contemporary sociology. As Daniel Hirschman told me, "The Du Bois approach was to get the facts right, even for [the goal of] social improvement." A prominent sociologist said the rediscovery of that history has sociologists "rethinking the canon in theory and not willing to tolerate a white male syllabus," realizing that the scope and methods of social research were largely defined by minority scholars who saw the benefits of standardization.

Some interpretivist critics of social science accept social explanations only if they are based on the meanings that the people being studied give to their social contexts.[99] The impulse for scholars to understand the situations they study as the subjects of their research see them can be a good one: empathy and position taking are important bases for theoretical diversity (though they are not usually practiced impartially as sympathetic social groups invite more research drawn from their perspectives). But that does not justify privileging the understandings of subjects in causal analyses of behavior. Human beliefs and actions often follow from contexts that individuals cannot see (or do not directly interpret), and self-understandings of behavior can be after-the-fact rationalizations rather than explanations. Minority scholars have long understood the importance of both hearing directly from the voiceless who are left out of majority-driven scholarship and assessing the role of social institutions, policies, and practices that may be beyond the view of those participants.

Critique of measures and assumptions built into social scientific methods can be valuable, but not if it becomes a theoretical conversation mired in conceptualization debates. Clear operational definitions enable measures to be repeated and understood. Researchers can determine distributions, sequences, and relationships and assess their connections to theoretical ideas. But the key is to find instantiations that can be widely analyzed, with progress through empirical analysis and theoretical comparison. Understanding the biases in our analyses but also the benefits of systematic study, minority scholars have historically been leaders in this process.

That matters for how we interpret contemporary complaints, such as the attempt to carry out an updated Sokal hoax. Even if disgruntled researchers can still punk humanities journals and throw shade on "grievance studies," social science is slowly but surely advancing due to its diversification—not in spite of it—expanding our data and enlarging our interpretation. Studies of race and gender have been important to the development of social science methods and their expanded scope. If critics see the focus on those two areas of diversity as misplaced, they would be better off expanding on their model to highlight other important aspects of human difference that are not fully recognized in social research. As researchers of human social behavior, we are all engaged in me-search of a kind. By uncovering biases in standard treatments and discovering new aspects of human life, identity researchers have provided a path forward for all of us to search for shared truth despite our partial views of the world.

5

Universities as Settings

The Chronicle of Higher Education, the main industry publication for academia, includes a "Review" ideas magazine that seems to specialize in sky-is-falling narratives about the state of universities and academic life. One issue included articles about digital search imperiling the superior learning previously made possible by card catalogs, social media destroying scholarly conversation, financial constraints breaking scholarly publishing, and—the perennial favorite topic—sadly observing the humanities in flames.

The mood is dire and dour, especially with datelines from the Modern Language Association meetings. But the same critiques are extended to American academia in general: there is too much pressure for metrics and financial success, the important topics do not get enough attention, technical sophistication is prized over true knowledge, and (to paraphrase a recent headline) it always seems to be time for radical reorganization. In these pages, colleges are cratering, faculty are in decline, and tenure is on the ropes—with the pandemic set to accelerate it all.

Specific coverage of the social sciences is no more positive. "How Political Science Became Irrelevant" seemed to be stimulated by the author's inability to gain access to foreign policy elites, without noticing any recent trends in public scholarship. It was widely panned, including in a response essay—but that might be the point.[1] The business model seems to be promoting scholarly self-loathing and infighting, stimulating angry blowback and repeating the cycle.

The *Chronicle* recently reran covers from its historical issues, demonstrating that the pattern may be perennial. A 1971 issue feared "attacks on tenure," an "era of crisis" for higher education, the televised university replacing face-to-face instruction, and controversies over sex discrimination. A 1975 issue bemoaned the rise in part-time faculty, the decline of jobs for graduates, limited federal funds for universities, conflicts of interest in research funding, and broken accreditation systems. A 1976 issue focused on computerized education as the wave of the future, also noting faculty critiques of research metrics and identity politics and politicization of controversial research.

Notwithstanding all the claims of crisis, American universities are a well-resourced global industry. Its dynamics and structures, including its long-standing and new challenges, are important for understanding the content and development of social science. Academia is the institution where social science lives. US universities are the center of that practice. The *Chronicle* and other observers are right to question how they direct and constrain research. Although social science is slowly internationalizing in topics and researcher collaboration, the American university system is still the source of the most research and the key setting where scholars debate its future. But the news is not all bad. Social science is still growing in American universities as well as elsewhere, especially by expanding into applied fields.

This chapter attends to the history of universities as the setting for social science and the incentives and opportunities they provide. The goal is to understand how the current context of social science affects the content of its research by reviewing the history of that relationship and the trends in academia likely to be operative today. We have a chance to learn from history about how institutional biases creep into our work and how shining a light on them can improve scholarship.

Social Science in the American University System

President George Washington proposed a national university to enhance the "education of our Youth in the science of government," and James Madison proposed including "to establish a university" in the list of constitutional powers authorized for Congress.[2] Although neither passed, there were proposals for a national system through the nineteenth century. The interest in higher education was strong, but the system that developed was based in states and churches.

The organizing principles of American universities evolved with their funders and personnel, but new goals were layered on top of old institutions more often than replacing prior missions entirely. A tradition of language recitation was up against a desire for practical skills training and an inferiority complex about scientific endeavor in Europe. As initial universities were founded to train religious leaders and initial professorships were often sponsored by local notables and businesses, US universities always advanced potentially conflicting interests. Research university traditions had to adapt to the traditional American college system, focused on rural settings for student spiritual development. American colleges were entrepreneurial and competitive, but the sales pitch had little to do with research or even social mobility through economic utility.[3]

Attempting to copy the German university model meant integrating research and certification and standardizing textbooks and instruction. It involved self-consciously building fields with shared standards and connecting them to associations and bureaucracies.[4] Graduate education, led by Johns Hopkins, built on a scientific model, but the need for donor and state support still promoted practical instruction.[5] The tenure system emerged as high-profile academics were dismissed over political or economic elite concerns. Complaints about the sources of funds for research, the randomness of evaluation, and the competition for student enrollment go back to Max Weber, especially tied to the Americanization of universities.[6] But even the first German universities also had their share of controversies over their mixed motivations, concern for social status, and inability to unify knowledge or impartially contribute to society.[7]

The twentieth century dramatically expanded higher education and research. Just from 1918 to 1941, enrollment surged from 118,000 to 805,000, while colleges and departments proliferated and government collected more statistics of all kinds.[8] As researchers constructed databases and ordering systems, they changed public and elite understanding of the scope of knowledge and signaled the key social role of data gathering for its own sake.[9] The explosion in academic literature overwhelmed libraries, which grew into university behemoths with specialized reference functions and broad collections of books and articles.[10]

The major expansions and transformations in social science, however, came from World War II's aftermath and the 1960s.[11] Public and policymaker support expanded, while an internal "academic revolution" made graduate education and research in disciplines large and permanent.[12] Federal research funds quadrupled from 1958 to 1964 as spending moved from an overwhelming concentration in defense and energy (87 percent in 1950) to a broad expansion of health and science research.[13] Foundation funding led to the creation of area studies programs and syntheses of research areas, including direct support for doctoral education and a large expansion in applied research at business schools (transforming them to PhD-led institutions). Most applied social disciplines were remade by social scientists in the image of social science, though at different levels (e.g., high in business, medium in education, and low in law).

Doctorates doubled from 1964 to 1969 and then plateaued, temporarily creating a very young faculty. Universities grew with the perception that humanity was entering a globalized "information age" with new economic rules that required "human capital" investment.[14] It is not an accident that the *Chronicle* crisis issues of the 1970s followed this revolution. Academia has been comparing itself against its temporary age of growth and unfettered support since that time.

Nonetheless, universities remain the center of research. Nearly three-quarters of all articles published in scientific journals come from authors working at universities, and almost 60 percent of basic research still takes place there.[15] Academia's central research debates revolve around the constraints of academic publishing: the quality and quantity of peer review, the pecking order of journals and their growth, assessing influence and impact, defining disciplinary boundaries and research topics, and the role of editors and gatekeepers.[16] Conference presentations have also expanded, but mostly serve as entrées into publishing communities. Growth has meant expansion of all research topics but also fear of competition in a winner-take-all system. In this clamor for attention, papers have become more visual and methodologically sophisticated across the sciences.[17]

Conservative economists argue that academics are blind to the core incentives driving their profession and institutions.[18] We believe in our own virtue and neglect trade-offs, budget constraints, and unintended consequences. Although incentivized by more than salary, academics still want self-expansion: more faculty and research funding with less teaching. Students, meanwhile, want credentials and leisure. That leads, they say, to an oversupply of faculty and lower-level administrators and distorted claims in academic advertising. We can convince ourselves that career options from our disciplines are plentiful while our social impact is critical.

But liberal critics also recognize how university financial incentives drive research. One study found that researchers quickly abandon unfunded research trajectories and easily justify their calculated moves on public-spirited grounds.[19] As environmental science federal funding dropped quickly, many related projects were abandoned. Research centers had to survive but did not state their obvious political and funding pressures as the reasons for their moves; instead, they repositioned centers toward a topic gaining more support, operating like private sector ventures.

The needs of the specific social institutions that accept social science graduates, like education, law, and health, also affect how they understand the division of scholarly interests and the need for coordination across fields.[20] The megatrend has been the expansion of social science research beyond the basic sciences toward applied fields, including business and education. Even at elite institutions like Harvard, most of the growth is in applied fields and professional schools.[21] While mainstream social science never quite accepted education and business schools as equal partners, they were often an easier sell to university administrators and students.

The Continued Growth of American University Research

Education historian David Labaree contends that American universities have always faced competing objectives and weak political support but have consistently muddled through.[22] One can find rationales for various decisions made by universities, he says, but they were built more by logrolling arrangements than by rationalized planning. Despite conflicting goals of knowledge, marketization, and status, they have emerged globally ascendant, with a socially important role.

Somehow, the United States came out on top. The American university system, initially last among major countries in Nobel Prize biography mentions, became the world leader by 1920, gradually gained further, and never looked back.[23] According to economist Miguel Urquiola, the system was uniquely effective in offering self-rule, free entry (of institutions), and free scope. He argues that this created a strong hierarchy of selectivity, concentrating great minds, in an expanding pool.[24] Top professors received less teaching duty, higher salaries, graduate student assistance, and time for research. Although many schools faced precarious positions, the system became the envy of the world.

As Max Weber long ago noted, large universities combine an enterprise in a capitalist system with an old faculty style; they contain many overlapping fields and lots of status competition; from the beginning, they generated complaints about cultural decay, abstract knowledge, and amoralism.[25] A 1975 nationwide faculty survey found that professors usually held conservative attitudes about change on their own campus even though they were liberal on national issues.[26]

But there has been change. The end of World War II created a large need for faculty (based on returning soldier undergraduates) and an associated increase in PhD programs while the Vietnam era overloaded graduate and undergraduate programs with students. Education historian Roger Geiger finds that students got more practical after the 1960s protest era, more concerned with job security and salaries, while still demanding diversity.[27] University students reported less interest in finding a "philosophy of life" and more in being financially well-off or famous. Universities diversified topics in part through new research centers, which grew by 30 percent in the early 1980s, and by hiring nonfaculty researchers (doubling in the 1980s).[28] Despite talk of the glory days of the postwar era, the largest rise in research spending was from 1980 to 2000, enabling a huge surge in publication.

Sociologist of education Steven Brint says research universities emerged stronger financially as well as intellectually; they advanced many of their competing goals—from intellectual growth to working with markets to expanding inclusion of underprivileged groups.[29] Universities professionalized and innovated, creating even more complicated organizational structures.

Undergraduate and graduate enrollment both doubled from 1980 to 2015, but research became more concentrated at the top. Research expenditures increased by a factor of 10 from 1979 to 2010, while publications nearly tripled. Citations more than doubled from 1980 to 2005, but inequality across papers and scholars increased. The top 200 research universities (5 percent of US colleges) now publish 80 percent of all peer-reviewed research.[30] Stratification of awards has also increased over time globally, with most award-winning social scientists moving among Harvard, Chicago, Yale, Berkeley, Stanford, Columbia, Michigan, and Oxford.[31] Inequalities in research output and attention could be producing a decline in diversity of perspectives in research, though there is some evidence that—like agglomeration effects in industry—concentration at particular universities may increase production and collaboration among top researchers.[32]

Although faculty numbers and salaries continued increasing, they were dwarfed by administrative growth. Administrative staff grew by 85 percent between 1975 to 2005, professional staff by 240 percent; they now outnumber faculty. Universities have also lately been on a huge building binge, with wide federal support.[33] Although faculty in most disciplines are stable or rising, there has been widespread concern about the decline of the academic profession. Professors became less satisfied with their careers and saw their autonomy declining.[34] But some of the complaints about constantly increasing expectations may be overstated. The number of publications has grown with the number of researchers, but individual scientists are only publishing more if you count their coauthorships as equivalent to all their prior single authorships.[35]

To illustrate the consequences for social science, I searched the secondary literature on these higher education trends, but I also wanted to use up-to-date data on the broad context social scientists face. I reviewed data on degrees awarded, faculty employment, and research expenditures, three key institutional trends that keep the social sciences going. Concerns about the rise and fall of disciplines or the changing constraints of academia need to be grounded in realities, including comparisons with other fields and trends over time.

To maintain the social sciences, even as research fields, they need to continue to attract students. Figure 5.1 illustrates data on undergraduate bachelor's degrees in the social sciences back to the 1970s. The top panel covers total degrees awarded in each year and the bottom covers the share of degrees awarded. Both compare degrees awarded in the social sciences (including the core disciplines reviewed in this book) with degrees in the applied social sciences, which here comprise (from largest to smallest) business, communication, education, criminal justice, public administration, and family sciences.

After falling in the 1970s and rising in the 1990s, social science bachelor's degrees have remained largely flat. Growth is understated because The National Center for Education Statistics (the data source) includes history in the social science category, which has seen larger falls than the social sciences. Psychology, which is tracked separately, has seen much larger gains than the overall social science category. Degrees in applied social sciences have risen considerably since the 1970s, but the increase has also recently flattened. Business and communication have seen the largest gains, while education has seen the largest fall.

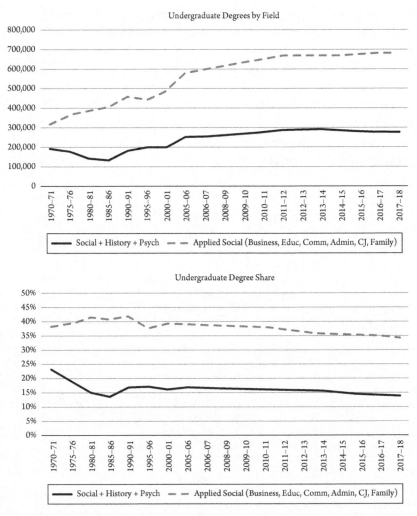

Figure 5.1 Undergraduate Degrees Awarded in Social Science Fields. Data from National Center for Education Statistics, Table 322.10; aggregated by author.

Given that degrees are increasing overall, however, the share of degrees awarded in social science and applied fields has long been flat or slightly declining (health professions have made the largest gains). As an undergraduate field, social science is thus stable but not the growth area. The evidence does not support categorizing social science with the humanities as slowly dying parts of the university, but it confirms that social sciences have grown more applied and lost relative ground.

The trends in doctoral degrees are somewhat distinct but are only partially consistent with perceptions that the social sciences are overproducing PhDs relative to undergraduate interest. Figure 5.2 illustrates PhDs awarded by year based on the same categories. The social sciences increased their doctoral degree production from 6,944 in 1990 to 11,411 in 2013 before declining slightly, with psychology again increasing more quickly than the social science category as a whole. But the applied social sciences have more than doubled their production since 1990 from 8,320 to 18,365 in 2017, with education and business leading the way within the applied category. And doctoral degrees overall have been increasing at universities, meaning that core social sciences now make up a smaller and declining share. Doctoral degree production has thus increased, but

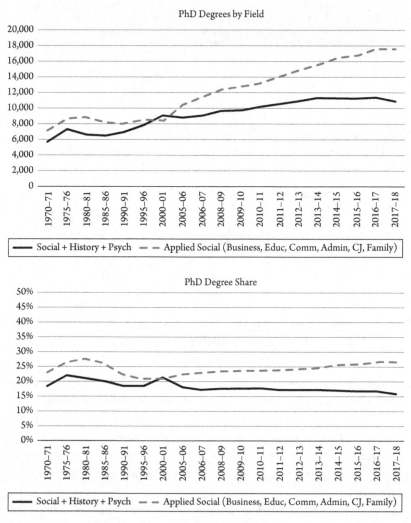

Figure 5.2 Doctoral Degrees Awarded in Social Science Fields. Data from National Center for Education Statistics, Table 324.10; aggregated by author.

it is concentrated in applied fields, is not especially recent, and does not stand out within the university.

Comparing the undergraduate and doctoral degree production, it is clear that social sciences still produce similar shares of undergraduate and graduate degrees. If the social sciences are producing too many doctorates relative to their undergraduate interest (and thus presumably the eventual market for academic jobs), that has been a long-standing pattern. But that may mask an important story. Applied social sciences are still underrepresented in PhD production compared to bachelor's degree production, but they are increasing their doctoral program share while their undergraduate share declines. It is the applied parts of social science that are developing higher ratios of graduate to undergraduate degrees, but they have not yet reached the ratios in the core social sciences. One conjecture is that social science PhDs used to be employed in applied schools such as education, business, and public administration, but now those disciplines produce their own PhDs to work in those fields, limiting the market for social science doctoral program graduates. Although not consistent with the simple story of doctoral overproduction, this might show how the success of social sciences in applied fields eventually undermined their expanding academic job markets as those applied fields grew on their own.

Social science disciplines have not all fared similarly. Figure 5.3 illustrates the number of faculty by discipline through two different measures: the top, from the Bureau of Labor Statistics (BLS), is based on general public surveys of employment and thus includes anyone who lists their occupation as a college teacher; the bottom, from Academic Analytics (a private firm that allowed access to these data), is based on (overwhelmingly tenure-track) faculty at American research universities. The BLS data go further back in time, but neither series had comparable data stretching back as far as the degree data. The BLS data indicate strong growth in many disciplines, concentrated before the other data series begins. Notice that the first chart tops out at 45,000, whereas the bottom goes to only 6,000; the difference is the many more faculty working outside of research roles in research universities, such as those working at community colleges and those in non-tenure-track positions. These data confirm that the growth in faculty positions has not been concentrated in tenure-track research university faculty, but do not show large recent declines.

Discipline-specific data also enable an assessment of some distinct institutional positions. Psychology and communication are the largest of the fields of faculty overall, but history is still the largest field within research universities. The rumored death of the humanities may not apply to history faculty positions, despite the decline in history majors. Communication appears to be on a long growth spurt, but one concentrated outside of research positions (likely due to its perceived utility). Of the disciplines considered closely in this book, the order by

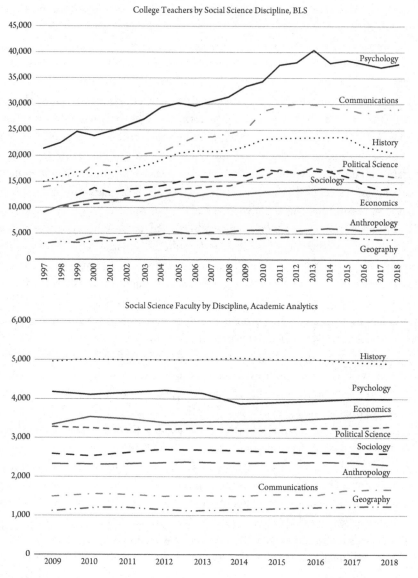

Figure 5.3 Faculty by Social Science Discipline. Data from the Bureau of Labor Statistics (*top*) and Academic Analytics (*bottom*).

size of research university faculty has remained the same since 2009: psychology is the largest, followed by economics, political science, sociology, and then anthropology, with a total range from 2,298 to 4,008. The research faculty base of these disciplines is thus small but stable. The range across all universities and faculty types is much larger, from 37,630 (for psychology) to 5,890 (for anthropology), and the order is somewhat different, with more political scientists and fewer economists. Anthropology appears to have few non-research positions. The total faculty workforce may respond more to changes in student demand than do research university faculty. Psychology is also likely growing in its more applied and less research-intensive sectors. Social sciences are thus mature fields with limited opportunities for growth in their most research-intensive sectors but are far more stable than usually perceived in the United States (even as they are expanding globally).

Research universities have also become big business over this period, though the gains are not concentrated in social science. If not through students, disciplines may also grow through research dollars. Figure 5.4 illustrates trends in research expenditures, as reported by institutions that spend more than $150,000 in research and development expenses (that they separately account for and send to the National Science Foundation). The top panel compares sources of social science funds, and the bottom compares social science with other research areas. The trends help explain the structural financial position of social science disciplines within the university. Overall, most research funding comes from the federal government. But social science research funds are more likely to come from other sources, including states, foundations, and universities; this non-federal share has been growing in recent years.

But research funding for the social sciences is paltry compared to those for other disciplines, especially the biomedical sciences. Notice that the social science funds, though increasing at a much higher rate than inflation in the top panel, barely register when compared with natural science or applied natural science (such as engineering and health). As federal research spending has exploded, funding for the social sciences has not kept pace. Although it is not true that the social sciences are losing funding, these data are more consistent with the popular image: social sciences are losing ground even as science gains national support. Science and technology disciplines can gain university attention and resources, even if they are not gaining in student demand (and some, such as computer science, clearly are gaining in both).

These data cannot account for other resource differences across disciplines, where the social sciences may falter. University funding allocations, based partly on indirect costs (especially notable in federal grants), may enable higher salaries, more graduate student support, larger start-up packages, and seed grants for natural science and applied disciplines. That could indirectly harm the production and success of social science research, reinforce inequalities, and stimulate grant chasing. Yet the limited social science federal grant funding may still be impactful and useful, as these fields otherwise generate limited support; every recent US economics Nobel laureate received NSF funding, and even limited NSF funding has helped keep fields like linguistics and archeology going.[36]

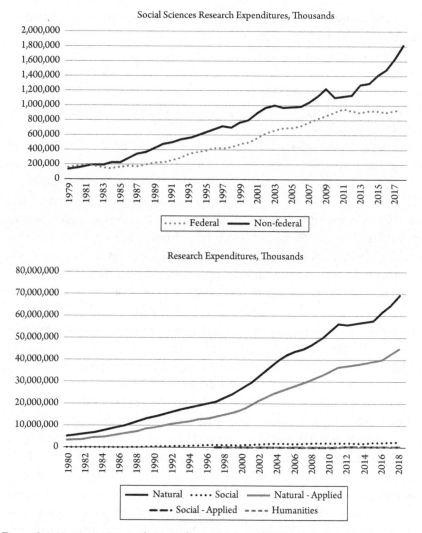

Figure 5.4 University Research Expenditures, Compared. Data from National Science Foundation, Higher Education Research and Development Survey.

These data help situate social science within the American university system. Although a stable field of education and employment, it has lost some ground to applied fields that now produce their own doctorates and can place faculty outside of research universities. In the university system as a whole, it retains a stable place but does not make much of a dent in research spending (getting lost among the dollars for the natural sciences). Social science research is moving forward, but within a university system where students prefer applied skills and administrators prefer natural science dollars.

American academia as a whole is facing increasing pressure to produce results from its research funding and a long-term trend of reduced high-school graduates to serve as potential undergraduates. Amid fears that the COVID-19 pandemic will decimate university budgets—from falling state support to low international enrollment—social science may not be as well positioned to weather the storm. But over the longer time horizon, social science grew dramatically as a research and teaching enterprise and is maintaining this size as a community of researchers and students.

Limited Internationalization

American universities, of course, do not constitute the full setting for social science, which is practiced around the world. Across the sciences, the growth is in other parts of the world. But Americans and American-educated researchers do still constitute a lot of its research workforce and output. A sociologist told me that the American centrism of research "shapes the structure of knowledge." Even as they lose some global share of researchers, American universities direct research through training, collaboration, and top journal control. Since researchers are not evenly distributed within US universities, we also fail to see the full picture of even the American system. Because regional comprehensives are systematically understudied, we miss the determinants of research content that are based more on practical local needs and may understate the importance of student job prospects in driving university investment in research areas.

American social science dominance is tied to its political dominance. As one analyst put it, "The enormous presence of the United States on the international stage (whether viewed in military, economic, scientific, or technological terms) enabled the nation's social scientists to enjoy a period of unparalleled importance worldwide."[37] Even in foreign universities, faculty training in the United States internationalized American approaches. As college attendance rates became higher in other nations, research remained disproportionately American.[38]

Although the exchange was not only one way, US cosmopolitan and global interests included a hidden Americanization, which disguised the extent to which Americans' global research concerns remained parochial.[39] International exchange was common across the social sciences through mobility of scholars, international associations and research outlets, and knowledge integration.[40] But despite rising indigenous social sciences in many continental European countries, social science scholarship remained overwhelmingly concentrated in English-language journals.[41]

The topics of social science studies have slowly internationalized, but Western Europe has remained the next most likely focus after the United States.

Two-thirds of published economics papers, for example, still cover well-off English-speaking countries, but empirical work focusing on the Middle East, Africa, Asia, and Latin America has grown.[42] Political science was extremely concentrated in North America and Western Europe but globalized over several decades. Some countries still received few citations, with differences based on language, income, democracy, and conflict.[43]

An analysis found that the countries scholars study were only minimally accounted for by US national security ties and trade interests or student course demands and demographics. It was mostly just the inertia of disciplines and institutional structures that determined focus, with especially slow internationalization in articles and dissertations.[44] Critics should thus not overstate the extent to which the US political worldview drives the American dominance of social science research. Much of our current research focus is more haphazard, based on trajectories of country-level scholarship and social networks of scholars from those areas. Internationalization of scholarly author teams is rising but is mostly a product of increases in coauthorship; it is higher in natural science, with more authors per publication.[45]

By comparing specific differences in university organization and practice across countries (along with their national administrative and funding apparatus), scholars can show differences that matter for the content of research. American science policy is adversarial, for example, whereas the British convene experts to reach consensus and the Germans appoint experts as representatives of social interests beyond their specific research.[46] Characteristics of the body of knowledge, the community of experts, and the institutional forms of adjudication create variation in scientific fields.

Social science disciplines are still dominated by Americans and American interests. The United States "strides like a giant over world sociology," says sociologist Michael Burawoy; most scholars are trained in the United States and most countries hold their scholars accountable to American journal rankings, associations, and norms.[47] A study of industrial-organizational psychology found American scholars dominant, despite internationalization, and samples and projects also focused domestically.[48] Even foreign researchers often transport theory and comparative data from US contexts. That means that seemingly broad research norms and theories might be tied to their American context. Anthropology's subfields were partially a product of the US field's early focus on Native Americans, but the field has evolved with researchers' interests in traveling abroad and their capacities and ties to each locale.[49]

There are differences across disciplines. More than half of economics PhDs now go to foreign students. Political science is second, but only at around 20 percent and declining; sociology, anthropology, and especially psychology are lagging further behind.[50] Differences are also apparent in research focus. In sociology, 80 percent of major journal articles feature US-focused data (with no major trend over time); in contrast, just over half of *American Economic Review* articles are US-focused and just under half of *American Political Science Review* articles are focused there.[51] Non-US countries of focus in major journals are overwhelmingly European, however, reflecting the country affiliations of the authors.

As scholars tend to generalize beyond their specific cases, they produce a biased view of global human behavior. This has led to concerns that psychology studies only apply to WEIRD (Western, educated, industrialized, rich, and democratic) contexts. In fact, the cultural sensitivity of results identified in advance did predict failures to replicate.[52] And psychologist Jay Van Bavel told me that the "many labs" tests "didn't really do justice to potential differences in institutions and behaviors" due to cross-cultural differences since they were designed to test easily translated universal phenomena. The centrality of US research "remains a blind spot," he noted; "even Europeans [much less non-Western nations] feel stigmatized and not in the trendy research." Psychologist Sanjay Srivastava agreed these tests were "unlikely to produce cultural differences in lab experiments," but he says we are "getting more thoughtful in our approach to culture [and] trying to design in differences [in studies]." A psychologist (and replication skeptic) agreed that psychology is "mostly a north American phenomenon, not much in Asia with 90 percent of the rest in Western Europe" and says American assumptions about representation, affirmative action, and social dominance may not apply elsewhere. Indeed, survey-based measures suggest the United States could be an outlier on many psychological dimensions, and the European populations studied next most often are likely to share similar biases.[53] If publications are biased toward Western country samples, that may limit the advance of knowledge and interventions for most of the world's population.[54]

Sociology also has controversy about its American focus, but Jeremy Freese says it is driven by undergraduate interests and unlikely to change. Sociologists expect less generalization of theory, he says, meaning they are less likely to make the broad claims of universal applicability that psychology studies make. Sociologist Daniel Hirschman sees a double standard in the discipline, with strong interests in domestic diversity but globalized work devalued. He says ideas based on international data usually face higher demands for theoretical interest, meaning they are often forced to make wider claims about generalizability. An international sociologist agreed: "I think sociology in the US is still fairly provincial—those of us who do research outside the US have to work much harder to justify why our research matters, and find that the bar for publication is higher because our research gets seen as niche. But research that is done in the US is rarely viewed as such. . . . I think this is a problem because it prevents us from having a more global outlook, and it means sociologists are not doing as much research on key global issues."

Economics is the most international in terms of students at American universities and the increase in global data. But even within Africa, economics research is highly concentrated in five countries, driven by international tourism, peace, and English-language use.[55] The historical lack of economics in Africa led important aspects of behavior like social trust and the legacies of slavery to be understudied, but a new African School of Economics is helping to fill the gap in research questions and data.[56]

Political science has a longer history of international studies and comparative political research. One scholar told me there is now more connection between American and international work, with many people studying the same questions and lots of people developing cross-national frameworks for comparison. Political scientist Amanda Friesen told me the old problem of having to study multiple countries if studies were not based in the United States is being overcome. There are now a lot more single-country studies elsewhere that are "changing the US centrism" of research, but she notes that the Global South is still underrepresented.

The structure of the university workforce inhibits global research. Comparative work is more difficult from a distance and often requires fieldwork that is not easy to balance with academic semesters. That means PhDs may gain a sense of a place at a particular time when they happen to be completing dissertation work or on sabbatical (which they might later implicitly take to be representative), with work rushed to meet university deadlines (rather than planned to match local social or economic events). Political scientists who did work at the end of the Cold War, for instance, had to reinvent themselves after the Soviet Union fell. More subtle influences based on time and place availability are more common than these easy-to-recognize abrupt changes.

When social scientists do go abroad, they may bring their American assumptions. Political scientist Alex Coppock observed that it is "definitely problematic to do field experiments in countries without much local participation and to have them concentrated in the places where they are allowed [and funded]." Political scientist Tara Slough told me that there are "lots of places where the assortment of researchers and the availability of support change how [and what] we study," noting a focus on Argentina within Latin America and Uganda in African field experiments. "We focus on certain countries and make stylized facts based on them. How much that affects conclusions is an open question. It is possible meta-analysis and macro level analysis can identify and fix [problems]. There is a bottom-up process that helps roughly harmonize [and] builds in community monitoring, negotiated with NGOs . . . but it's hard to make similar across-the-world studies." It is "optimal to have a mix of people from the place [studied] and outsiders," she notes. There are "problems with studying the poor everywhere. [We] want to give voice to [their] concerns but don't involve them." European-centric scholarship also led to an overemphasis on the role of military superiority (and an underemphasis on disease) in global history.[57]

The disproportionate focus on the United States and Europe is often taken as an anachronism. But research elsewhere is also biased by American and European applied interests and self-conceptualizations. In anthropology and political science, international research was at many times consciously colonial. Our geographic focus is better viewed as one aspect of our inherently applied motivations: social scientists study countries and places relevant to our own, just as we more often study our own time period, our own social groups, and our own social problems, because we are motivated by what we want to achieve with the knowledge rather than mere curiosity about timeless social behavior. These geographic biases, however, are increasingly recognized—especially when scholars make controversial global claims (see Chapter 7). Just like universities helping the local community or economy, focusing on domestic concerns may still be justified as a strategy for relevance and impact, as long as it isn't accompanied by unevidenced claims of generalizability. But increasing globalization is part of the successful advance of social science to address diverse concerns and better represent human behavior.

How University Incentives Affect Research

Social scientists are a product of the peculiar growth and dominance of the American university system. In the late nineteenth century, the country had more than 800 scattered colleges but only twenty-six that had more than 200 students or a large, trained faculty.[58] In 1904, just fifteen elite schools accounted for one-fifth of US college enrollments. But the number of American high schools increased from 2,500 to 14,000 from 1880 to 1920, increasing the demand for higher education.

The Morrill Act famously spread federal government funding (in the form of land to be sold off) to every state. But even private universities relied on government largesse. Harvard, Bowdoin, Williams, Columbia, and Pennsylvania all received early state appropriations. MIT received Morrill Act funding. But today, public universities rank dramatically lower on international rankings.[59] There are now more than one million faculty, but only 20 percent of them are at R1 research universities.[60] But those universities have outsized influence. Harvard alone has altered the history of social science, institutionalizing the use of operational definitions for theoretical concepts.[61]

It was not always clear that universities would combine professional training with scientific research and higher learning, as they were initially tied to churches.[62] But American faculty visited Germany and universities pioneered graduate education based on the German model, which incentivized academic disciplines. College professors did not monopolize social science disciplines early in the process, with many local branches incorporating practitioners and amateurs, but academic societies professionalized around university-based researchers.[63] Debates within universities nearly always combined organizational and procedural disputes over recourse allocation with larger concerns about the relative importance of sectors of knowledge and their unification.

The changing economic incentives of universities affected their research and operations, but universities were active participants in the move toward what sociologist Elizabeth Popp Berman calls the "market university."[64] University science came to be seen as an engine of economic growth, alongside the idea that innovation drives the economy, leading to faculty entrepreneurship, patenting university inventions, and university research parks. Universities had many incentives to evolve from basic science discovery to application in industry. Sociologist Patricia Gumport says the market logic ascended inside universities while traditional bureaucratic and faculty professional authority declined, leaving the economic value of research and student consumerism to guide decisions.[65]

The role of the federal government remains strong because research is dependent on grants. Some researchers spend half of their time on grant writing, which promotes promising more than you can deliver and limiting risk.[66] The correlation between scores on grant applications and later citations is low, as is inter-reviewer reliability.[67] Generating external funding means focusing on topics that are trendy or have institutionalized support. Rather than study the fundamentals of human history, geneticist David Reich had to claim to be addressing contemporary diseases.[68] Grant funding is a high-stakes lobbying game, with biomedical sciences best organized.

Non-governmental funding can also direct research. When industries seek to limit regulation or costs, they find scientists who will support their propositions. An entire industry has developed to find and promote industry views, complete with journals and consulting firms, in areas like health and the environment.[69] Funding from private foundations may also come with many strings attached. Foundations, for example, drove academic debates over standardized testing, charter schools, and district control.[70] And there is a long history of universities and professors managing relationships to try to avoid being redirected by their individual rich benefactors.[71] Although conflicts of interest and ties to specific project funding must often be disclosed, authors do not have to report broader university funding, including ties to philanthropy, grants, or federal agencies.

Funding perpetuates inequalities. The Gini coefficient for faculty salaries has more than doubled over the last few decades.[72] Inequalities across institutions, scholars, and departments rise together. Those from high-prestige departments and universities receive more grants and citations, reinforcing their dominance later.[73] Even when there is some benefit in citation potential to pursue innovative research, it is risky; only already-established scientists can usually afford to do so.[74] The inequalities are compounded because universities that are less competitive for research grants rely more on tuition and thus privilege student credit hours, reducing research capacity.

The journal publication process also increases inequality. Journals were created to speak to specialized audiences and gain legitimacy.[75] They systematized authorship and articles as the units of scientific discoveries, replacing the public meetings that preceded them. As in grant competition, much of the peer review process in academic writing is about the trendiness of ideas and the boundaries of disciplines and fields. The competition for funding and research output tends to concentrate resources at the top universities, where funding potential and collaborators are more plentiful.[76] Studies of peer review in grantmaking show it is driven by standards of "excellence" and "fit," often irreconcilable across disciplines; participants favor their own styles of research but need to believe that they are applying agreed-upon standards.[77] Researchers depend on scientific communities to reinforce shared ideas and promote their own future funding, which large team science further enables.[78] The size of author teams has increased from 1.9 to 3.5 authors per paper, with high-status authors increasingly collaborating.[79] Academic conferences, theoretically more open, are often pay-to-play opportunities that standardize ideas and make hierarchies concrete.[80]

Scholarly views of research ethics also affect the state of knowledge. Social psychology history shows the influence of human subjects standards. Many high-profile studies, such as the Stanford prison experiments (where fake guards abused fake inmates), the Milgram shock experiments (where participants supposedly delivered electric shocks), and the Robbers Cave experiments (where teams of campers harassed one another), continue to be cited in social science textbooks but would not pass today's standards for human subjects research. They are thus harder to debunk, even though recent reviews have found the results more tenuous than previously believed.

Cold War Social Science

The effects of university institutional interests and American dominance are hardly new to social science. It is easier to accept how social context affects the direction of university research through historical examples—and it also suggests that institutional and geographic biases were previously even more rampant and only slowly recognized.

Federal funding for science began controversially. Social science demanded inclusion in initial science funding under the presidency of Franklin Roosevelt, hampering the creation of a science agency. Critics within the social sciences worried that funding would distort priorities, displace other research, and make disciplines dependent on government.[81]

But World War II accelerated the links between government and universities. "Science, the Endless Frontier," a report to the president by engineer Vannevar Bush in 1945, advocated a federal science agency and investments in research and the scientific workforce to advance basic science, even for the proximate war-related purposes of national defense, disease prevention, and economic rebound. Federal university research funding grew sixfold from 1955 to 1967, with the federal share of university funds increasing from 54 percent to 74 percent.[82]

This helped create what C. Wright Mills called the "scientific-military-industrial complex," expanding on President Dwight Eisenhower's phrase and warning that "public policy could itself become the captive of a scientific-technological elite." Large military contracts included social science databases and consulting arrangements, creating twenty-one think tanks and hundreds of research institutes, with federally funded centers tripling between 1951 and 1967.[83] Even natural scientists expected that any World War III was more likely to be driven by social science and psychology. But Congress viewed social science with suspicion, pointing to examples of support for communism or revolution as well as early wasteful projects.

McCarthyism tended to "depoliticize" social science, according to one review, "adding one more incentive for scholars and university administrators to emphasize technical tools of science and to insist on its independence and detachment."[84] But these claims to objectivity were, in another sense, political stances that hid a large collection of social science research performed on contract: "scholars working on such diverse topics as scientific creativity, race relations, human instincts, and gender roles claimed their work was needed to strengthen the foundations of American society, institutions, and culture in the anxious nuclear age."[85] Many scholars did not have to be convinced to oppose communism and support American nationalism, seeing their scholarly and national contributions as aligned. Modernization theory, in particular, was advanced as a justification for the active US role in developing other nations assumed to be behind in following its trajectory.

Government support endangered the objectivity of social scientists, especially in international affairs. As student protests and public opinion shifted against the Vietnam War, there was a backlash. And critics charged that mid-century ideas such as systems analysis were based on military and American government values. Meanwhile, the State Department resented the expansion of social science into what they regarded as the diplomatic craft.[86] The most controversial and specific research left campus for contract research centers in the 1970s, pursuing models tied less to academic research and more to military operations.

The most famous example was Project Camelot, an Army-sponsored project at American University integrating psychology, economics, sociology, and anthropology to produce assessments of many countries. The project angered Latin American academics and State Department personnel and was eventually canceled (at least in name), leading social scientists to seek more professional autonomy.[87] Philosophers of science saw McCarthyism and Cold War politics as a reason to profess value-free commitments.[88] Military minds, meanwhile, decided that broad social research was less relevant than direct government studies on operational needs.[89]

A proposal for a National Social Science Foundation was introduced in Congress every year from 1966 to 1969. In 1965, only 2 percent of federal support went to the social sciences. But social science support for a foundation was surprisingly mixed, with some scholars fearing increased government interference.[90] NSF instead cautiously expanded into social science, with tepid support from natural scientists. Scientists and politicians repeatedly questioned whether the social sciences were driven by leftist values and whether they could be thought of as sciences at all, with NSF worried that social science funding would cause controversy in Congress. To insulate itself, NSF prioritized those fields most closely tied to biology and those involving the most math and computers.[91] But all federal research funding grew with Cold War concerns.

The Organisation for Economic Co-operation and Development then internationalized the argument for greater research and development spending, including more government-funded university research across countries.[92] The US pattern, more than that in use in Europe, was to promote objectivity. This meant that models tended to mix social and natural science in an integrated risk management perspective.[93] Basic science was tied to classified research, for example, guiding the earth sciences toward satellite-intensive research. The precarious position of social science in federal funding meant it attached itself to both a military-driven agenda (criticized for conservative ideological views) and later to the war on poverty (criticized for liberal ideological views).

In both sectors, there were many actors who went in and out of government, private research centers, and universities. Global researchers had incentives to promote many national security threats while economists sought to become known as institution designers.[94] Changes in military strategy helped codify the place of psychological and sociological concerns, especially in counterinsurgency, and raised the country's cultural mission (visible in initiatives like the

Peace Corps).[95] American dominance in European reconstruction after World War II tended to advance academic perspectives on modernization as well as topical missions in area studies.[96] Although the country focus of research does not follow from changing US national security needs, the early focus on certain countries self-perpetuates through the building of associated scholarly communities.[97]

Domestic policy entrepreneurs learned from defense, with administrators creating offices for research, plans, programs, and evaluation based on RAND.[98] Evaluations of Head Start (early childhood education) and community action programs copied the model, with the same social science that had been used to build President Johnson's war on poverty later used to limit its claims of success under President Nixon.[99] There were 250 new interdisciplinary social science institutes created in the twenty years following World War II, many using an engineering model.

Cold War social science began in the age of systems analysis and optimism around grand unified theories but ended by emphasizing more specialized pursuits. Science historian Hunter Crowther-Heyck finds that the first federal patronage system helped create the behavioral revolution in social sciences through interdisciplinary syntheses, but the second focused on specialized concepts and techniques, fragmenting the disciplines.[100] Harvard's Department of Social Relations, designed to combine interests in anthropology, sociology, and psychology, did not survive intact.

The funding efforts nonetheless helped the social sciences triple in size by the 1960s, based on the growth of scholarly associations. Whereas only one in thirty psychology articles had a funding support acknowledgment in 1940, twenty-five of thirty did by 1955.[101] That promoted quantitative behavioral research and formal theory. Throughout science, in fact, journal peer review processes were adopted largely to justify public scientific support during the Cold War, only later being seen as emblems of scientific practice.[102] There was a social science establishment that rotated between the Ford, Rockefeller, and Carnegie foundations; the naval research, air force, and operations research federal offices; and think tanks like RAND.

By the 1970s, however, large, ambitious projects and sweeping book titles were replaced by concerns about the failure of grand theory. In tandem, federal funding stopped growing (in constant dollars). Today, both Canada and Europe still provide more independent support for social science than the United States, with separate federal foundations. Based on concerns of international competition, federal research funding also became more pluralist and less motivated by national security. Foundations also shifted toward practical evaluations of existing programs. A rising sense that broad technocracy brought unmet promises led to more socially aware and applied research projects.[103]

Research on the Cold War history of social science and related science studies scholarship provides clear examples of federal funding influence on research topics, aims, and interpretations, driven in part by its ties to natural science justifications. The story was anticipated by critics and not too difficult to understand: as federal money became available, it increased the size and ambition of social science research and redirected it toward first military and then domestic national political goals. That expanded the ability of researchers to study other nations but compromised their open inquiry in foreseeable ways. Similar methods and approaches were then used to fight the war on poverty, also with clear effects on what scholars researched and what they expected to find.

Challenges in the Contemporary University

If the contours of US government policy and the direct interests of universities in research funding had large effects during the Cold War, the same is likely true today—even if the consequences are less visible. But the complaints have shifted to emphasize the difficulty of sustaining a continued expansion of research in the face of less political support.

University presidents widely perceive stress associated with increasing costs and decreased support and several key trade-offs: between research, teaching, and outreach; between basic knowledge and applied work; and between global and close-to-home interests.[104] The main solution has been to focus on rankings and grant dollars, while building academic administration to address student concerns for service learning, engagement, inclusion, and careers. Given declining state support for public universities, the federal government has become even more influential alongside endowment gifts and foundation funding.

Interestingly, faculty nationally say they are still spending a lot of time on teaching, while they have become less interested in becoming an authority in their field.[105] Initial fanfare around massive online open courses (MOOCs) replacing traditional education gave way to reality, as few students paid or completed coursework. They established a more specialized niche in corporate training, with new forms of credentials concentrated in technology learning. Faculty who are less successful in research tend to take up other causes, including local service and teaching.[106]

In an international survey of political scientists, the primary complaints were about job security, administrative duties, and university pressures.[107] Scholars saw the quality of methodological skills, social diversity, interdisciplinarity, and collaboration all improving, while university life had become more burdensome. The long-term trend, however, is toward less faculty involvement in university administration, with the rise of associate deans and professional administrators and a reduced direct faculty role in governance.[108]

Universities have increasingly aimed to evaluate themselves relative to others, which has produced some questionable metrics. Most central of them all is *US News and World Report* rankings of departments (based on graduate program reputations) and universities (based on undergraduate data including test scores).[109] Although resisted and critiqued by schools, the metrics cause schools to redirect resources and sometimes fudge the numbers. Since reputation is so important, they also tend to be very sticky. As students select based on them, they also reinforce hierarchies and increase inequality across institutions.

Even though university origins differ, they are increasingly chasing the same model. The US system was layered among four major types: liberal arts colleges, state universities, land-grant practical universities, and the graduate-based research university.[110] But they are all increasingly competing with one another over faculty, students, and research dollars, looking less distinct. They are shooting for accessible learning as well as knowledge integration, real-world application as well as social advance. Social scientists are having to show they can do all of the above.

Academic job market concerns are justified, though social science may actually be in a comparatively better position. In sciences, nearly everyone has to go through multiple postdocs to get a still-rare permanent position.[111] This very long ladder makes it difficult to predict and react to scientific needs. In the humanities, jobs are even more scarce while doctorate production continues. But across departments, career entry has become more difficult, with growth concentrated in contingent faculty.[112] Academic departments are notorious for hiding accurate and representative placement information and tend to emphasize any success, rather than the often-long paths from graduate school to first job to permanent position and the many who drop out along the way.[113]

Yet some research indicates that the replacement of academic researchers by part-time teaching faculty is overblown. The ratio of full-time professors per student is instead staying relatively constant, while part-time faculty are added to take on more teaching responsibilities.[114] Remaining general education requirements are slowing the transition from liberal arts to applied disciplines. Universities are producing more doctorates than jobs available, but mainly because falling disciplines are still producing nearly as many. The federal and state governments are still supporting university research and graduate training at high levels, but universities are producing graduates mostly based on student demand regardless of job availability.

Once employed, researchers face increasing tenure demands, which could affect the content of research. Many researchers show a rapid rise in research production, an early peak, and a gradual decline based on the tenure system, though there is substantial variation—with the common (average) pattern describing only about one-fifth of faculty.[115] Universities may thus be incentivizing quick-hit research that only works well for the research agendas of a minority of faculty. The tenure system may also disincentivize the sharing of code and data, as researchers try to get all they can out of anything they collect, but there are signs that young researchers can gain status through sharing.[116]

As they have historically, the incentives of academia will continue to affect research. By integrating research on the university system and its history, social science researchers can better perceive their incentives and limitations—without waiting for the next generation to uncover them. We now have better evidence on how university structures affect scholarship and we are starting to build institutions to address downsides. The most significant challenges are in the limitations of the job market and the associated increases in competitiveness. But even here the competition is partially a product of increasing standards for research and the success of top-tier researchers in large-scale research efforts. And neither the social sciences nor the American universities where they often live are as precarious as sometimes alleged. As social scientists explore well beyond their shores and pursue larger and broader research, often in collaborations across subfields and disciplines, they are learning more—even while inhabiting imperfect university institutions.

|| 6 ||

Opportunities and Constraints
of the Disciplines

In the early months of the COVID-19 pandemic, some economists grew frustrated with the epidemiological prediction models that were guiding public policy responses. George Mason economist (and public intellectual) Tyler Cowen raised tough questions for the epidemiologists, covering not only their prior track record but their salaries, training, and standardized test scores.[1] Their early models were driving policy decisions, including widespread economic shutdowns, without fully justified assumptions. Despite widespread agreement that the models were reliant on incomplete data, Cowen's posture was greeted with incredulity: economists were again running headlong into a new field, assuming expertise without regard to their lack of content knowledge.

Although perhaps typical of the smug imperialism economists are (only somewhat unfairly) known for, Cowen's outburst actually illustrated how economics has learned from other fields.[2] It criticized epidemiologists for faults traditionally associated with economics: modeling with strong assumptions, ignoring variability across individuals and nations, and disregarding important descriptive data. The public spat hid some important collaborations between epidemiologists and economists to measure the effects of anti-virus policies and consider the trade-offs between economic recovery and the spread of disease.

It was not the first or last economics-epidemiology dust-up. Economist Emily Oster had argued that typical recommendations for breastfeeding are based on flimsy evidence, eventually authoring her own popular guides to pregnancy and parenting based on independent reviews of the evidence. Although it was another example of economists being quite willing to traverse field boundaries, here too the intervention showed increasing worries about theory-based public advice without high standards of causal inference. Some of the initial turf protection from epidemiology gave way to reconsideration of the evidence, but breastfeeding guidelines did not change. Oster later angered some epidemiologists by collecting data on COVID impacts of childcare centers and schools—but that project too presaged a softening expert consensus on school-based spread.

This chapter covers the constraints that disciplinary boundaries place on research as well as the limited role of interdisciplinarity in alleviating them. Political science, economics, sociology, psychology, and anthropology each offers a different vision of human nature, with accompanying ideas about topical importance and methodological rigor. Interdisciplinary work that tries to integrate the best of each discipline, especially in applied fields, has been valuable. But each discipline's historical objectives and boundaries still guide its research practices. Social science is still mostly dependent on their central ideas to govern its scope and ambitions. Dismantling and rebuilding disciplines is neither feasible nor advisable. Instead, self-aware disciplines that know their own limits and exchange with others are the best path forward.

Inheriting the Disciplines

Although most universities maintain traditional disciplines, some occasionally try to refashion them. Arizona State University features a School for the Future of Innovation in Society, a School of Sustainability, and both a College of Integrative Sciences and Arts and a New College of Interdisciplinary Arts and Sciences. Most faculty likely still consider themselves attached to their disciplines, but there is always a marketing niche for reinvention.

Sociologist Nicholas Christakis recommended breaking up the traditional social sciences altogether in favor of new disciplines: biosocial science, network science, neuroeconomics, behavioral genetics, and computational social science. Probably not coincidentally, these happened to be strong interests of Christakis's. Three of his five disciplinary ideas appear more like protestations of social science's aversion to its biological underpinnings—another common Christakis theme. Many scholars could likely create a similar list of topics they would like to see covered more, with proposed reorientations for others.

If we were building the social sciences from scratch today, we would not arrive at the current division of basic sciences. In fact, newer applied disciplines in communication, information, cognitive science, education, business, public health, and public policy are arguably attempts to redesign the social sciences around today's concerns. Though notice that they are quite a bit more applied, with substantive topical interests, than the list from Christakis.

But just because social science disciplines are historical constructions does not mean they provide no useful structure for study. They have proven enormously successful at regenerating scholars, cataloguing spheres of knowledge, and advancing methods, without forsaking new potential avenues of research that cross boundaries.

All academic topics are intellectual characterizations as well as social institutions with traditions and communities attached to them.[3] They each approach an amorphous set of problems and concerns and are often preoccupied with setting their boundaries and topical hierarchies. Every standardization of topics into categories removes important context and meaning, but it also provides the basis of building infrastructure for scholarly communication.[4] Professionalizing education in disciplines, including attaching applied interests to them (such as criminology and demography to sociology), allows disciplines to grow.[5]

Today's academic fields, both disciplines and internal subcategories, are practical divisions of labor rather than fundamental ontological or epistemological categories; they provide simplified strategies for pursuing knowledge within communities of interest.[6] But they also organize careers around traditional hierarchies and institutions, meaning they have the potential to corrupt free investigations by supplanting the search for knowledge with strategies for personal advancement.[7]

Disciplinary boundaries arose, among a broader proliferation of occupational and demographic categorizations, as claims to turf and social importance and as the basis for organization of work and careers.[8] Most social sciences have developed a disciplinary history community that seeks to understand how their development constrains current thought, especially since standard histories of science leave out the social sciences.[9]

The Cold War era that built the social sciences into large and well-funded juggernauts left its mark. The social science pioneers of mid-century sought to build "strong social disciplines whose rigor and independence made real objectivity possible" as well as the "academic departments and advanced doctoral training [that] defined the institutional structures of self-consciously professional science."[10] Membership in the American Sociological Association rose from 3,241 in 1950 to 14,156 by 1970. From 1947 to 1967, the American Political Science Association grew from 4,598 to 14,687 members; the American Economic Association grew from 7,529 to 23,305; the American Anthropological Association grew from 1,692 to 6,634; and the American Psychological Association grew from 4,661 to 25,800.[11]

Despite lots of changes in American society and the university system, all of these disciplines remain large today, with a presence at most universities. Other large social science disciplines, such as education and communication, still often hire doctoral recipients from these fields rather than their own (whereas the core social sciences still hire 90 percent of their faculty from PhD programs in the same discipline).[12] Few interdisciplinary social science fields established themselves across lots of universities, though fields that pursue applied work like social work and education have been more successful.

Psychologist Donald Campbell challenged the "ethnocentrism of disciplines" in a call for "fish scale" knowledge with overlapping specialties.[13] He crudely mapped the existing disciplines as lineages of historical patterns of study: anthropology from exotic land travel, sociology from the problems of European industrialization, psychology from the study of mental illness, political science from improving government, and economics from an ideal man built for commerce and math. Evaluation and organization, he feared, are often based on arbitrary boundary judgments based on these idiosyncratic histories rather than current research needs.

Disciplinary distinctions indeed come up when social scientists convene to judge one another, but most still defer to expertise in other disciplines and seek pluralism in perspectives.[14] And the disciplines have also had somewhat analogous internal divisions, especially fights between qualitative and historical methods and quantitative approaches. Each discipline recognizes some outside critiques as matching at least some scholars within their own tradition.

Political scientist Scott Page, who has been involved in many interdisciplinary debates, told me each social science leaves out some pieces of the puzzle on purpose. In the best circumstances, they recognize that others are there to examine issues they leave in a black box: "The world is high-dimensional, and you have to leave some things out. Psychologists and economists both have areas they say are not up for debate. . . . But now people are more aware [that what they leave out is the main interest of others]." Economists take preferences as a given, but we still need to know how they are developed. Disciplines mix arbitrary intellectual decisions with reasonable divisions of labor. They each came to prominence in part because they added something important to the discussion, not only covering new topics but honing go-to methods. Acknowledging their roles and their blind spots is useful—and they can better learn from each other if they reflect on their backgrounds.

The Basic Social Sciences

Each of the social sciences has its own internal conversation about how its self-image shapes its studies. In importing German graduate education models, they each brought a Wissenschaft, or ideas about a core set of systematic methods. None of them is still associated with a single unifying paradigm but they have commonly shared assumptions about what to study and how to study it. They differ in the importance they place on boundary setting, on shared theoretical and methodological allegiances, and on the role of their historical inheritance in their current work. I review each in turn based on its self-definition and self-reflective literature.

Psychology

Herman Ebbinghaus argued that "psychology has a long past, but only a short history." Its concerns are long-standing in human life, but it took time to become a self-conscious intellectual community. It has long been seen as a "fragile science" dealing with the many unknown intricacies of the human mind, but one that nonetheless needs to be put into immediate practice to improve mental health.[15] Psychology has a strong focus on empiricism and experiments; it is among the most comfortable with strong distinctions between facts and values and subjects and objects because the study of the mind has required clarity about divorcing the researcher from the researched.[16]

Psychology also has a heritage in philosophy departments. Its American national tradition was based in pragmatism, gradually expanding to new fields: social and behavioral, personality, cognition, and neuroscience. That differed from its traditions in Germany, based in physiology; the UK, emphasizing comparative work; France, drawing from psychiatry; and Austria, highlighting psychodynamics.[17] The United States led its further scientific, biological, and evolutionary transformations.

Because its subject is the individual, psychology has a strong tendency to be influenced by folk ideas about the mind. Memory, for example, is both a specific topic within psychology and a long-standing concern of lay individuals in common conversation—changing humanistic metaphors concerning memory have altered how psychology thinks about it.[18] The same is true of everyday concepts like emotions, meaning that lay notions influence the development of theories and psychology is easily popularized in self-help form. It continues to be influenced by popular psychology and psychotherapy, despite being practiced as a science in a very different form than the popular imagination. But psychological concepts still often represent folk categories, rather than discovered packages of human traits or behaviors.[19]

Since neuroscience is a rising field, psychology as a scientific discipline also has close ties to related natural sciences. Psychology departments contain wet labs and work on animal models. The discipline has also mostly inherited some initially interdisciplinary fields, such as cognitive science, providing ties to all of the cognate fields (including philosophy, computer science, and linguistics).[20] Psychology journals have higher average impact factors than those for the other social sciences, with psychology-adjacent journals in other fields also cited more often.

Although there is a disciplinary history of psychology, it is the least historicized in its regular studies compared to the other four core disciplines. There is little historical psychology about how human thought or behavior has changed over time; "universality is a default assumption" when it comes to whether studies apply across places and time.[21] Cross-cultural research is encouraged, but most studies do not consider subjects representative of their country or social group. Evolutionary psychology tests (often speculative) stories about natural selection on contemporary subjects, but it also tends to underplay the role of institutions and each time period; it assumes the most generalized human behavior, especially across time.[22] One analysis found that 89 percent of psychology results are described with generic statements about humans, even where samples are specific (readers judged those generic statements more important, suggesting a reason for overgeneralization).[23]

The structure of psychology is somewhat unique compared to the other social sciences. To see how each discipline is internally organized (and how opinions differ based on what scholars study), I asked US research university professors to define their major research subfield in an open-ended question (though some named more than one). Figure 6.1 illustrates psychologists' answers in a word cloud of the most frequently used words (removing the discipline name and connecting words); I also include our qualitative categorization of their answers.[24]

Psychologists have reasonably well-defined subfields. Cognitive, social, and developmental were the most common fields mentioned, with neuroscience and clinical also mentioned frequently. I also observed some differences in opinions of research trends across these fields. Social psychologists were unsurprisingly the most attentive to reproducibility difficulties, the most likely to see a replication crisis, and the most supportive of reforms. Clinical psychologists were the most convinced that the discipline was becoming more empirical, quantitative, and causal; they also tended to think that conflicts in the discipline were declining. Overall, psychology stands out for its universalist ambitions and its ties to natural science.

Sociology

Sociology is the broadest and most amorphous of the social sciences, stemming more from France than from Britain. Emile Durkheim consciously sought to establish it as an autonomous science, complete with a textbook on rules of method in 1895. His study of suicide argued that it must be explained by tendencies of the social group, rather than as a series of individual actions. Society also involved collective material and symbolic histories, he said, which were associated with collective impulses and social obligations.

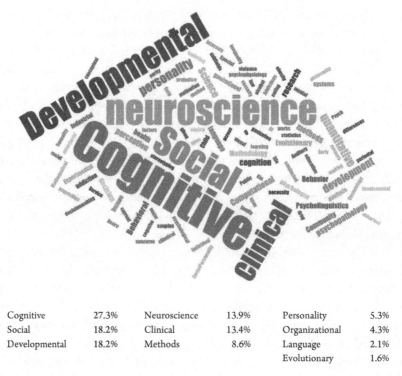

Cognitive	27.3%	Neuroscience	13.9%	Personality	5.3%
Social	18.2%	Clinical	13.4%	Organizational	4.3%
Developmental	18.2%	Methods	8.6%	Language	2.1%
				Evolutionary	1.6%

Figure 6.1 Psychology Fields. Data from the author's 2020 survey of social scientists at major US research universities. n=1,141.

Early US sociology courses were focused on social problems, social progress, social institutions, and race and nationality, marked by concern with the social order.[25] The Chicago school's reformulation of sociology sought to separate it from social work and reform. W. E. B. Du Bois tried to maintain both social reform and objectivity goals while cutting ties to social Darwinism (which excused current structures as preordained and natural).[26] These conflicts over method and scope gave rise to sociology's two top journals: the *American Journal of Sociology* at Chicago and the *American Sociological Review* (designed to be divorced from Chicago's dominance). Sociology temporarily developed canons based on symbolic interactionism and structural functionalism, but then diversified in traditions and topics.[27]

Sociology is the most aware among the social sciences of its theoretical history, with graduate students often still reading "great books" like Marx and Durkheim as a part of their training (a practice mostly absent in psychology, economics, and political science outside of political theory). But sociology still sees itself as having lost the public voice that it should have (primarily in an assumed conflict with economics, even though economics also had its own public influence from the beginning). Sociology is still surprisingly disconnected from anthropology, honoring a sort of détente where sociology focuses more on contemporary industrialized societies.

Sociologists have been less faddish than other disciplines about methods changes. As one sociologist said, "Sociology has taken stock of methodological debates, but it hasn't gone as far as political science in chasing tight causal inference at all costs. We remain a methodologically pluralist field, even if the trends here are contradictory—pressure for rapid and frequent publication using existing data vs. arguably greater respect for qualitative research than there was a decade ago." Another told me they can unite the best of both worlds: "We're a 'big tent' discipline informed by both humanistic and scientific traditions of inquiry. At our best, this is a huge strength—we can learn from each other to produce work that is both interpretively adequate and scientifically valid and reliable." Sociology's lack of clear boundaries also makes it open to applied work. Several journals with the top impact factors in the discipline are even in education and tourism.

Sociology may be the most openly politicized discipline, with activism more accepted and a strong interest in the pursuit of social change. One unifying theme is understanding and responding to inequalities and another is attentiveness to how people understand their multiple social identities; both are becoming increasingly aligned with the ideological left in contemporary politics. That means sociological engagement often entails social movement advocacy.

On my survey, sociologists were the most internally diverse in their self-definition. Figure 6.2 uses sociologists' subfield answers to picture their most frequently used words and then lists our categorization of their answers. Demography seems to be the only well-defined field moniker. But the largest fields study race, politics, and demographics, followed by specific policy issue areas, inequality, and organizations. Even combining fields into these composite categories did not create broad subfields to match the other disciplines; the closest we came to defining a large subfield was the category of social identity interests broadly conceived (including race, gender, and class). Sociologists do tend to embrace their focus on inequality and identity. But demography represents the only topically constrained subfield with a shared self-definition.

Sociologists' responses had the highest number of words used by few people (more than one but less than five), suggesting a balkanized discipline based on topical interests (or more optimistically, one open to many subjects). Sociology also has small subfields that serve as connectors to each of the other social science disciplines: political, economic, cultural, and social psychology (as well as other fields with ties to applied disciplines). Sociology is thus an open and diverse discipline but lacks a shared domain of practical application.

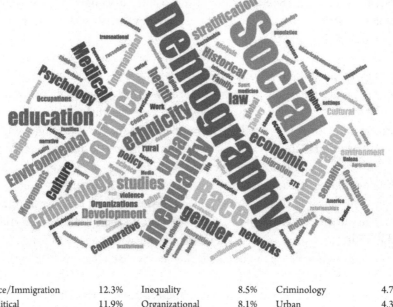

Race/Immigration	12.3%	Inequality	8.5%	Criminology	4.7%
Political	11.9%	Organizational	8.1%	Urban	4.3%
Demography	11.5%	Comparative	7.2%	Culture	3.4%
Education/Health/		Gender/Family	6.0%	Social Psychology	3.0%
Environment	9.8%	Economic	5.1%	Methods	3.0%

Figure 6.2 Sociology Fields. Data from the author's 2020 survey of social scientists at major US research universities. n=1,141.

Economics

Economics was a popular science of the 1800s, with Adam Smith having directed it toward more abstract and rigorous investigation. But it never lost its potential for inclusion in political debates and its reputation as the "dismal science," earned from the catastrophic demographic musings of Thomas Malthus and the impersonal political economy of David Ricardo. It quickly became a strong theoretical discipline, led by Alfred Marshall's *Principles of Economics* (1890) and eventually replaced by Paul Samuelson's canonical *Foundations of Economic Analysis* (1947). But its theoretical base was tied to a strong interest in statistics and data gathering.

Conceiving of an economy as separate from a society or polity was itself a political position of Marshall, who wanted to place economic decision-making at the center of social and political life, though to the modern eye he featured a lot of philosophy and policy discussion.[28] Both the political slant and theoretical interests shifted over time, especially with economist John Maynard Keynes and his influence on aggressive government policy. But a new generation of economists then sought to resurrect free-market views, from the monetary economics of Milton Friedman to the rational expectations models of Robert Lucas to the rational choice theories of social problems of Gary Becker.[29] Economics has also been willing to ignore many aspects of human life until they can be codified in mathematical models, seeing the advance of methods as a necessary trajectory independent of current explanatory power.[30] Paul Krugman argues that economics is the study of humans where their motivations are most simplistic.[31]

But economics has also been the most imperial of the social sciences, some-times forthrightly. Edward Lazear argued that economics was the only "genuine science" with pure theories and refutable implications and tests, which allowed it to invade other intellectual territory successfully, even winning over adherents in law and business schools.[32] But there seems to be little reflection of the ob-vious biases involved in broadening theories of the economy and economic be-havior to social or political acts. Even as economists have increasingly accepted revisions to their models of individual behavior from psychologists, there has been less attention to the many factors absent from most economic models that are commonly studied in sociology, political science, and anthropology. Economists also share a self-conception of having a way of thinking, rather than just a subject or method, often producing books and columns about thinking like an economist.

Economics is more hierarchical than the other social sciences in its journal ratings, its star system, and its governance (by faculty at the top institutions).[33] Economists have more in-group pride than other social sciences and prize tech-nical skill. But economics courses seem to make students more selfish and more likely to free-ride, conforming to the predictions of theories more than other students.[34] Economists' internal labor market also conforms to theory, with a strong hierarchy in hiring with a clear department pecking order.

Although economics has a stereotype of being divided between microeco-nomics and macroeconomics, that division does not necessarily match scholars' self-definitions today. Figure 6.3 maps economists' answers regarding their major subfield in a word cloud of the most frequently used words (removing the dis-cipline name) along with a subfield categorization. Labor and macroeconomics were the most used terms, but applied economics and microeconomics were the largest categories once answers were combined in categories. International and development economics was also a popular field.

Economics thus has strong subfields but may be diversifying through increas-ingly applied work. Applied economists were the most convinced that their dis-cipline is becoming more empirical and causal, perhaps because they are leading the charge. Microeconomists were unsurprisingly the most likely to remain taken with theory over empirics. Economics curiously has no fields naming the other social sciences (such as sociological economics), though it does have a historical

Applied	19.1%	Macro	15.4%	Methods	7.4%
Labor	16.7%	International	11.7%	History	5.6%
Micro	16.0%	Public	9.3%		

Figure 6.3 Economics Fields. Data from the author's 2020 survey of social scientists at major US research universities. n=1,141.

subfield and long-running interests in political economy. It usually recognizes the topics of other social sciences as its own, however, rather than seeing them as alternative lenses for analyses of economic behavior. Economics is changing but still stands out among the social sciences in its dedication to mathematics and its commitment to extending its own theoretical structure.

Political Science

Political science is a combination of many different traditions, some based in moral philosophy, others in constitutionalism and law, others in administration and governance, and yet others in comparative study.[35] Early reading lists borrowed from the Greeks and Romans. Political science is the only social science discipline to retain philosophers (though they now view themselves as political theorists). But it also worked, from the beginning, in the service of the state with an applied aim, reflecting the current issue agenda in each time period. It was shaped by racialized views of state development, with early negative verdicts on immigration and reconstruction.[36]

Political science is the only social science to call itself a science in the name, but that was not born of an effort to purify it from current concerns or even of insecurity that its studies would be considered partisan. It instead instilled in the name an argument that government could be perfected through knowledge, with an etymology stretching back to proto-sociologists and proto-economists for centuries. Few contemporary political scientists would sign on to these aspirations, but the turn to scientism (in the sense of prizing objective empiricism) was historically much later.

The cliché is that political science shares only its dependent variables: government or politics. It does not tend to have a paradigmatic theory or method, consciously borrowing from most of the other social sciences. It also lacks a debated philosophy of science or canonical history, probably because its foundations are left to political theorists more interested in the bases of politics than of political science.[37]

The closest to a shared enterprise it achieved was behavioralism in the mid-twentieth century, a loose set of ideas around searching for and verifying quantitative regularities across societies and governments. The discipline is now, political scientist Michael Haas argues, "a jigsaw puzzle nobody wants to solve."[38] The majority of the discipline has long been empirical, though formal theory rose in the 1970s and 1980s. The main decline in the aims of political science articles has been in policy recommendations, which tended to conclude political science papers in the early twentieth century. The discipline has also seen a traditionalist backlash; though its trajectory is empirical, it retains historians and commenters on public law.

Political science is the only social science discipline that maintains an "American" major subfield (like history), even though "comparative" also includes the United States and now studies domestic politics everywhere. The subfield can be seen as a historical relic of its role in championing American government or a product of contemporary undergraduate teaching needs, but it can also be seen as a recognition that studying one's own political system is epistemologically distinct from studying others from a bird's-eye view. As a result, non-Americanists are more likely to have to study more than one country's politics and view each country as a case on international spectrums.

Political science still has strong subfield boundaries based on the countries that scholars study. Figure 6.4 illustrates political scientists' self-definitions of their major research subfield, both in a word cloud of open-ended responses and my categorization. The vast majority of political scientists identify as being either in American, comparative, or international relations. Theory (or political philosophy) is usually considered the fourth major subfield, but it is small and losing ground at major research universities. Some political scientists also identify based on their connections to economics, policy, or psychology. Adam

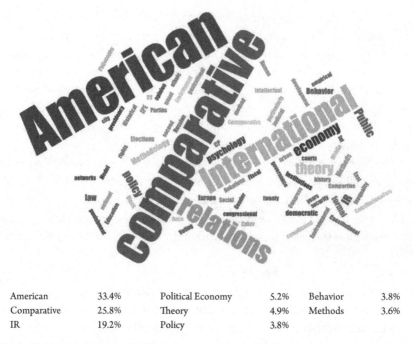

American	33.4%	Political Economy	5.2%	Behavior	3.8%
Comparative	25.8%	Theory	4.9%	Methods	3.6%
IR	19.2%	Policy	3.8%		

Figure 6.4 Political Science Fields. Data from the author's 2020 survey of social scientists at major US research universities. n=1,141.

Berinsky, an Americanist who does work in international relations and with comparativists, told me, "At a structural level, the subfields have not changed. But at an intellectual level, they have become more integrated [around similar questions]." Political scientists did not differ much by subfield in their opinions on the direction of the discipline or its methods, though there were some differences based on generation. They stand out among social scientists in their narrow topical focus.

Anthropology

Anthropology is the most consciously historical of the social sciences and its studies cover a much longer time period of humanity. It is also very aware of its own history—especially the conflict between studying other societies and comparing them to the scholar's expectations based on their own society. Although there are few pure relativists today, nearly all scholars are aware that our attempts to learn human history by studying (supposedly more "primitive") societies is a fraught enterprise that reflects contemporary and national values.[39]

Anthropology may be the most tied to its roots in Europe. It refers back to its own history in European conquest and travel and it maintains traditions tied to the UK, France, and Germany, despite American anthropology's being large from the beginning.[40] The American tradition is most closely tied to Franz Boas and socio-cultural work on complexity and diversity, based on empirical field-work and historical particularism.

Anthropology is also the most internally divided of the social sciences, with especially strong subfield differences between biological and cultural anthro-pology. It retains paleontologists and primatologists who see themselves as nat-ural scientists. Developments in human evolution from genetics research are especially controversial, but many anthropologists are central figures in debates over biological and cultural evolution.[41] Despite the conflicts, each subfield is advancing and now more aware of where it lacks the capacity to review other subfields' work and where disagreements are semantic rather than founda-tional.[42] Anthropology is also the only social science with a museum-oriented side, collecting materials and storytelling for public display.

Anthropology still contains divides over nearly all scientific attitudes (not just by subfield but also by gender and political ideology).[43] The shared sus-picion of Western representations of faraway lands is a large part of the field's development. Though there is broad agreement that science has a positive in-fluence on life and policy, one-third of anthropologists endorse some relativism about science relative to other sources of explanation, and one-fifth say science is no more valid than other ways of knowing.[44] Anthropology could be seen as a counterexample to my claim that reflexivity about social research is useful, though its conflicts seem to stem more from lack of integration than the act of self-criticism.[45]

One anthropologist was optimistic about the future of integration, citing a "recognition within the discipline of a body of knowledge that crosses over the subfields of anthropology—both qualitative/cultural data and scientific data on [the] human past and physical [remains]. So, there is wide acceptance of cross-disciplinary work." But the discipline combined subfields in part based on the misnomer that studying less developed societies today helped understand human history, a justification it now largely disowns despite therefore giving the discipline less coherence.

But anthropologists are of two minds. They endorse the view that the disci-pline reflects the power and interests of researchers and society, but they also fear that anti-science views are undermining the field.[46] There are especially strong divides on theories of culture and sex differences, but there is a shared fear that anthropology has long been used to advance racist views. That puts anthropologists in a good position to be reflective about their discipline's assumptions and historical role. But it also leaves anthropology less able to con-nect as a discipline with the other social sciences in methods or analysis.

As we have seen, anthropology is the most starkly divided social science by its subfields. Figure 6.5 illustrates how anthropologists at major US research universities see their research fields. Although archeology was the most used word (beyond the discipline's name, which is excluded), that is because each of the two traditional other fields go by multiple names: biological or physical anthropology and social, cultural, or socio-cultural anthropology. Linguistic anthropology is also considered a major field but is smaller (and sometimes practiced in linguistics departments).

The social/cultural subfield stands out in my survey as not perceiving a move toward empirical, quantitative, or causal inference research. Many participants said they still conduct mainly qualitative research. The archeology subfield stands out as seeing more conflicts about the generalization of research and the correct methodologies, perhaps because it partially serves to integrate the biological and cultural poles of the discipline. Anthropology is unique in its combination of strong subfields with distinct views of science.

These composite sketches are hardly meant as full analyses of large and diverse scientific disciplines. But they do suggest that many different approaches, topical interests, and categorical combinations are available within the core social sciences. Each could draw more from the formulas on offer in the others and learn from their internal divisions. Social knowledge would be weaker

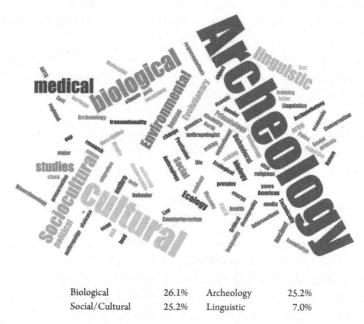

| Biological | 26.1% | Archeology | 25.2% |
| Social/Cultural | 25.2% | Linguistic | 7.0% |

Figure 6.5 Anthropology Fields. Data from the author's 2020 survey of social scientists at major US research universities. n=1,141.

without any of their contributions, and none should be written off as unscientific. In conducting social science on questions that inevitably relate to those considered in other disciplines, researchers should be mindful of when their answers are limited by their disciplinary norms. But as with other long-standing concerns, the trends are positive: toward interdisciplinary cooperation and learning.

Interdisciplinarity

Claims that disciplines create artificial boundaries for addressing multifaceted problems and questions are often associated with calls for interdisciplinary research programs. Interdisciplinary research is increasing over time, alongside multi-author research generally. Interdisciplinary work is also higher and rising faster in the social sciences than in most natural sciences or humanities disciplines.[47] The rise in interdisciplinary articles and citations is associated with the increasing number of coauthors per paper since 1975, though most coauthorships are still between closely neighboring disciplines.[48]

Although there are now connections between researchers studying similar topics in different disciplines, there is still more parallel work than collaboration, with continued discipline-specific jargon.[49] Funding pressure and physical proximity can incentivize interdisciplinary research, but forming new applied subfields with associated journals and conferences is often necessary to build permanent ties—and even then, many interdisciplinary efforts are not sustained.[50] Government and foundation funders have increased their requests for creativity in combining fields. Universities have dutifully increased their cluster hiring programs, often with direct ties to funding initiatives—but these hires across departments have proven difficult to manage and maintain.[51]

Research consortiums and interdisciplinary centers are often products of government demand, even if they incentivize private sector collaboration. The earliest research contributors who build centers become spokespeople for expanding their initiatives.[52] Across 25 leading research universities, there are now more than 100 research centers per school designed around interdisciplinary research endeavors.[53] A large part of that expansion in the social sciences was the dedication of area studies centers that would combine social science and humanities knowledge of particular world regions or countries. That still leads political scientists and other international area specialists to be more tethered to history and language disciplines than other social sciences.

But the results of forced interdisciplinarity often do not live up to the hype. A review of 900 center-based scientists found that interdisciplinary centers result in lower productivity with increasing cognitive and administrative challenges, though occasional success stories suggest they may be high-risk, high-reward ventures.[54] Follow-up reports on interdisciplinary cluster hires are even more negative: they often die or are barely operating five or ten years after their founding, and their participants take longer to publish and are less likely to receive tenure.[55] Cluster hiring is mostly driven by development- and grant-chasing considerations as well as applied problem solving (though diversity and inclusion initiatives are an exception to the financial aims).[56] Despite the signs of failure, nearly all universities claim to favor interdisciplinary research, with a lot of administrative discussions about removing silos and breaking down boundaries.

The trouble is that sustainable interdisciplinary initiatives tend to require building new fields, rather than simply incentivizing connections across them. The most obvious potential collaborative areas across social science, however, are decades old and present in applied schools covering education, public health, public policy, and business. That does not mean no new fields are possible, just that they are usually well trodden. Data science is gaining widespread recent attention for its potential to combine computer science, math, and engineering with social and natural sciences. It has proven successful, at least at generating grants, publications, and paying students.[57]

Interdisciplinarity for its own sake, however, is probably not a useful goal. In fact, many interdisciplinary efforts fail because they do not account for the strong gains that our imperfect existing disciplines bring in policing shared standards and codifying argumentation. The largest basic and applied social sciences can and do learn from one another without always pursuing cross-field authorship or building new interdisciplinary fields. Although often treated as a difficult abstract discussion about knowledge accumulation, the lessons of research on interdisciplinarity are relatively clear: scholars should read and build ties outside of their disciplines (and be aware of outside views), but not try to re-create already institutionalized fields.

Calls for interdisciplinarity are often part of competitions over resources and efforts to move peripheral concerns in one discipline to the forefront of a newly defined terrain, but they invite practical challenges in understanding the ethos of each discipline they combine.[58] Some initiatives fail to create new areas and evolve into subsets of existing disciplines. Cognitive science, initially an ambitious effort to combine philosophy, computer science, psychology, and neuroscience, has mostly become a subset of psychology—while neuroscience has become a much larger and well-funded independent field.

When scholars do engage with other disciplines, there are often benefits even if the integration is impossible or short-lived. Researchers who have contact with another discipline develop more favorable attitudes toward it, for example.[59] But multidisciplinary panels still defer to disciplinary expertise, often favoring pragmatic logrolling alliances and a vague support for pluralism over integration.[60] Proposals to unify the social sciences under the umbrella of one of them do not usually work, leading to fragmentation within the disciplines (such as new psychological sections within other social sciences).[61] Behavioral economics has had a fantastic rise, but it consists mostly of economists taking in psychological assumptions rather than a merger of the disciplines of psychology and economics.

As social science center director Gary King told me, administrators like interdisciplinarity as an idea even when there is little reason to expect the underlying disciplines to work well together. Their inclination is correct: the disciplines are only legacies and today's categories would be different. But that does not mean it is easy to build new research areas or the communities that make them thrive. Social scientists can recognize disciplinary particularities without proposing dissolution.

Reconciling Views of Human Nature

Many interdisciplinary social science conflicts are tied to disagreements over human nature, with each discipline emphasizing different parts: economics the maximizing strategic actor, psychology the emotional and thinking person, sociology the context-dependent creature of habit, political science the follower of leaders or causes, and anthropology the emblem of cultural practice. Social scientists, meanwhile, are in conversation with biologists (or biologically inclined fellow social scientists), who perceive human nature as more closely associated with our cognate species and more a product of our underlying genetics and physiology.

The longer debate over evolutionary explanations for human behavior and the relative roles (and interactions between) cultural, social, and biological development still provokes fierce responses. But the wider sociobiology debates (discussed in Chapter 10) have also wound down, as almost no one entirely discounts the role of genetics or social influence in human behavior. A prominent psychologist told me that the discipline no longer understands "what the fuss is all about; the wars of the 1970s ended; the biological basis of human nature is now mainstream." A behavioral economist told me they are now more open to biology studies involving genetic data, as they have learned what they can show and their limits.

Disciplinary particularities are easier to see in these interdisciplinary debates. Studies of "nature versus nurture" debates on aggressive and sexual behavior show that many researcher choices—from causal explanations and tests to

measurements to concern with representativeness—are the product of disciplinary norms about where in time and space explanations should focus, such as
whether studies are trying to explain the existence of behaviors or how to affect
their current prevalence.[62] Studies of terrorism unsurprisingly emphasize mental
states in psychology, resources and incentives in economics, social pressures in
sociology, government structure and response in political science, and culture
in anthropology.[63] More complete explanations come from integrating these
viewpoints. But even psychology retains considerable disagreement about
human nature, despite shared opposition to rational choice theory and new
sensitivities to social context.[64]

The social sciences differ in the extent to which they incorporate research
from the other core social science disciplines. In citation patterns, political science and sociology are the largest importers (more than 25 percent and 20 percent of citations, respectively), primarily from economics (though sociology
also imports from psychology and political science while political science also
imports from sociology and psychology).[65] Psychology imports the least, with
sociology and economics (the top imported fields) both constituting only 1 percent of psychology citations. Economics is starting to import more often, primarily from political science, though citations to the core social sciences still
constitute only approximately 6 percent of its citations. Anthropology imports
modestly from sociology and psychology but is not a major source of citations in
any core social science. External citations are increasing over time in economics,
psychology, and sociology (while holding steady in the others), but no social
science draws a lot from each of the others.

Social sciences also share vocabulary with adjacent disciplines in the hierarchy of the sciences (often drawing from each other), but disciplines seek credibility by repurposing words from natural science, mathematics, and computer
science.[66] Sociology shares most words with psychology, but psychology shares
most words with biology. Economics and political science share most words
with mathematics, but few have the same meaning across disciplines. Social sciences could still learn more from one another, but they are neither silos nor cut
off from other sciences.

Integration in Applied Fields

Interdisciplinarity has gained the most ground in applied fields, where the
assumptions and common methods of different fields can be brought to bear on
the same substantive questions and outcomes. The term "interdisciplinary" and
concepts associated with it are increasingly used in the titles of articles, especially in fields like education and medicine.[67] The National Science Foundation's

Integrative Graduate Education and Research Traineeship (IGERT) program explicitly asked universities to produce interdisciplinary collaborations to train students to solve specific problems. But universities have also built interdisciplinary programs on their own, especially with the rise of applied departments.[68] This has helped core social sciences become PhD exporters to applied fields, though less often once these fields develop their own larger doctoral programs (see Chapter 5).

Within the social sciences, these fields often produce complicated models of human behavior, including non-linear relationships, multilevel models, and far-from-equilibrium dynamics.[69] Cognitive science reveals the practical and intellectual challenges of combining disciplines, but also demonstrates that fields can rise and fall with new technologies (from computer models to replacement by neuroscience via the advance of brain imaging).[70]

Interdisciplinarity's concentration in applied fields also means that it often answers to a broader public and economic community of supporters, which tends to incentivize what science historian Theodore Porter calls "extremes of standardization and objectivity, a preoccupation with explicit, public forms of knowledge."[71] Whereas interdisciplinarity is promoted as a way of diversifying theories and methods, its use in applied fields often means the metrics must be standardized for use in government or the private sector.

Education, public policy, and business schools all combine economists with sociologists and psychologists but have moved toward economic models and metrics when performing for the public or government, often formalized in the use of cost-benefit analysis. Communication, another advanced field that still hires PhDs from core social sciences as well as its own programs, has borrowed less from economics and more from sociology but still moved toward quantitative metrics of public and commercial interest.

The use of core social science concepts and methods in applied fields also has important limits. Psychology theories often move from limited experimental support to discussion in popular psychology venues to institutionalization in applied disciplines like education, criminology, or policy.[72] But later critiques of the initial findings within psychology are not reflected in public knowledge or the applied work. Applied fields may run with the implementable applications, even as the basic science evidence deteriorates. Examples include strong theories of left- and right-hemisphere brain functions, the plasticity of brain development, the expansion of attention-deficit / hyperactivity disorder, and the role of delayed gratification and grit in human development.[73] In all these cases, an initial idea was codified in both school-based applications and popular knowledge even as social scientists poked holes in the causal inferences and generalizations of the initial studies.

Exchange among Strong Disciplines

There is a long history of filling gaps left by disciplines with new interdisciplinary ventures, which then become the new sites of knowledge production. Foucault argued that studies of political economy, language, and biology emerged as new fields because they were not covered by the traditional focus on wealth, grammar, and natural history. Out of the Enlightenment, we then gained concepts like "the economy" that enabled the formal social sciences to develop. But these were initially applied disciplines as well.[74] For Adam Smith, political economy was the "science of the statesman or legislator." The existing social sciences, despite being our inherited structures, are themselves efforts to fill holes in understanding social life, responding to social change, and mixing applied and pure science objectives.

Our current organization of knowledge was not inevitable. The discipline of geography, for example, was a popular science of the nineteenth century with public support. Its development in Britain and America was closely tied to publicity surrounding international expeditions and potential commercial exploitation.[75] It retains a foothold at several universities and spans the social and natural sciences, but it has not kept up with other social sciences in students or faculty. That may be partially due to idiosyncratic history. When Harvard eliminated its geography department in 1948, due in part to conflicts over science and in part to personality conflicts, it prompted other universities to do the same and reduce its stature.[76]

Fields of research have long been battles for intellectual attention, with disciplines competing against more amorphous groups; boundary changes are driven by movements that produce new agreed-upon knowledge circulated in communities of shared interest.[77] Success in field building or transforming comes less from the coherence of new ontological or epistemological principles than from practical action to generate public and institutional support.[78]

During these intellectual conflicts, the traditional disciplines are far more dynamic than typically conceived. The metaphor of "silos" never fit data on citation patterns across disciplines, which showed far more interdependence and shifts that start in one discipline and move to others. But the key to interdisciplinary movement is that a set of ideas gains credence within its home discipline before spreading to others.[79] The web of both specialized communities and interconnections in scholarship has grown with journal proliferation and applied work, but there is little evidence of disciplines walling off their ideas or failing to notice revolutions elsewhere. Instead, disciplines birth and develop ideas that then flow to other cognate fields.

A recent review found evidence of productive interdisciplinary exchange leading to accumulation of findings in areas such as loss aversion and social preferences in behavioral economics and disease spread and informational in-fluence in social network analysis.[80] The most effective integrations added new types of data and integrated theories from multiple disciplines.

Disciplines still have standard approaches that can make translation difficult. Adam Berinsky told me that, even for the same data from multiple experiments, psychologists tend to use multilevel models, economists collapse them and cluster by participant, and political scientists analyze each experiment separately. But it often makes little difference, and it is helpful to show that results do not depend on these style choices. By collaborating, he has been able to learn each. Interdisciplinary team science leads to innovation not because it invents new knowledge but because it combines conventional tools from widely differing contexts.[81]

Disciplinary infrastructure, including associations, journals, departments, and conferences, instantiates the informal communities of people and shared ideas. It is not easily dislodged. But looking over decades, there is considerable change and responses to anomalies in findings or category breakdowns.[82] When enough people seek a break from established ideas, they either form a new com-munity or redesign an existing one.

There is accompanying change within disciplines. Anthropology's disagreements have led to strong subfield divisions, with physical anthropology (now usually called biological anthropology) most separated from cultural studies. Archeology lives on intact; linguistics has evolved as both a subfield and a new discipline (in some places); and an applied field like forensics can advance as well. Sociology, the most amorphous of the social sciences, has developed a cohesive and growing core since the 1960s (as judged by its coauthorship net-work), with overlapping specialties and a large rise in coauthorship and data.[83] There is now more consensus on methods and approaches within the core, with remaining differences by topical focus that can be linked via coauthorship. Yet there is still room for innovation. Sociology articles that integrate rarely connected subfields get more citations; the growth in association sections also provides new opportunities to link disparate fields.[84]

Each of the five core social science disciplines is advancing human knowledge and each has particularities that limit their perspective. Each could better recog-nize and adjust where their norms make them outliers. Economics, for example, can be less imperial and more integrative of diverse assumptions. Psychology can be more aware of the temporal, social, and national context of its findings. Interdisciplinary research can help disciplines learn from each other, but each discipline should be treated as a valuable forum for cumulating questions, tools, and findings.

Each can also help analyze and respond to biases in social research. Psychology is best positioned to understand cognitive biases but poorly trained to understand cross-national and time-series variation. Sociology is traditionally superior in analyzing social group differences and understanding knowledge generation processes, but worst in recognizing how its political motivations drive research and how theories drive case selection. Economics has developed the best methods of causal inference and generalization but has the largest unrecognized disciplinary biases and overconfidence. Anthropology is the best equipped to analyze cultural variation and very long human time horizons; it seems the least prepared to build consensus across subfields and cumulate knowledge. Political science is the best at cross-national variation and at integrating institutional history and mass behavior in its explanations, but it is among the worst at disciplinary self-reflection and incorporating scholars' own positionality.

American social science remains dependent on its traditional disciplinary lenses, but it is not so constrained that ideas cannot travel, cumulate, or layer. The willingness of economists Tyler Cowen and Emily Oster to challenge epidemiological models in the face of COVID-19 can be a useful impulse if it stimulates new theory and empirical findings. Cowen has highlighted models from across the disciplinary spectrum, helped organize funding of new ventures, and tried to engage scholars in a new interdisciplinary project on "progress studies" to understand long-term economic and public health improvements.[85] Although he has an economist's tendencies and attitude, he draws from many disciplines and wants to integrate knowledge. Meanwhile, Oster has teamed up with epidemiologists and collected original data that matter for prioritizing public policy responses. If scholars can communicate across their divides and recognize limitations, disciplinary borders sometimes deserve to be broken down.

But the urge to rebuild entirely is misplaced. Scholars gain from the disciplinary communities that have developed over time, as long as they recognize that their go-to ideas reflect some arbitrary histories and boundaries along with the wisdom of codified knowledge. Social science is advancing through both disciplinary and interdisciplinary knowledge, as many scholars connect within their traditional homes and some set out for distant shores.

Multiple Levels of Analysis and Time Scales

The shocking 2016 US presidential election almost immediately stimulated a large academic literature, oriented around the motivations of Donald Trump voters. The early scholarly debate played out in public. Political scientist Diana Mutz, for example, received widespread academic and media attention for her study, "Status Threat, Not Economic Hardship, Explains the 2016 Presidential Vote," even though it confirmed the developing scholarly consensus.[1] Sociologist Steven Morgan did not accept the conclusion. He quickly distributed a rejoinder, arguing that Mutz's data were insufficient to draw her conclusions, that other interpretations of the evidence were possible, and that economic interests might still play an important role in Trump support.[2] The authors exchanged testy journal responses and stimulated other academics to join the fray.[3]

In some ways, the debate bore the hallmarks of other heated public academic firestorms. It was first conducted on social media and via shareable headlines, with Mutz's article treated as definitive evidence that Trump voters were scared of racial minorities and Morgan's response initially titled "Fake News." Due to the authors' differences, the debate was sometimes treated as emblematic of disputes between disciplines or even genders. Both authors combined accusations of statistical errors with broader critiques of the other author's tangentially related work.

And yet scholars learned several important lessons from the exchange. It became clear that there simply were not enough cases of party-switching voters in Mutz's panel data to draw definitive conclusions. But other panel data later confirmed that prior immigration views and attitudes toward Muslims were important in driving Trump vote switching.[4] The most important coding decisions in the dispute turned out to be substantively critical interpretations—especially whether immigration, trade, terrorism, and China policy positions were best seen as examples of status threats or real economic interests—rather than analysis details. That helped subsequent scholars tone down grand theories of "status threat," replacing them with more specific theories based on particular issues and candidate appeals. Further studies also sought to explore how actual local economic conditions could still matter, but because they influenced racial and social attitudes rather than economic views.[5] Other differences between 2012 and 2016, like a reduced partisan division over resentment of the rich and sympathy for the poor, suggested that Trump may have neutralized a normal Democratic advantage by reducing the importance of economic attitudes.[6] The timeline has also been revised: some attitudes mattered for Trump support in the primary (such as Social Security views) but were swamped by partisanship in the general election; some, like racial resentment, mattered more in 2016 but as part of a long-term increase in partisan division rather than as a Trump-specific pattern; other attitudes, like liberal views on immigration, started changing most after the election.[7]

Our understanding of the election dynamics and of the motivations of supporters of Trump and Clinton has grown considerably since 2016. Scholars have not only compared the election to historical and international examples and described the chronologies in detail, but also probed the longer-term trends leading to the election and identified several minor but pivotal election-specific factors. The 2020 election, where few voters changed sides but the vote switchers constituted enough to alter the outcome, provided more data on Trump voters and their distinguishing attributes. Then the violent aftermath again raised concerns about Trump's strongest supporters; even if most Trump voters were typical Republicans, a minority apparently viewed themselves as soldiers in his army.

These debates raise the critical issue of what question we are trying to answer: are we interested in the narrow question of the characteristics of the minority of Americans who changed their votes from one partisan side to the other over four years, the broader question of how leaders like Trump can be elected anywhere, or a question that narrows the geographic and temporal perspective but is less focused on individual voter decisions and more on the wider political culture? The example raises long-standing social science debates over human agency and social structure. Potential explanations for human behavior can include factors at multiple levels of analysis—from individuals to groups to nations—as well as across different time scales: the proximate events, the historical trajectory, or even the evolutionary context.

This chapter argues that philosophy of social science has reached a consensus against strict individualism: influences on social outcomes stem from individual and collective units, each with influential histories. Models of individual interaction can guide theory, but they do not imply that social processes ever start at a particular time or that all social structures derive from individual action. Instead, people are influenced by the groups and institutions that came before them and we are never able to fully divorce structure and agency.

Many of the ostensibly methodological debates about the 2016 election revolve around questions of responsibility that imply different timelines and scales. Scholars want to know why Trump won when Mitt Romney did not, but also why he was ever in a position to win; how individual behavior was influenced by group identities like partisanship, race, and gender; and how his victory fits into broader global patterns of populism. Unfortunately, even narrowly specifying the question does not absolve scholars of considering the higher-level or longer-horizon processes that brought it about. Although an endemic problem of social science, understanding that we are looking at the same problem from different vantages helps scholars jointly expand their knowledge.

Trump Studies

Trump's election might have been unexpected, but the large scholarly literature that developed around it was foreseeable. As political scientist Amanda Friesen told me, the 2016 outcome was treated with "shock and awe;" many scholars focused more on race and gender as well as rural and conservative views. As a scholar of religion from a Red state, she saw Trump's victory as a plausible outcome but found many others surprised enough to shift views.

Scholar diversity—of lack thereof—is an important consideration in the reaction, but it is nearly impossible to approach the 2016 election with full objectivity. We could not exclude researchers with clear views on Trump or Clinton (essentially every scholar). We would not want to essentialize scholarly perspectives based on social group memberships. And those are hardly the only biasing motivations at work: scholars want to publish clear findings and offer definitive explanations, they want to connect the latest events to their prior theories, they have deeply held views about their countries and human nature, and they want to offer useful knowledge for improving democracy.

Political science has also learned from explanations for Trump's rise from other disciplines: psychology offered useful interventions based on personality, identity, anxiety, and social dominance; communication pointed to rhetorical and media innovations; history gave plenty of comparative examples; and economics contributed useful measures of trade competition. But none of that substitutes for our knowledge of voting structures, political motivations, and American campaign dynamics. It is likewise useful to know that basic biological processes or aspects of human nature are relevant to contemporary political behavior, but that is not the same as analyzing a specific campaign trajectory or electoral outcome. The reasons people are attracted to demagogues or to conformity to in-groups are important considerations, but they do not demonstrate what mattered more in a particular election.

Part of the commotion was the surprise. Polling misses in presidential elections have long produced recriminations among journalists and pollsters, always intertwined with public interest in and skepticism about social research.[8] From 1936 onward, each election miss produced methodological reinvention, worries about data influencing voters, and excuses galore. Scholars typically react by trying to separate their research from public polling, but critiques of polling misses often apply to core social science difficulties of measurement, inference, and generalization. If election polls are several points off, our estimates of unemployment and trust in government may be as well. If we fail to notice social trends culminating in elections, what else might we be missing? Election prediction tools, after all, have long been hyped as proof that people can be studied scientifically. Computer models of elections in the 1960s, for example, were touted as the "A-bomb of the social sciences," with failure indicting prominent social scientists of the era.[9]

How and why Trump was elected in 2016 is among the clearest example of a parochial concern driving contemporary scholarship. But we still want to know the answer. That includes not only the specific proximate factors that led to the associated voting behavior but also the ties between common political aspirations and human tendencies and our current predicament. We should never forget that we are asking such questions within a particular social context and as particular researchers, not from a God's-eye view with perfect objective research practices. But that knowledge is a strength of scientific methods and communities, not a reason to abandon either.

It should also be clear that we have chosen a difficult question and characterized it in a way that makes it less amenable to research. Common research design advice reasonably suggests that scholars limit research questions to more answerable puzzles. This has often led to recommending designs that look at the effects of a cause, rather than the (usually multiple) causes of an effect, which makes causal inference easier. Gary King, Robert Keohane, and Sidney Verba recommend choosing questions and theories that apply to many different cases, rather than a single instance, as this makes both causal inference and generalization more plausible.[10] Nevertheless, both researchers and our multiple outside audiences (e.g., students, other disciplines, practitioners, and citizens) are often drawn to difficult-to-answer questions and sometimes appreciate incomplete and uncertain partial answers to those questions over full and reliable answers to others.

There are many identified factors and explanatory lenses useful for understanding the 2016 election, many of which invoke long-standing human nature or recent global change. But it is natural to start from the most proximate features. The United States has a closely divided two-party system, and anyone nominated by one of the major parties has a good chance to win the general election. Donald Trump slightly underperformed models based on fundamental factors such as presidential approval and economic performance. His victory in the Electoral College was made possible by outperformance in the Upper Midwest. He won mostly with traditional Republican voters, but voter switching was concentrated in increasing support from less-educated, conservative-leaning white voters. Although economically distressed geographic areas were associated with increased support, there is little evidence that individual economic standing or perceptions influenced vote choice. Instead, cultural attitudes related to race and gender, issue attitudes related to immigration, and general populist attitudes toward government and elites seemed to matter most.

But there are also reasonable efforts to compare and connect Trump's election with the rise of right-wing populism in other parts of the world as well as the long history of conservatism's ties to reactionary movements.[11] Social scientists were reasonably frightened by Trump's treatment of the media and some minority groups, with rhetoric and behavior sometimes analogous to the world's despots. With time, some of the most outlandish prognostications associated with Trump's rise have given way to more tempered criticisms of trends in progress and warnings of their potential continuation. But events after the 2020 election suggest scholarly warnings were far from misplaced.

The real world has also produced new data. Since Trump's election, American voters have moved leftward on a variety of policy issues (especially starkly on issues related to race, immigration, and trade), signaling not only that our old theories of thermostatic responsiveness (the tendency for public opinion to go against the direction of policy and the president) are intact, but that idiosyncratic factors related to Trump's rise may not continue.[12] Policymaking under Trump, which initially seemed full of aberrations, has also been thoroughly analyzed, with scholars able to pinpoint where those departures from norms were most pronounced, where they were a continuation of trends visible in prior congresses or administrations, and where they mirrored long-running continuities.

Acknowledgment of scholars' many biases is an important part of this process. Conservatives are right to critique some scholarly practices as reflecting liberal bias. The most obvious are the names of survey scales such as "racial resentment," "hostile sexism," and "authoritarianism," all of which could imply that any move from the most liberal endpoint is morally suspect.[13] The scales each include attitudes beyond prejudice, and we may have underestimated the importance of related attitudes toward political correctness, the salience of minority group concerns, and social traditionalism. All of these views are important to understanding contemporary political change and Trump's victory—and there is no doubt that differences in prejudice also divided voters. We are rectifying our inadequate prior attention to racial and gender dynamics of American campaigns.

Similarly, we should be concerned that the concentration of scholars in the United States in the current historical moment is affecting our views of Trump. We can welcome comparative analysis and longer-term historical investigations. The recent influence of media coverage on our early research, with its emphasis on simple stories from definitive takes, is also worthy of critique. Research that conforms to news values, such as declaring a fundamental realignment or seeing an election as an inevitable reflection of a dark human nature, may discount historical continuities and idiosyncratic factors. We can both broaden the lens to see the fundamental issues at stake in Trump's election and also observe that many contributors to his victory reflected common political patterns or quirks of American institutions rather than emblematic cultural touchstones.

These difficulties are hardly unique to studies of Trump's election. Many similar critiques of biased social science reasoning and practice are being addressed at its methodological frontier, in the daily interrogations of empirical researchers, and in the communities that police and integrate research findings. Even in our aspirations for global and timeless knowledge about human affairs, we are part of a collective human effort to understand our own time and place.

Knowledge is still accumulating, even where we should expect researcher biases to be strong and critiques unheeded in the pursuit of headlines. We are learning through the traditional tools of social science, subject to the same constraints as usual. But excluding evidence from any time scale or level of analysis, or believing we must finish each analysis alone, is not a recipe for progress.

Individual Agency and Social Structure

As philosopher of science Brian Epstein notes, "From the beginning, the social sciences have been bitterly divided about the right 'level' for social explanations."[14] Some researchers have always been skeptical of broad societal forces, while others have conceived of individual behavior as inseparable from them. A reductionist assumption suggested that building from the bottom up was most fruitful: explain societies as collections of individuals, with individual behavior a product of lower-level biological processes. But successive moves downward have not proven useful for scientific progress, only occasionally as a guide to theory building.[15]

These debates have been somewhat different across social science disciplines. In psychology, it is focused on the relationship between (internal) mental and external states; in sociology and anthropology, it is a conflict over how much to focus on social norms or culture; across disciplines, subfield divisions are often premised on boundaries between levels of analysis.[16] In economics, the desire to specify individual-level processes manifests in micro theories of macro behavior; in political science, is it often the request for behavioral microfoundations. Analytical sociology seeks to specify micro-macro links as the individual-level mechanisms for macro outcomes.[17]

Part of Du Bois's intervention in sociology was to measure individual and structural factors and their interactions, believing that specifying group-level social outcomes limited opportunities for change but that ignoring systemic features often led to blaming the victim. He wanted to both preserve human agency and acknowledge structural inequality.[18]

More recently, scholars of emergence and network structure have attempted to combine levels of analysis. Sociologist Duncan Watts argues that most scholars now recognize a need to "consider more than one scale at a time." "In practice," he says, "methodological individualists have lost the battle, and not just in economics."[19] Watts is part of an effort to use simulations as well as illustrative networks to understand cascades of behavior, but he still recognizes that real societies have histories and interacting forces that cannot be easily modeled, meaning that models always select a few salient higher-level factors to explain without exhausting the real-world interactions between social forces and individual action.

Whenever social scientists move from models of individual interaction and collective behavior to specific societies, they encounter the influence of their historical trajectories and local differences. The alternative impulse to universal models is comparative history, with close attention to the details of places and time periods (and usually the accompanying assumption that all or most of them matter).[20] Analogous to modelers' requests for microfoundations, historically minded scholars seek to know the specific individuals and event orderings that put a particular place on a different path from others. Starting with individuals thus does not imply an approach based on law-like social behavior; it might instead be based on the supposition that particular individuals led a larger social group toward a different path.

Social science has proceeded down several dead ends designed to demarcate individual and social action.[21] Functionalism, with a long tradition in sociology and anthropology, sought to place all emphasis on the structural features of society and how they work together (often to produce stability). This resulted in confusing an outcome with a cause, without investigating whether the result of a social pattern was recognized in advance and part of its development. Philosopher John Searle's argument that social life was a product of "speech acts" led to overextended claims about the social construction of reality. At the other extreme, Mendelian evolution was haphazardly applied to social behavior, even though few if any social differences are the product of single genes.

These debates thus mix ontological ideas with methodological views about the components of an explanation. But philosophers of social science have mainly settled on a realist acceptance that both social forces and social groups can be useful for explanations and predictions. Even if some of these collective entities could in principle be reduced to group constituents or an identifiable construction, they are best treated like any other simplification (such as a typology of individuals or a scale of variation in behavior) necessary for social science explanation.[22]

Like practicing social scientists, philosophers have accepted that assemblages can have continuity and change, with the behavior of composites difficult to understand based on their components; effects can be probabilistic and complex, with influences from different scales and from both material and mental factors.[23] Viewing social life as exclusively either constructed by collective views or by individual interactions was far too constricting for real explanations. Even ontological individualism has faded in popularity among philosophers, as simple real-world groups and institutions are difficult to explain without reference to collective forces.[24]

Findings Are Not Universal or Believed to Be

Although a few social scientists have long made broad claims about the forces driving human history across time and region, most have stuck with more modest claims. Trade books and news reports traffic in the broadest debates, but social scientists tend to work on particular locales and time periods and only slowly generalize from them. To assess current opinion, I asked social scientists at research universities to evaluate in which direction research was moving over the last decade: toward "Broad claims of global scope" or "Specific claims about particular geographies," as well as toward "Broad claims about humans across time" or "Specific claims about temporal periods" on a five-point scale from −2 to +2. Figure 7.1 reports the results by discipline.

Across all five disciplines, research is reportedly becoming slightly more geographically and temporally specific. The trends are not overwhelming in any discipline; they are slightly less pronounced than the perceived trends toward quantitative or causal research (reviewed in Chapter 3). Psychologists perceive a greater increase in temporal than in geographic specificity; psychology has traditionally been the least historical social science, so that could suggest some movement toward the others. Although hardly revolutionary, these trends should temper any claims that social scientists are pursuing ever-grander theories that do not account for context.

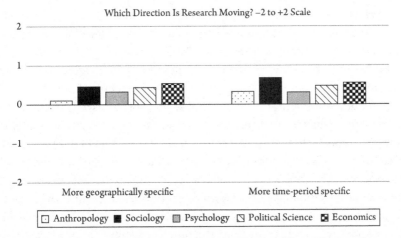

Figure 7.1 Perceptions of the Temporal and Geographic Specificity of Research. Data from the author's 2020 survey of social scientists at major US research universities. n=1,141.

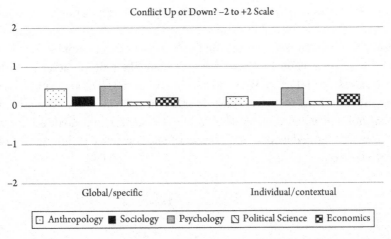

Figure 7.2 Perceptions of Conflict on the Scope and Levels of Research. Data from the author's 2020 survey of social scientists at major US research universities. n=1,141.

I also asked social scientists the extent to which conflict had intensified or lessened in their disciplines along two dimensions: the "global vs. geographically specific focus of research" and the "individual vs. contextual determinants of human behavior." Figure 7.2 illustrates the results by discipline, which are arrayed on a five-point scale from −2 to +2. In contrast to the decreasing conflict seen between qualitative and quantitative approaches or historical and contemporary research (reviewed in Chapter 3), social scientists see slightly increasing conflict on these two dimensions. But here the trends are less pronounced. Psychology, in the midst of debates over the cross-cultural validity of findings from WEIRD contexts, sees the largest increase in scholarly conflict. One sociologist told me that the debates come from increased awareness: "The importance of social context, structural factors, and social processes seems to be increasing. Perspectives . . . are being questioned for their tendency to ignore or discount social or relational factors that shape processes and outcomes."

In addition to assessing trends in their disciplines, I also asked social scientists directly about whether findings generalized across countries and time periods. Figure 7.3 reports the results, which run from strongly agree (+2) to strongly disagree (−2). Scholars across disciplines were unlikely to agree with either form of generalizability. Only 8 percent of anthropologists, 6 percent of sociologists, 18 percent of psychologists, 16 percent of political scientists, and 16 percent of economists agreed that most findings generalize cross-nationally. The low rates of agreement were similar for generalization across time periods: 12 percent, 10 percent, 16 percent, 12 percent, and 18 percent, respectively. Even the most confident disciplines about generalizability, economics and psychology, are thus not very confident.

In combination, these results suggest that there is a strong norm of assuming that findings lack generalizability in social science despite perceived conflict on these issues. That suggests social scientists see (but often do not believe) broad claims in their disciplines. These claims now invoke more disagreement than consensus as disciplines move slightly toward more historical and national specificity. Social scientists aim for generalizable claims, but they are accustomed to poking holes in global and eternal theories. They can agree that context matters but use that knowledge to identify the most relevant scope conditions for each pattern they observe.

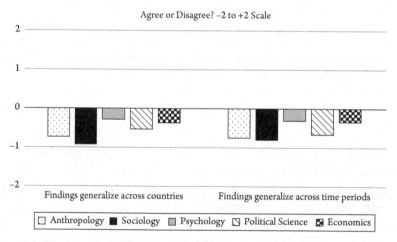

Figure 7.3 Perceptions of Generalizability across Time and Country. Data from the author's 2020 survey of social scientists at major US research universities. n=1,141.

This matters for our aspirations and whether we can achieve them. The inability to find that all swans are white from observing white swans alone is often seen as a central problem of induction; only once Europeans observed a black swan elsewhere, the fable goes, could they learn it was false. But it can also be seen as a problem of unwarranted generalization: if Europeans had just said that swans tend to be colored white recently in Europe, they would have been correct. Most current social science defines the scope of its claims in a more sensible fashion. Induction with a comparison of competing models can be justified as the optimal learning strategy applied to particular problems, even if its philosophical justification remains debated.[25]

Levels of Analysis and Time Scales

In practice, social scientists work at multiple levels of analysis, from as far down as parts of the brain and body to individual human beings up to social groups and organizations and all the way up to nations and global arrangements. The common call for specification of microfoundations of higher-level phenomena has been paired with two different impulses: an appeal to naturalism and unification with biology or rational choice modelers' discarding of claims of cultural or institutional influence without clear individual-level mechanisms.

The traditional reconciliation has been to argue that, although states, institutions, and cultures might result from individual behavior, it is still productive to talk about higher-level relationships that can result from multiple underspecified lower-level dynamics.[26] This resolution also implicates longer time horizons: if a macro-level social feature like a cultural norm or an institutionalized practice is the product of numerous individual actions over multiple generations, it may make more sense to assume its continued impact, rather than precisely map out how it developed. The Electoral College, for example, dramatically influenced the 2016 election; although it was a product of particular interactions among individuals and states long ago, it is at this point better treated as a stable rule of the game. It could still be important to investigate as a manifestation of Americans' divided appeals to state and nation or of white supremacy's role in compromises based on slave dehumanization, but neither is necessarily central to contemporary explanation.

Most social entities have these kinds of properties: they are not just temporary groups established by a confined set of knowing agents for one purpose. They sometimes leave non-social marks like buildings, resources, and environmental impacts; they are passed on generationally, have historical legacies, are known by outsiders, and are taken for granted by insiders. Group-level cultural traits can be reasonable elements of explanations because human societies evolved to take lots of cultural knowledge for granted; group knowledge, layered and developed over time, was better for survival. That means we respect tradition and rely on a store of codified knowledge at social levels.[27] We can productively talk of the impact of "political parties" or "media coverage" without fully specifying their components because of shared cultural meanings.

Racial group identity is another important and controversial example. Asking people to identify as White or Black; choosing between the Latino, Hispanic, and Latinx identity categories; or deciding whether to call groups ethnic or racial identities can all raise important issues, but endless conceptual debates should be paired with acknowledgment and use of imperfect measures. Current empirical approaches measure in multiple ways and assess the differences or compare answers to open-ended and categorical response options. We can assume that most respondents will recognize and apply racial categories without endorsing a false biological theory of racial division.

Our disciplinary biases, however, may still cause us to focus on particular levels of analysis and time periods. One way of seeing mid-century behavioralism in political science is as a move from a prior bias assuming stable rule-focused national institutions to a new bias premised on public action through partisan and interest group intermediaries. That, in turn, stimulated an effort to "bring the state back in" and refocus on higher-level institutions like governments.[28] Scholars can also be misled by particular temporal norms, especially if born of data availability. We often treat the beginning of survey data as the beginning of the public opinion time series, for instance, even if the initial period of data availability was an outlier (as mid-century America, the start of the survey boom, was on many dimensions).

Our chosen focus is not necessarily optimal. Social science is generally presentist and applied: we want to understand current behavior and possible changes. In thinking of the 2016 election, we focus primarily on what is necessary to explain its differences compared with the last few elections and to anticipate its potential for marking lasting change. Historians are familiar with this problem, always trying to move further back in the timescale of explanation. They know that history is reinterpreted in light of the current moment, but they question the influence of current views and regularly seek to reinterpret past views in light of other time periods. Cultural anthropologists also see human relations as products of group histories, interpreting far-flung findings as indicting simplifications about the inevitability or superiority of contemporary life.[29]

Especially for social problems that involve influences from many social levels and temporal timelines, it makes less sense to continually construct new elaborate and allegedly universal theories than to expect heterogeneity in time and space. As science accumulates, it also becomes harder to make our existing theories consistent with all known observations than to come up with a new key test of a novel idea. Historians' approach, essentially listing influential factors at individual and societal levels in each time period while attending to specific chronologies and agents, might be a model in a more systematized form. Contemporary social science is more accepting of contingency and path dependence in sequences, with individual, social group, and societal variation.[30]

Research now usually includes implicit scope conditions on how well theories travel across time, space, and groups.[31] Occasional attempts to reconfigure social science as an aspect of biology still conclude that we make too many assumptions about even individual-level integrated behavior.[32] Similarly, claims that all social life is a product of collective intentions and performances have given way to more complicated models of the interaction of mental, physical, and social life.[33]

Evolutionary biologist Kevin Laland finds that there was no straightforward linear evolution of the human mind, with substantial social learning and copying as well as trial and error in behavior.[34] As well as through adaptation, culture can advance via fads, overlearning of key lessons, or translating behavior born in one environment to another. Understanding human learning, intelligence, language, cooperation, and computation, he acknowledges, will require all the tools of social and natural science. Even the human body developed from systems first optimized for fish, with lots of stark evolutionary changes enabled by regulatory genes and recombination.[35] That is not to suggest that you need to fully understand a lower-level process or an evolutionary time scale to explain a contemporary social pattern. Researchers can stop to do a deep dive on the origins of a repeated human behavior only when necessary. Physical spaces, individual life-cycle processes, shared communication, event experiences, and social institutions are always potential factors in explanations, but we do not need to rewrite the full story of humanity in each area of social life.

Political scientists Christian List and Kai Spiekermann have attempted to reconcile individualism and holism for their discipline, arguing that some social regularities cannot be fully explained by individual-level descriptions because they have multiple potential realizations from different lower-level processes.[36] This is true, but it hardly exhausts the roles of higher-level variables. Particular physical environments or distributions of other social actors or patterns of connection between individuals can all affect social phenomena, even if they are a product of one unknown sequence of individual actions. And the historical particularity of higher-level causes such as colonialism or wars can change individuals far removed from their initial construction.

Multiple Time Scale Causes

Social science points to causes at multiple time scales. A social arrangement may have both a particular developmental history, a broader context for the development of similar entities, and even a deeper evolutionary trajectory. Each university has particular founders and builders but is also the manifestation of global trends in learning, research, religion, commerce, and politics; each of these trends, in turn, reflects fundamental human tendencies developed over evolutionary time. Even at the individual level, traits considered relatively stable, such as personality, are still affected by historical events and changing personal life circumstances as well as developmental patterns.

Past distributions and associations may not predict future events in any context where causal patterns change over time and most social worlds are nonstationary.[37] Most models that include changes over time in both attributes and causal relationships will suggest lots of uncertainty. And many global theories mistakenly discount long-term forces and the importance of developmental trajectories, which make current circumstances likely to be idiosyncratic consequences.[38] In seeking testability, we often simplify both causal mechanisms and the similarity of contexts across time.

We should be wary of our temporal bias. As Adrian Currie put it, "We occupy an often unrepresentative, atypical sliver of time. Our immediately accessible sample is biased, extremely incomplete, inadequate to answer questions at long scales."[39] "Temporal validity," whether a finding applies beyond the period in which it was studied, is an important aspect of external validity.[40] A nonreplication can always be a product of a changing temporal context; it may not be feasible to replicate and aggregate research findings in fast-changing areas. But even in areas where we do not expect much change, social science's extreme concentration in recent decades, with most research being conducted during the same social conditions and late state of technological development, should serve as a caution against generalization across time.

Studies that do incorporate diversity in temporal causes tend to closely analyze a few cases. Institutional theories in social science have moved from holism and functionalism to a series of "new institutionalisms" designed to incorporate ideas about path dependence in developmental trajectories.[41] The epistemological difficulty is explaining the current situation as the product of a trajectory when we lack multiple counterfactuals, especially for every step in the process. The more we believe an outcome is contingent, the more difficult it is to demonstrate. But historical accounts are not the only place this happens; evolutionary theories in social science also explain already known outcomes as the product of natural or mate selection over very long temporal scales.[42] Yet the interactions between genetics and the environment may have changed more across human history than they differ between us and our closest relative species today.[43]

Unfortunately, even social science that is attentive to problems of generalization often aims for simplistic world-historical theories. Joseph Henrich (who popularized the problems of psychologists drawing samples from WEIRD populations) is a lumper when it comes to human history, attributing human differences to a mostly unidimensional development driven by a few big causes like religious practice, even though he is a splitter when it comes to contemporary life, seeing most evidence as culturally and temporally specific.[44] Marriage institutions, social trust, market institutions, and long-term regional variation may all be important to human innovation, beliefs, and cultural development, as he argues, but it is unlikely that there is a generic effect of complex variables like education or religion across time and space (or that other variables can be ignored).

Narrative history explanations are often too neat, responsive more to the human love for stories than social science standards of evidence.[45] Data requirements are extensive even to parse generational, age, and period changes in opinion or behavior, much less to assess the sources of changing influence over time and generations. There has even been a revival in taking the personal characteristics of individual leaders more seriously in driving historical events, an approach previously uncommon in social science though common in history.[46] But history has mostly left systematic empirical work to the social sciences, content to specialize in interpretive chronologies. Historians recognize that history changes in each period as it is motivated by contemporary concerns, but they see that as a way to learn anew. They speak of reading archives "against the grain," framed as an opportunity to uncover biases of previous researchers, rather than for the benefits of hindsight.

Historian and political scientist William Sewell argued that the social sciences can learn from historians' perspectives because of the "fundamental historicity of social forums."[47] Even when historians and social scientists are studying the same phenomena and period, their disciplinary cultures move them in different directions: history to documentation of chronologies and potential influential factors and social science to structural models with as few variables as possible. Historians see long-term and short-term structural forces mixed with individual agency, even in an explanation of a single event. Social scientists do not necessarily reject these complexities in causality, but they see them as very difficult to test and historians' desires to complexify opening them to confirmation bias. Happily, the historical sections of social science disciplines (such as political development in political science or economic history in economics) strike a reasonable balance: they recognize the possibility of influential sequences and long-term causes but attempt to assess them using the broadest available data and, where possible, tests that enable causal inferences.

One path social scientists take is to continually refine and debate concepts, with debates about short- and long-term causes often stuck in definitional controversies. Democracy, for example, has been defined dichotomously, unidimensionally, and multi-dimensionally, with different implications for its distribution, stability, causes, and effects.[48] Repeated conceptualization and measurement debates are usually unproductive, but identifying that scholars are having a debate over a concept or measure rather than its causes or effects is an important realization. Often, scholarly consensus can develop around relationships once semantic debates are set aside. In the democracy example, the periods around the two world wars featured large increases in the number of democracies, though the qualities, types, and levels of democracies remain varied. We can also recognize recent democratic backsliding around the world without descent into autocracy. Scholars thus learn from the patterns present, given multiple imperfect definitions, and recognize the importance of refining them to explain different trends.

The Death of Methodological Individualism

Many social science gains have come from a softening of demands for low-level explanations. Despite a half-century of dominance in the social sciences, methodological individualism is now seen as a misguided project in philosophy and practice. In each area of scholarship, there are ongoing debates about remote and proximate influences, levels of explanation, and appropriate models and methods, but there is no reason to privilege individuals and individual-level factors without assessing the weight of the evidence.[49] As economics has moved away from insisting on rational choice models, the social sciences have faced fewer attempts at unification based on individualism. Objections that collective entities cannot have agency carry less weight when even individual agency is now seen more as a convenient fiction than a fact.

Philosopher Brian Epstein has recently done the most to nail the coffin shut on individualism, arguing that even ontological individualism is wrongly assumed and explanatory individualism (the idea that social facts are best explained by individual interaction) cannot make sense of even simple real-world groups and institutions.[50] Defining every term in a social theory in terms of individuals "has almost never been successfully accomplished," he argues, and there is little reason to privilege that project. Besides, "Social objects only rarely even come close to being intrinsically individuated. . . . Building the social world out of people, or modeling by starting with people, is a gross distortion."[51]

Even if states, institutions, and cultures result from underlying individual behavior (which should not be assumed), that does not mean individual-level factors provide a full explanation for collective behavior. There may also be social forces that operate at a higher level (such as power and competition in an international system) regardless of the distinct individual- and group-level factors that produced the interacting entities (such as nation-states).[52]

Social science theorist John Elster, who popularized individualism, claimed that explanations should show how collective behavior arose from individuals—but he softened over time to accept that collective entities are often "harmless shorthand" and that many collective outcomes do not result from rational individual behavior.[53] Nonetheless, his methodological individualist project was mainly a defense of rational choice theory's preeminence, rather than a study of what kinds of explanations work best. He sought to incorporate everything from subjective perceptions to probability errors to motivated belief formation to emotional responses into a rational choice model, but ultimately his advice was to assume an individual rational model and then modify based on its inadequacies.

But basic models of representative agents in interaction came under fire from inside and outside economics.[54] The general equilibrium model at the macro level is also still treated as a useful starting point but is also the butt of jokes about an economy with one worker, one owner, and one consumer who plans ahead and lives forever. The reformulation is not limited to economics. Scholars are realizing that one's ideas about the proper level of analysis are mostly products of how the social science disciplines and fields were constructed and the focal points of our interests, rather than a coherent model of when individual, group, national, and international forces are most relevant for our explanations.[55]

Updating Philosophy of Science

Since current philosophy of science controversies are usually new versions of old disputes, it is difficult for social scientists to attend to trends relevant to our research.[56] Philosopher Daniel Little nonetheless sees change in the community studying philosophy of social science, associated with some actionable advice.[57] Philosophers haven't resolved disputes, but they have recognized heterogeneity in social group composition and dynamics and contingency in historical development. Individual actor-centered approaches can be useful but cannot be fully separated from social settings or normative systems. Philosophers of social science have mostly agreed on what not to do: avoid naturalism and strong metaphors from natural science; avoid dichotomies of physical and mental causes; and avoid reductionist demands for lower-level explanations for every social phenomenon.

Like Epstein, Little shows that any moderately complex social entity, such as a legislature, a church, or a labor union, is an assemblage that has continuity beyond the individuals within it and that develops an institutional history with social practices and shared beliefs. But social scientists do not give up in the face of the complexity: they continue defining concepts and creating schemes, measuring influential factors at the individual, group, and broader levels. They do not discount the individual-level interactions that helped produce a group but see them as instances of broader patterns of collective action and particular histories of mobilization and communication.

Philosophers of social science have followed debates in modeling, as researchers complexified rational choice theory and invented tools like agent-based modeling to understand emergence of collective phenomena from simple individual-level dynamics. But they have also followed empirical progress in understanding social causation and accept that some collective rules and institutions have irreducible influence.[58] Their contemporary social scientific realism also suggests that descriptions or models can be useful if approximately true or incomplete, in predictive success as well as other desiderata for understanding and application.

Philosophers of social science have also been active in developing and promoting methodological advances in specifying counterfactual and potential outcome models, using Bayes nets and acyclic graphs, measuring average treatment effects, assessing probabilistic causation, and taking advantage of natural experiments.[59] Although they do not uniformly side with variable-oriented over case-oriented approaches or prioritize causal inference over other aims, they see value in these innovations.

Unfortunately, quantitative- and causality-focused social scientists tend to associate higher-level social causes with qualitative historical work, especially given the history of social construction as an airy critical perspective that assigns thoughts and agency to society as a whole.[60] Methodological individualism was developed as a defense of social science against less-than-scientific theories like Marxism and psychoanalysis.[61] Even if not all theories can be stated at the individual level, social scientists want to avoid anything-goes grand views of history and society.

As philosophy of science moved from studying physics to biology, it also found that many theories based on a search for general laws did not fit well.[62] That left philosophers of social science with an opening to show that contingency and theories of local scope in time and space are prevalent throughout the sciences. Scientists try to generalize findings but recognize limits quickly. It might be the history of physics, rather than the social sciences, that is the outlier in how theories are developed.

Helen Longino's studies of the interaction between biological and social sciences to understand similar questions show that each approach is partial and not easily reconciled with the same data, especially given definitional disputes, the use of proxies and limited models, and the influence of political, disciplinary, and moral ideas on scholars' interpretations.[63] But recognizing when scholars disagree because they are working at different levels or time scales, rather than due to different findings, has been critical to reconciling these perspectives.

Complex and Successful Social Science

Both social and natural sciences encounter simple patterns as well as complex multilevel processes. A fun way to compare their challenges is to choose two topics that humans often want to understand: the traffic and the weather. The former is mostly a social phenomenon, the latter mostly natural (though both have some influence on the other). But knowledge of each is important and actionable, so much so that they are both covered on some news radio stations every ten minutes and are among the most used functions on smartphone and smart car systems. Interestingly, we are also making great progress on both, measured in terms of prediction and broader understanding.

Weather involves both long-term climatic considerations and shorter-term and less predictable forces, but we have nonetheless made lots of practical progress. Weather reports are more accurate, severe weather influence is more trackable, and data are more abundant. Traffic is a cumulation of individual human tendencies, laws and practices, social institutions and trends, and the built and natural environment but it nonetheless obeys common patterns and we can make useful predictions. Indeed, we now have a lot more real-time and in-depth traffic data, better metropolitan-level models of policy or construction changes, and innovations for individual and governmental decision-making. In both cases, lots of progress is made simply through observational generalization, updating models with data and new findings, and putting more tools in the hands of more researchers. Precision in calculation, breadth of observation, and advances in simulation guide investigations of regularities and theory building.[64]

Also, in both cases, most of our complaints involve our inability to change the world, not to understand it: we have made only modest progress in intentionally altering the weather, and our efforts to reduce traffic or improve flow do not move fast enough for frustrated motorists. Yet initial attempts to make traffic management into solely a physical engineering problem have been less successful than integrating human behavior. Adding a lane to a road often just increases traffic, but governments now communicate effectively via a large increase in roadside signs and technological tools to effectively re-route motorists.[65]

We have even made progress in understanding our frustration, both from theories of mass psychology and movement and from self-sampling ideas (you are more likely to be in the slower lane because more people are in it).[66] Sophisticated mathematical models, computer simulations, traditional observational analysis, simple geographic and temporal comparisons, and big data algorithmic learning are also used in both fields, though no one technique has crowded out others.[67]

Both fields also exemplify science realism. As Adrian Currie points out, meteorologists use feedback, tweaks to their models, and simulations without necessitating a complete understanding: "a meteorologist predicting the weather need not be so concerned with whether her model represents the causal dynamics of weather systems. Rather, she can focus on whether it provides true predictions." The same is true in social systems where "only those causal details influencing the target system to the level of approximation required to support or undermine the hypotheses . . . concern us."[68] And weather and traffic both suffer from practical problems of measurement based on changes in human behavior. During the COVID-19 pandemic, for example, declining aircraft use led to a deterioration of surface meteorology forecasts.[69] Similarly, large increases in working from home not only led to declines in traffic but less predictable effects of construction backups.

Policymakers call on science in both areas, but that does not mean scientists can move beyond informing decisions to directing them. In areas like tornado prevention, enough shared goals can legitimate evidence-based advice. But scientists often pretend that other areas have the same widely shared values as natural disaster preparation, even though many are more contested.[70] Perhaps we do not all want to improve traffic flow, after all, if it will lead to more car commuting that eventually affects the weather through pollution and climate change.

Coupled Social and Natural Systems

Thankfully, natural scientists are increasingly recognizing that social dynamics are key factors in what they study and often cannot be understood with the same assumptions and tools. Climate modeling has been at the forefront of this movement, with recognition that forecasting requires modeling a coupled social and natural system with short- and long-term influences, local and global.[71] The necessity of social science to address science and engineering problems was central to social sciences gaining a foothold in federal research funding.[72]

Many engineering and science problems involve coupled natural, technical, and human systems. Humans both develop technology and interact with it alongside natural surroundings they can also alter. Humans are complicated parts of these systems, no less important or connected than other parts. Geography, a discipline that crosses social and natural sciences, was founded on thinking at both social and natural timescales about local and global variation. Its tools and insights have been just as common in understanding human as natural geography, and it is likewise moving toward understanding their interaction.[73]

Part of the success of the social sciences during the Cold War came from the recognition of their importance and utility even in seemingly technical problems. Electronic advancements, for example, required transforming humans as well as making tools; many failures came from neglecting to think through how people collectively designed, operated, and maintained systems.[74] Practical considerations then fed back into social science model building, with theoretical ideas reflecting the role of science in society and the economy as people adapted to knowledge and technology.[75] In this way, larger and interconnected human populations have facilitated the accumulation of knowledge.[76]

Coupled human and natural systems are not just forcing engineering disciplines to adapt, but also changing views about the uniqueness of social science (and its relative impossibility). Joint analyses, such as models of watersheds, fail to show a bright line between thinking about human behavior and environmental behavior.[77] It is a common challenge that social agents can react to scientific findings and thereby change them, but neither our impact on the world nor our consideration of the political and societal implications of our findings is unique to social phenomena.

Knowledge and Action

Audiences do not just want knowledge for its own sake, they want to see progress in application. As Currie reports, "The public, policymakers, and so forth want clear epistemic dividends on their investment."[78] They are less keen on hearing about unsolvable problems or inevitable trade-offs. It is often easier and more popular to address human behavior through a technological workaround than to attempt a broad social change; there are social and policy solutions to problems like inequality or environmental damage, but we may still prefer techy alternatives.[79]

Knowledge of basic science, awareness of likely blind spots, and joint efforts to solve problems are all useful and rising, but that does not guarantee easy solutions to human challenges. In fact, analyses of scientific breakthroughs show a decline in the pace of innovations that have large economic impacts (despite significant public investment).[80] But our desperation for speed and novelty might be part of the problem. Significant progress might follow from application of already-known social research, but it would often take the form of policy and guidance that would seem like common sense in retrospect (e.g., incentivizing group travel to reduce traffic and pollution).

Even in response to crises, social scientists need to pragmatically build and modify models, working back and forth among inductive and deductive approaches, with close attention to temporal and spatial context. The particularities of humans matter, even if their responses to unpredicted events are often difficult to understand.[81] Since we are in a boat together, we have to collectively figure out what is going on and adjust along the way in order to safely reach the shore.

8

All History and Policy

In the midst of the Great Recession, former Federal Reserve chair and economist Alan Greenspan made a stark admission to a congressional committee: "I have found a flaw [in my economic ideology]. I don't know how significant or permanent it is. But I have been very distressed by that fact." He pronounced himself in "a state of shocked disbelief" that banks could not regulate themselves out of their own self-interest after "going for 40 years or more with very considerable evidence that it was working exceptionally well."[1]

The re-evaluation of fundamental economic premises was not limited to Greenspan. The economic crisis provoked a broader rethinking of the failure to anticipate the crisis, leading to changes in how economics is studied and taught. Forty-one economics student protest groups from nineteen countries argued that "The real world should be brought back into the classroom, as well as debate and a pluralism of theories and methods."[2] The discipline's core theories, they said, had been too closely tied to an ideology that failed in policy and prediction. Books like *What's Wrong with Economics, Crisis and the Failure of Economic Theory*, and *The End of Theory* argued that economics was hopelessly attached to inadequate models.[3] Nobel laureate Paul Krugman was left to ask: "How Did Economics Get It So Wrong?" His answer: the discipline had mistaken beauty in formula for eternal truth, building models based on a narrow reading of US history for use in policy debates.[4] Harvard reformulated its economics classes to incorporate more empirical data and theories from psychology and sociology.[5] Economists tried to revise standard models but found that humans may be a lot less calculating and optimizing and more responsive to narratives than the models assume.[6]

Like Greenspan, economists also realized that too much of their discipline's views had been tied to the past few decades of economic behavior in the United States. They returned to analyses of the Great Depression and inequality in global history. Also like Greenspan, they acknowledged that purpose-driven models for policymaking too often combined ideological ideas about the role of government with ontological precepts about human behavior.[7] These twin realizations revisit social science's historical divorce from its two antecedents: history and policy. Economists' desire to build a general model of human behavior from limited history is hardly an outlier; it is a microcosm of the trajectory of American social science from subdisciplines of history to their scientific ambitions. Likewise, economists' hidden merger of policy advice and theories of human behavior was visible from the foundations of political economy. The social theory that guided the development of social science was born of political contestation, long including debates about whether economics' focus on self-interested behavior should guide public decisions over other collective ambitions.

This chapter uses social science's origins to investigate its incomplete divorce from history and policy. Social scientists began studying history and seeking to influence social decisions, but they used a scientific self-image to unattach themselves from historians and social reformers and raise their relative status. Social scientists still work with the same historical variation and they are still judged by how well their findings translate into policy. If patterns change over time, social scientists are limited to the same periods to study as historians. And all of us are driven by collective social goals colored by our ideological views.

Given that social scientists must consider explanations over short- and long-term time horizons and operating through groups and societies as well as individuals, that leaves us in a difficult predicament. We are motivated to inform action today but limited by the historical variation available (and we expect heterogeneity across time and place). Learning from the patterns of history does not lend itself to informing collective decisions unless we are careful about the conclusions we can draw and the non-empirical motivations that guide us. We privilege our point of view in the present moment and assume that widely seen recent patterns are timeless or eternal.[8]

But that hardly leaves us hopeless. Historians consider theories more as thematic elements of narratives, tending to accept some role for many pieces of the story. Social scientists want to divvy up the explanatory power of each element, in part to assess when and how outcomes can be changed. Scholars can also draw from our desires for reform while recognizing that they change our scholarship. Social science was created to systematize historical investigations and intervene in the contemporary world, learning from natural science to specify and limit the biases of the researcher. It should not seek to replace traditional history or policy debate, but its efforts to structure and organize knowledge remain quite valuable to both. Despite discounting one another's work, for example, historians and social scientists eventually converged on similar chronologies and causal mechanisms for major international conflicts.[9]

The current moment will always intervene on our values and disrupt our prior theories. After a decade of economic growth following Greenspan's remarks, the global economy was hit by a pandemic-driven recession in 2020 that reignited debates over whether economic theory was too narrow, whether economists should guide policy over other disciplines, and whether scholars can build general knowledge or simply react to the circumstances of the latest events. Instead of learning only particularized lessons about what was missing in anticipating these events, social scientists can aim to permanently acknowledge the role of our policy ambitions and historical knowledge in understanding human society. Thankfully, today's historical analyses in social science are more careful and today's policy interventions are more cognizant of our limited role in the making of society's collective choices.

The Separation from History

Historian Dorothy Ross argues that American economics, sociology, and political science all slowly separated from history from the late nineteenth century to the 1920s, spurred by modernization and a belief in American exceptionalism. Social scientists came to view social life as both a natural process and a controllable evolution toward social goals.[10] In her periodization, a crisis of exceptionalism from 1865 to 1896 characterized by Gilded Age economics and a socialist threat stimulated a historicist challenge to budding social science. It was answered by a progressive social science from 1896 to 1914; pragmatism rose alongside scientific aspiration, manifesting in marginalism in economics, social control in sociology, and realism in political science. From 1908 to 1929, science ambition rose further in a conflict with the last gasp of historicism: institutional and neoclassical perspectives fought in economics, instrumental positivism arose in sociology, and pluralist group conflict replaced constitutionalism in political science. Emulation of the natural sciences eventually enabled a turn away from both the practical politics of progressive reformism and the final separation from history as a less systematic pursuit. Ross finds this was visible in associational politics within each discipline as well as in their public feuds.[11]

This trajectory holds critical lessons: the initial break with history was less a turn away from politics than toward it. Sociology's rise was not based on a tempering of the policymaking ambitions of economics, but a desire to expand them beyond the economy to social behavior writ large. As historian Mary Furner argues, claims of scientific status were advanced in order to gain status in these public debates, as university professors took over social science associations from reformers.[12] Industrialism and urbanization raised the profile of society-wide problems; social scientists wanted to defend the desirability of American society but argued that reform was needed to retain its advance.

Political scientists built schools and institutes to advise government while developing a more systematic study via statistics and experiments.[13]

The American Economic Association was founded under the auspices of the American Historical Association at a joint meeting with the American Social Science Association (initially a Boston-based group sponsoring civil service reform), with economics the least committed to the reform movement and more academically oriented.[14] Separate disciplines arose as social scientists gained authority and as all moved from humanitarian causes to advocacy of new methods. The institutional origins of psychology and anthropology differed from the shared history of economics, political science, and sociology, but hardly because they were less applied in orientation. Instead, both were partially manifestations of government projects: the regulation of mental illness and the advance of imperialism. Scientism in each discipline reflected a technocratic vision and a demotion of social reform (driven more by women), even though philanthropic foundations and local government continued their interest in the on-the-ground practical ambitions of social efforts.[15]

Social science's separation from history, then, was based on its interest in informing action. Its move from reformism to broad and systematic social schemas was, in turn, a product of raising the mission beyond local interests to guiding broader society. Scholarship, of course, continued to reflect the goals of its time period and its understanding of history. But history as the center of inquiry was discarded because of society's newfound problems and social science's view that it could be the source of their solution.

The Relationship with History

Today, social science has reincorporated history via a systematizing of its findings. On the theoretical side, it moved from historical stories to models of set dependence (where a single turning point changes a trajectory) and path dependence (where each step along the way changes the next).[16] On the empirical side, it is increasingly using key historical events to map long-term changes and effects, especially where they can be seen as natural experiments (such as an agricultural disease forcing migration) or if the order or application of events was random (such as a military draft) or as-if-random (such as a policy implemented geographically in stages).

When social science departed from history, the discipline of history evolved with the rise of archival methods. The norm of traveling to archives fragmented historical scholarship and limited generalization, in turn stimulating systemic collections and related fields.[17] The backlash against studying elites and culturally dominant groups within history was partially justified by a methods critique that the archives are written by those shaping their own memory. But social history eventually expanded the content of archives themselves and their interpretation.

Inherently historical sciences like archeology have long centered the question of what kinds of traces will remain for long-past events based on factors like what materials and artifacts degrade, what records were made, and the number and diversity of descendants.[18] But each event can create ripples, some dispersing over longer physical and historical distances. That means parochial histories are always part of the combined investigation of human life, and different models of sensitivity to initial conditions limit potential confirmation. By regularly considering history, archeologists try to distinguish between generalizable and local patterns.

But given that major cultural evolution in humans has only come in the last 10,000 to 12,000 years, it is not easy to generate even basic timelines or definitive social patterns; many claims about hunter-gatherer societies, conquests, and migrations remain contested.[19] This should not be surprising. Writing the history of dogs or other domesticated animals also requires a lot of social and historically contingent background knowledge alongside systematic genetic and archeological trace data. And we still lack the complete non-human history.

Geneticist David Reich, author of the grandly titled *Who We Are and How We Got Here*, makes many anthropologists uncomfortable given his global history ambitions and assumed generalizability of his cases and methods.[20] He attempts to learn over broad swathes of human history but acknowledges that what archeologists collect remains mostly in close-by sites and more recent periods.[21] That means scientists are always reasoning from fewer specimens the further away and back we go from the here and now—and we have less accompanying archeological and historical evidence to interpret and align with the genetic findings. Even though Reich is using ancient DNA to quickly change understandings of human history, he is working with archeologists and linguists and often confirming prior views of mass migrations and population mixtures. Where he departs, he often makes the story more complicated by showing more and earlier movement and mixing than others have documented. In other words, he is adding historical contingency and complexity rather than writing one narrative. Rather than products of an evolutionary model that adds a few cultural regularities to our shared genetic ancestry, contemporary human similarity and diversity are consequences of many historical and geographic factors that could have gone different ways.

Political scientist James C. Scott argues that we fundamentally misunderstand human history based on the tales and records of the victors.[22] Since agriculture has been widespread for only 240 generations, he says, our ideas about urbanization, the development of government, and conflict and cooperation are all based on the particular crops we developed (and where they were planted) and the social arrangements that they required. How societies organize commerce, count inhabitants, draw borders, fight wars, tax and distribute resources, and interact with their environments, he says, are all partially dependent on prosaic needs of staple grains.[23] Since the states that develop also record and measure, they also control the accessibility of historical records. The decline of written records could have coincided with productive overthrows of unequal regimes, but we see them largely as falls of civilizations.[24]

Systems of slavery were built on the basis of agricultural and military needs as well as human social views. Slaves, especially women, were treated as the spoils of war to raise armies. Slavery also became endemic in areas where it was useful for farming. As sociologist Orlando Patterson has found, human slavery was born of group distinctions, with a group that did not belong, but was often expedient. This included women slaves exported before the African slave trade and some societies that had elite slaves.[25] Our eventual abhorrence toward slavery made us rewrite history to see it as less useful, seeing the Northern states as efficient emblems of capitalism and Southern states as backward-looking traditionalists more as myth building than history.[26] Scholars can also err in their corrections, however, making slavery appear overly central to economic growth. But the blossoming of social science concerned with history has uncovered our faulty memories and enabled debates over topics such as the relative importance of cotton in the American South's development and the dominance of women in slavery's global history.

We are also retelling the related history of inter-state violence. War and violent revolution were central mechanisms for reducing inequality, whereas both government-led development and commercial expansion are tools for upward redistribution.[27] If liberals and conservatives seek to claim little trade-off between development and inequality or both want to stand opposed to violence and in favor of equal growth, views of history that do not fit either ideological box may be left out. But attention to these trade-offs is rising.

A simpler example of historical views and political motives may help. At the time of the American Revolution, East and West Florida were also considered American colonies but they have been excluded from our history because they sided with the English.[28] This is not just an exemplar of the cliché that winners write history, but also a reminder that our historical stories are tied to our self-conceptualization. Social science can theoretically be more systematic in its use of historical data, but by default (and without any self-correction) it is subject to the same biases. And history always matters to current analysis because the provenance of data changes what it tells us, and the trajectory of what we are studying influences what we can learn about it today.[29]

Limits of Scientism

Despite the partial turn back to history, social science remains infatuated with the natural science example. Naturalism (the idea that social science reduces to natural science) has long been seen as a polar alternative to more historically informed traditionalism, though both assumed that social scientists also had some practical ambitions.[30]

Even with social science's methodological advances, we are still left with studying either empirical regularities from history or the efficacy of interventions. Inference from history depends on the nature of historical processes (how randomly and interrelatedly they occur). Inference from interventions relies on how well our experiments adapt to new contexts and scale up to broader domains. Each is a product of the degree of variation and complexity in the human world and thus cannot be separated from the classic tools of describing variation and trajectories.

The impulse to systematic investigation is the core of the social science tradition. But we still sometimes get caught up in confusing the image of science with its usefulness. For example, the National Institutes of Health funded a huge rise in both candidate gene research and fMRI brain studies, even though there was a very low probability of replicable findings given small sample sizes.[31] There are still incentives for splashy science—which often means connections to natural science like brain imaging and genetics. But many of the findings so far suggest the same complex processes found in social sciences: many different areas of influence, with some persistence and some changeability but limited success in intervening to change human behavior.

The Relationship with Policy

Social statistics were invented by participants in policy arguments and political disputes, motivating each side to further invest in persuasion via "political arithmetic."[32] Statistics eventually migrated to official government agencies, but never lost their influence in policymaking. The social sciences themselves also developed as outgrowths of public debates over collective decisions.

Scientists' proper role in policymaking is usually conceived as being an "honest broker" of information, rather than an arbiter of decisions, an issue advocate, or a pure researcher.[33] They should move beyond research findings to clarify decisions and potential consequences and suggest new options, the thinking goes, but not cross the line to pure advocacy. But scholars, publishers, and grant makers all seek projects with "policy implications" that can go well beyond the expertise of the researcher, without necessarily asking them to accumulate or weigh alternative views.[34]

The usual audience for social science is bureaucratic, with the "acquiescence of elected officials" with lingering doubts about the motives of scholars.[35] American social science associations' initial political goal was civil service reform, which they saw as helping to rationalize policymaking.[36] Scholars like Du Bois had to thread the thin line between policy relevance and objective research, gaining funding by directly addressing public problems but having a manuscript destroyed by the US Department of Labor because it "touched on political matters."[37]

Today, public expectations of science remain focused on collective problem solving. Focus groups are surprised to learn that scientists direct their own research, choosing topics of interest, rather than being directed to solve particular problems.[38] Even in the most applied contexts, however, government agencies more commonly choose among proposals from scientists than direct research from the top down. Research funding is often justified with reference to an innovation cycle modeled on industrial labs. Models of stages from basic to applied research to commercialization, however, have lost favor to ideas about promoting systems and cultures of innovation.[39] These often require public-private-academic alignment; yet tight relationships between universities, foundations, think tanks, and government agencies are also often critiqued as emblematic of an establishment looking out for its own interests.[40]

Economic models have had the most success in policymaking circles, not only in classic decision models but also in designing mechanisms to incentivize behavior.[41] Most social science requires significant translation to serve as an input in the policymaking process, but economics has created bureaucratic institutions and procedures to enable its input.[42] Influential public-spirited economists still worry about the weakness of their academic field, however, believing that they are trusted more for their data analysis skills than for their theoretical inheritance.[43]

Even as it evolves its theories and preferred methods, economics continues to have broad policy influence beyond economists. Law professor Cass Sunstein, the most cited active legal scholar, promoted a revolution in the use of cost-benefit analysis in government, the continuing advance of social statistics, and the rise of "nudge" policies based on behavioral economics.[44]

The rise of economics in government was part of a broader technocratic movement based in agencies and think tanks. An initial (mostly liberal) expert community in the 1960s was critiqued by an antiwar movement on the left, but was eventually challenged by an upstart conservative movement in the 1970s that sought to replace expert consensus with contests between credentialed ideologues.[45] Although conservatives initially saw the infrastructure of scientific advising as another unelected branch of government working toward its own expansion, they eventually challenged the system on its own merits, seeing demands for open data and evidence as effective tools for slowing regulation.

Policies can also build or redesign associated expert communities. Medicare and Medicaid helped expand and professionalize university medical schools.[46] The huge decline in state mental hospitals, with patients declining 80 percent from 1955 to 1985, transformed mental health as a field and nationalized its funding sources.[47] Food and Drug Administration trials support a large number of researchers but also incentivize pharmaceutical over therapeutic treatment.[48] Research on several drugs that are used recreationally, meanwhile, was put on hold for decades despite early scientific success, partially because of high-profile adventurism by university affiliate Timothy Leary.[49]

The political context surrounding research affects how scholarly debates develop. Since criminal justice research and core sociobiological studies of aggressive and sexual behavior raise legal issues, researchers weigh how findings will map onto social desires to blame or excuse activity.[50] Policy debates over terrorism, infectious disease, and climate change are also sites of contestation over both the barrier between science and policymaking and the internal lines of relative expertise within the sciences.[51] The adversarial legal and regulatory practices in the United States make establishing who is an expert, what kinds of evidence are permitted, and which communities need to come to consensus on standards into core political issues. Courts and agencies cite generic standards of scientific expertise and evidence nearly as often as specific cases analogous to each dispute. Science has responded to judicial needs with new ideas about measurement, codifying uncertainty, and establishing causation.[52]

Political Unrepresentativeness

Given their important policymaking role, social scientists should be particularly mindful of the potential for political bias. The public views social science as partly a "guided pursuit of evidence in favor of scientists' personal ideology" on controversial topics.[53] Republicans have less trust in university-created knowledge, especially if they perceive faculty as more disproportionately liberal.[54]

Steven Lubet's critique of ethnography argues that scholarship starts from the ideological perspective that police are bad actors, defendants are often framed, and criminals are needlessly caught up in a bad system; all of those premises could be correct, but they can lead to a search for confirming evidence, with the field judging from ideological premises over evidentiary standards.[55] Conservative critic of social science Jim Manzi also argues that social scientists seek to justify their view of the world (and are not diverted from it absent undeniable evidence); he sees randomized controlled trials as the only solution, but even there contends that social scientists assume far more potential for scaling up studies than is warranted based on their hope for more government action.[56] But Manzi's solution, to stick with non-government action absent overwhelming evidence of program effectiveness, is less an epistemological principle than a return to his different ideological precepts.

Recent critiques of liberal academia come in the wake of a generation-long attack on the independent and nonpartisan standing of academic social scientists by conservative think tanks, who argued that they were simply providing studies from an alternative perspective born of conservative principles.[57] But that is not a reason to fully dismiss the critiques. Experts are indeed ill equipped to make predictions even in fields closely related to their academic work, often due to their affinity with the assumptions of activists and ideologues.[58]

Within social psychology, there has been an active effort to determine the impact of political biases. A recent collection finds pejorative naming and interpretation, assuming that liberal views are the norm rather than one endpoint of a scale, and aversion to any explanation involving evolutionary motives.[59] These public interventions in psychology caused scholars to organize around studying perspectives missing from current debates and provoked responses from others saying the concerns were overblown (who also systematically studied the role of politics in scholars' findings).

Many of the social psychology examples are related to topics also studied in political science, such as prejudice and conservatism. A recent special issue of the journal *PS* drafted scholars to comment on the effects of ideological bias; most of the examples were similar. They argued that we often misdiagnose conservatism and use uncharitable interpretations based on poorly designed survey scales, especially when investigating relationships with personality and prejudice.[60] They cited instances of misunderstanding and self-censoring and called for more ideological diversity. But even for cherry-picked examples, the clearest cases were a simple fraud and a coding mistake, rather than biases in questions or interpretations. And two articles in the symposium provoked thoughtful follow-ups that suggested concerns may have been misplaced. One found that evidence of the effects of anti-man attitudes on voting was absent from the literature because of null findings, rather than scholarly bias.[61] Another said a data error (ideologically important but mostly irrelevant to the paper's findings) had been blown out of proportion by conservative media.[62]

Political science has a long tradition of treating parties and groups from each ideological side equivalently for model tractability, so the biases may not manifest similarly. Nonetheless, most of its theories and evidence would expect partisan and ideological biases in scholars' interpretation of information.[63] In predictions, experts are often worse than amateurs, especially when their work carries an ideological perspective with it.[64] Social scientists are not representative

of their nations' publics in ideology or partisanship—and they may move leftward during their professionalization. A study of partisan change in the 1960s
shows that 40 percent of faculty changed their party identification, mostly by
converting to Democrats. Of professors whose parents were Republicans,
60 percent converted to Democrats; only 20 percent of those with Democratic
parents converted to Republicans.[65]

Critics from the left and right could both be right about the ideological
roles of social scientists. Political diversity may be limited and left-skewed by
partisan and ideological metrics, but the kinds of liberals who stay in academia
may also have a status quo bias (given their placement in organizationally conservative institutions). Self-selection into staid institutions with cultures that
nonetheless question everything may produce political liberals but disciplinary
conservatives.

It is easier to see the potential effects of political biases in another time period. Social science was closely affiliated with the "war on poverty" in the 1960s,
including both its liberal impulses and its conservative views on the effects of
African American family structure and the impact of the "culture of poverty."[66]
Social scientists were affected by the availability of grants, prevailing views of racial differences, and the ideological appeal of discussing culture rather than class.
This did not produce uniformly liberal responses but was guided by the liberal
aspirations of the Great Society.

It also provoked a conservative backlash to social welfare policy scholarship,
premised as much on the bankruptcy of expert-led anti-poverty policy evaluation as on the actual ineffectiveness of redistributive programs. The long debate
over poverty birthed many social-science-supported social welfare policies but
also the counterrevolution of Charles Murray's *Losing Ground*, which suggested
these policies made things worse. Social science was central to both a new political consensus on welfare dependency in the 1980s and the reinvention of
place-based policies led by William Julius Wilson's *The Truly Disadvantaged*.[67]
Today's biases may similarly be mixes of conservative and liberal assumptions
rather than a simple discounting of conservative views.

The American Association of University Professors, known for its work
defending tenure, has a long history of defending faculty rights to participate
politically. The social science associations supported these efforts but had different ethical concerns. Anthropologists were concerned with relationships to
government funders, political science with disclosure of funders and data, and
sociologists with politicization of academic evaluations.[68] But social scientists'
remaining ties to conservatives have been politically important. NSF social science funding was repeatedly threatened by concerns about liberal bias, with
150 congressmen complaining by 1965 and NSF responding with funding
restrictions.[69] An early Reagan administration effort to cut social science out of

the NSF was stopped due to intense mobilization, especially by conservative economists touting its nonideological benefits, but NSF remained wary of social science and became more economics-focused in response.[70]

Conservatives have long been more critical of "eggheads," academic experts driving policy—but the role of elite intellectuals also divided Democratic constituencies.[71] In the Trump era, anti-intellectualism again became ascendant but even more concentrated among Republicans. Democrats have become more likely to defer to scientists and scientific research, but perhaps only based on the issues currently associated with expertise.[72] A majority of Republicans believe that scientists are just as biased as nonscientists.[73] Research shows that scientific communication can help acclimate public partisans to scientific information, connect to diverse cultures, and establish the importance of consensus, but that is no match for a political elite that sees scientists as taking a side and wants to intervene against their influence. Conservative messaging has also reached the right-leaning public, with increasing concerns about free speech and bias in academia.[74] But another conservative strategy, exemplified in the move from creationism to "intelligent design," is to emulate scientific concepts and create new expert communities, fudging a court-imposed line between science and religion.

It is not just courts that have trouble distinguishing ideological views from scientific ones. In one study, economists stated that only the content of a statement—not the speaker—should be judged, but when put to the test they did not follow that script.[75] When presented with identical economic statements attributed to left and right sources (e.g., Karl Marx or Adam Smith saying the same aphorism), economists evaluated them based on the source. And the biases were stronger in the most policy-relevant fields. Ideology is also associated with research topic selection, citation networks, faculty hiring, methods, specializations, and departments. Although economists usually show wide agreement on policy questions, ideology divides them when they do disagree.

The influence of the politics of scholars in each time period is also evident in psychology. Its scales of survey questions and go-to interventions and measurements are products of their specific historical motivations, such as studying "obedience to authority" and measuring "authoritarianism" in the context of the Holocaust. Core psychological concepts like personality, motivation, attitude, and emotion are hardly "nothing but socio-historical constructions," but they are also not "natural kinds" that can be interpreted outside of the history of particular research aims.[76] The long debate over intelligence testing, for example, involves both (some) liberal blindness to the consistency and impact of cognitive ability and an aggrieved conservative view that liberal skepticism is born of a broader ideological conspiracy to accuse conservatives of racism. But the interesting pattern is that all kinds of related studies continue, despite common claims of silencing or self-censorship.

Psychologist Jay Van Bavel told me there is reason to be concerned but grounds for hope: we should "look for conservative people or views being squeezed out, but we didn't find liberal studies less likely to replicate. People predict bias but need to be specific about when and where it might come about. It's more likely on topic selection where we don't have institutions to protect us." Sociologists seem more open about their ideological views, with more reason to be worried about their influence. Jeremy Freese called the lack of ideological diversity "an existential issue for the discipline." "We wouldn't even know the conservative view [in some areas and we're] . . . bad at presenting conservative arguments. [That means we] leave things unexplored." Judging findings as "appropriately sociological often means [whether they're] practical for left politics. That's not consistent with organized skepticism," one sociologist told me. "Most people don't care; I think it's not healthy . . . no question that the topics the discipline is interested in are shaped by political values." Mark Mizruchi points to examples of sociological findings being dismissed not due to their evidence but because they did not fit with liberal worldviews, causing public backlash.[77]

Political scientists pointed to how scholars actively participate with liberal partners on field experimental research. Jessica Preece, one of the few political scientists who has worked with conservative partners, said, "Our first job is to describe the political world and the way people operate. That is hard to do if our experiences are all the same. It is harder to understand when our experience with or as conservatives is so limited." When she worked with a state Republican Party on a gender field experiment, "people were amazed but we had to use their help in designing the experiment; we couldn't [motivate women to seek office based on the] need for diversity; we needed to emphasize families and communities."

A political scientist summed up broader worries: "At this point it is almost impossible to find political scientists who voted for Trump, even though about half of the US population voted for him. This breeds a dangerous groupthink, conditions the type of questions people ask, and leads to overly facile explanations of political phenomena." Alex Coppock told me, "We should be very worried about political complexion of disciplines . . . but it's a real issue because we are culpable for both political and professional ethics." Gary King said political science has long dealt with political bias affecting its insecure relationship, with government and those worries are spreading to other fields: "We study government and politics; we should think about diversification of viewpoints."

The Trouble with Recognition of Ideological Bias

Although scholars recognize their dominant political perspectives and see some potential for bias, it has not generated the same level of concern as other biases.

Conservatives have complained, but their calls for greater representation have been limited (as have other scholars' appetite for it). There can be no doubt that social scientists are politically unrepresentative. I asked social scientists at major US research universities to identify their partisan and ideological perspectives, using the standard seven-point scale of party identification (asked in two questions) and a matching seven-point ideological scale from left to right. Figure 8.1 illustrates the distributions.

More than 80 percent of social scientists in all disciplines identify as Democrats. The percentage of Republicans range from 8 percent of economists to 1 percent of anthropologists. In fact, more respondents wrote in that they were a form of socialist than identified as Republicans. There was limited variation on the ideological scale. Among anthropologists, 94 percent placed themselves on the left side and less than 1 percent placed themselves on the right side; among economists, it was 68 percent on the left and 13 percent on the right. Almost no one was more conservative than center-right, but many placed themselves on the far left of the scale (including 38 percent of anthropologists and 36 percent of sociologists). The modal category in every discipline except economics was one notch toward the center from the left end of the scale (more economists placed themselves on the center-left). In the American public, there are slightly more Democrats than Republicans, but more people identify as conservatives than liberals (though the public in many other countries is more likely to place themselves on the center-left). Very few members of the American public place themselves far on the left.

This is an extraordinary level of scholar political concentration, given plenty of evidence that partisanship and ideology cloud judgments of facts and evaluations of evidence. Despite widespread critiques of faculty liberalism, the American public (even Republicans) dramatically underestimate the lack of ideological diversity (with 15 percent believing there are more conservatives than liberals and another 20 percent perceiving an even split).[78] Academia is designed to counter individual biases through collective introspection and feed-back, but these levels of ideological and partisan conformity likely make that difficult. Although the patterns may reflect selection into the professorial occu-pation more than discrimination, they may still produce incentives for conser-vative faculty and graduate students to stay quiet about their political views.[79] International surveys have also found values and identifications of the political left to be much more popular with social scientists—with political distributions far more concentrated than for other professions.[80]

Social scientists are somewhat aware about the potential for ideological bias. I asked social scientists to what extent (on a scale from 1–5) the political ideology of researchers influenced the content of research in their discipline. Figure 8.2 illustrates the results. Interestingly, sociology and anthropology are the most

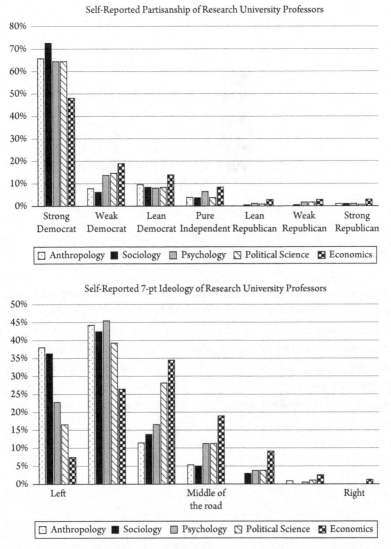

Figure 8.1 Partisanship and Ideological Self-Placement of Social Scientists. Data from the author's 2020 survey of social scientists at major US research universities. n=1,141.

cognizant of ideological bias. They may recognize that they are the most left-wing disciplines, though some respondents may still perceive their disciplines as too far right (a few complained about neoliberal views in their open-ended responses). Overall, the perceived influence of ideology is just below that of race and gender (as reviewed in Chapter 4).

I also asked faculty to assess the extent to which their disciplines are increasingly recognizing the potential for partisan or ideological bias in research (on a

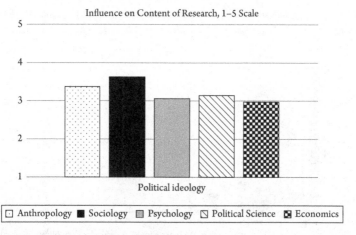

Figure 8.2 Perceptions of Ideological Influence on Research. Data from the author's 2020 survey of social scientists at major US research universities. n=1,141.

1–5 scale from "a lot" to "not at all"). Figure 8.3 illustrates the results. For a comparison, it also includes their assessments of the extent to which their disciplines are recognizing confirmation bias. All disciplines are reportedly recognizing both forms of bias to some degree, though recognition of partisan or ideological bias is just below the midpoint in most disciplines and it is below recognition of confirmation bias in all disciplines except anthropology. These ratings are also well below the recognition of racial and gender biases.

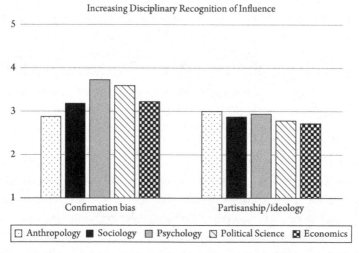

Figure 8.3 Social Scientists' Perceptions of Confirmation and Ideological Bias. Data from the author's 2020 survey of social scientists at major US research universities. n=1,141.

Scholars thus see the potential for research biases related to partisanship and ideology but may not recognize the degree of underrepresentation of conservative views. Even economics, which is perceived to be a right-leaning discipline based on some of its public intellectuals, is only conservative relative to the other social sciences; relative to the public, it is decidedly on the left. The long history of social science shows that these ideological perspectives do not foreclose the possibility of representing the perspectives of conservative interests, such as the American military or business sector. And conservatism in the American public may be an outlier globally, suggesting scholars are (at least slightly) more representative of global publics. But scholars are likely still too quick to see conservative influences and not cognizant enough of the way partisan and liberal ideological views seep into their questions and investigations.

Scientific identity, social norms of collaboration and skepticism, and institutional practices of review can all limit ideological groupthink in social science.[81] But our applied goals may still be limited. As a vocation initially mobilized by reform goals, where does that leave us? Being cognizant and up front about our (normally liberal) goals, including how widely they are shared within the population we inhabit, can be a starting point.

But the level of unrepresentativeness suggests we should also search the conservative scholarship we do have for objectives, such as social cohesion, economic freedom, and shared morality, that might deserve more attention as outcomes. Political unrepresentativeness should give rise to niches for conservative hypotheses or interpretations to further test and develop (analogous to those found by women scholars entering fields dominated by men). Initially discounted conservative-aligned ideas, such as the negative effects of divorce on children or the underwhelming performance of implicit bias measures in predicting behavior, will be more accepted as scholars make recognizable progress working from out-of-the-mainstream viewpoints. Because political science studies multi-sided affairs like elections and policymaking, it has often been able to learn from at least the political efficacy of both sides, even when scholars share only one side's goals. The same is likely true in studies of conservative moral foundations in psychology or conservative social movements in sociology. The danger is not in learning from scholars motivated by goals like remedying economic inequality but in failing to learn from scholars focused on goals like improving stable families. We need both communities checking each other's assumptions.

One concrete step is to support efforts within academia to hear from conservative (or ideologically diverse) scholars, including their challenges but also their research approaches. I am a member of Heterodox Academy (heterodoxacademy. org), an organization of nearly 4,000 academics that provides resources, research, awards, and a community for scholars concerned about ideological diversity.

Participation is concentrated in the social sciences, with active members across the five core social sciences discussed here. The organization has enabled liberals to see some of the concerns that drive other scholars. In my own area of research on party and ideological differences, it has helped minority-viewpoint scholars coalesce around projects to investigate whether prior findings depend on the particular survey question wordings and topics used in previous work (they often do).

The Trump era, including the associated rise of education level as a larger correlate of partisanship, obviously made it more difficult for liberals to find common ground with conservative scholars—or even for conservative scholars to identify with the Trump-led Republicans. Economist David Autor told me, "There's almost no academic influence in the Trump administration. That's not healthy . . . but it's not that economics has changed; the Republicans have." Trump's behavior after losing the 2020 election (justly) further alarmed scholars, who saw the nation's failure to peacefully transfer power as a sign that their critiques of Trumpism were prescient warnings built on firm evidence from other nations and American history, rather than ideological biases.

And many liberals now see racist or sexist views on the American right that they cannot countenance. They also object to attacks on universities associated with conservative scholars, including caricatures of social science research and racial minority student concerns. Part of the aversion, however, may stem from hearing the loudest conservative objectors rather than from the diversity of objectives they bring.

The Niskanen Center (niskanencenter.org), where I am affiliated as a senior fellow and host of the Science of Politics podcast, is another example of an institution making progress on this front. It has become a home for scholars of a libertarian, center-right, or center-left tilt who were alienated by the Trump administration and the state of the Republican Party. It pursues direct policy change but is also open to highly theoretical discussion merging academic and policymaker concerns, giving a hearing to conservative views. Jeffrey Sachs's painstaking efforts to track university speaker disinvitations and faculty firings related to political views responded to conservative complaints but showed them to be overblown, with attacks not concentrated against the right.[82]

Other scholars can make their own decisions about affiliating with political organizations. I suggest only that they acknowledge how their own political goals affect their scholarship, imagine how a community with different policy objectives might approach their research questions, and take advantage of the shrinking remaining political diversity to uncover blind spots in their research areas. Scholars should not have to give up on the social justice or egalitarian goals that drove many of them to scholarship (they were there from the beginning of the social sciences), but they should want to know if different policy goals would produce a different empirical view of what they study. We should not simultaneously argue that race, class, or gender have major effects on our scholarly viewpoints and that our political views and ties are irrelevant. We never fully split from our reformist compulsions, and they still affect how we see the world.

Systematizing Our Limited History and Acknowledging Our Policy Goals

Neither social science's interest in influencing collective decisions nor its inheritance from history are inevitable downsides to systematic investigation. Knowing that both impulses were there from the beginning contextualizes current concerns and our ongoing ties with the discipline of history and the policymaking community. We still aspire to guide decisions based on the limited human collective experience. Like astronomers, we are trying to understand a broader universe from a peculiar place in space and time. But unlike them, we are attempting to realign the stars in our community based on our knowledge. Both that motive and that vantage constrain our objectivity.

Historian Andrew Jewett finds that attacks on science from the left and right have repeatedly re-emerged since World War II and taken surprisingly similar form, often overgeneralizing about the effects of a scientific worldview and ignoring internal scientific self-reflection on limits and values (especially in the social sciences).[83] Critics have long been concerned mostly about technocratic social engineering, supposedly born of modernizing hard science views applied to human life and ignoring the role of values and inequality. But many social scientists share similar concerns and scrutinize the broadest claims, questioning quick knowledge applications absent public debate.[84]

Social science might be able to learn from muckraking journalism, which initially had institutional ties and similar values to our early associations. Journalists have long faced the challenge of staying normatively focused on oversight but "taming the potentially distortive" risks of that effort.[85] Their solution is to work hard to make the pieces of stories fit together while acknowledging trade-offs between uncertainty and actionable information. Social scientists similarly provide information for public decisions but seek information from unbiased investigations. Our tools for doing so are more immense, but the difficulty of constraining our impulses is the same.

We can also learn from our past. As historian Oscar Browning put it, social science "coordinates the most interesting facts of history; it gives method to investigations" that make them interesting to decision makers.[86] In the early days of social science, there was more back and forth between broad social theory, historical reflection, and data analysis than we remember. We are all engaged in a similar effort to tell the human story based on what has come before. Social science never completed its divorce from history or policy, but it developed the resources, methods, and communities to develop independently. We can fulfill multiple roles as long as we remain cognizant of how our political and presentist outlooks both intentionally and unintentionally guide our understanding. Through self-reflection and efforts to diversify goals and practices, social scientists are improving both our scholarship and the potential applications of our lessons.

Motivations of a Practical Orientation

WIRED magazine editor Chris Anderson declared "The End of Theory" in 2008, arguing that "big data" had rendered traditional scientific theory and testing irrelevant.[1] Even for the often-triumphalist magazine, Anderson's claims were quite over the top. Examples like Google's advertising and search algorithms, he claimed, showed that the scientific method was obsolete. With enough data, correlation was enough to assess causation. And near infinite experiments could be run without explaining or predicting their results. The explosion of biological and genetic data was showing that the tools of the technology industry would soon reign in science as well.

The thesis was "deeply wrong," political scientist Gary King told me. There is "no way to eliminate theory because you need a lens" to look at easily downloaded data. We have made progress in one part of the empirical end of science: we have a lot of new measurement tools that allow us to "estimate new things, to gain in one specific area." Indeed, social science still needs models to interpret and generalize data. Anderson's claims were odd even for Google itself, given that its search engine was created by graduate students applying sociological theories of citation networks and its advertising sales market was the product of economists advancing auction theory. Google itself shows that the words we use and the connections we make between them are growing every year; the search engine is forced to evolve with us.[2]

Another home for bluster about big data is the financial industry, which has become increasingly quantitative as it has taken a larger share of the American economy. But after an original burst of theory-light tinkering, contemporary quantitative finance now relies on a lot of PhD-level econometrics as well as knowledge of human cognitive biases. High-profile failures like the crash of Long-Term Capital Management and the mortgage derivative market made financiers cognizant of their dependence on short-term unreflective data and how their interventions often changed the underlying dynamics they were trying to understand.[3] The long-term rise of "quants" in financial markets, including the importation of PhDs, seems likely to continue with revisions.[4]

From racial bias in photo recognition software to gender biases in automated résumé reviews, we are learning that biases in initial training data can be codified by algorithms that supposedly let data speak for themselves. If you rely on pictures that are not representative or try to get software to emulate your prior decisions, computers will do what you ask them to do but will do so based on the letter of the code rather than the spirit of your intentions.

Many errors come from researchers' qualitative wrangling with their initial data, rather than the computer's search for solutions. Since these algorithms drift forward (incorporating their initial steps) and eventually put many of their choices in black boxes, they can hide the biases that we might uncover in traditional data analysis. As data scientist Andrea Joes-Rooy points out, data science projects perpetuate (if they do not uncover) "systematic errors, errors of choosing what to measure, and errors of exclusion."[5] Advances require close looks at the data-generating and data-analyzing processes. The availability of big data makes it more likely that scholars make false discoveries while making basic data literacy more important.[6]

Political scientist Robert Kubinek told me that younger scholars are very open to using large online and text data for both exploratory and descriptive work and for testing critical theories, but they are conscious that it may be "more precisely estimating bias." Although causal inference tools are advancing alongside big data, it is an "awkward marriage." And just like companies rebranding themselves as dot coms (in a previous era) or artificial intelligence plays (in the current era), universities are also "responding to resource availability" by "reframing" themselves as data science specialists to take advantage of the student and commercial interest. Since online platforms enclose users' experiences and measure for internal purposes, however, social science knowledge based on their data makes compromises in representativeness in ways (at least implicitly) directed by the platforms.[7]

Despite the hype and the dangers, there are real gains. And some stem from productive exchange between scholars and real-world appliers of social science knowledge. Many of the industries of today (and tomorrow) are built on social science insights and scholarly tools. Social scientists want our studies to prove useful, both to help institutions carry out their current responsibilities and to transform or replace them to better achieve their aims. Political scientist Adam Berinsky, who has worked directly with technology companies on research, says they are now very interested: "I like talking directly to the platforms for real impact. The 2016 moment, it made them real interested [in issues like misinformation]." And reporters followed: "Now they want to know the research. Reporters are more interested in learning what do we actually know."

And it turns out research is almost always conducted in the context of practical concerns. Social science was divorced from history not for the sake of general knowledge curiosity but to intervene in social life (as Chapter 8 reviewed). In considering our goals, scholars need to account for how our desire to apply knowledge affects how and what we study (what I call application bias in Chapter 1). This chapter reviews social science's desire to change the world in addition to studying it, focusing on the history of our practical goals and their impact.

The social sciences did not develop as pure basic sciences, only to later be transformed for applied pursuits. Instead, practical motivations were there from the beginning—and those aims were not always defensible. Most glaringly, American social science played a central role in promoting eugenics, the racism-inspired view that humankind should direct its reproduction to increase desirable genetic characteristics. That history is important not just for historical accounting, but also for how we should interpret our motivations today. If we can see that the racist impulses of prior generations led to poor research design and misinterpretations of evidence, we can also see how our desires for social change and usefulness influence our conclusions today. Thankfully, scholars are becoming more cognizant of the trade-offs among their applied and scientific goals.

Application Came First

Social science was put to practical use before it became a scholarly pursuit. John Graunt, the seventeenth-century pioneer of demography, produced public health statistics in demographic categories with the aim of comparing social systems. His friend William Petty, one of the first economists, was concerned with critiquing groups that were public charges, influencing fiscal and trade policy, and justifying English action in Ireland. In doing so, they made lots of estimations from limited data and assumptions about cultural group differences and values. They often estimated wildly from London statistics alone, for example, and then assumed its stereotypical differences from elsewhere.

Systematic social statistics were first collected to influence policy and reflected the assumptions and aspirations of their political goals. As historian William Deringer put it, "Britain's new quantitative age was not fashioned by dispassionate scientific practitioners seeking 'objective' knowledge about society or the economy, nor by diligent bureaucrats trying to advance the interests of the state. Rather, political actors of various stripes, from eminent ministers and members of Parliament to hack writers and out-of-work accountants, found that numerical calculation offered an especially useful tool for carrying out political arguments."[8] They were especially important in partisan political debates, with each side investing in expertise.

Government statistics came from core debates over economic policy concerning redistribution, war, and depression. State (referring to government) is the root of the word "statistics," as it initially referred to aggregate information about nations, especially the character of their aggregate social life.[9] But individuals and private organizations preceded government in data collection. Data collection reflected prejudices about social groups as well as attempts to deflect responsibility and compare one's government and society favorably to those in other places.[10] Even "pure" mathematics advanced primarily through attempts to solve particular human problems.[11]

As historian Theodore Porter finds, the broad role of social science in practice continued into the nineteenth and twentieth centuries: "statistics was itself a social science for most of the nineteenth century, and in many ways it was the prototype of empirical, problem-oriented social science. Law, administration, poverty relief, public works, crime, even revolution were all topics of social science, as practiced not just by academics but by officials in treasury ministries or bureaus of labor and trade, by prison superintendents, poor law commissioners, public health officers, and other state bureaucrats, as well as reformers of all kinds. These men and, in growing numbers, women were seen not merely as applying or dabbling in social science, but as practicing it."[12]

Social science helped to institutionalize the idea of public social problems in need of solution through the invention of aggregate social data, such as crime and employment statistics.[13] Statistics were developed and advanced as much through applied social science as through natural science or mathematical questions.[14] Early social science helped to advance war planning, census and bureaucratic administration, and city life, in the process moving quantitative comparisons of value and social categorization to the forefront of public life. That, in turn, made it important to intervene on what was measured and how, which both advanced the science of sampling and made it more likely that measurements would be challenged on criteria of what worked in political disputes.[15]

Philosopher Michel Foucault expanded on these details to claim that social knowledge itself was almost purely constructed by power. The human sciences, he found, did not proceed from an already mapped domain of understanding but from the practical threats of industrialization and revolution.[16] We studied labor, life, and language to intervene to protect and justify the established order, he thought, and thus hid the history of that development. Straightforward reading of early social science certainly suggests it was often dedicated to justifying inequality and the governing order (Petty and Graunt are good examples)—though the early social science tradition also produced Karl Marx.

The institutional development of economics was driven by railroad expansion and repeated economic crises. From the beginning, academics and
regulators were learning the lessons of the prior crisis, which created problems if
the circumstances surrounding them (such as a bank run or a commodity price
drop) changed each time.[17] Early economics also showed that failures of prediction did not necessarily deter additional input: if a new crisis developed, economic thought and models were still needed to address it. Economists shifted
with the times and retained their influence.

Social science in Western Europe remained more politically diverse and
bound by traditional practices of historians, but American social science came
into its own role attached to new social professions and policy reformers.[18]
The first generation of discipline-based social scientists, according to historian Dorothy Ross, were motivated to "reconfirm the traditional principles of
American governance and economy" on the basis of scientific knowledge.[19]
They reacted to the problems of the Gilded Age, including the socialist threat,
but merged apparently timeless principles with American aspirations, hoping to
secure and justify American progress.

Sociologists W. E. B. Du Bois and Max Weber supported the settlement house
movement for social and economic integration, including Jane Addams's work
combining social science with a new profession of social work and public administration.[20] A second generation of sociologists, however, dismissed Addams's
work as a "do-gooder" who failed to live up to objectivity.[21]

Political science developed in the context of public administration in cities. In
1912, only one out of five American Political Science Association members were
professors or teachers; more were lawyers and businessmen seeking practical
work.[22] Political science was able to separate from history because of interest
in public administration, which raised the status of the early discipline.[23] It long
maintained a civic responsibility, but its early subfields of administration, history, and law were eventually replaced by new emphases on methods and international relations.[24] In Scandinavia, its name etymologically implies "knowledge
of the state" (e.g., in Swedish, "statsvetenskap") due to its role in training officials.

As economics separated from applied work, other disciplines arose to fill in
the holes it left. That is part of the back story of why the annual meeting of the
discipline is still called the "Allied Social Science Associations" meeting even
though it is run by the American Economic Association: many focused applied
groups developed, and economists wanted to stay linked to these groups without
compromising its independent scientific aspirations.[25]

All social sciences slowly moved away from application and toward empiricism, but with some discipline-specific trends.[26] Economics was most responsive
to periodic recessions and gained public recognition as its topics expanded to
incorporate growth and social welfare. Sociology always combined empiricism

and application but increased its theoretical ambitions. Political science was the most focused on American national goals but gained preeminence with the rise of survey research on political behavior and broad analyses of political power. Anthropology was more divorced from this history, tied to studies of non-literate communities and natural history in the public mind but increasingly trying to apply its theories to contemporary domestic society. With clinical work, psychology remained the most tied to practice without necessitating a policy focus (though psychology studies were heavily influenced by trends in policy, such as deinstitutionalization).[27]

Social science disciplines gained funding and (temporary) bipartisan legitimacy in the 1960s due to the rise of what historian Alice O'Connor calls the "poverty research industry."[28] That meant a return to its original roots in studies of unemployment, urban life, and labor, but updated with its scientific ambitions and national government support through new departments and think tanks.

Economists have taken the lead in driving policymaking, first convincing policymakers to focus on economic growth and development and only later growing concerned with addressing inequality.[29] Economists changed common policy ideas and arguments on both the ideological left and the right—in both public debates in the media and behind-the-scenes analyses just for policymakers. Even economic ideas that sounded morally questionable to the public, such as valuing human lives, become standards as all sides of debates saw incentives to quantify their preferred costs or benefits and add new considerations to decision-making models.

The popular vision of the scientific approach became more circumscribed. Widespread ideas about the contents of the "scientific method," including the use of that terminology, were developed in popular science writing and via commercial applications, rather than drawing the boundaries for scientific research within universities.[30] The more that science could be broken down into a clear set of followable steps (such as hypotheses, experiment, and confirmation), the more it gained public acceptance, even if real scientific disciplines were messier and contained more diverse sequences. By codifying naturalistic scientific steps, social science sought to lead social improvement.

Psychology gained public status based on its assumed usefulness in personal growth and solutions to public problems. But it has always borrowed from popular concerns: words like "learning," "perception," "depression," and "stress" all entered disciplinary research early with their ordinary meanings and continue to have the highest usage in psychology journals.[31] Psychology history shows that practical applications often came before theoretical and methodological innovation, with basic research later adopting tools from applied work.[32]

That also meant continuing ties to psychiatry. Conceptions of mental illness tracked by the *Diagnostic and Statistical Manual of Mental Disorders* (first introduced in 1952 and updated in 1968, 1980, 1987, 1994, 2000, and 2013) reflected changing cultural and social mores with each new edition—most famously with changes in views of homosexuality.[33] As the practices of psychiatry and therapy evolved during the 1960s and 1970s to focus more on social and family change, psychology became part of a broader evolution of popular culture that tied it more closely to public life with theories of social change that were more consistent with the other social sciences.[34]

Application Today

Health eventually became the central application of science. As federal and private health spending expanded dramatically, it became the dominant source of scientific funding and concern. Health research funding is now ten times greater than general science funding; partially as a result, applications to health have come to dominate research and even basic science prizes.[35] Until the 1980s, most Nobel Prize solicitations were for simplifying through broad theory, but they have increasingly moved toward constructing applications, even in physics and chemistry.[36]

But the medical profession still maintains sovereignty over the application of health ideas. Even with the growth of evidence-based medicine, it has been difficult to stop procedures that are known to be worthless.[37] Medical assumptions and needs also feed back into basic science understanding. Horizontal gene transfer, for example, was long dismissed or minimized as inconsistent with evolutionary theory before its usefulness in understanding antibiotic resistance.[38]

Most ideas about science application still involve a model of stages where ideas move from basic to applied to development research.[39] Social science helped build these models to justify investment in research, not only within economics but also in the anthropology of innovation and the sociology of modernization.[40] But social science lacks a "development" field because its applied work is rarely associated with products for industry. Technology and product development constitute proofs of scientific success in the public mind; credit eludes social science for social technologies, even those in wide use like messaging, surveys, deliberations, trainings, and software.[41] Much of the technological innovation in energy, public health, and transportation, however, comes from gradual, recombinant, and cooperative efforts based on small improvements and work with practitioners, rather than predesigned development sequences.[42] Practitioners can often see recent trends and shifts in acceleration, while social scientists are focused more on stable patterns.[43]

Humans can also react to social science knowledge by changing behavior, especially in policy and widespread practice—and not always to the benefit of social science. "When a measure becomes a target, it ceases to become a good measure," goes Goodhart's Law (as written by Marilyn Strathern).[44] That means once social science identifies a goal, whether it is low poverty or high subjective well-being, the measurement of that goal becomes gameable and politicized, undermining its value. The more we demand that social science provide actionable prescriptions and measurable progress, the less it can objectively describe the social world.

But social scientists still see value in their research having a role in informing public policy. Although less enthused than natural scientists about directly developing products and services, they observe and champion increasing policy-relevant knowledge. My survey asked research university professors to assess whether their disciplines were becoming more or less policy relevant (on a −2 to +2 scale). Figure 9.1 illustrates the results. All disciplines perceive policy relevant research as increasing. This trend is perceived at similar levels to the rise of randomized controlled trials and network data (discussed in Chapter 2), though is reportedly less pronounced than the rise of big data. Compared to other indicators, this measure has lower variation across disciplines.

The question asked respondents to consider the last decade, so it is possible that social scientists would still recognize that their disciplines have a long history of practical research. But the examples scholars gave suggest that they also perceive their recent shifts to policy standing out. Rather than the lists of policy recommendations and arguments that used to form the basis of political science articles in the early twentieth century, for example, today's policy-relevant research includes studies of how policy is implemented in different states, whether existing policies reach their professed goals and have unintended consequences, and whether they feed back positively by helping the politicians who pass them.

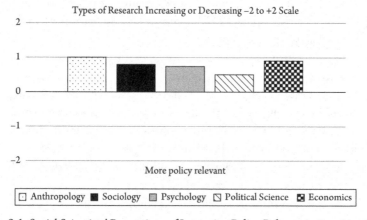

Figure 9.1 Social Scientists' Perceptions of Increasing Policy Relevance. Data from the author's 2020 survey of social scientists at major US research universities. n=1,141.

This policy-relevant research is important for basic social questions, rather than a sidelight, and draws more explicitly from social science expertise and data.

The practical ambitions of social science do not necessarily set it apart from natural and biological science. There are many engineering disciplines that focus on translating science into applications, including some with clear social goals like civil engineering and conservation biology. Disciplines can clearly apply scientific ideas to social goals like bridge construction and maintaining biodiversity without sacrificing their claims to objectivity in conceiving or applying knowledge. But the policy focus of social science, especially without a guiding light beyond social improvement (infused with liberal ideology), deserves more introspection. There is certainly reason from social science history to be skeptical that it can pursue social application without prejudice.

The Lessons of Eugenic History

Social science was central to the eugenics movement, which sought to improve human genetics through promoting reproduction among individuals or groups thought to be superior and limiting it among those judged inferior. It was made virulent by an associated "race science" that sought to order human groups on the basis of their supposed genetic superiority and inferiority. It justified widespread new policies in immigration restriction, forced sterilization, and birth control. It was used to justify traditional social hierarchies and blame the poor for their condition. Before being discredited through its application by the Nazis, eugenics was a broadly popular political and social scientific goal endorsed by everyone from economist John Maynard Keynes to statistician Karl Pearson to sociologist William Graham Sumner. It is only a slight overstatement to say that statistics developed mainly by directing gambling theory toward the pursuit of eugenic goals. Eugenic aims were foundational to many innovations in statistics, and statistical advance was inseparable from the project of understanding and shaping society based on eugenic conceptions of social science.[45]

This history is important because it shows that social scientists, from the beginning, engaged in motivated reasoning based on prejudiced ideas, biased by their topical interests, peer networks, and emotional reactions.[46] It is easy to dismiss as the product of outmoded ideas, but it developed from the same inherent problems of scholars seeing what they wish to believe and seeking social improvement through standardized measures and evidence-based policies. The literatures ignored disconfirming evidence, tied beliefs to political needs, and favored monocausal stories.[47]

Eugenics history does not invalidate the statistical methods invented to assess and achieve its goals or all of the ideas about cultural difference, social hierarchy, and social and political change that were tangentially associated with it, but that does not mean the history should be pushed under the rug. As political scientist Mirya Holman told me, "It's important to know about biases foundational to the discipline to uncover the need to recalibrate [the bases of our own ideas and intended applications]."

Francis Galton, the father of eugenics, was instrumental in the rise of empirical and mathematical social science. He sought to compare across social groups and classes, drawing on both prejudices and available data. He invented the concept of regression to the mean to describe the problems maintaining height and intelligence from one generation to the next. Herbert Spencer, the famous social Darwinist, was also an innovator in social statistics and an originator of sociobiology. He coined the phrase "survival of the fittest" to describe social progression, which influenced popular ideas about biology and sociology.

But eugenics gained particular political ground in the United States from biologist Charles Davenport, who established a record office and the eugenics policy agenda. This entailed collecting a lot of population data, helping to advance social professions and the use of institutional data, writing on the genetics of social behavior, and becoming the progenitor of cost-benefit analysis justifying current spending through future benefits.

Eugenic ideas and data were important in public debates and policymaking, particularly in a nation where centuries of African American and Native American oppression had to be justified. Historian Ibram Kendi, however, has found that racist ideas were often produced in response to racist policies, justifying them afterward rather than emerging beforehand to enable their passage.[48] Economic and cultural interests drove many policies, he says, later attributed to these racist ideas.

Historian Theodore Porter has found that administrative data from insane asylums were important in the development of statistics, social data collection, and genetics. The aims to cure madness and eugenically advance humanity were central to the scientific infrastructure of understanding heredity, rather than a secondary application of evolutionary ideas.[49] We began systematizing institutional data and creating family and social group data to evaluate the success of mental institutions and treatments, innovating in social statistics and arguing over what could be learned despite selection effects, mismeasurement, and biased self-reports. The broader development of public health infrastructure was also built on racist ideas and imagery, including early materials used by the public health workforce and for the public justification of policy.[50]

Philosopher Robert A. Wilson sees the ambitions of social science in this eugenic history.[51] It was science tied to a utopian social movement as well as practical data-informed decision-making. It relied on tabulations of statistics to confirm common beliefs about talent, group differences, and social improvement. Eugenics was also part of a sociological move from individuals and families to broader social groups and an associated change in social scientists' practical ambitions from influencing philanthropic good works to public policy. When social movements are attached to scientific data, seemingly innocuous discussion of human improvement can go off the rails quickly.

Eugenic methods, beyond related statistics and data sources, were key to social science development. Craniometry was common in anthropology, and intelligence testing was central to the development of psychological metrics. Judging people and groups on cognitive ability, in part to rationalize social hierarchies, was always an important motivation for social science. More troubling, the idea that social life could be improved through systematic social data collection and analysis, with science-guided application by social institutions—found primarily in a popular eugenics movement—was central to the rising esteem for social science. If we could improve human society with the same scientific rigor used for agriculture and animal breeding, the thinking went, that justified a large role for social scientists.

This cautionary tale is central to current conflicts over sociobiology. In the long debate over *The Bell Curve*, opponents charged that the authors were merely rehashing eugenic ideas: intelligence largely determines life outcomes and is inherited, different across groups, and largely immutable. Because of this inheritance, scholars favoring nature over nurture explanations for human behavior now take pains to distinguish their ideas from eugenic history, sometimes saying new biological data help discard eugenic views. Geneticist David Reich argues that contemporary genetic data are valuable for disproving discredited ideas: it makes clear that human populations substantially overlap on traits; their diversity does not match popular racial categories, with variation within a group six times greater than the average difference between groups.[52]

But eugenic history should not merely offer a critique of genetics-based social science research. The realization that ideas about racial hierarchy were central to social science institutions and methods does not mean we should just discard those ideas, but also it demonstrates that scholarly ideas often combine popular prejudices with scientific aspirations, especially when intended to inform social improvement. Social science was born of the dual claim that human life could be studied with similar precision as the natural world and that the knowledge learned could be applied to advance society. Since those ambitions are still with us, biases based on the crude popular ideas of our own era and the social aspirations of experts are influencing our studies today. Disclaiming hypotheses shared with eugenicists does not absolve scholars from considering their own overconfident interventions. But today's scholars are more cognizant of this history and less apt to repeat it.

Because scholars widely share the biases of human societies, however, it is difficult to see how our scholarship is constrained by them. Only the latest 5 percent of humans had access to settled life in cities, for example.[53] Populations without settled states had their histories written by those with states, who stigmatized nomadic peoples as barbarians while minimizing their own problems of disease and their dependence on slavery.[54] Non-state peoples we recognize may not even conceive of themselves as groups; tribal names are often just the names of places created by states. The collection of systematic data by the winners was part of the effort to define social difference and herald change. Our analyses may be biased toward cities, governments, and settled agriculture in our historical understanding and ideas about the progressive inevitability of social arrangements.

That makes the history of overturned ideas useful in understanding how our intended applications drove our knowledge. We are hypervigilant for repetitions of eugenics-style movements, but there is reason to be wary not only of their direct descendants but also of the triumphalism that comes from efforts to improve society through science. In applying science to contemporary concerns, we should be wary of ideas that advise simple technological fixes to complex problems or invoke the inevitable progress of new techniques to sidetrack questions of our collective goals.

The Triumphalism of Technology Influence

Today's leading candidate for overclaiming in social science is application in the technology sector. Promoters of social science revolution point to firms like Google, which have run thousands of experiments and made hundreds of business decisions based on them.[55] Google and the marketing departments of large companies like Procter & Gamble employ more people than social science disciplines, philosopher Brian Epstein points out, drawing a broader lesson: "It is only a slight exaggeration to say that the world economy is transforming into a massive system for doing social science. For all our talk of the 'information economy,' the 'knowledge economy,' and the 'technology economy,' a more accurate name for the present epoch is the 'social sciences economy.' "[56]

Historian James Cortada argues that information has become the pillar of American society, the democratic political system, and the capitalist economic system—and that the Internet has accelerated it all.[57] Many people now work in information industries, and many others are tied to those industries and increasingly tied to masses of social data. Contemporary individuals are interconnected with current institutional practices—from social network platform data collection and self-presentation to government reporting and taxation—and, through participation, tacitly morally implicated in their common data collection and analyses.

These are not new worries. Jürgen Habermas argues that the instrumental rationality of bureaucracies and markets in government and industry colonize the scope of practices and attitudes acceptable in everyday life, legitimating a consensus social view and restraining others from appearing in public debate.[58] Technology is changing, but not its ability to direct our collective goals and behaviors well outside of the context where it developed.

As objections to technological advance arise, engineers are adept at promoting technological fixes to social problems, including adjusting to the unintended consequences of their own advances.[59] They often cross into social theory to combine their technological know-how with public promotion of efforts to redesign institutions, from transportation systems to communications networks. These efforts have long involved claims that traditional disciplinary lines (and divisions between science and practice) are obsolete and must give way to a culture of interdisciplinary social engineering. Alongside large anthropological exhibits designed to showcase colonial receipts, for example, the great World's Fairs displayed technological marvels and future socio-technical plans.

Social science has long been tied to these projects, as well as to their broader technocratic principles and governance. It has recognized (and helped regulate and organize) risk for both the problems of society it directly studies and the consequences of natural science technologies.[60] Social science sees itself as addressing the downsides of technological societies by designing better institutions and improving public education.

But corporations have long sold us a sense of the future by claiming to put science into practice. From General Motors to General Electric, public presentations were full of glorified corporate research on automation and scientific advance.[61] Disney built Tomorrowland to imagine the future and Epcot Center to highlight its global scale. But today, the imagineers have moved to Silicon Valley, where they create global tools and platforms, largely on the basis of social data. Corporate science labs help guide research, as it is more difficult to jump from pure science to application.[62] And companies are today willing to hire social scientists (as are governments and universities), with more than half a million individuals now working as social scientists.[63] The Organisation for Economic Co-operation and Development has helped to popularize the role of science and innovation and the information economy in economic growth throughout the world, further expanding the domain of social science applications.[64]

The knowledge sector of the economy has grown from one-quarter to nearly one-half of US gross domestic product. Some professors are now serving as consultants and experts within knowledge economy institutions. Concepts from social science have also become mainstays of corporate life: stakeholders, social capital, communities of practice, self-efficacy, emotional intelligence, implicit bias, coping strategies, and decision biases are all in wide cultural and economic usage.[65] One analysis found that three-quarters of major technological innovations involved academic researchers, with others coming from associated nonprofits. They involved many different universities and lots of federal funding—and some social science.[66] Social network centrality scores, for example, were key to Google's search engine and early patents.[67] And the Internet economy has helped produce a broader shift in social science toward network models, with ideas like diffusion and contagion coming more quickly to the public and academic mind.[68] Social scientists have been instrumental in raising the salience of concepts such as "human capital," including their measurement and use in industry and government, through institutions like the National Bureau of Economic Research.[69]

Firm surveys suggest public research has more of an impact on large firms as well as small start-ups.[70] Many firms report using academic publications and reports, public meetings or conferences, and consulting. Hiring graduate students, forming joint ventures, and using patents or licenses are less common. The rise of technology and finance industries over manufacturing has made social science research more relevant. As other industries like automotive become more dependent on software and algorithms, they also become more concerned with social interaction.

But not all science business applications have been successful. In finance, many academic models failed to work over a long period in the real world, while others created so many imitators that they quickly lost their edge and a few others caused calamities as everyone followed the same (no longer reliable) signals.[71] Drug development has been limited by differences between animal and human tests, long timelines, problems in compliance, strong placebo effects, and differences across social groups. But overall, universities do produce large spillovers into the broader health economy.[72] The public embraces technology only when they see long-term payoffs, however, because they are wary of disruption; even beneficial changes usually require broad acquiescence and legal change, not just new technological tools.[73]

Social science business data applications have also produced mixed results. The story of Google Flu Trends also offers a useful example. It was initially seen as better than Centers for Disease Control (CDC) data at finding local upsurges in flu-like symptoms quickly, but Google did not dedicate employees to long-term upkeep and it became less reliable over time even as the CDC data was corrected to make it better.[74] Users also responded to the availability of the data to make searches unrelated to their symptoms, causing trouble for the algorithm. Applications of quantitative analysis can often advance more quickly than those of other forms of social science research, but qualitative changes and interpretations are still critical for real-world impacts.

When scholars use business data, it also creates new potential biases. Twitter offers a case study: it is easily scraped (automatically converted to data), but not representative of human communication and it often loses meaning outside of its original context.[75] Users are often unaware of all the research uses of their online data, raising ethics concerns; on the other hand, using only public data leads to more unrepresentativeness, as only some types of users control their privacy. Internal corporate data can be better, but access is difficult and can lead to other biases: companies can support research that makes the company look good or helps its bottom line.

Economist Joel Waldfogel has tracked the use of social science in cultural industries and used a lot of data from companies to test social theory.[76] When college students began downloading music from Napster, he found, the music industry produced many poor estimates of how much it was costing them. But as they began to produce better estimates and potentially responsive policies, the industry kept changing to new business models that required new assessments: while downloading became common, singles gained on albums and live performances gained value; eventually, streaming became central. In the end, he finds that the cultural industries lost control to our collective benefit: quality and quantity improved in music, movies, and books.

Legal proceedings have also helped create new expert categories based on social science knowledge, including in the music industry cases. But courts usually try to make new technologies fit into prior categories, wanting to categorize downloadable songs as either home tape recordings or radio plays. And courts may now be subject to a "CSI effect," where people expect DNA evidence or cell phone data because they have seen it on television, even when other evidence is stronger.

Social scientists are increasingly used as witnesses and brief writers. But not everyone is convinced. Chief Justice John Roberts recently rejected what he called "sociological gobbledygook" (actually a political science model) in a Supreme Court case on gerrymandering. In other words, there are problems with giving too much credence to scientific evidence but also times when it is too quickly dismissed by those who do not understand it or see it as unsupportive of their goals.

While it may be overstatement to label a new social science society or economy, contemporary technology does use social science theory, methods, and data. And big technology companies are facing a backlash over privacy and concentrated power, especially over their use of social data. There are also broader concerns that the aspirations of companies like Facebook and Google to change society in their own image may take their influence too far; they are guided mostly by the ethics of what is possible technologically. The tendency to immediately apply social data is familiar in social science history. Scholars can step back to consider whether and when social goals might conflict with corporate or technological aspirations.

Applied social sciences in areas such as education, business, and communication have all seen a backlash to technological determinism and Silicon Valley hype, and they often consider ethics more forthrightly than the core disciplines. By stepping back from application to pursue global empirical knowledge, core disciplines can lose track of the goals that guide them. It is a benefit to be able to broadly consider social welfare and the distribution of gains from technology, but only if we recognize our implicit goals.

I do not mean to normatively compare the advance of social science applications in technology businesses to the eugenics movement that was central to social science development. But letting the possible application of social theory and data drive what we want to learn can have deleterious consequences. And we have erred historically in recognizing what assumptions guide our collection and interpretation of evidence in ways that later seem obvious. In celebrating the role of social science theory and method in enabling tools like social networks and search engines, we should be conscious that their social effects may turn out to be quite mixed. It remains to be seen how much history will repeat itself.

How Social Science Proves Useful

Social science is more important than ever. It is less expensive than natural and biological science, meaning a lot of research can be finished before we collectively decide whether we share researchers' aspirations. And social science, as the study of ourselves, is inherently more political—with fewer effects through direct technological development and more through ideas about how to organize society, especially through public policy. Application biases thus may enhance other researcher biases, such as those tied to our political goals and the dominant ideas of our time period.

When scholars seek to change the world, more of their biases enter into their investigations. That social science has real-world applications should be celebrated—but our ability to enact social interventions no more decides their desirability than nuclear science justifies atomic weapons. Many industries and public concerns of the future will require social science knowledge. That makes both the research and the consideration of its associated goals more critical. Experts often share a vision of society and government while failing to recognize that their consensus reflects their interests and social position.[77]

Social scientists are still often reformers, seeing institutional changes as important for remedying unfairness or recovering democratic values. But scholars can also learn from their evidence. After a long period of studying negativity in campaign advertising and election turnout, for example, they discovered that the relationship was conditional and likely small, by no means topping the list of factors for understanding political participation (even if distasteful). Similarly, campaign finance research has shown less influence on election and policy outcomes than reformers anticipate, suggesting that reformers focus more on parties, media, and voting rules.

Environmental activism has long used science in support of proposals for political action. The evidence has become drastically more politicized as the proposed solutions, especially for climate change, have become larger and more aligned with the ideological left. The good news is that energy technology is advancing so that societies may no longer have to choose between lower consumption or environmental damage; but that will also require changing pessimistic social models of resource depletion.[78] And social science is helping understand policymakers' and publics' aversion to plans to address global warming, assessing interventions to increase public support, comparing alternative policies to intervene, and tracking the results around the world.[79]

The dominant modes and progress of science have long been important in understanding and acting globally. Political scientist Bentley Allan argues that scientific aims have been central to worldwide development and the international order. A period dominated by astronomy and mechanical ideas from 1550 to 1815, he finds, led governments to think in terms of the balance of power. Then a period from 1860 to 1950 influenced by Darwinian views led them to emphasize historical development and change over time. Since 1945, governments have borrowed more from engineering and its model systems. Both the dominant ideas and organizational mechanisms of each era, he says, came from their associated sciences.[80] The historical and statistical sciences enabled the League of Nations and British imperialism alongside the rise of social questions like public health. But then economics, and the systems thinking that rose with it, helped form the backbone of institutions like the World Bank and a focus on technical modernization. Our current era is one of data-driven decision-making, legitimated by the "East Asian miracle" economies, he says, where quantification of social ends has enabled a shared focus on growth.

That world-historical periodization may be too simplistic, but it does show that the ideas of a period matter to how we build institutions and think about the progress of mankind. And the ideas of our own time are largely about social science questions. Our shared aims, like public health and economic growth, can become so ingrained that we may not consider them applications of specific knowledge, including ideas about how and why we produce it. And even those who dismiss social science are often acting based on it. As Keynes famously said, "Practical men who believe themselves to be quite exempt from any intellectual influence, are usually the slaves of some defunct economist. Madmen in authority, who hear voices in the air, are distilling their frenzy from some academic scribbler of a few years back."

While scientists can point the public toward technological inventions, social scientists have more trouble pointing to tangible instantiations of their progress. But inventions may be an overhyped form of progress. Whether based on social or natural science, improvements in energy, public health, and transportation have more often come from accumulated small improvements and commercialization of existing knowledge than from lightbulb moments.[81] Many single inventor stories are myths propagated for branding rather than the true roots of social advance. Translating between practical work and basic knowledge requires balance between overhyped general claims and undertheorized applications.[82]

Social scientists are thinking about their roles in understanding and improving social life. Sociologist Michael Burawoy argues that scholars have to collectively engage in four types of work: professional, policy, public, and critical.[83] They each depend on and complement each other: professional sociology depends on engagement, but is most accountable to peer review, instead of clients, the public, or intellectuals. Social science maintains the civil society connections that it held from the beginning, he says, but its public engagement is globalizing. The critical and professional sides of sociology (and social science generally) can discipline the public and policy aspirations, noting when empirical regularities are translated into suggestions for action and what can go wrong.

It should be a strength of social science application that it tends to require social contestation and collective planning. Rather than being easily patented and applied by a single company, most social science research suggests changes in public policy or social practice that require broader input. That may frustrate social scientists and make it harder for the public to see that our knowledge has applications, but it enables reflection before implementation.

The public-facing role of social science is foundational to the land grant university system pioneered in US research universities. Education professor Stephen Gavazzi and college president Gordon Gee argue that universities still need to act out that model, being relevant to citizens, responding to community needs, and solving problems.[84] But they acknowledge that researchers are not representative of their communities and need practical ties. They recommend a seven-part test for engagement: responsiveness, respect for partners, academic neutrality, accessibility, integration, coordination, and resource partnerships. Although these are reasonable desiderata, the history of social science shows that they are difficult to achieve in unison. We often do not know when our neutrality is compromised and when our partners indirectly adjust our aspirations. Thinking through these trade-offs is important work for social scientists. Because we study social cooperation and collective decision-making, we can help universities consider the implications of their work across the scholarly spectrum. Although university promotional offices tend to feature natural sciences and medicine, universities contribute to society by being a hub of natural and social science activity (alongside the humanities); that continually distinguishes them as places people want to be around.[85]

Social science will be a large part of whether universities can succeed in their goals. And social science research will be central to how the domestic and international systems respond to humanity's changing needs and technological opportunities. Acknowledging our aspirations for social change, which have been with us from the beginning, is an important first step to useful intervention and self-understanding. We should continue to shoot for the moon, but not without noticing how our perspective changes on the way up and on the way down.

10

Popularization and Consilience

Psychologist Steven Pinker brought good news to the world in 2011: violence was in a long-term and global decline while our progress in human rights was continually marching forward.[1] The claims brought significant controversy, which Pinker seems to covet. Critics charged that a central trend, a decline in inter-state war deaths since 1950, was already known, whereas the broader claims were more difficult to establish.[2] Going further back in time, Pinker earned the ire of some anthropologists for seeing war as endemic in prehistory and among non-human primates; but he seemed to be opening the door to more cultural evolution than he had previously countenanced.[3]

Rather than temper his optimism, Pinker followed up with the broader claim that we are achieving ever-greater human enlightenment—not just peace but progress in health, knowledge, prosperity, and happiness.[4] He faced not only continued scrutiny of his data and identified trends, but also complaints from scholars of the enlightenment thinkers he had tried to emulate.

But look beyond the incentives for grandstanding, and the Pinker debates showed the promise of public scholarship. He went well beyond his areas of expertise to bring key global social trends to scholars' attention, gathering evidence across many different time periods and societies. Large claims tend to attract counterexamples that clarify what can be documented and what remains to be debated. He established a broader audience for debates in human history by associating it with fundamental philosophical viewpoints and current political perspectives. And by claiming to overturn a bias toward pervasive pessimism, he also brought forward critiques of his own biases.

When social science becomes part of public debate, many worry that scholars are prioritizing publicity over truth. But popularization also enables interdisciplinary conversations and ties between arcane academic topics and real-world issues. Social science occurs not only in universities and journals, but in popular media and public conversation. That has altered scholars' motivations and changed what they study as they see the implications of their work. This chapter reviews the role of popularization in academic debates, seeing it as sparking academia-wide integrative research. I use the example of sociobiology studies: scholars with different perspectives on humanity have now held a decades-long conversation about the relationship between biology and social development, one I see as progressing from broad unevidenced claims to the potential for an evolutionary consensus. Many scholars like to take shots at the overstepping outsized claims of big thinkers, but the broader debates they spark help scholarship advance.

Popularization

Popularization of social science is nothing new. British social statistics began as weapons in public political debates, developed to be shared broadly to justify political ideas rather than to objectively investigate the social world.[5] *The Economist* newspaper further popularized social science work for policymakers and the public, a role it still serves after 177 years. In the United States, social science influenced urban policy from the beginning. And Woodrow Wilson was an accomplished political scientist and university president before becoming president.

But it was survey research that made social science central to popular culture. Historian Sarah Igo finds that the *Middletown* studies of life in Muncie, Indiana, were influential bestsellers, the early election pollsters George Gallup and Elmo Roper were central to political discourse, and the human sexuality studies of Alfred Kinsey changed our understanding of ourselves.[6] They collectively popularized an idea of the Average American and deviations from it—becoming the standard against which Americans judged themselves. And despite their mixed receptions in traditional social science disciplines, they instilled a broader acquiescence to aggregate statistics and—despite common public dismissiveness—trust in systematic investigations of social life.

Middletown (1929, with a follow-up in 1937) was designed for public consumption, but was also filled with statistics, documentary materials, and many interviews. It attempted both a critique of the American class system and a representative picture of American life. Opinion polling flourished in the 1930s in private, political, and scholarly worlds, gaining first in market research and later in university centers. Kinsey conducted thousands of interviews, but his books (1948 and 1953) were written as catalogs of oddities designed to shock due to their apparent normalcy. Anthropology also became a popular product in the twentieth century, especially with Franz Boas and his student Margaret Mead contributing to contemporary issues with tales of differences in faraway lands, influencing American social movements and popular understanding.[7]

Psychology eventually flourished most with the American public. By the early 1970s, nearly one in six bestsellers were in the self-help category that relied on popular psychology, and it still retains a mass market (at least in a sanitized version).[8] Economics flourished most with policymakers and in news coverage. From references and lectures to magazines and nonfiction books, it gained an elite audience and became the go-to discipline for interpreting social trends and policy debates.[9]

Social science theoretical ideas like social capital, the creative class, and the clash of civilizations also became mainstream terms and areas of public concern. A recent study found that these and other "social science ideas become public ideas when they are used as objects of interest (being the news)" or "are used as interpretants (making sense of the news)," such as books to explain elections or economic trends.[10] But there is no one path to prominence; each example had a different trajectory and distinct receptions within academia and the public. In digestible format, social science remains popular. Malcolm Gladwell's *Talking to Strangers* and Yuval Noah Harari's *Sapiens* were among 2019's top-ten nonfiction books. Then *White Fragility* and *How to Be an Antiracist* made the list in 2020.

These popularized works have often been subject to critique. Many have repeated or emphasized research results that did not survive the replication crisis.[11] The results that sell tend to suggest that life-changing alterations are possible in a few easy steps. Both poor research practices and poor communication of results can leave the public version of research far from the disciplinary version. News about sex, cancer, or money; simple answers to complex problems; and easily quantified metrics make better copy.[12] Neither the scientists nor the reporters and popular commentators seem to have incentives to get their exchanges right—and there are incentives to produce the "theory of everything," to cause controversy, and to tie theories to technologies or schemes for personal gains.[13]

Science studies has focused on a notorious incident from the natural sciences in 1989, when electrochemists claimed to have discovered cold fusion energy.[14] Even then, the boundaries between scientific publication and media communication were breaking down, leading to large claims, backlashes, and competitive science. After two months of chaotic reporting, interest declined before replication failures and government debunking. But it raised concern that any scientific communication—from grant proposals to public talks to textbooks to policy reports—can become fodder for a large public debate with lots of overclaimed results.

Sociologists of knowledge have moved from studying intellectuals as a social type to studying how ideas move into the public sphere.[15] The initial concerns about intellectual radicalization and undefined social roles have been replaced by difficulties in defining academic and public boundaries and creating useful interactions between scholars and the public. A new field of scientific communication has blossomed, especially around climate change, specifically to use social science to advise scientists on public pronouncements about research.

That is a far cry from historian Russell Jacoby's 1987 contention that public intellectuals were an endangered species because academics had become too specialized and radical. Current concerns also differ from those in legal scholar Richard Posner's 2003 update, which bemoaned specialists talking outside of their field replacing broadly read intellectuals.[16] Both might say that the current generation of public social scientists still lacks the punch of literary and philosophical intellectuals. France, where public philosophers supposedly still have cachet, is often the implied comparison case. But given the rise of popular nonfiction and expertise-driven journalism, it is hard to argue that the United States has no public intellectual life—the genre is just inherently open to criticism.

Geographer Jared Diamond, with his books on human evolution, development, and decline—especially the bestseller *Guns, Germs, and Steel*—has attracted notoriety and criticism for his increasingly broad claims about the rise of the West and the impending collapse of human civilization. Although accepted as storytelling and theory-building, his claims have attracted alternative theories and criticism for stepping well beyond the evidence.[17] But the debate has reinvigorated "big history" and interdisciplinary conversations between anthropologists (who see more contingency in the rise and fall of civilizations and a Western bias), economists (who see institutions and political developments mattering more), and political scientists (who found his composite political histories error-prone). The conversations have nevertheless helped develop more nuanced assessments of the role of environmental damage and agricultural pests in human history as well as how scholars see eras of Chinese and Islamic dominance relative to Western history.

Political scientist Daniel Drezner has recently argued that public intellectuals have been replaced by "thought leaders" with dim qualifications and grand theories.[18] Although poor examples of public scholarship are not hard to come by, this is essentially a new version of the perennial trade-off between talking beyond narrow expertise and tackling large and contemporary questions. In an age when scholarly blogs are attached to mainstream news organizations, data journalism and explanatory journalism with plenty of academic references are on the rise, and scholars regularly promote their work in the public sphere and engage criticism, it seems like the same criticisms are still forwarded despite the diversity of new voices. If you want narrow specialists translating their research, there is plenty of that. If you want eclectic broad-read visionaries, that is also an option. Both obviously entail some limits, but the public conversation allows them to interact.

A recent large conversation about the Anthropocene (a name for the current world-historical period of earth that emphasizes its dominance by humans) shows the results. There are dissenters even to the initial claim, arguing that bacteria or bugs are more dominant than humans. But it has also provoked concern that we are undergoing a new large (sixth) extinction event, synthesizing a lot of trends in scientific history.[19] Like human history comparisons, any effort to link five large and different events to a current ongoing transformation is fraught. Evidence on species extinctions is accumulating, but scientists are also investigating how much their awareness and investigations also change over time. Hyped ideas can thus turn out to be quite useful in public debate and in science, as the Anthropocene proposal has already moved research forward across far-flung areas.[20]

The primary concern about the lack of public intellectuals in the older era, that intellectual specialization had choked off analysis from generalist experts reading major newspapers and comparing work across fields, seems less relevant. It is still useful for scholars to read science and social-science-relevant news and commentary and to take advantage of reading in disparate fields to juxtapose and combine ideas.[21] But current media trends are more consistent with a large class of intellectual readers divorced from the less-attentive masses than they are with claims of decline in science or social trend news.

A prominent political scientist told me, "There are a lot more places to get publicly relevant research results out and not just narrowly or instrumentally. Explainer sites and deep interviews with scholars are exciting." Political scientist Kevin Munger said that "Publicity is necessary but risks politicization and makes it easier for actors to change behavior in response to knowledge." That brings back the long-running fear that social science can change society (but it is near the opposite of the fear that we are losing influence).

There remain useful conversations about whether and how journalists should be trained to interpret news, how scholars and university public relations departments should promote their work, and how far scholars should tread outside their areas of expertise. An experiment with press offices at universities, journals, and funders found that news claims and headlines about studies could be better aligned with their evidence (with more caution and caveats) by making narrower claims in press releases—without reducing press interest in the research.[22] But social science journalism is also improving and public intellectuals are abundant. Economist David Autor told me, "The media does create some shortcutting of the referee process. But economics journalism is much better. . . . A lot of us have learned from them how to present data." And that has helped the discipline: "For a long time economics was seen as aloof and haughty, but it is now more seen as connected to journalism and detective work."

The science that reporters cover also influences the studies that are conducted and promoted. Professors, like others, are attracted to fame and public influence. Because their reputations are tied to respect as well as notoriety, however, the desire for coverage does not usually overwhelm other motives.[23] In economics, this produced a "Freakonomics phase" sparked by the popularity Steven Levitt gained around his series of books applying economic analysis to fun topics such as drug dealing, in collaboration with journalist Stephen Dubner.[24] Autor told me this produced "a blip of research on cute topics [that often did not hold up] but that's calmed down a lot."

Reporters select which research trends the public hears about. Political scientist Tara Slough told me there are "problems translating the best research to the media conversation and getting results too early," such as the lack of coverage of null results. On the plus side, she says, media coverage of early results helps get reactions from stakeholders. A psychologist was more optimistic that reforms in research will translate into better popularized scholarship: "There is a much greater awareness of the limitations of the inferences that can be made from a single study and, I hope, a greater humility about the scope and robustness about one's findings. This may restrain impulses to make large, publicity-seeking claims." Meta-scientific studies and public data are enabling more credible debunking of misleading popularized science, but the public's goal of using scientific findings for self-help or self-justification makes dislodging claims more difficult.[25]

Social scientists have mixed feelings about the popular discussion of research. In my survey of US research university faculty, I asked professors to evaluate the quality of research discussion in several different popular spheres: Twitter, Facebook, mainstream news stories, op-eds and opinion journalism, scholarly blogs, podcasts, radio and television interviews, and "TED-style" public talks. Figure 10.1 illustrates the results, with each measured on a 1–5 scale from poor to excellent.

The average discipline rated blogs (3.5) and podcasts (3.2) the highest and Facebook (2) the lowest, though most platforms were rated just below the median. There was not much differentiation by discipline, though economics was surprisingly negative about blogs (where it is quite prominent). Scholarly led discussion in the public sphere was generally rated more positively than news, though podcasts were the only format to receive high ratings in each discipline.

One political scientist is more optimistic about involving the public in discussion: "The availability of the human experience to everyone via social media has turned everyone into a social scientist of sorts (either contributing observations, theory, analysis, etc.). This is exciting as it makes our research important and interesting to a larger part of the public. This is good for civic education, for us as researchers, and for the public at large. The death of gatekeeping is good." Although public misinformation is difficult to correct, effective messages are possible. A meta-analysis found that immediate and coherent corrections from ideologically matched and trusted sources can reduce misinformation.[26]

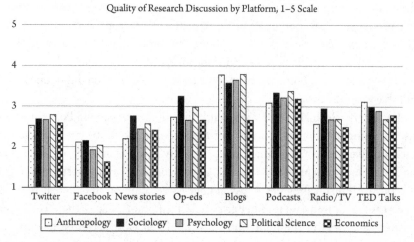

Figure 10.1 Social Scientists' Views of Popular Discussion Platforms. Data from the author's 2020 survey of social scientists at major US research universities. n=1,141.

There are also efforts to improve the public discussion of social science. The nonprofit Scholars Strategy Network (of which I am a member) has built a large community of social scientists seeking to provide evidence for public policy discussion. It generates substantial media interest in research and has also gained a voice with policymakers. Each member is asked to provide a memo that is used to promote research for reporters and policymakers. Local chapters have been active in training researchers how to prepare information for journalists and policymakers. Not only is media coverage a potential route to policy influence, but also it serves as a training ground for researchers to translate their research for real-world concerns.

How Popular Discussion Feeds Back In

Popularized social science also provides an opportunity for large interdisciplinary debates that involve more stakeholders. One strand of science and technology studies has called for a broadening of scientific participation or a democratization of science through public engagement or even "citizen science." Indeed, the public offers an interdisciplinary audience that may not defer as much to established theories and authorities, forcing scholars to justify their approaches.

Popular psychology, for example, drew from interest in academic work but also from suspicion of psychiatry, including its emphasis on pharmaceutical treatments and its increasingly social diagnoses of personal problems.[27] Studies that aligned with journalistic accounts of mistreatment, even if conducted poorly and without sourcing, gained more credence.[28] Popular psychology retains tendencies to look for get-rich-quick personal improvement schemes, but popularization has also served to review the rise of new diagnoses and the evidence base for homeopathic approaches. And not all efforts have been failures: many of the main precepts of cognitive behavioral therapy, the main evidence-based therapy, have been incorporated in bestsellers and effectively communicated to mass audiences.

Intelligence testing has not always lent itself to productive public discussion. Some popular accounts argue that intelligence determines life circumstances, with national differences in intelligence even said to explain good governance and economic growth across countries.[29] Others argue that any talk of intelligence is inherently eugenicist and bound to perpetuate inequality.[30] This makes even standard reporting of intelligence testing research seem untoward, while leading scholars question the motives of otherwise prosaic research.

Open science reforms were also driven by a large public debate. Although reformers were skeptical of several high-profile public pronouncements, they also organized to publicly question them, spread knowledge of problems in replication, and organize a community to address it.[31] Psychologist Robert Nozek told me, "We are getting better at having public debates." There were "jerks in all directions initially," he said, but "we're realizing [replication] is an ordinary part of science [and we can] engage productively."

Scholars view popularized research as both a threat and an opportunity. Political scientist Amanda Friesen told me, "We do have sensationalized findings and it's hard to explain nuance, but social science blogs and Twitter help bring concerns together [regarding] publicized work. And it's good for scholars to [have to] explain [their work] to general audiences." She sees problems with small-sample psychology studies being overpromoted, but she has also reached out to psychologists with relevant findings, enlarging and diversifying her research network.

Political scientist Mirya Holman cited The Monkey Cage, a political science blog hosted by the *Washington Post* (where I have also contributed regularly). It has made scholars "value thinking about how to communicate broadly," she said. She has gotten useful feedback from public scholarship and believes it may be helping scholars communicate better in journals as well. Indeed, the blog has expanded into the main forum for public discussion in the discipline, with hundreds of contributors. It provides scholars with regular entrées into current events discussions and enlivens debate among scholars and with practitioners and reporters.

It is part of a renaissance of "smart" journalism that draws more from social science research to reach a more educated general audience, including "explainer" sites like Vox.com (where I previously contributed to a blog) and "data journalism" sites like FiveThirtyEight.com (where I am now a paid contributor). Traditional op-ed pages have also made increasing efforts to reach scholars. Many universities have bought into an effort called The Conversation, which publishes scholarly commentary that can then be republished in traditional media outlets.

Social scientists have been quite active in sharing research publicly. They constitute nearly half of the scientists on Twitter, even though they are only 21 percent of the scientific workforce.[32] But the active social media universe still does not represent a majority of social scientists. Approximately 30 percent of political science faculty at doctoral universities are on Twitter, with American parties and elections and development and policy the most well-represented fields.[33]

Political scientist Cyrus Samii told me the "Twitter network is more diverse in geography, discipline, and institution," but he cited the "downside is the addictive quality and fragmented attention." More academics get to have a voice, but conversations do not always cumulate toward research clarification or productivity. Political scientist Jessica Preece said, "Academic twitter has helped on a practical level, opening the water cooler conversations. . . . You . . . see people care about ideas . . . [and are] able to see conversations in motion."

Popular Nonfiction

The university press book market, though small in typical sales, has continued to serve a vital role in scholarship. Political scientist Kevin Munger told me that "books are an example of quantitative/qualitative [divides] softening." Although social science books can now include plenty of previously rare quantitative models and figures, they are still a place for "big think" integrated scholarship. Even mostly quantitative researchers tend to pepper their books with examples, aiming for a broader audience than with a journal article. Munger says, "The object itself influences research," becoming a marker of interest and shifts in scholarly focus.

University presses, under strain to gain revenues, are expanding their marketing and promotion. Social media and specialized online media like podcasts and blogs have enabled broader coverage and online ordering, and e-books allow scholarly books that would not make it to traditional bookstores to be sold into global but specialized markets. In the process, books that might have been marketed in only one subfield or discipline are now more widely known to others studying related topics from other disciplinary perspectives.

But academic arguments are not left only for academic books. There has been an explosion of trade nonfiction books tackling research topics, including social science. The nonfiction market has grown bigger than fiction overall, including more academic authors.[34] Researchers can now promote their books across disciplines and to interested subsets of the general public, including large audiences for science, economics, politics, history, sociology, the environment, and psychology. The books, in turn, are widely discussed in popular media— making journalism responsive to scholarly debates and calling on more scholars for interpretation in book reviews and commentary. Popular books are increasingly emphasizing creativity, including working out ideas through incubation of new models as well as ideas for verification.[35] Science has long taken cues from literature and storytelling in its ideation; long-form writing is the primary opportunity for breakthrough ideas to spread from home disciplines to wider audiences.

Think Tanks

Another venue for academic influence in popular debate is think tanks. Long influential in military contracting, organizations known by that label expanded dramatically from the 1960s to the 1980s, becoming more media savvy and political in orientation.[36] Conservative upstarts like the Heritage Foundation joined staid regulars like the Brookings Institution, in the process making the field more recognized for hybrid research products like policy briefs and transition manuals.

Academics had long joined Washington institutions as (temporary, resident, or affiliated nonresident) scholars to add intellectual heft to their products. But conservatives began to see them as alternatives to (liberal) academia, a place to make broad policy-relevant arguments and to be influential even if dismissed by university-based researchers.[37] Sociologist Steven Medvetz finds that conservative scholarship filtered through these institutions, from the "broken windows" approach to policing to arguments against social welfare policy, influenced thinkers on the left and right.[38]

Today, they still open space to bring scholarship to policy discussions, but they also bring academic work into a polarized political climate. In the best circumstances, this might allow research products to respond to readers who do not share their political predispositions. But it also means scholarship can be produced for political impact, often to the detriment of full exploration.

Interdisciplinarity in Popular Debate

Public scholarship should be a step toward consilience, with evidence from different fields converging toward a consensus explanation. But public scholars tend to bring strong views that the consensus should move in their direction.

Sociobiologist Edward O. Wilson, who promoted that goal, believed that it would lead to more biologically informed social explanations.[39]

Consilience is useful in principle, though the social sciences should have a strong role in collective judgment. And scholars can inform public debate without necessitating a move toward scientific unity. Unless staged in interdisciplinary conferences, scholars looking at the same questions from different disciplines and levels of analysis often do not talk enough to each other to clarify their differences.[40] Battles over framing in popular media often take place only after a set of questions gains notoriety, forcing fields to interact (and ideally confront their assumptions).

Thomas Piketty's bestseller *Capital in the 21st Century* and his broader work on inequality have helped to popularize measures of the top 1 percent share of income and wealth, especially by incorporating history, sociology, and political science alongside economics. But it also allowed counterevidence to accumulate, with alternative historical timelines suggesting a less pronounced inequality increase and different specifications implying a wealth effect specific to housing. Without the initial popular claim, it is doubtful that these data would have been picked through as much or that alternative theories would have accumulated as fast. Many debates about the limits of growth, including the roles of technology, trade, and inequality, are likewise based on interpretations of unexplained changes in productivity, with publicly contested assumptions of data comparability.[41]

Psychologist Jay Van Bavel told me there are trade-offs with public interdisciplinary scholarship, but they often self-remedy: "All disciplines have blind spots and come at it from their training. When you go into a new field, you miss core citations and have a superficial understanding of key concepts. Social media and the web make it easier to find related information for the open-minded. [But we are] more public facing than ever and get more credit and feedback from sharing."

The Good and Bad in Sociobiology

The most controversial arena of public social science debate has been over the extent to which social science can be reduced to biology. There is, of course, a long history of debates over naturalism within philosophy and science, but the contemporary manifestation was marked by Wilson's *Sociobiology: The New Synthesis* in 1975. Yet Wilson has changed his tune somewhat: he is unhappy with the constant focus on science, technology, engineering, and math disciplines and believes everyone overreacted to his initial claims; he now sees himself as a pluralist for influence from multiple fields.[42]

Wilson's intervention came from research on social animals like ants and bees. In decades of research on the potential for group (rather than individual) natural selection, evolutionary biologists had found many ways that apparently groupish behavior, such as coalitions, inter-group conflict, regulation and outlaw policing, and coordination, reflected individual-level mechanisms such as kin selection.[43] This debate was long conducted in the shadow of assumed human differentiation: if social practices could be a product of individual natural selection, human behavioral differences were likely to be overestimated. Wilson saw analogous behavior in many social animals, helping to explain the individual-level mechanisms that created them, but eventually sided with those who saw the possibility of group selection in humans and other animals. Group selection remains unpopular with biologists, but the proliferation of definitions means scholars are often talking past one another; efforts to analogize from eusocial animals have had mixed success.[44]

Evolutionary theory, however, has transformed through the understanding of nonstandard mechanisms: shared developmental paths leading to convergence across species, plasticity leading to unselected differences across lineages, nongenetic inheritance through care and environment choice, horizontal gene transmission, coevolution of multiple species, epigenetic inheritance, and niche construction with environmental development.[45] Some biologists see these as small updates to traditional evolution, while others see them as grounds for a new synthesis.[46]

In parallel, social scientists (especially anthropologists) had been developing theories of gene-culture coevolution, arguing that humans' shared records of experience, ability to teach over generations, and cultural records helped create much wider human groups for coordination. These processes might not rely on group genetic selection, but instead on cultural themes developing and stabilizing within human societies. This has reignited debates over how much humans stand out from other species, with findings of similar social traits but no comparable package. In human behavioral ecology and related fields, social scientists investigate human variation as a product of development, reproduction, mate selection, and parental caregiving in different environments based on models of social interaction. In paleoanthropology, researchers look at the biological development of modern humans and their closest relatives. Anthropologists and geneticists also continue to study the trajectory of specific human populations, from ancient to recent, sometimes finding particular historical breaks (like those based on invasions or disease). The accelerating rise of ancient genome research has quickly confirmed the complexity of human social history, but not been able to escape traditional problems of generalizability and causal inference.[47]

The popular discussion can be somewhat divorced from trends within social science disciplines. Recall (from Chapter 3) that scholars in every discipline that

I surveyed are more likely to see a decline in nature-versus-nurture conflict than an increase. That may be because trends are not moving as readily as sometimes assumed. I asked social scientists at major research universities in what direction research was moving in their disciplines (on a scale of –2 to +2): toward genetic determinants of human behavior or toward social determinants. Figure 10.2 illustrates the results. There is almost no perceived change, with slightly genetic moves in psychology and slightly social moves in all other disciplines. In fact, the modal answer in every discipline was no change. Anthropologists were the most likely to see a strong social move (16 percent) and psychologists were most likely to see a strong genetic move (5 percent), but those were still small minorities.

Sociobiologists may say that this represents the blinders of social scientists unopen to new tools and findings. But given that they perceive both less conflict and no strong moves in their fields, it seems more likely that social scientists just do not perceive the prophesied revolution. Instead, they may see the same recycled criticisms of social science and the same examples of biological influence, without necessarily seeing the findings as transformative.

Despite the diversity and nuance of updated views, popularized sociobiology debates are still often based on straw men and exaggerated claims of evidence. Anthropologist Pascal Boyer recently claimed that social scientists had made little progress because they had not borrowed from natural science.[48] But he acknowledged focusing on social questions most likely to reflect biological bases, such as sex differences and conflict, and focusing on their similarities across time and space (rather than the continuing differences less likely to be explained by biology). His reviews of far-flung literatures, such as those on racial

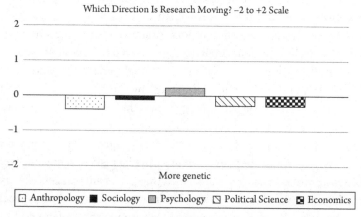

Figure 10.2 Assessments of the Direction of Research toward Genetic or Social Determinants. Data from the author's 2020 survey of social scientists at major US research universities. n=1,141.

bias and ideological differences, ignored the specificities of the countries and time periods they sought to study in favor of just-so stories based mainly on game theory. Although there are still social scientists who deny some universal ingrained human behaviors, there is also a sociobiological tendency to argue that they are all you need to explain very particular outcomes. For example, it is not enough to know that humans form in-groups to understand American racial segregation (which has changed over time and area as a product of policy, economics, sociology, and culture), but the same simple model (which does not explain these differences and predicts near-absolute segregation) is repeatedly raised.

Sociologist Nicholas Christakis similarly recently argued that social scientists deny cultural universals, arguing that more could be explained by biology.[49] But he again selected cases on the dependent variable, acknowledging that he was focusing on a human universal social suite of identity, love, friendship, cooperation, solidarity, dominance, learning, and social networks. If you seek to ignore all human variation and thus define concepts as generally as possible, you will certainly advantage less social or developmental explanations. Christakis does allow more mechanisms of cultural transmission than Boyer, especially through the selection of teaching and learning behavior. But he also gravitates toward explanations involving human universals in explaining contemporary phenomena.

Similar patterns are evident in some neuroscience. Kevin Mitchell argues that biological explanations are winning the war in social sciences, but he frames the counterargument as belief that social behaviors have no basis in genetics or neurosciences.[50] He repeatedly discusses human capacities and tendencies as encoded programs, but notes the failures to directly map simple biological processes for human differences such as personality traits. Contemporary genetic analyses with genome-wide association tests, he accurately summarizes, typically find many different parts of the genome linked to phenotypic outcomes, such as educational attainment, with both ultra-rare and common variants contributing. But even the most successful mappings explain a minority of social outcomes, usually within countries or even racial groups and always within the same time period. Education is a simple example of the limits of the biological approach, since it is obvious that national and (especially) time period effects (such as more schools) explain more variation, with attainment rising substantially over time alongside opportunity.

Philosophers who review sociobiology debates, such as Alex Rosenberg, tend to cleanly separate the biological and social explanations and see attempts to analogize biological and cultural change as fraught.[51] Since popularized sociobiological accounts have titles like *Blueprint* and *Innate*, it is not surprising that social scientists and commentators see strong assumptions. Neanderthal research, for example, has repeatedly faced difficulty divorcing moral ideas about human exceptionalism from empirical claims, but findings of interacting small differences are nonetheless accumulating against expectations that one key difference will explain human uniqueness.[52]

Popularized books on human distinctiveness tend to emphasize a few factors to explain relative human success. This can sometimes lead back to twists on craniometry. Psychologist Suzana Herculano-Houzel argues that human brains are seven times too large for our bodies compared to average, but do not stand out enough to explain differences—instead pointing to our oversized cerebral cortex as allowing neuron density.[53] But anthropologist Richard Wrangham argues that humans saw a 10–15 percent reduction in our brain size due to being self-domesticated (along with other signs like narrow faces, small teeth, and a feminization of male skulls and skeletons).[54] Comparing human hunter-gatherers and non-human primates, he finds more cajoling, ostracism, ridicule, and separation, arguing that human groups achieved domestication of alpha males. Social scientists should not rule out either of these hypotheses based on distaste for biological explanations, but there is a danger in conceiving each theory of human development as a new theory of everything for social science. There are many contributors to human universals and differences.

Economist Garrett Jones even argues that intelligence differentiates societies, with higher-productivity human groups able to save and cooperate more, build markets and technology, and imitate the best approaches.[55] It is not surprising that critics' ire is raised by the continuing tendency of these popular sociobiological approaches to indiscriminately come back to brain size and intelligence.

But that also gives critics of sociobiology an opening to argue against the most extreme examples. Biologist Kevin Laland argues that human cultural evolution is evidence in favor of the extended evolutionary synthesis (including multi-level selection, transgenerational epigenetic inheritance, niche construction, evolvability, evolutionary developmental biology, and molecular genetics).[56] Human culture, he theorizes, created coevolutionary feedbacks because the scale of required cooperation was much larger. Humans' abilities to teach and communicate have much broader scope. Their behavioral diversity is high, even though genetic diversity is low. Humans have uniquely had a cumulative culture of wide scope, with improving educational technologies. Indeed, no one trait present in humans and absent in other animals can explain our superior cognitive performance; humans are flexible all-around cognitive athletes, with interactions and reinforcement of our skills across cognitive domains.[57]

Psychologist Cecilia Heyes similarly argues that cultural evolution is based on social learning.[58] Humans refined and created varied versions of what other animals have, she says, enabling cultural development. She says language is just one aspect of cognitive functional tools humans developed, such as causal understanding and social learning. She gives the useful examples of reading and fishing, which both required educational transmission and were shaped over generations and did not occur simultaneously across human societies.

Anthropologists Clive Gamble, John Gowlett, and Robin Dunbar also focus on human differences derived from large-scale social life.[59] They find an increasingly social brain from primates up to great apes, hominins, humans, and modern humans, with social group size increasing with brain size. They acknowledge that current understanding is limited by the fossil record: archeologists cannot find fossilized friendship. But they identify a social turn even in archeology, with its traditional focus on food and materials expanded with speculation. They point to intentionality as a human difference, alongside self-awareness, a theory of mind, beliefs about others' beliefs, connections to ancestors, seeing real and imaginary worlds, and engaging in complex symbolism.

Biologist Mark Moffett argues that overlapping social identifications are unique to humans, with society mergers, slavery, and economic trading unheard of in other animals. Humans developed larger social scales, he argues, eventually creating states with provincial capitals and administrations.[60]

These big-think popular books, as should be clear by now, are often speculative. But popular culture may be the only place to have such wide interdisciplinary conversations. Animal behaviorists have also been active, arguing that whales and many other species have cultures involving social sharing and group communication that differ across geographic areas based on cultural learning.[61] The behavioral models we use for other animals tend to emphasize their bodies over their brains, but we are equally susceptible to seeing the world through our bodily strengths and limitations.[62] Working through the details tends to show fewer findings at odds and more disagreement on the relative importance of different factors in human differences from other species.

Biologist Joseph Henrich finds that humans are no better at cognitive tasks and worse at mixed-strategy strategic games than chimps, but we are better at social learning and we copy behavior often (sometimes to a fault).[63] Rather than produce causal models of the world, we evolve cultural understandings and then rationalize our behavior afterward with simplified models. Cultural evolution can then shape the biology of our brain and hormones in areas like reading or in domains like the placebo effect in health care. For hundreds of thousands of years, human evolution has been more driven by these cultural changes, such as the use of fire and language. And eventually these cultural changes cumulated to enable complex social entities such as laws and courts.

Psychologist Michael Tomasello has produced one of the best recent syntheses of research on how humans are different that shows the value of broad interdisciplinary learning.[64] It is a developmental psychology approach using ape-child and cross-cultural comparisons, revealing that human children up to age seven uniquely develop shared intentionality for cooperation, cultural learning, prosociality, norms, and morality (as brains are maturing and children are more dependent on adults than in other species). This enables cultural groups to develop and change over time, with early caregiving enabling later self-monitoring. Comparing chimps and bonobos with human children shows humans' unique ability to share agency, see from different perspectives, and pursue pragmatic joint action and communication. Across cultures, humans develop unique senses of fairness as part of group mindedness and manage others' impressions of them. Humans develop the ability to differentiate subjective and objective conditions and to coordinate perspectives through emotion sharing, iconic representation, gestures, and role playing. They give reasons for their actions in terms of cultural norms, which they then enforce. They treat resource distribution games as an issue of being treated with respect, meaning they do not conform to expectations of economic games as well as chimps.

Geneticist Adam Rutherford has also translated human evolutionary theories and findings for popular audiences, without overselling their usefulness in replacing social science.[65] He argues that biology's pillars of universal genetics, cell theory, metabolism, and evolution enable progressively improved knowledge, but that humans did change dramatically through recent cultural change (despite interbreeding and similarity with other hominins). Separating cultural evolution as a separate domain is unhelpful, he argues, but socio-cultural factors certainly matter for the cognitive revolution in human behavior (that he dates to 45,000 years ago) and are important in human developments like weapons, fashion, painting, and tools.

Popular sociobiology, when it is not overstated in its application, can be useful for social scientists. Evolutionary views were built from popularized scholarship from the beginning. Charles Darwin was inspired by Alexander von Humboldt's naturalism and travel writing and drew from Humboldt's efforts to bring together disparate elements of existing knowledge, not only to develop and test new ideas.[66] We will nonetheless continue to face controversial findings, especially in genetics, but that is part of our shared project to understand humanity. As David Reich puts it, "We geneticists may be the barbarians coming late to the study of the human past, but it is always a bad idea to ignore barbarians."[67] Especially when seeking to understand universal human tendencies or important differences like those based on sex, it is unhelpful to ignore relevant biological research. Anthropology is the social science central to these debates. We need both its improvements in biological knowledge of humans (and related species) and its understanding of cultural evolution.

But I am less persuaded that most social scientists are ignorant of codified knowledge that will replace their dominant explanations. To use an analogy, sociobiology is only rarely central to art history: true, all painting involves the same underlying physical processes and archetypal human expressions, but that is not typically useful for explaining changes in art in a particular nation over a short time scale. The same is true for most human sciences, especially when it comes to our interests in specific recent events. Where biological data are relevant and growing, in areas like fertility, addiction, and educational attainment, they are quickly being incorporated into social science, though usually with small effects and lots of gene-environment interactions.[68] In using new genetic data and methods, social scientists are also increasing their reach into biological disciplines like medicine that increasingly recognize social determinants of biological outcomes.[69]

Sociologist Aaron Panofsky, who studied the interdisciplinary rise of behavioral genetics (the use of genetic data to analyze psychological and social outcomes), finds that it has been regularly mired in political debates (especially over race and homosexuality), making it a more popularized field, at the cost of internal diversity and connections with non-human animal research.[70] Sociobiologists sometimes see evidence from heritability estimates in twin studies as slam-dunk cases for the biological basis of human behavior. Almost no matter the trait, they tend to show some heritability, small effects of shared environment, and significant variation explained by neither (even oddly showing higher heritability estimates than animal studies with controlled environments). But these estimates allocate variance within the population studied, usually the residents of one country at a particular time. As Panofsky says, the measure is "always local"; it is "linked to a specific group of individuals, with a particular distribution of genotypes experiencing a particular range of environments."[71]

Psychologist Paige Harden argues that does little to undermine the project. Genetic influences on social life stem from combining many small and conditional factors, but polygenic scores are useful for assessing both genetic and environmental factors and how they change by national and temporal context.[72] Lay estimates of genetic influence mostly match heritability estimates from twin studies, but social scientists and the public still contemplate much more direct influences than the evidence finds. Analogies to social variables are instructive: a composite individual-level variable like socioeconomic status also likely combines many small influences that are dependent on context. An aggregate variable like inequality is likewise also a snapshot that compresses many stable and dynamic factors.

Even strongly genetic traits like height can be accounted for by genetic differences within a population, but still vary greatly across societies and over time due to circumstances like food availability and public health.[73] When it comes to estimating complex social outcomes like educational attainment, the point is even more obvious: while genetics are associated with the outcome within countries in a particular generation, the broad patterns across time and country are attributable to the opportunities made available to students. Improvements in GWAS studies and epigenetic arrays (with markers of actual gene expression) are helping to identify particular genetic pathways, but the results have also been less transformative than originally suspected. Sociobiologists are always predicting a biological revolution in social science, while even applied fields open to natural science such as medicine, business, education, and policy seem to be moving more toward social determinants and environmental interactions.

Less triumphalism could also serve research well. Research on genetic determinants in political science and psychology both went through unproductive "candidate gene" phases, where many studies made claims of large effects of single mutations that were later discredited. Economist Daniel Benjamin told me economists never went through that phase, instead emphasizing small effects on outcomes already of interest, and they are now prepared to incorporate more as data expands exponentially. But we should expect modest results even with large increases in data. As Panofsky quotes one behavioral geneticist, "The impact of genetics on the overall undertaking of behavioral science has been and will be less than everybody thought it was going to be. And that in fact is what happens when the traditional problems in psychology meet a new technology, it's not that the technology transforms the old problems into new science, it's that the complexity of the problems transforms the technology into social science of the old kind."[74]

Contemporary societies have repeatedly faced new biological understanding in arenas like policy and courtrooms, not without incident but without complete reinvention. From neuroimaging and DNA testing to new ideas about insanity or the influence of addiction, we have accepted new tools and evidence but also noticed their limits.[75] Neuroimaging experts did not want to use their tools for diagnosis, but they found that people gave undue deference to their products.[76] Social scientists are similarly acknowledging the potential gains, but wary that biological explanations will be privileged beyond their scope of evidence.

Political scientist Scott Page told me he sees a softening in these debates: "Fewer people are saying it will change everything," but some sociobiology ideas are integrated and "inescapable." Sociologist Aaron Parofsky told me he sees "convergence on both sides." Behavioral genetics' "center of gravity is now complicated mixtures of nature and nurture and sophistication about what genetics does." Social science genomics has meanwhile moved from "fragmented islands" to an "integrative project."

Political scientist Amanda Friesen also sees softening, based on the limits of biological methods: "There is now more of a sense of what we have already done; we're still learning from twin studies but adding lots of new methods. . . . There is some narrowing of theory and it's all gene-environment interaction and developmental and longitudinal." The "candidate gene" era of understanding human differences was largely a dead end, but we have quickly moved on. Since the same transformations were present in other applications like medicine, it should not be taken as a permanent roadblock to biologically informed social science.

I am also an optimist on the field. As a nonexpert, I have hardly done justice to research on human evolution or biological determinants of human behavior. But as someone who reads widely in the field both for recreation and for potential insights for contemporary social science, I have benefited from a flourishing conversation that is advancing over time. It is accessible for application by nonexperts like me because it is in the wider public domain, written by authors who are also looking to make an impact across fields. I have tried to give a flavor of that literature as the most prominent example of a controversial and yet cumulative example of public scholarship.

When these authors try to apply their knowledge to issues where I do have expertise, such as understanding interest group or electoral politics in the United States, I of course find the insights rather limited. I expect the same is true of researchers working on socioeconomic inequality or contemporary family life, but I do not think any of us should discount the possibility that human universals from our evolutionary inheritance are parts of any of these puzzles. Hearing the broad claims in public debate is the way for specialists to find the most relevant pieces but push back against the broadest unevidenced claims.

The Popular Conversation and the Advance of Research

Social science research is now a major part of the public conversation. Social scientists are directly employed by media companies and train the data and explanatory journalists of the future. Quotes and analysis from economists, psychologists, sociologists, and political scientists are more prevalent in recent years in the *New York Times* and in popular books.[77] The educational attainment of the public is growing, producing a larger audience of nonfiction readers able to follow social science debates. Social scientists debate both public social issues and interdisciplinary scholarly controversies in the public eye and with public attention. Nonacademic public intellectuals such as newspaper columnists and television commentators now regularly seek to integrate social science research and are asked to produce more evidence for their claims or respond to others' evidence.

This has changed scholarly incentives as well as public knowledge, sometimes leading researchers to privilege TED Talks and influential op-eds over credible research. But it has also opened an interdisciplinary conversation, increasing the diversity of researchers addressing similar questions and aware of the alternative viewpoints. Popular writers like Steven Pinker may still be able to shape news coverage with his own incomplete readings of scholarly literature, but he will face pushback from other scholars and be asked to reconcile opposing evidence. Scholars can now comment immediately on others' forays into popular debate and insert themselves when they have evidence to share.

As with increasing policy relevance, social scientists have to be wary of the biases that popular criteria bring back into research. The public often wants easy answers to complex problems and tires of nuance. But scholars aware of the trade-offs can enlarge their disciplinary conversations. From tracking the decline of violence to understanding the differences between humans and other animals, social scientists are tackling big questions and benefiting from the public eye.

11

Reasons for Cautious Optimism

Economist Raj Chetty has developed quite a partnership in public data-driven scholarship with the *New York Times*. His work on social mobility—from neighborhood effects to racial and gender inequality to the role of colleges—has been transformed into localizable (and clickworthy) content with detailed maps.[1] As popularized, open, and big data, it reflects several of the positive trends discussed in this book. It takes advantage of new access to useful and precise information from tax authorities. It has helped begin discussion across disciplines and the public sphere about myriad issues from education policy to family structure. It enables specialists to propose new explanations for findings in particular geographies or aspects of social life.

The primary downside might be overhype: readers may accept easy causal narratives or see the outcomes as permanent aspects of geographic areas or social groups. The findings are instead specific to one nation, one data source on life outcomes, and one time period. Understanding social mobility requires complicated research on diverse topics like human capital, political capture, assortative mating, and segregation, all integrated in comparable models.[2] But even from the vantage of a few decades ago, it is amazing that these data on economic outcomes across generations and the country are available alongside evidence of many related factors. We can learn that inequality and social mobility are related, that racial composition still matters independently of income, and that mobility is still low for most children. And note that the progress Chetty has enabled came mainly from descriptive data, not methodological wizardry.

These data are open to challenge and distinct interpretations within the social science community. Analyses framed as evidence of Black children's wealth disadvantages, for example, might more accurately be seen as indices of dynastic wealth among whites.[3] Descriptive analyses of racial differences might seem to imply joint responsibility, rather than discrimination and privilege. With public data and analysis helping to build fields and stimulate policy efforts, we can gain by combining our greater access to information with an acknowledgment of our biases in asking questions, collecting data, and interpreting results.

As exemplified by these data, social science is well situated to improve. There has been a wide increase in data collection and availability on social life coinciding with an expanded academic sphere now better connected to the real world. Theoretical innovation, with more humility than in prior generations, and methodological pluralism, with new tools and more scrutiny of old ones, are both on the upswing. And it could not come at a better time. Humanity will need to address collective problems such as climate change and infectious disease and has the opportunity to alleviate poverty and accelerate our improved well-being.

This chapter ends with the grounds for optimism, but not ignorance of the difficulties. Though scholars are on a collective search for truth, they face numerous individual and social biases that systematically thwart their efforts. The impulses to reform and diversify social science have proved fruitful, but collective understanding of our predicament and attention to our biases will work in tandem with any changes in our composition and our procedures. In our shared project, descriptive inferences of generalized patterns, causal inferences about relationships (local and global), and qualitative explorations of new or idiosyncratic observations will all be necessary. While noting the potential harms of assuming we have finally solved the puzzle of self-understanding, scholars should commemorate how far we have come.

Efforts to condense large scholarly literatures cannot do justice to their intricacies and are inevitably colored by the biases of the summarizer. But the quickening growth of both social research and meta-scientific studies relevant to its advance means synthesized lessons are still needed. By distilling researcher biases, I have shown that social science is a difficult enterprise that advances through self-reflection. By evaluating reforms, I have highlighted paths forward but tempered claims of universal methodological solutions. By tracking science critics, I have tried to find a middle ground in the shared project to confront but minimize bias in the pursuit of truth. In uplifting diversification, even instantiated in increased me-search, I have argued that our efforts to address demographic biases can serve as a positive example.

Where social science biases remain, I have surveyed the landscape for practical lessons and toned down depressing claims about science. American university institutions face some turmoil, but they have long managed to muddle through with diverse goals; they remain a good home for a slowly globalizing social science. The basic social science disciplines each offer useful tools and exciting terrain and are interacting more productively, rather than remaining caricatured silos. Endemic battles over the global and eternal scope of research claims are giving way to both an acknowledgment of the scope conditions of our research and an openness to causal forces emanating from many levels of analysis and time scales. Social science's incomplete divorce from history and social reform leave us open to learning from each, but also cognizant of the presentist and progressive biases of our practical goals. Our increasingly public conversation leaves us open to poor incentives, but also enables integrated knowledge.

This book has catalogued research biases and assessed efforts to confront them—from methodological reforms to increasing diversity. It has argued that metascientific research from philosophy, history, STS, and higher education all have lessons for our pursuits, but that these fields are more open to the pluralist evidence in contemporary social science than it might seem from their critiques. It has repeatedly found that acknowledgment of related biases is better than a faux objectivity. I have seen social science as unrepresentative in its disciplinary concerns, its primary domain in American research universities, its social group identifications, and its political goals. But in each case, I have noted signs of progress. We are innovating not only in method and data collection, but in understanding how our community and our practices collectively shape our view of the globe. Although divisions remain within social science, I have found surprising alignment in understanding our biases and committing to address them. Others have noticed many of the same positive trends in social science. There are systematic reasons to be hopeful.

Reasons for Optimism

As Adrian Currie articulates, there is more reason to be optimistic about accumulating knowledge than about finding the one big theory or earth-shattering discovery.[4] The most straightforward reason, he points out, is that our "epistemic resources" are growing: we have better techniques, better data, and improved capacities. Because pronouncements of optimism are sometimes misread as broader than needed, he articulates several versions. The clearest evidence is for a general trend toward increasing knowledge over time. But there are also reasons to bet on scientists, who now have more resources, to better understand their particular areas and even broaden the context to which their findings apply. It is likely too much, he says, to bet that we will learn everything of interest or even that we will be able to articulate the specific reasons why some things will remain unknowable. But that bar seems a lot higher than most expect from social science.

There are also reasons to bet on improved human understanding. Intelligence is increasing globally; the largest increases recorded by intelligence tests are for creative abstract tasks similar to those pursued by scientists.[5] We are more connected and better able to compare across knowledge categories and epistemic communities. Most scientists are also optimistic about the future of science.[6] Their concerns are about the institutions in which they work and compete, rather than our ability to generate knowledge—where they see continued upside.

Overconfidence is a threat, but so is unwarranted pessimism. People are naturally attentive to negative information. It usually takes hearing four good things to overcome one bad thing in our evaluations.[7] Our pessimism usually comes from overpromising results and setting expectations too high. And contemporary therapy tries to help people tone down their negativity bias and reset those expectations. Perhaps we should do the same.

Economist Tyler Cowen and software entrepreneur Patrick Collison have recently called for a new "science of progress" to correct our negative predispositions and understand how human societies have made tremendous gains in recent history.[8] Although these economic, social, and health gains are studied across many disciplines, organizing scholarship (and funding) around them might stimulate new insights, they say, pointing to the success of climate science as an interdisciplinary field. More research with a new frame is likely to be productive. But a better precedent might be positive psychology, which attempted to correct for psychology's focus on correcting mental health problems by understanding happiness. That did lead to important findings, but it also produced some unreplicated scholarship and popular misinformation, possibly related to its organization of science around accentuating good news and easily implemented strategies.

There is some reason to be wary of too much optimism. Because people have seen past improvements, there is an assumed progression in scientific work. People think more recent published findings are better, for example, even if there is no indication that they have moved closer to the truth.[9] The idea of progress is especially firm in the American mind, where linear narratives from a disowned past to an imagined future are common.[10] But finding areas of subjectivity and pervasive uncertainty is not enough reason to doubt the scientific project, even as it is applied to human self-understanding. Nearly all worries, including those about the biases of social science, can be articulated as slippery slopes from one reasonable concern to a fundamental roadblock. But close monitoring and occasional intervention are usually enough to stop a moving ball, even on a slippery slope.

Recent unexpected events, from the financial crisis to Trump's election, have shown that social scientists were too dependent on single categories of models with strong assumptions. But that is less an argument for abandoning theory than for working from multiple perspectives: models remain useful for articulating analogies and imagining alternative realities.[11] And even unexpected events provide new data that drive new research to fill in the full picture of social life. We now know more about recessions than we did in 2008 and more about voting and elections than in 2016.

These perspectives were widely shared by the researchers I spoke with. Political scientist Arthur Lupia told me, "Now we can have the conversation and be able to question our process. It is a form of service with increasing diversity and rigor. We now know the potential for greater uncertainty." It is "easier than ever to question science," he told me, but social scientists should be able to point out difficulties without discarding knowledge generation.

There is also a shared sense that methods are improving. Political scientist Alex Coppock told me, "We have great tools." We're "not returning to the bad old days of regression and interpretivist stories." His goal is to further educate people on the "properties of their designs," having co-invented simulations to help them do so. Psychologist Jay Van Bavel told me, "Past work was flimsier than we thought and now we're more skeptical, but that's progress in science. It is better than letting zombie ideas go uncontested with no forums for pointing them out. It now feels better and easier to admit the need to adapt."

Political scientist Christina Wolbrecht sees "new opportunities for scholars to study and communicate." "Social science is hard but slow," she says, seeing particular value in the progress toward diversification: "we have moved from critiques of underrepresentation to real findings [missed by previous scholars]." But Neil Malhotra told me to watch out for inevitable remaining inequalities, especially those between institutions. "You feel it as a journal editor, your goal can't be to correct it, but it is plausible that requests for more statistical power and bigger designs will increase inequalities." But he sees it as "part of rising thresholds of good science" and sees some promise in "shared datasets with equalized access."

Explosion of Data

The clearest reason to be optimistic is the growth of data, broadly conceived. As biologist Stuart Firestein points out, "Advances in measurement techniques almost always precede important new discoveries."[12] Scholars have to be able to see the world to effectively analyze it. The rise of data stretches beyond science: increased availability of information has generated new uses and industries, further stimulating collections of descriptions and numeric data.[13] Economic expansion, especially in finance and services, and the growth of computers and information technology have spread the collection and analysis of data—from charts and graphs on desktops to advanced data analytics.[14]

This includes biological data. The costs of producing genome-wide data have dropped even faster than expected, quickly enabling new discoveries.[15] Improved dating technologies and new finds from language to archeology have linked with this data to provide a better picture of human history.[16] We have reached a data-driven era, critics and celebrants agree.[17]

But we have also seen that "big data" is hardly a panacea. It is only as good as its source, and numerous errors can come from just putting it in usable form. Often, the same discoveries could have been made with basic descriptive data that do not bring the associated fanfare. More data means we need more and better interpretive models.[18] It does not allow us to dispense with the hard work of measurement and interpretation in social science.

Yet economist David Autor told me the big picture is that "the quality of evidence is so much better," and that this coincides with studies that are "so much broader and more creative." Adam Berinsky agreed: "We can do so much more. The kind of stuff I can run in a week is so much richer [than what used to take much longer]. The opportunity to do research is so much greater." Political scientist Gary King told me that all the new data have "empowered us to do large-scale policy evaluation and invention," generating more interest from government and industry. But social scientists still lack access to most private sector and government data, often creating trade-offs between broader use and protecting company and agency interests.

Neil Malhotra sees a danger that the "descriptive approach might be being crowded out" by the twin gains in machine learning and causal inference. It may "undermine gains" from "the hard work of data collection" if researchers settle for subpar but available data, such as information from social media posts instead of internal communication. Mirya Holman agrees: "It would be better if we were more open to descriptive work. . . . We need long-term progress on data [building] because [collection is still a] messy process."

But as political scientist Justin Grimmer reported, "The dismissal of description is ironic because much of the empirical work of political scientists and theories that they construct are a direct product of description."[19] Indeed, creating and describing measures is a core habit of effective social scientists that leads to large citation counts and prestige. As a result, he notes, data science is coming to resemble social science: "the big data revolution also is a recognition that the problems addressed by quantitative social scientists—measuring quantities of interest from noisy data and inferring causal effects—are abundant."[20]

Social outcomes and relationships are difficult to describe, much less explain. Given the space of theoretical possibilities, describing distributions and relationships alone can narrow the scope of possible explanations, improve prediction, and raise new questions. Recognizing our limits and compiling what we know represent an important advance, even if our claims to knowledge are more constricted than before.

Expansion of Academia and the World of Ideas

The rise in social science is part of a long-term broadening of research in the information age. Increasing human interconnectedness and information exchange has long been central to large-scale change, including the takeoff of population and economic growth.[21] Then as humanity published ever more books, kept more records, and eventually stored more data over the course of the twentieth century, educational attainment rose quickly. Research and development became mainstays in the public and private sectors. Social science degrees and professors expanded along with the rising public and corporate salience of research.[22] Just since 2002, the world's professional scientists have grown from 5 million to 8 million; 90 percent of scientists of all time are still alive today.[23]

But the expansion has not meant easy solutions to old puzzles. Whereas scientific article production has grown exponentially, the unique topics and ideas used in them have grown linearly (at least as measured by the phrases used in them).[24] It is now possible to investigate global history and differences, but the accumulation of knowledge in all directions makes integration difficult—and we retain many of the same disagreements.[25] But humanity has faced similar challenges before. The expanded scale of human life and the difficulties of integration have been central to major revolutions in human behavior. Each time we expanded our population and our degree of interconnectedness, we learned and applied new knowledge even as we faced new conflicts.[26]

And everyday citizens are also now interested in participating in scientific work and debate. The expansion of preprint servers and commenting systems has made knowledge transfer faster and easier, though the take-up and usage differ by field.[27] The social sciences, which still have more disagreement and less quick consensus on innovation, still rely on the imprimatur of journals and older gatekeepers in conferring credibility. Like the natural sciences, we thus have more data and more analysts; but unlike them, we still rely on relatively crude processes for codifying and building on new findings. Yet scholars are now more integrated in a wider field of knowledge generation and an interdisciplinary contest of ideas stretching across research and practice.

Methodological Innovation

Among the most important sources of consensus in the development of knowledge is methodological advance. While maintaining diversity in method, scholars should acknowledge gains from new approaches, especially in quantitative domains where past errors can be corrected and new measures and tests invented. Shared communication via mathematics has been central to the faster development of science in some areas, due to the growth of research technologies.[28]

Even proponents of traditional models and methods have found it hard to keep up with the proliferation of new tools—but there is no doubt the toolbox is growing. From descriptive advances like multilevel regression with

post-stratification (for creating local estimates from aggregate data) and automated text analysis (for inferring dimensions of differences across texts),
we are now better able to assess difficult-to-measure variation. From natural
experiments to the full suite of quasi-experimental approaches to causal inference, we are also able to assess associations, orders, and causes. Steady methodological progress has been critical to social science's move away from attractive
but under-evidenced theories like psychoanalysis and Marxism.[29]

There may be inherent limits to our ability to understand human history
and variation, but perhaps they are less dramatic than feared. Ancient DNA
researchers see a million-year limit to preservation, but quite a lot of ground
can be covered with already available tools.[30] We cannot observe every human
action, but we are now gaining access to very detailed chronologies, as well as
opinion, administrative, and behavioral data that fill in a lot of previous holes.
With new methods advancing alongside new data, we have a lot of potential.

Social Scientists' Views

I also asked social scientists at major US research universities for their views
on what makes them most optimistic about the future of research in their
disciplines. Table 11.1 lists the most popular answers to these open-ended
questions among the thirty-seven different answers given. Thirty percent of
respondents listed nothing; among those that did, we coded an average of two
answers. Approximately one-third of all answers concerned the topic content
of research and another one-third touted the methods; 17 percent cited people
in the discipline (mostly the top answer, referencing young people); 12 percent
cited institutions; and only 4 percent cited external audiences.

The most popular answers covered the topics reviewed in this book. Scholars
are especially optimistic about the new generation of researchers, including
their graduate students. A political scientist cited "the creativity and ambition of
emerging scholars, as well as the speed with which new studies are developed."
Another said, "I am really encouraged by the attitude of my younger colleagues
at both my own institution and beyond. They are interested in political science
because they want to make the world a better place—they are clear-eyed but
not opportunistic or cynical." A psychologist cited "the younger generation and
their openness to new methods and new ways of doing science."

Younger researchers were often mentioned in conjunction with other factors,
such as the use of new methods or sources or increased diversity. An anthropologist said, "There seems to be a generational shift in faculty within universities,
and changes will lead to more diverse training, inclusivity of voices, and richness
of publications challenging accepted theories and practices." A political scientist

Table 11.1 **Social Scientists' Reasons for Optimism**

New generation of scholars	146
More data or sources	97
Reproducibility reform	88
New methods & analyses	81
Interdisciplinarity	80
Methodological pluralism	80
Improved methods/rigor	78
Diversity & breadth of topics	71
Addresses real-world problems	68
Diversity of people	65
Important questions	55
More public discussion	46
Better training	45
More critical of society	41
More empirical	30
Theoretical pluralism	29
Humility/revising old knowledge	23
Larger/better samples	23
More experiments/causal inference	21
Uncovering/addressing biases	20
Recognizing limits of causal inference	19
Increase in favored topics	18

Data from the author's 2020 survey of social scientists at major US research universities. n=1,141.

said, "As incoming cohorts of graduate students and assistant professors grow in diversity (across dimensions such as age, life experience, gender, race, nationality, religion, etc.), diversity of thought will follow. Our discipline will grow as contributions from multiple perspectives bring new theories, critiques, and methods to the fore." A sociologist cited "a mega talented generation of junior and mid-career scholars who are less hung up on artificial debates (e.g., quantitative vs. qualitative) and more interested in advancing the discipline as a science with important stakes in political questions." A political scientist cited "some great young scholars coming up who defy trends, cross discipline boundaries,

[and] engage important theoretical issues. Also, some who are deeply engaged with our real-world problems." A psychologist cited "a new generation of graduate students and junior scholars who are bringing new perspectives and lived experiences into the field and rethinking traditional approaches to long-standing questions and posing new lines of inquiry."

Many social scientists made references to diversity and pluralism, including of data sources, methods, disciplines, people, and topics. A sociologist cited the discipline's "openness about method. I like being in a discipline with scholars doing causal inference, ethnography, and archival research. Ideally, this would help us to generate more complete explanations." A political scientist said, "I believe that the discipline is becoming increasingly representative of the public, though it has a long way to go. I expect this will improve the quality of discussion and the relevance of our research questions."

There were also many references to better methods, including reproducible research with new and better training. A psychologist said, "I think the open science movement has brought a lot of good reforms. I also think 'big data' has expanded our ability to ask new and interesting questions." Another cited "sincere and widespread efforts to improve research practices." Another psychologist also saw progress: "Psychology underwent very rapid and systematic reforms in the face of the replication crisis. Practices have improved dramatically, and most grad students today take these reforms for granted, so they will be even more widespread among upcoming researchers." An economist cited "availability of good quality data for many years and countries. More access to data used in published research so that replication is possible." Another economist cited "the rise of empirical research. This emphasis has improved standards of empirical work and brought very productive attention to providing data for verification, replication, and revelation of methodology. The quality of work and expectations of scientific clarity in empirical research have greatly improved over the past decade and more." A sociologist listed "technological advances providing new avenues for more rigor in data collection and analysis [and] increasing recognition of the value of multiple methodological approaches."

Many scholars were also optimistic about addressing real-world problems and important questions, even in public. A political scientist said, "We're seeing a renaissance of communicating our findings to the public." Another agreed: "Political scientists are becoming much more effective at communicating our research to a broader audience and being connected to policy debates. There are some risks in these trends (i.e., great politicization of research), but on the whole I think it is positive." A sociologist said, "More departments are open to research that has 'real world' implications," noting they previously had to hide those interests.

Several answers combined the benefits. One scholar said, "The quality of training has improved. The discipline is better oriented around good research designs. It is much easier to get good data on the cheap. And many scholars are interested in promoting their work to the general public." A political scientist said, "Access to research findings has improved to such a degree that we are building specialized scholarly communities that span boundaries that were previously difficult to bridge, across geography, disciplines, and types of institutions." Another listed a "well-trained rising generation of scholars addressing good research questions with a range of appropriate methodologies; their collegiality and willingness to collaborate; their diversity re: race, gender, and nationality."

One economist tied many of the gains to reform: "It's becoming more transparent, with publicly posted data and code required for publication (to the greatest extent possible). Statistical methods are also getting better, as are data sources. There is reduced reliance on simplified models and existing models now have added complexity. The field is slowly diversifying, which leads to better research as researchers often study areas that relate to their personal experiences but would have otherwise been missed."

A psychologist cited data availability and its important implications: "With the advent of Big Data and access to large, diverse samples through the internet, psychology research will become more representative and more generalizable." A sociologist pointed to both inevitable increases in research opportunities and an improved interdisciplinary orientation: "My optimism is based on the huge growth in availability of no-cost data for analysis; the enormous increase in the availability of free and low-cost software for data analysis; the ever-increasing power, and ever-decreasing cost, of computing; and the ever-increasing awareness by economists that they are a social science discipline addressing questions of human behavior that have occupied sociology, social psychology and psychology for a century."

An anthropologist also saw more integration and awareness of bias: "Increasing attention to self-critical analysis and bias. Increasing interdisciplinarity. Decrease in 'theory wars' that were tearing departments apart." A psychologist saw methods improving along with awareness: "Increases in interdisciplinarity that contribute to different perspectives and methods, keen awareness of representativeness (and limits of that) in samples, and attention to specific samples with greater cultural awareness/competence."

An economist was optimistic about how discussions of diversity have improved the discipline, citing "the recent discussion within the profession about the continued underrepresentation of women, and [minority] racial and ethnic groups, and a willingness to see that this absence affects and colors the questions the profession asks as well as the answers it gets."

An anthropologist pointed to many increases in methodological awareness and rigor: "More heightened awareness of the importance of systematic research design and implementation, whether in qualitative or quantitative modes of research. Initiatives to continue the methodological training of PhDs and to extend the training available to graduate students in various techniques, for instance, the quantification of qualitative data and in more rigorous techniques in analyzing data collected from interviews, conversations, etc. Also, integration and triangulation of GIS and geographical methods in ethnographic research in which matters related to space and place are germane."

An economist pointed to better theoretical and empirical integration: "Continued dialogue between empirical researchers exploring new sources of data and theoretical researchers finding frameworks to interpret that data, with empiricists keeping theorists grounded in reality and theorists preventing empiricists from chasing pure noise, at least in some fields of Economics."

A sociologist summed up the end of methods disputes: "The increasing interest in multiple data sources and diverse theoretical frameworks. Instead of relying on our old bread-and-butter of individual-level surveys, sociologists are, more than ever, thinking about how new sources of data (both quantitative and qualitatively) might be used to ask new questions or better answer old ones. As a younger researcher, I also note how many in my cohort (broadly construed) do not care for the old quantitative/qualitative divides and instead 'use the right tool for the right job.'"

A political scientist was optimistic about both the people and their methods: "The field is getting bigger and bigger, people have more and better access to data and methods training, and the theory development and testing seems as vibrant as it has been; if not more so." A psychologist made a similar summary: "Our diversifying methods, theories, interests, and corpus of scholars, both substantively and in terms of representation across meaningful identities." In short, there is a lot to be optimistic about, including most of the trends identified in this book.

Reasons for Pessimism

To be fair, I also asked social scientists what made them most pessimistic about the future of research in their discipline. Table 11.2 lists the most popular answers out of a total of forty-eight different answers we coded. Funding worries dominated, but there were many critiques. Twenty-seven percent of respondents listed nothing; among those that did, the average respondent was coded as giving two answers. Many more people listed factors related to external audiences as negatives than positives (they constituted 12 percent of negative answers, three times as many as positive); these comments often mentioned the political environment, public attitudes toward expertise, or public discussion. Institutional factors, constituting 32 percent of answers, were also mentioned

Table 11.2 **Social Scientists' Reasons for Pessimism**

Low/decreased funding or grants	103
Too much focus on causal inference	58
Too narrow in topics/questions	56
Low standards/lack of rigor	55
Subfield division/fragmentation	54
Left bias/activism/political correctness	54
Negative public image/decline of expertise	52
Politicization/political environment	51
Inequality within discipline	51
Too quantitative/too little substance	47
Resistant to change	46
Decline of universities/administration	46
Decline of theory/too empirical	44
Too methods-driven/convenient questions	43
Biases of researchers	41
Poor public discussion/social media	38
P-hacking/replication crisis	37
Poor training	34
Too little applied/irrelevance	33
Publication pressures	33
Lack of jobs	32
Poor incentive structure	30

Data from the author's 2020 survey of social scientists at major US research universities. n=1,141.

three times as often as negatives than positives. In addition to funding concerns, these included subfield fragmentation, inequality in the discipline, and university administration. This is somewhat surprising given that the survey targeted scholars at the most well-resourced universities. But even they perceive pressures on institutional resources. Concerns related to research topics (23 percent) and research methods (26 percent) were mentioned less often as negatives than positives (though still constituting nearly half of the answers). Compared to the distribution of positives, less than half as many negative citations concerned people (with the most frequent concern being their resistance to change). Social scientists like their fellow scholars, but not their institutional constraints.

Funding concerns, comprising pressures to get grants, declining university support for their disciplines, and lack of federal and state support, topped the list of negatives by a long shot. No other reason was listed by more than 5 percent of respondents, with answers widely distributed across many other concerns. A psychologist combined worries about funding and inequality: "The incentive structure within psychology (and academia in general) often hurts labs with less funding or junior researchers. While there's a push to change the field (open access, preregistration, preprints), I worry many of the changes may still hurt these same groups." Another psychologist agreed: "As the demands for larger sample sizes increase, there will be consolidation of psychologists at large state institutions who can provide these resources. Programs at smaller private institutions will no longer be viable." A political scientist also cited inequalities: "The continued reinforcement of status hierarchies in training, hiring, publishing, promotion, and professional accolades; the uneven (across subfields) efforts to address implicit and explicit biases and their effects."

Another political scientist pointed out that open science reforms may exacerbate inequalities: "The fact that many solution[s] will harm scholars from less-prominent institutions because of their relative lack of resources. If a grad student from a non-Ivy preregisters and doesn't find the 'right' results, then they will be in deep trouble." Another cited general methodological requirements for increasing funding fears: "Much modern research work tends to be highly resource-intensive, exacerbating resource disparities between scholars at places with deep pockets versus others; declining grant funding will only make this worse." A psychologist also cited expensive methods trends: "Seems increasingly 'trendy' whenever a new technology comes along . . . and those technologies tend to be expensive, effectively reducing the number and variety of research projects that can be funded."

Many of the secondary concerns illustrated remaining conflicts within social science. Some professors thought there was too much emphasis on experiments and causal inference identification, others thought lack of rigor or low standards was the problem, and still others pointed to the narrowness of topics. Recall that other respondents had voiced each of these same points as a positive about the future of research in their field. Similarly, some researchers cited activism as a problem whereas others had seen it as a positive.

On one side, researchers feared method-driven research. A political scientist cited "narrowing of the field around methods-driven micro-level research questions, with less attention to macro-level substantive political importance of research questions." Another political scientist concurred: "The trade-off with a good research design is that sometimes the scope conditions are severe (the treatment effect is highly local). And sometimes too much research seems engaged in fairly narrow questions rather than speaking to broad and relevant topics." Another reported that "the current obsession with causality is leading to a lot of plodding, a-theoretical research about uninteresting issues, and it is currently too often rewarded. We are not teaching our students nearly enough social theory and too many graduates are idiot savants who are technically really good and yet totally incapable of interesting theorizing." And still another cited "prioritization of quasi-experimental methods and [experimental] approximation as 'standard' for useful research, leading to a lot of effort looking for randomness explaining isolable variable relationships rather than understanding situated actors in context or important cases/broader trends." A similar comment noted, "The increasing focus on causal identification and experimental methods leads many more researchers to study problems that are tractable but of relatively little broad significance for politics, raising the possibility that we will lack understanding of issues that cannot be studied experimentally."

An economist cited the same potential trade-off between causal work and important work: "The focus on causality can be a bit of a double-edged sword. It sometimes pushes us to choose topics based on data quality or availability of natural experiments, which can lead to well-estimated results of little consequence or generalizability. And it makes it harder to publish work that takes on big questions in, necessarily, a less quasi-experimental way." But other complaints about methods focused less on causal inference. A sociologist said, "I am most pessimistic about what feels like a bloat of new research that is not particularly advancing scholarship more than an inch per article. . . . I see the high growth of quantitative research to have allowed a burgeoning group of articles (often using surveys) that are not particularly innovative, creative, or even have much bearing on theory. My sense is that the rise in quantitative work is a double-edged sword."

A psychologist combined resource and methods concerns: "There is a money bias and an 'excitement' bias that both work against improving the field. It can be tough to get large samples and to conduct many studies without enough funding, but decisions about hiring and [tenure] are primarily based on number of pubs. Thus, for people with little startup funds or whose work is not as exciting to funders, it is hard to get enough and good enough data to crank out publications. This is part of what creates a fundamental disconnection between what we want as a field—good theory, high power, replication, diverse samples—and ability to achieve these goals." Another psychologist also saw a quality-quantity trade-off: "Incentive model that motivates quick and easy instead of slow, steady, and careful science. There seems to be an impatience for results now, which is contrary to how science should be done. Science should focus on the quality of the generated information and not the quantity. We should value training over producing, but we seem to value products instead of the scholarly process. Scholarship is threatened where new scholars are unfamiliar with older questions and debates and reinvent the wheel poorly because of a lack of understanding of what was done in our discipline's history."

An alternative theme was social scientists who feared their field's activism and political perspective. One sociologist said, "Sociology has become a partisan and highly ideological field, mostly concerned with 'intersectionality.' The state of the art in qualitative sociology, has, if anything, decayed as ideologically driven and biased work dedicated to 'proving' conclusions which have already been reached proliferates. Sociologists no longer believe that a truth claim can be evaluated without reference to the identity of the speaker. Science dies at that point." Another sociologist said, "Anti-scientific voices and those favoring activism over science have increasingly louder voices. On the whole, this will not be a positive development for the social sciences."

One political scientist compared their discipline negatively with others: "The discipline is hopelessly fragmented, and that is not going to change. There is an enormous diversity of views on fundamental matters—like how graduate students should be taught and what constitutes good scholarship. . . . Contrast political science departments with either economics departments or psychology departments. Faculty in those other departments are far less varied in terms of their training and their views on fundamental matters. This lack of variation has a downside—it makes it easier for pathologies to take root—but I think that, in some ways, the intellectual environments in those departments are more vigorous as a result." This is generally consistent with (though exaggerated compared to) my survey results on disciplinary differences. Yet more faculty see pluralism as a virtue than a vice. And other political scientists saw opposite trends, with one citing an "extreme narrowing of substantive foci, popular methodologies, and theoretical scope of most research." Given the variety exhibited on the survey, this also seems overstated.

Scholars' external concerns tended to be about social science's devaluation in the wider society. An economist said, "The decrease in respect for experts more generally may also lead policymakers to rely less on academic economists, and instead turn to hacks who say what the politicians want to hear." One sociologist said, "Sociology (and other intellectual disciplines) are on the 'wrong side' of the 'cultural wars' for a large segment of our society. These people no longer value 'expertise' of any kind and don't seem to realize that facts and truth are NOT 'relative.' Depending on political outcomes, support for both sociology and higher education may decline." Another sociologist combined these with institutional concerns, listing several worries: "Outsider perceptions of sociology as pure identity politics. Some of the lower quality public facing opinion talk on the internet and social media by sociology faculty and graduate students. The general decline of public funding of higher education. Partisanship surrounding education and higher education."

A psychologist directly compared social science research with social media: "The fact that behavioral science doesn't seem to have a good handle on the answers to address the world's big problems, many of which are inherently behavioral in nature. Our research and interventions don't have the reach of entities like Facebook for changing perceptions and behavior." And a political scientist cited it among several trends devaluing social science: "What makes me most pessimistic is increasing political polarization, social media fragmentation, and manipulation of the public through misinformation campaigns.... If any evidence counter to a position (on right or left) is angrily dismissed as 'fake news,' I do not see a future for our field."

An economist combined these with other institutional and external worries: "Publication lags for the most rigorous work means that the work which is best suited for influencing public policy is generally not available to policymakers until after the immediate situation has passed. Other voices then get prioritized based on availability, and these voices often are significantly more biased." A political scientist focused on lack of institutional support for otherwise positive trends: "The state of academia overall makes me pessimistic. I worry about reductions in tenure track hiring. Reducing the supply of tenure track faculty can negatively impact research production. This would be unfortunate at a time when our discipline is thriving with new data and broader public outreach."

Many social scientists were cognizant of trade-offs or mixed outcomes in research trends. Several even referred to the same methodological innovations as making them optimistic and pessimistic. But I would be remiss not to share some of the widespread concerns. In particular, neither the open science reform movement nor the causal inference revolution has full support across the social sciences. And the concerns critics raise are hardly mere sour grapes about being left behind. There is a perceived trade-off between tackling the most answerable and narrowly conceived questions and contributing to wider debates over the most important general questions. That said, I find many of the perceptions of reformers off-base. As I found in Chapter 2, they are aware that preregistration cannot be a universal solution and have also learned through the process that more of their own research is exploratory. Debates about identifying causes versus generalizable patterns are also long-standing in social science, with plenty of recognition of downsides on each side.

I also find the perception by a minority of scholars that identity politics has gone wild in academia off-base, as do many scholars touting the gains from diversity. Whatever the wider world of politics brings, the trends in scholarship in these areas are toward increased rigor, new theoretical perspectives, and open debate. Even highly politicized topics like the role of racism and sexism in Trump's election are now investigated with the latest methodological tools and competing (usually reasonable) interpretations of evidence.

Overall, the positives cited by social scientists are mostly about a new generation armed with better tools, data, methodological innovations, and more malleable theory. Some of the negatives concern downsides of those trends, but many others focus on resource constraints and institutional inequalities. Of course, these trends can interact, with methodological innovation driving consolidation of research in the top tier. But unequal career and university outcomes may have dual effects, offering productivity and network gains from concentration while limiting diversity from institutional perspectives. The very real problems of funding constraints and increased competition are stemming largely from an increase in demands for better evidence and scholars working hard to meet those demands. When each paper contains more, it raises the competitive bar.

Although I have painted with a brighter brush here, I have also sought to remind social scientists to learn from their critics—especially those who have seen overhyped advances before. There is value to the common arc of excitement and overpromotion followed by discovery of difficulties and limits, but only if scholars recognize the long-standing fundamental difficulties explaining a social world that they inhabit. By recognizing our continued biases, but also giving the benefit of the doubt to many efforts to correct or adjust for them, we can build a research world closer to the one envisioned by the optimists.

The World Is Depending on Social Science

That is important because social science will play an important part in the human future. We face cataclysmic risks to our environment and our public health, but we have tremendous opportunities to pull millions out of poverty. Managing risks and making gains will both require understanding human behavior. Our technological advances alone will not be effective without policies and behavioral change made possible by social knowledge. From controversies over vaccination to climate change, both social science research and attention to its biases and limits will be critical to guide society—but the usable answers often lie in the details.[31]

The good news is that we are equipped to use knowledge for human gain. Although we tend to assume that crises bring out the worst in human nature, they actually tend to accentuate our pro-social behavior and our desire for action. The trouble is that we are trained to search for and notice selfishness: humans assume that others take a dimmer view of others, even if they take a positive view.[32] Humanity faces crises, but that can enhance our cooperation in learning and action. There is thus reason for hope, though social science can make no claim from its own studies that its insights will be usefully incorporated into public opinion or governance. Scholars have appropriately shown the limits of knowledge outside academic life, with areas of study dedicated to the difficulties of scientific communication and the limits of evidence-based policymaking.

Human progress has required an interplay of basic and applied knowledge, enabling our demographic and industrial revolutions. To improve human happiness, we will need a similar match between social ideas, policy, cooperation, and social understanding.[33] The United States, where social science resides most prominently, may not even be the best political system to gain from the advance of social science, which tends to advise building and refining regulatory and welfare states.[34] That means further globalization of social science is critical for finding successful interventions as well as gaining a more representative understanding of the world's cultures, societies, belief systems, economies, and governments. A social science finding suggesting development of public spaces is not as easily implemented or credited as an engineering success.[35] That does not mean no one is listening, but that public engagement and adaptation to local circumstances will remain important.

Solving problems like the opioid epidemic, for example, requires multiple methods and data sources to understand markets, user behavior, and health outcomes as well as often-complicated models of transmission and interaction.[36] Even in what is regarded as a major issue for medicine and public health, psychology, sociology, and economics are all critical for understanding the scope and determinants of the problem while political science is necessary for evaluating feasible solutions.

Climate change research has also needed significant input from social science, as scenarios, impacts, and potential adaptation all crucially depend on policy and social behavior.[37] Far-afield discoveries, such as looking at patterns during long-ago periods of planetary warming, have also been quite relevant in depicting the scope of change.[38] A cottage industry of social scientists aids with scientific communication and policy evaluation and advocacy on climate. It is not the lack of alternative energy that is holding us back, but our inability to come to consensus on policies and behavioral changes that become self-reinforcing, a hard—but largely social scientific—problem.

The spread of COVID-19, at first seen as a problem best left to epidemiologists and virologists, again showed the importance of incorporating social science. The proliferation of COVID research quickly demonstrated that social factors were central to the problem and potential solutions. Using sophisticated data collection from smartphones and store visit tracking, economists showed how consumer behavior adjusted in response to policy, changes in norms, and local conditions. Sociologists used social networks and contextual data to understand why the disease hit minority communities and particular sectors especially hard. Political scientists showed how partisanship mattered for both the policies implemented and compliance with them (and how global outcomes responded to government capacity). The pandemic also showed the importance of lots of basic social science research, even in untrendy topics. In political science alone, that includes bureaucratic decision-making, gubernatorial power, legal compliance, and public procurement. Policymakers sought to fund new COVID research, but the real underfunding may be in longstanding areas where social and natural systems interact and where the application is policy and public information.

When the world's attention moved to racism and police violence in the wake of the Minneapolis killing of George Floyd, social science was also central. Books on racism, white identity, and implicit bias became bestsellers. But scholars also pushed back against easy answers like human resources trainings and officer cameras; they were influential in congressional discussions. Claims of evidence that police violence was not discriminatory also drew new scrutiny. And the crises surfaced the rising scholarship on the broad lifelong impacts of the carceral state.

Although evidence-based policy is catching on in many areas like education, criminal justice, health, and social welfare, it critically depends on social science. And systematic reviews of evidence and comparison across study types remains more the coin of the realm than one-study discoveries. Most impact evaluations in the public, private, and nonprofit arenas cannot use randomized controlled trials. Their critical needs instead come down to measurement of key outcomes and determinants. The advice practitioners usually need is about identifying and avoiding common biases like participant self-selection as well as creatively testing among alternatives.[39]

When it comes to major risks to humanity, we can often understand the causes of prior crises, but it has been devilishly difficult to predict the circumstances of the next. The Great Recession was a story of overleveraging in finance, but a long period of growth and recovery was then a victim of a public health crisis via global integration. Humans are unique in our ability to react to our beliefs about the future, integrating our collective rationality and our intuitions.[40] But responding to future risks is more difficult than learning about those we have already faced.

As society changes, social science has to revise its tools to study new developments in motion. Even when having to learn on the fly, however, social science is improving. Media effects research is a good example. The classic historiography is that scholars moved from assuming huge effects of radio, television, and newspapers (in the aftermath of Nazi propaganda) to finding few, and then settled on a pattern of some media effects (such as setting the issue agenda rather than telling people what side to take) in some circumstances (such as when the information flow is bipartisan). But contemporary media effects research also has a lot more tools, such as using the random assignment of channel numbers to evaluate the effects of Fox News viewership.[41] It also has a lot more data, such as observing users' browsing and clicking patterns that do not always match their professed behavior. Scholars are now better prepared to assess even new developments. Technological innovations like online platforms may not always bring net positives for social welfare, but social science is now equipped to advise both media companies and policymakers.

Social science is usually part of a wider democratic discussion, where public opinion matters as much as scientific evidence. That means even if social science does point the way to a reasonable solution—or foresee a dramatic risk—it cannot expect to be automatically heeded. But just as failure to take medical advice does not prove that health research is incorrect, social science may be advancing where its findings have to compete with other influences on behavior. Even in evidence-based medicine, citizens and doctors seek information but want to avoid mandates and sometimes trust their own judgment over clear evidence.[42]

Nevertheless, scholars tend to overstate how gullible humans are and to understate how often they request sources, examine methods, and require signs of trustworthiness.[43] The public learns information over time from expert signals and facts on the ground, especially where few issues become politicized.[44] Where they do misread evidence, it is often from overresponsiveness to threats, rather than not heeding warnings.[45] Social science has responded to the questioning of scientific evidence by providing more information about public communication and policy processes alongside issue-specific advice. But the nature of our exercise and our potential influence requires regular engagement across value orientations and practical orientations, including with citizens and leaders not inclined to trust our evidence.[46]

Moving Forward

Open science reformers sometimes argue that better science is necessary to convince the public or policymakers to attend to our evidence or heed our advice. But Ken Miller, an expert on the public understanding of science, told me there's not much evidence that internal scientific debates matter for public opinion. The public does not know how the practices of science work, such as where funding comes from or what research is conducted in universities, much less care about journal policies, data sharing agreements, or peer review practices.

Other reformers point to an open science future where scientists are less needed—previous knowledge in the scientific literature is mined by artificial intelligence, scientists work at global scales, and knowledge is curated in the worlds of media and policy.[47] But despite many efforts, science is still not easily mapped by outsiders, anticipated by algorithms, or replaced by letting data speak for itself. Instead, it is driven by curiosity, from following up on the unexpected.[48] Academia is still the community where the truth is consciously pursued, and consensus is messily reached.

Reformers have implemented useful guidelines and achieved quick and tremendous take-up on methods of improving social science research and checking its accuracy afterward. But all of social science will not fit under one umbrella of rules. As one political scientist told me, even assuming the highest success in changing journal policies, there will still be options in books, proliferating journals, and public outlets. And some people who painstakingly collect original data will still balk at handing it over. If social science is to continue improving its practices, it will have to do so based on the curiosity of researchers to know the truth, not only the enforcement of outsiders.

This book has highlighted diverse organizational efforts to advance social science. I am supportive of the Center for Open Science and other direct reform organizations. But the multiple biases I review here suggest that seemingly unrelated efforts like highlighting racial, gender, and political diversity in social science or efforts to help social scientists hone and share their public ideas may be just as important. That means organizations to hear new voices, from Women Also Know Stuff to Heterodox Academy, are also part of the solution. Social scientists can contribute through quiet self-assessment, organized mobilization, or even just listening to the field in motion.

I hope this book has given you some tools to move forward as a better observer of the social world and a conscious evaluator of trends in social science. Attention to frontier methodological tools is important if combined with skepticism about overclaiming and openness to also seeing advances in small steps (such as a new paper archive). Beware of claims that science is essentially one type of method or based on one style of theory construction, especially if accompanied by assertions that it is a settled philosophical issue (when philosophers are still working to justify and extend our many methods and viewpoints). Rather than envying (a caricature of) physicists, look for the perspective that social science offers. Archeologists, for example, have to think like historians and area specialists but also be open to firm physical and biological evidence and global claims about human advancement; they have to both divorce their contemporary interests from the evidence they uncover and recognize how their interests color their judgments.

Social scientists should be proud of their efforts to improve the world, but they should pause before judging society incapable of following their advice. Scholars are one voice in the human conversation. We are using our expertise to provide evidence others can heed, but we are not in full control (and our history gives reasons to doubt that we should be).

Most important, social scientists can better understand the uphill battle they are waging, to understand complex human societies from inside of them and to collectively assemble an accurate picture of humanity from our many distorted mirrors—but also acknowledge how far we have come. Social science advances because it innovates in gathering, analyzing, and integrating information. I have argued that it can learn from the long-standing concerns of its philosophy, history, and sociology and the research on its context in universities. But restating the same philosophical (or worse, definitional) disputes will not make social science progressive.

Social scientists want to take advantage of the more and better data they can now collect and the proliferating and ingenious methods they now have at their disposal. The only thing holding them back is the possibility that more information will not be effectively integrated, given the biases of researchers and the scientific community. But scholars are revisiting fundamental debates about what is possible in social science to acknowledge and overcome their biases. We cannot expect perfection, but our advances should raise our expectations about what social science can achieve.

Social scientists are subject to myriad human biases that they are coming to better understand. They are improving in their ability to counter those biases and to police their community as it produces shared knowledge. But the largest gains may come from the simple advances in collecting and analyzing new information and recognizing its limitations. Knowing which questions remain unaddressed or only partially answered is an important part of the battle. But endless critique is less useful than acknowledgment of bias with strategies to address it.

After all, there are important regularities in the social world—and we are finding them. There are ways to intervene to improve society—and we are using evidence to assess them. Social science deserves its close scrutiny, but also credit for its incremental progress in accumulating useful knowledge. To paraphrase Winston Churchill (speaking about democracy), science is the worst method of understanding the social world except for all those others that have been tried.

ACKNOWLEDGMENTS

I made an unusual decision during my sabbatical that made this book possible: I returned to college. That did not mean living in dorms or joining the meal plan, but I did take two in-person undergraduate classes, sit in on seminars and reading groups, spend considerable time searching university libraries and reading in coffee shops, talk to professors and students in open-ended conversations about their fields, and engage in broad reading and thinking on new topics.

That was possible because of my year in Cambridge, Massachusetts, where I had access to the resources of two amazing institutions. I was officially Visiting Associate Professor in the Department of Political Science at the Massachusetts Institute of Technology and Visiting Scholar at the Institute for Quantitative Social Science at Harvard University, but I had no real responsibilities. Thanks to Devin Caughey and Gary King for arranging my time there, as well as all my temporary colleagues and helpful support staff. Thanks to Sheila Jasanoff and William Deringer for letting me sit in on their classes (and my fellow students for welcoming me). I am also indebted to librarians and staff at the university libraries of Harvard and MIT, the public libraries of Boston and Cambridge, the Radcliffe Institute for Advanced Study, and the COOP, MIT Press, and Harvard book stores. I also benefited from numerous public lectures, series, and conferences as well as early conversations and reading recommendations from Nicole Nelson.

This book was mostly written after I returned back to East Lansing, Michigan. It was motivated by the incredible work by faculty and graduate students I see every day in my Department of Political Science, the College of Social Science, and throughout Michigan State University. My colleagues in political science, including Ben Appel, Janice Beecher, Ryan Black, Eric Chang, Erica Frantz, Eric Gonzalez Juenke, Nazita Lajevardi, Ian Ostrander, Chuck Ostrom, Josh Sapotichne, Ani Sarkissian, Cory Smidt, Jakana Thomas, and Michael Wahman, have been influential in my thinking. The book is dedicated to Steven Kautz, a political theorist and great friend who passed away during my sabbatical. Steve and I always had long, varied conversations that inspired broader and deeper thinking but also kept my most outlandish claims and aspirations in check.

I serve as Director the Institute for Public Policy and Social Research (IPPSR), which connects university research with the practice of state government and public affairs. That means I regularly seek to translate the findings of university research for policymakers, media, and the public to serve immediate practical ends. Keeping a foot in the real world has been valuable for understanding the place of social science in public life. My work is made possible by tremendous IPPSR administrators, especially Arnold Weinfeld (who took over while I was away), Linda Cleary, Lin Stork, AnnMarie Schneider, Cindy Kyle, Iris Harper, and Milly Shiraev.

I also serve as a Senior Fellow at the Niskanen Center in Washington, where I host the Science of Politics podcast. My colleagues there have also influenced my thinking. Keeping up with research by interviewing colleagues every week is also a great way to see the advance of the field beyond my immediate research interests.

I interviewed many scholars for this book, including some anonymously when requested to speak more freely. I thank them all; even when direct quotes are missing, the conversations influenced my thinking and the book. I benefit from Twitter as well, interacting with many social scientists and the research reform community. Hundreds of scholars at major universities also took time to contribute to my survey, including offering detailed comments. Even those who do not appear in the book helped it be more broadly representative of scholarly views.

I benefited from amazing research assistance in completing this book. I want to especially thank Karen Clark for programming and administering the survey and Madeleine March-Meenagh for analyzing verbatim responses. Thanks also to Brendan Cantwell for helping formulate, acquire, and analyze data on universities and disciplines and providing comments. Thanks to Manal Saleh, Frederik Georg Hjorth, and Andrew Roberts for commenting on chapters. Thanks to Lilliana Mason and other participants at an American Political Science Association annual meeting panel for useful comments on a draft of related material.

My Oxford University Press editor David McBride also provided useful comments on the book, from idea to completion, as did anonymous reviewers. It is quite a privilege to be given both the opportunity to comment generally on developments throughout the social sciences as well as the advice to make my expansions into new areas worthwhile.

Thanks are also due to my undergraduate and graduate school professors and fellow students at Claremont McKenna College and the University of California,

Berkeley. Although I have long focused my interests on American politics, I have always been encouraged to keep up with my side interests in higher education, philosophy of science, anthropology, sociology, and social science history. My short forays at the Santa Fe Institute were also influential in keeping those interests alive. The initial idea for a related book happened on a long-ago visit with my friend Joanna Lower.

I also thank my family. My father and mother, Larry and Jan Grossmann, helped guide my interests, education, and career. My wife, Sarah Reckhow, is both my life partner and my colleague in political science, and thus has to listen to hours of half-baked ideas and keep me grounded. She influences everything that I think and write. My daughter, Norah, sometimes shares responsibility for keeping me level-headed and brings me joy. My son, Ari, has developed an early interest in science and history, even challenging me to explain how my work fits into his own investigations. This book was finished in the early months of the COVID-19 pandemic, when everyone had to quickly adapt to limited time and new responsibilities at home. My family heroically allowed me the time and space to complete the book and gave me some new inspiration for working efficiently. I have long dreamed of writing a broader book on social science and I am thankful to have the support to make it possible.

NOTES

Preface

1. Miles (1978) explains the origin and usefulness of the law.
2. Jacobs (2013).
3. Herbst (1993).
4. Igo (2007).
5. Deringer (2018).
6. Cortada (2016).
7. Causal identification strategies are research designs and statistical procedures to mimic the benefits of randomized experiments using non-experimental data. They are discussed in Chapter 2.
8. Collini, Winch, and Burrow (1983).
9. Haas (2017).
10. Sigelman (2006).
11. Haas (2017).
12. Desch (2019); Farrell and Knight (2019).
13. McIntyre and Rosenberg (2017).
14. Pozzoni (2020).
15. Weber (1946).
16. Harding (1992), 70.
17. Little (2016).
18. I interviewed 29 social scientists and 3 philosophers who were both active substantive researchers and important actors in debates about social science methodology and research trends. Some asked to remain anonymous. More than four in five were tenured, with full professors overrepresented, but I also tried to interview up-and-coming younger researchers. In addition to these interviews, I also draw from a survey of social scientists at major US research universities (described in Chapter 1), which also included open-ended questions about research trends.

Chapter 1

1. Kotlowitz, Alex. (2014, June 29). "Deep Cover: Alice Goffman's On the Run." *New York Times Sunday Book Review,* 14.
2. Goffman (2014).
3. Lubet (2017).
4. Dingwall (2018).
5. Rojas, Fabio. (2019). "Steven Lubet vs. the Entire Field of Ethnography." Orgtheoryblog, https://orgtheory.wordpress.com/2019/05/15/steven-lubet-vs-the-entire-field-of-ethnography/

6. Lubet (2017).

7. Morris (2017), 33.

8. Porter (1996).

9. Harding (1992).

10. Epstein (2019).

11. Fuentes (2019).

12. Henrich (2015).

13. Page (2017).

14. Mercier and Sperber (2019).

15. Derex and Boyd (2016).

16. Muthukrishna (2016).

17. Nielsen (2014).

18. McIntyre (2019).

19. Kida (2006).

20. Merton (1979). The four Mertonian norms are known as communism (common ownership), universalism (knowledge independent of individual status), disinterestedness (for common benefit), and organized skepticism (critical scrutiny).

21. In the range of 90 percent of National Institutes of Health grant recipients agreed with the norms in one survey, though they doubted community adherence. See Anderson, Martinson, and De Vries (2007).

22. Bruner and Holman (2019).

23. Mercier and Sperber (2019), 11.

24. Mercier and Sperber (2019). They provide the cautionary tale of the Unabomber who solved math problems and commanded logic in a solitary life, only to later live in a shack reading about contemporary politics and justifying a killing spree.

25. Mercier (2020).

26. Wray (2011).

27. Mercier and Sperber (2017).

28. Dehaene (2020).

29. Oreskes (2019).

30. Intemann (2019).

31. Scott Page, personal interview.

32. Potochnik (2017).

33. Currie (2019).

34. Scott (2017).

35. Furner (1975).

36. Lewis (2003). The book focused on the Oakland Athletics and was made into a popular movie in 2011.

37. Feynman (1974).

38. Currie (2018).

39. Fanelli and Granzel (2013), 1.

40. Sociology can even be conceived as the most central because it incorporates analysis of scientific practices and knowledge production. See McCarthy (1996).

41. Bonaccorsi et al. (2017).

42. Jaffe (2014).

43. Simonton (2015).

44. Simonton (2015).

45. Benjafield (2020).

46. Currie (2018), 318.

47. Page (2018).

48. For a useful recent example applying theories of cooperation to cancer, see Aktipis (2020).

49. Douglas (2014).

50. Gamble, Gowlett, and Dunbar (2014).

51. Currie (2018).

52. Watts (2011).

53. Herbst (1993).

54. Of course, social science research occurs outside of these disciplines, outside of the United States, and at institutions below this tier of research university. Professors at other institutions or in other fields may have distinct views of social science trends. I was primarily interested in very high research output universities with PhD programs in all five disciplines because I am studying trends in social science research most visible at the highest research universities and in graduate training. My experience surveying political consultants and interest groups also suggested that responses were biased toward the least active in concentrated areas. But in a book about bias, I should note that viewing social science from its most research-focused corner necessarily understates other views on the same trends—as does viewing it from the United States alone.

55. I also report subfield differences where relevant and consider each discipline in turn in Chapter 6.

56. We included the members of the American Association of Universities, an association of major research universities with very high research activity, as well as five universities that ranked highly in multiple social sciences but were not members: Boston College, Arizona State, Notre Dame, Georgetown, and Florida State (and appeared to be excluded for organizational, rather than reasons of research prestige). None of the results changes substantially after excluding these universities. Response rates were similar across universities. The survey is only representative of researchers in core social science disciplines at these universities, who complete the bulk of research and graduate training in their fields in the United States. It does not reflect the international diversity of these disciplines or the diversity of teaching and learning in the disciplines. More information about the survey and additional results are available at mattg.org.

57. For this reason, I report results by discipline in this book. I report complete results for individual questions in a report available at mattg.org.

58. As a reviewer of this manuscript pointed out, social science does not require majority rule. Minority perspectives are also important and can continue to be advanced in research communities. But sometimes disciplines do evolve with changing community standards, and several key trends are reflected in top-line results. The book does not include multivariate analyses of each result; where there are large disagreements beyond discipline, I have noted them in the text. They are mostly straightforward, with younger researchers more involved in the trends acknowledging them more than other researchers, but there is no appropriate causal identification strategy for determining the sources of researcher views.

59. See Soss and Weaver (2017).

60. Douglas (2009).

61. Reich (2018).

62. See Blatt (2018) for a review of the impact on political science.

63. Stoker and Jennings (2013).

64. Wolbrecht and Corder (2020).

65. Brown and Samuels (2018).

66. See the *American Political Science Review* editorial team statement and discussion at https://www.santafe.edu/news-center/news/righting-balance-new-apsr-editors-meet-sfi-discuss-gender-and-race-scientific-publishing.

67. Kurzman (2017).

68. Henrich (2020), 1.

69. Latham (2000).

70. Schrodt (2014).

71. Kevin Munger, personal interview.

72. Collins (1985).

73. Watts (2001).

74. Mlodinow (2008), 153.

75. Jasanoff (2018).

76. Wilson et al. (2020).

77. Bardon (2010).

78. Watts (2001).

79. Mercier and Sperber (2017).

80. Mercier and Sperber (2017).
81. Mercier and Sperber (2017).
82. Mercier and Sperber (2017).
83. Best (2012); Wheelan (2013).
84. McIntyre and Rosenberg (2017), analyzing John Stuart Mill.
85. Latour (2004).
86. Smithsimon (2018).
87. Pearl (2018).
88. Kida (2006).
89. Schuurman (2020).
90. Rosling (2018).

Chapter 2

1. The video is available at: https://www.ted.com/talks/amy_cuddy_your_body_language_shapes_who_you_are. The review of this incident is taken from Dominus (2017).
2. Simons, Nelson, and Simonsohn (2011).
3. Forsell et al. (2019).
4. Hoogeveen et al. (2020).
5. Publication bias means that published research is more likely to feature positive and statistically significant findings, while null findings or negative findings are less likely to appear. Reformers have found ways to look for the absence of published findings by looking for unpublished or "grey" literature or by looking at the distribution of p-values in published research. Low statistical power means that studies might not show statistically significant results even if there is a real relationship because the sample is too small to observe it. Reformers recommend larger samples with calculations in advance based on hypothesized effect sizes. P-hacking means that researchers have run many unreported statistical tests, such as other dependent variables, data subsets, or missing data strategies. Reformers suggest preregistered studies or a full articulation of decisions made in the research. HARKing means that hypotheses are not developed before data analysis. Reformers suggest preregistration or honesty about exploratory analysis.
6. Bishop (2019).
7. Broduer, Cook, and Heyes (2019).
8. Ioannidis (2005).
9. The result, however, might apply more to studies of rare diseases than to social science studies of reasonable hypotheses. See Bergstrom and West (2020), 227.
10. Nicole Nelson. (2020). Public talk, Radcliffe Institute for Advanced Study, Harvard University. Available at: https://www.youtube.com/watch?v=DEZl0e0J9rs.
11. Scott Alexander review available at: https://slatestarcodex.com/2019/05/07/5-httlpr-a-pointed-review/.
12. Collins (1985). This connection was made by Nicole Nelson.
13. Edwards and Roy (2017).
14. Earp (2016).
15. Motyl et al. (2017).
16. Motyl et al. (2017).
17. Sassenberg and Ditr (2019).
18. Pallesen (2018).
19. Manzi (2012).
20. Fanelli (2018).
21. Gilbert et al. (2016).
22. Gilbert et al. (2016). More information is available at: https://thehardestscience.com/2016/03/03/evaluating-a-new-critique-of-the-reproducibility-project/.
23. Fanelli (2018).
24. Fanelli (2017). Christensen, Wang, and Paluck, et al. (2019).
25. Oreskes (2019).
26. For an annotated list of findings, see pigee, "Robust Findings in Personality Psychology." Available at https://pigee.wordpress.com/2019/11/12/robust-findings-in-personality-psychology/.

27. Jacobs et al. (2021).
28. Spanos (2018).
29. Mayo (2018).
30. Leahey (2005).
31. Fanelli (2012).
32. Broduer, Cook, and Heyes (2019).
33. Amrhein, Greenland, and McShane (2019).
34. Washburn et al. (2018)
35. Banerjee et al. (2020).
36. Christensen, Freese, and Miguel (2019).
37. For a review of the history and use of these techniques, which are each valuable in different contexts, see Marks-Anglin and Chen (2020).
38. Tetlock and Mitchell (2009).
39. Batmen et al. (2005).
40. Christensen et al. (2019).
41. Bernhard and O'Neill (2017).
42. Mantzavinos (2020).
43. Wernimont (2018).
44. Leahey (2008).
45. Leahey (2008).
46. Brice and Montesinos-Yufa (2019).
47. Schwert (2020).
48. Walters (1997).
49. Watts (2011).
50. Latham (2000).
51. Watts (2011).
52. De Souza Leao and Eyal (2019).
53. De Souza Leao and Eyal (2019).
54. Cartwright and Deaton (2018).
55. Gelman and Loken (2013).
56. Gelman website.
57. Imai and King (2008).
58. Angrist and Pischke (2010).
59. Angrist and Pischke (2010).
60. Angrist and Pischke (2009). Instrumental variables use variables that are correlated with the independent variable of interest but not with the potential confounder to estimate relationships. Panel data designs rely on changes over time across the same units, with effects estimated by comparing changes in the independent variable in some cases but not others. Regression discontinuity uses cases close to a threshold that arbitrarily produces a large change in the independent variable. Quantile regression, which is also covered in the book but not as commonly used for causal inference, is a substitute for linear regression when major assumptions are not met.
61. Nakamura and Steinsson (2018).
62. Imbens (2019).
63. Synthetic control uses a weighted comparison group that is not affected by the hypothesized cause.
64. Imbens (2019).
65. Pearl (2018).
66. Conjoint experiments assess the impact of many different factors on a choice by randomly assigning many different characteristics at once, such as choosing between candidates of all combinations of genders, races, and parties. Initial concerns that online samples were unrepresentative were tempered by early studies showing limited treatment effect heterogeneity from odd samples.
67. Cartwright (2017). In many situations, it is difficult to separate exogenous factors and assume invariance, independence, and a stable set of relationships and causal orders.
68. Spiegelhalter (2019).

69. Potochnik (2017).
70. Even knowledge from field experiments can decline readily if the world changes quickly. Relationships in observational data are usually somewhat time- and country-limited. See Munger (2019).
71. Brannigan (2004).
72. Kubinek (2019).
73. See the *PS: Political Science & Politics* Symposium "Big Data, Causal Inference, and Formal Theory: Contradictory Trends in Political Science?," especially Monroe et al. (2015) and Grimmer (2015).
74. McIntyre and Rosenberg (2017).
75. Ribes (2018).
76. Bozeman and Youtie (2017).
77. Nielsen (2014).
78. Bakhouse and Fontaine (2010).
79. Shapiro (2002).
80. Currie (2018), 138.
81. Firestein (2012).
82. Lohse (2016).
83. Devezer et al. (2019).
84. Baumberg (2018).
85. Soloman and Fernbach (2017).
86. Hedstrom and Ylikowski (2010).
87. Bergstrom and West (2020), 102.
88. Acharya et al. (2014).
89. Jarvie and Zmora-Bonilla, eds. (2011).
90. Tetlock and Gardner (2015).

Chapter 3

1. Latour (2004).
2. Protest signs are available at: https://qz.com/966436/march-for-science-the-best-signs-from-protests-around-the-globe/.
3. See Morris (2017) for a review of this history.
4. Walters (1997).
5. McIntyre and Rosenberg (2017).
6. Goldman (2014).
7. Renn (2020).
8. Gross and Levitt (1994); Bloom (1987).
9. Segerstrale (2000).
10. Segerstrale (2000).
11. Stehr and Meja (2005).
12. Collins (1985), 167.
13. Jarvie and Zmora-Bonilla, eds. (2011).
14. Harding (2015), 50.
15. Thomas and Thomas (2020).
16. Latour (2004).
17. Cartwright and Montuschi (2014), 5.
18. Pennock (2019).
19. Pennock (2019).
20. Pennock (2019), 210.
21. Douglas (2009).
22. Jay Van Bavel, personal interview.
23. Neil Malhotra, personal interview.
24. Ross (1992).
25. McIntyre and Rosenberg (2017).
26. Jarvie and Zmora-Bonilla, eds. (2011).

27. Mayo (2018).
28. Rosling (2018).
29. Fay (1996).
30. Longino (2013).
31. Backhouse and Fontaine (2010).
32. Jarvie and Zmora-Bonilla, eds. (2011).
33. Epstein (2019).
34. Wernimont (2018).
35. Erikkson (2012).
36. Deringer (2018).
37. Gigerenzer (2015).
38. Hacking (1990), 91.
39. Herbst (1993).
40. Wernimont (2018).
41. Porter (1996), 115.
42. Solovey and Cravens, eds. (2012).
43. Everett (2017).
44. Strogatz (2019).
45. Ellenberg (2014).
46. Shapiro (2002).
47. Lamont (2009).
48. Einstein and Hochschild (2017).
49. Mantzavinos (2009).
50. Small (2019).
51. Schwemmer and Wieczorek (2019).
52. Jamison (2019)
53. Rodrik (2008).
54. Manzi (2012).
55. Pritchett and Sandefur (2015).
56. Yarkoni (2020).
57. Fabrigar, Wegener, and Petty (2020).
58. Scheel et al. (2020).
59. Jarvie and Zmora-Bonilla, eds. (2011).
60. Spiegelhalter (2019).
61. Pearl (2018).
62. Mayo (2018).
63. Currie (2018).
64. American Statistical Association, "Statement on Statistical Significance and P-Values." Available at: http://amstat.tandfonline.com/doi/abs/10.1080/00031305.2016.1154108#. Vt2XIOaE2MN.
65. Page (2018).
66. Page (2018).
67. Bevir and Blakely (2018).
68. To take two examples, they argue against Steven Levitt's claim that abortion led to a reduction in crime by citing the contingent historical meaning of both abortion and crime. They further argue against Steven Pinker's view that violence has declined by recategorizing incarceration and verbal comments as violent. These are decidedly weak-sauce arguments compared to the large empirical literatures that have sprung up to contest and clarify these relationships.
69. Jewett (2020).
70. Kay and King (2020).
71. Haas (2017).
72. Haas (2017).
73. Becker (1976).
74. Elster (2015).
75. Jarvie and Zmora-Bonilla, eds. (2011).
76. McIntyre and Rosenberg (2017).

77. Rosenberg (2008).
78. Mercier and Sperber (2017).
79. Hedstrom and Ylikowski (2010).
80. Mercier and Sperber (2017).
81. Matthews (2019).
82. Epstein (2015).
83. Bookstaber (2017).
84. Page (2018).
85. Leys (2017).
86. Lents (2018).
87. Laland (2017).
88. Derksen (2019).
89. Roth in Jarvie and Zmora-Bonilla, eds. (2011); Oreskes (2019).
90. Oreskes (2019).
91. See the introduction and examples in Whitcomb and Goldman (2011).
92. Cartwright and Montuschi (2014).
93. Rosenberg (2008).
94. McLevey et al. (2018).
95. Morris (2017).
96. Harding (1992).
97. Oreskes (2019).
98. Potochnik (2017), 6.
99. Collins and Evans (2002).
100. Douglas (2014).
101. Douglas (2009).
102. Currie (2018), 26.
103. Currie (2018), 138.
104. Cowles (2020).
105. McIntyre (2019).
106. Little (2016).
107. Jarvie and Zmora-Bonilla, eds. (2011).
108. Page (2018).
109. Shapiro (2002).
110. Page (2018).
111. Epstein (2019).
112. Tetlock and Gardner (2015). See also Tversky (2019) on the gains from perspective taking and diversity in groups.
113. Smith (1998).
114. Longino (2013).
115. Leifer (2018).
116. Davies (2019).
117. Jarvie and Zmora-Bonilla, eds. (2011).
118. Mulgan (2017).
119. Haas (2017).
120. Haas (2017).
121. Shwed and Bearman (2010).
122. Norris (2019).
123. Firestein (2012).

Chapter 4

1. Lagerspetz (2020).
2. Tversky (2019).
3. McIntyre and Rosenberg (2017).
4. Little (2016).
5. Collins (1998).

6. Rosenberg (2018).
7. LeDoux (2019). See Harris (2019) for an intellectual history and perspective.
8. Goff (2019).
9. Cartwright and Montuschi (2014).
10. Jarvie and Zmora-Bonilla, eds. (2011).
11. Kusch (2002).
12. Soloman and Fernbach (2017).
13. Laland (2017).
14. Renn (2020).
15. Barash (2018).
16. Firestein (2012).
17. E.g., Wernimont (2018).
18. Porter (2006).
19. Whitcomb et al. (2015). This section draws from a multi-instructor massive online open course on Intellectual Humility, available from the University of Edinburgh through Coursera.
20. Roberts and Wood (2007).
21. Krumrei-Mancuso and Rouse (2016).
22. Hill et al. (2015).
23. Kusch (2002).
24. McIntyre (2019).
25. Foucault (1969).
26. Foucault (1970).
27. Foucault and Deleuze (1972).
28. Jarvie and Zmora-Bonilla, eds. (2011).
29. Bourdieu (2004).
30. Nisbet (1980).
31. Harding (1992).
32. Harding (1992), 70.
33. Scott (1998).
34. Stasavage (2020).
35. Danziger (2010).
36. Olson (2008), 295.
37. McCarthy (1997).
38. Kusch (2002).
39. Wilson (2018).
40. Mannheim (1936).
41. Fay (1996).
42. Fricker (2009).
43. Knorr and Cetina (1999).
44. Whitcomb and Goldman (2011).
45. Currie (2018).
46. Poundstone (2019).
47. Rutherford (2019).
48. Laland (2017).
49. See Dan Hirschman. 2019. "The (Dis)embeddedness of Academic Action in Social Structure," Scatterplot blog. Available at https://scatter.wordpress.com/2019/01/22/the-disembeddedness-of-academic-action-in-social-structure/.
50. See an automated analysis of text from 130,000 Twitter users across 3,500 occupations. Catherine Armitage, "Scientists Are Curious and Passionate and Ready to Argue," *Nature Index*, 12 February 2020. Available at https://www.natureindex.com/news-blog/scientists-are-curious-and-idealistic-but-not-very-agreeable-compared-to-other-professions?utm_source=twitter&utm_medium=social&utm_content=organic&utm_campaign=NGMT_USG_JC01_GL_Nature.
51. Rios and Roth (2019).
52. Rosenberg (2008).
53. McCarthy (1997).

54. Wallerstein (2004).
55. Cartwright and Montuschi (2014).
56. Crenshaw et al. (2019).
57. Folbre (1993).
58. Silverberg, ed. (1998).
59. Wolbrecht and Corder (2019).
60. Gowera et al. (2019).
61. Rutherford (2019).
62. Intemann (2019); Saini (2017).
63. Horowitz, Yaworsky, and Kickham (2019).
64. Eagly (2018).
65. Leahy (2006).
66. Lockhart (Forthcoming).
67. Epstein (2007).
68. Epstein (2007).
69. Geiger (2019).
70. Brint (2019).
71. Brint (2019).
72. Rojas (2007), 94.
73. See Soss and Weaver (2017) for a review of policing research in political science.
74. Patterson (1985).
75. Smithsimon (2018).
76. Roberts et al. (2020).
77. See the controversy over University of Chicago economist Harald Uhlig. Casselman, Ben, and Jim Tankersly, "Protests Intensify Push for Diversity in Economics," *New York Times*, 11 June 2020, B3.
78. Gary King, personal interview.
79. Yadon and Ostfeld (2020).
80. Key and Sumner (2019).
81. Intemann (2019).
82. Jarvie and Zmora-Bonilla, eds. (2011).
83. Hofstra et al. (2019).
84. Guetzkow, Lamont, and Mallard (2004).
85. Lamont (2009).
86. Harding (2015).
87. Cartwright and Montuschi (2014).
88. Walters (1997).
89. E.g., Lilla (2017).
90. Perry (2020), 15.
91. Oreskes (2019).
92. Nightingale (1859).
93. Du Bois (1899).
94. Morris (2017), 7.
95. Morris (2017), 110.
96. Addams (1895).
97. Donato and Gabaccia (2015).
98. Morris (2017).
99. See Bevir and Blakely (2018) for an overview. The heightened attention to self-understanding in social explanation is portrayed as an effort to respond to the unique circumstance of studying fellow humans. But I did not uncover similar defenses among historians of social science. It may instead be an effort to justify humanistic theory perspectives as central to the empirical project of social science (even if that role is less emphasized in historical or sociological studies).

Chapter 5

1. Desch (2019).
2. Thomas (2014).
3. Labaree (2017).
4. Whitley (1984).
5. Ross (1992).
6. Weber (1946).
7. Menand, Reitter, and Wellmon (2017) collect the original documents, often referenced by American university presidents, and comment on both the myths behind them and the many complexities they reveal.
8. Cortada (2016).
9. Lemov, in Camic, Gross, and Lamont (2011).
10. Abbott, in Camic, Gross, and Lamont (2011).
11. Bakhouse and Fontaine (2010).
12. Geiger (2019).
13. Geiger (2019).
14. Schuster and Finkelstein (2006).
15. Stephan (2015).
16. Baumberg (2018).
17. Baumberg (2018).
18. Brennan and Magness (2019).
19. Jeon (2019).
20. Richardson (2017).
21. Gary King, personal interview.
22. Labaree (2017).
23. Urquiola (2020).
24. Urquiola (2020).
25. Weber (1946).
26. Ladd and Lipset (1975).
27. Geiger (2019).
28. Geiger (2019).
29. Brint (2019).
30. Brint (2019).
31. Jiang-Liu (2020).
32. Urquiola (2020).
33. Stephan (2015).
34. Schuster and Finkelstein (2006).
35. Fanelli (2018).
36. These data cover 1998 to 2016. See Solovey (2020).
37. Solovey and Cravens, eds. (2012).
38. Geiger (2019).
39. Swidler and Arditi (1994).
40. Heilbron, Guilhot, and Jeanpierre (2008).
41. Heilbron, Guilhot, and Jeanpierre (2008).
42. For an overview, see "Where Economists Focus Their Research," *The Economist*, 10 December 2020. Available at: https://www.economist.com/finance-and-economics/2020/12/10/where-economists-focus-their-research.
43. Wilson and Knutsen (2020).
44. Kurzman (2017).
45. Coccia and Wang (2016).
46. Jasanoff (2012).
47. Burawoy (2005), 18.
48. Bajwa and Konig (2018).
49. Hannerz (2010).
50. Healy (2019).

51. Jacobs and Mizrachi (2020).
52. Motyl et al. (2017).
53. Muthukrishna et al. (2020).
54. Mulimani (2019).
55. Porteous (2020).
56. "Trust, Slavery and the African School of Economics," *The Economist*, 21 May 2020. Available at: https://www.economist.com/middle-east-and-africa/2020/05/21/trust-slavery-and-the-african-school-of-economics.
57. Sharman (2019).
58. Labaree (2017).
59. Labaree (2017).
60. Labaree (2017).
61. Isaac (2017).
62. Collins (1998).
63. Haskell (1977).
64. Berman (2011).
65. Gumport (2019).
66. Piper (2019).
67. Piper (2019).
68. Reich (2018).
69. Michaels (2020).
70. Reckhow (2012).
71. Menand, Reitter, and Wellmon (2020).
72. Stephan (2015).
73. Morris (2017).
74. Foster, Rzhetsky, and Evans (2015).
75. Csiszar (2018).
76. Baumberg (2018).
77. Lamont (2009).
78. Soloman and Fernbach (2017).
79. Stephan (2015).
80. Camic, Gross, and Lamont (2011).
81. Geiger (2019).
82. Stephan (2015).
83. Rohde (2013).
84. Solovey and Cravens (2012).
85. Solovey and Cravens (2012).
86. Rohde (2013).
87. Solovey (2001).
88. Harding (2015).
89. Godin (2017).
90. Rohde (2013). But see Solovey (2020) for the view that social scientists were more supportive.
91. Solovey (2020).
92. Godin (2017).
93. Jasanoff, in Camic, Gross, and Lamont (2011).
94. Camic, Gross, and Lamont (2011).
95. Latham (2000).
96. Heilbron, Guilhot, and Jeanpierre (2008).
97. Kurzman (2017).
98. Originally created by an aircraft company, RAND was the center of defense research. See O'Connor (2001).
99. O'Connor (2001).
100. Crowther-Heyck (2006).
101. Crowther-Heyck (2006).
102. Baldwin (2018).

103. Jasanoff (2012).
104. Gavazzi and Gee (2018).
105. Brint (2019).
106. Brint (2019).
107. Norris (2019).
108. Ginsberg (2013).
109. Espeland and Sauder (2007).
110. Crow and Dabars (2020).
111. Baumberg (2018).
112. Schuster and Finkelstein (2006).
113. Stephan (2015).
114. Brennan and Magness (2019).
115. Waya, Clauseta, and Lorremorea (2017).
116. Neilson (2014).

Chapter 6

1. For a review of these debates, see "Why Relations between Economists and Epidemiologists Have Become Testy," *The Economist*, 14 November 2020.
2. For Cowen's review of the subsequent debate, see Tyler Cowen, "Economics and Epidemiology, Revisited," 16 November 2020. Available at: https://marginalrevolution. com/marginalrevolution/2020/11/economics-and-epidemiology-revisited.html.
3. Jarvie and Zmora-Bonilla, eds. (2011).
4. Mulgan (2017).
5. Labaree (2017).
6. Potochnik (2017).
7. Wallerstein (2004).
8. Lamont and Molnar (2002).
9. Schabas (2002).
10. Solovey and Cravens, eds. (2012).
11. Crowther-Heyck (2005), 336.
12. Jacobs (2013).
13. Reprinted in Derry, Schunn, and Gernsbacher (2005).
14. Lamont (2009).
15. Wilson (2018).
16. Danziger (2010).
17. Saugstad (2018).
18. Benjafield (2019); Danziger (2010).
19. Brick et al. (2021).
20. Nunez et al. (2019).
21. Danziger (2010).
22. Sapolsky (2017).
23. DeJesus et al. (2019).
24. Across all disciplines, full professors were more likely to respond. Subfield categorizations may thus understate recent change.
25. Calhoun (2007).
26. Morris (2017).
27. Calhoun (2007).
28. Collini, Winch, and Burrow (1983).
29. Burgin (2012).
30. Krugman (1995).
31. Krugman (2020).
32. Lazear (2000).
33. Fourcade, Ollion, and Algan (2015).
34. Javdani and Chang (2019).
35. Collini, Winch, and Burrow (1983).

36. Blatt (2018).
37. McIntyre and Rosenberg (2017).
38. Haas (2017).
39. Eriksen and Neilsen (2001).
40. Eriksen and Neilsen (2001).
41. Wrangham (2019).
42. Chibnik (2020).
43. Horowitz, Yaworsky, and Kickham (2019).
44. Horowitz, Yaworsky, and Kickham (2019).
45. Eriksen and Neilsen (2001). The tradition of reflexivity in anthropological writing, led by feminists, played a role in the social turn in philosophy and offered some of the more concrete debates in science studies.
46. Horowitz, Yaworsky, and Kickham (2019).
47. Milojevic (2019).
48. Porter and Rafols (2009).
49. Derry, Schunn, and Gernsbacher (2005).
50. Derry, Schunn, and Gernsbacher (2005).
51. Derry, Schunn, and Gernsbacher (2005).
52. Strathern, in Camic, Gross, and Lamont (2011).
53. Jacobs and Frickel (2009).
54. Leahey, Beckman, and Stanko (2016).
55. Brint (2019).
56. Brint (2019).
57. Ribes (2018).
58. Efstathiou and Mirmalek, in Cartwright and Montuschi (2014).
59. Urbanska, Huet, and Guimond (2019).
60. Camic, Gross, and Lamont (2011).
61. Ambrosino, Cedrini, and Davis (2019).
62. Longino (2013).
63. See a useful thread of literature reviews in each discipline by international relations professor Paul Poast at https://twitter.com/ProfPaulPoast/status/1159506072211808263.
64. They thus show an aversion to economistic theory but an openness to sociological views, which are incorporated in the discipline via social psychology. See the survey and data at http://academic-priors.herokuapp.com/.
65. Angrist et al. (2017).
66. Benjafield (2020).
67. Jacobs and Frickel (2009).
68. Jacobs and Frickel (2009).
69. Byrne and Callaghan (2014).
70. Derry, Schunn, and Gernsbacher (2005).
71. Porter (1996), 229.
72. This can sometimes take extreme form. Admittedly fraudulent papers even continue to be cited in applied fields after retraction. Fernández and Vadillo (2020).
73. Staub (2018). See also Toppo (2019) on learning styles.
74. Schabas (2006).
75. Morin (2011).
76. Smith (1987).
77. Frickel and Gross (2005).
78. Frickel and Gross (2005).
79. Jacobs (2013).
80. Buyalskaya, Gallo, and Camerer (2019).
81. Crow and Dabars (2020).
82. Derry, Schunn, and Gernsbacher (2005).
83. Moody (2004).
84. Leahey and Moody (2014).
85. See Cowen and Southwood (2019).

Chapter 7

1. Mutz (2018); media coverage reviewed in Morgan (2018).
2. Morgan (2018).
3. See Mutz (2018b), Morgan (2018b), Green et al. (2018), Gelman (2018).
4. Griffin and Teixeira (2017).
5. Cerrato, Ferrara, and Ruggieri (2018).
6. Piston (2018).
7. Sides, Tesler, and Vavrek (2018).
8. Campbell (2020).
9. Lepore (2020), 4.
10. King, Keohane, and Verba (1994).
11. Levitsky and Ziblatt (2018).
12. Wlezien (1995) and the related literature it spawned have shown that public opinion regularly moves against the direction of policymaking and the party of the president. Elections prophesied as revolutionary moments for one side more often produce a backlash in the other direction.
13. I discuss this more in Grossmann (2018).
14. Epstein (2015), 6.
15. Rosenberg (2008).
16. McIntyre and Rosenberg (2017).
17. Jarvie and Zmora-Bonilla, eds. (2011).
18. Morris (2017).
19. Watts (2001), 67.
20. Mantzavinos (2009).
21. These are reviewed in McIntyre and Rosenberg (2017).
22. McIntyre and Rosenberg (2017).
23. Little (2016).
24. Epstein (2015).
25. Schurz (2019).
26. List and Spiekermann (2013).
27. Henrich (2015).
28. Jarvie and Zmora-Bonilla, eds. (2011).
29. See King (2019) for an overview of Franz Boas and his students and their efforts to tamp down on generalization and critique assumptions of universality.
30. Little (2016).
31. Morris (2017).
32. Boyer (2018).
33. Jarvie and Zmora-Bonilla, eds. (2011).
34. Laland (2017).
35. Shubin (2020).
36. List and Spiekermann (2013).
37. Kay and King (2020).
38. Bevir and Blakely (2018).
39. Currie (2019), 2.
40. Munger (2019).
41. Jarvie and Zmora-Bonilla, eds. (2011).
42. Byrne and Callaghan (2014).
43. Vince (2020).
44. See Henrich (2020), which relies on long-term associations between the spread of churches and contemporary variation on individualist beliefs and nepotistic behavior to explain human history.
45. Rosenberg (2018), 18.
46. Krcmaric et al. (2020).
47. Sewell (2005).
48. Collier and Adcock (1999).

49. Jarvie and Zmora-Bonilla, eds. (2011).
50. Epstein (2015).
51. Epstein (2015), 247.
52. List and Spiekermann (2013).
53. Elster (2015).
54. Bookstaber (2017).
55. Potochnik (2017).
56. Rosenberg (2008).
57. Little (2016).
58. Little (2016).
59. Jarvie and Zmora-Bonilla, eds. (2011).
60. E.g., Searle (2010).
61. McIntyre and Rosenberg (2017).
62. Mantzavinos (2009).
63. Longino (2013).
64. Blum (2019).
65. Cortada (2016).
66. Poundstone (2019).
67. Bookstaber (2017).
68. Currie (2018), 265.
69. Chen (2020).
70. Pielke (2007).
71. Land and Schneider (1987).
72. Solovey (2020).
73. Byrne and Callaghan (2014).
74. Solovey and Cravens, eds. (2012).
75. Godin (2017).
76. Rutherford (2019).
77. Currie (2018)
78. Currie (2018), 294.
79. Jasanoff (2018).
80. Baumberg (2018).
81. Bookstaber (2017).

Chapter 8

1. Quotes from the hearing are available in: Michael M. Grynbaum, "Greenspan Concedes Error on Regulation," *New York Times*, 23 October 2008. Available at: https://www.nytimes.com/2008/10/23/business/worldbusiness/23iht-24greenspan.17202367.html.
2. Phillip Inman, "Economics Students Call for Shakeup of the Way Their Subject Is Taught," *The Guardian*, 4 May 2014. Available at: https://www.theguardian.com/education/2014/may/04/economics-students-overhaul-subject-teaching.
3. Skidelsky (2020); Bertocco (2017); Bookstaber (2017).
4. Paul Krugman, "How Did Economics Get It So Wrong?," *New York Times Magazine*, 2 September 2009. Available at: https://www.nytimes.com/2009/09/06/magazine/06Economic-t.html
5. Dylan Matthews, "The Radical Plan to Change How Harvard Teaches Economics," *Vox*, 14 May 2019. Available at: https://www.vox.com/the-highlight/2019/5/14/18520783/harvard-economics-chetty. On the longtime role of standard economic assumptions in the course and its impact, see also Noah Smith, "Harvard's Econ 101 Will Never Be the Same," *Bloomberg*, 12 March 2019 Available at https://www.bloomberg.com/opinion/articles/2019-03-12/gregory-mankiw-steps-down-at-harvard-ending-an-era-in-economics.
6. Kay and King (2020).
7. Skidelsky (2020).
8. Goff (2019).
9. Sharman (2019).
10. Ross (1992).

11. Ross (1992).
12. Furner (1975).
13. Heaney (2007).
14. Haskell (1977).
15. Silverberg, ed. (1998).
16. Page (2018).
17. Grafton, in Camic, Gross, and Lamont (2011).
18. Currie (2018).
19. Laland (2017).
20. Reich (2018).
21. Reich (2018).
22. Scott (2017).
23. Scott (2017).
24. Newitz (2020).
25. Patterson (1985).
26. Patterson (1985).
27. Scheidel (2018).
28. Davis (2017).
29. Curie (2020).
30. Jarvie and Zmora-Bonilla, eds. (2011).
31. Brent Roberts on Two Psychologists podcast. Available at: https://fourbeers.fireside.fm/22.
32. Deringer (2018).
33. Pielke (2007).
34. Lubet (2017).
35. Porter (1996).
36. Haskell (1977).
37. Morris (2017).
38. Baumberg (2018).
39. Godin (2017).
40. Kabaservice (2004).
41. Page (2018).
42. Cartwright (2017).
43. See an interview-based study by Reay (2007).
44. Sunstein (2018).
45. Medvetz (2012).
46. Stephan (2015).
47. Staub (2011).
48. Jasanoff (2018).
49. Pollan (2018).
50. Longino (2013).
51. Jasanoff (2012).
52. Jasanoff (2012).
53. Hannikainen (2018).
54. Marietta and Barker (2019).
55. Lubet (2017).
56. Manzi (2012).
57. Medvetz (2012).
58. Rosling (2018).
59. Crawford and Jussim (2018).
60. Gray (2019); Campbell (2019).
61. Utych (2020).
62. Velhurst and Hatemi (2020).
63. Rom (2019).
64. Rosling (2018)
65. Wright, Motz, and Nixon (2019)
66. O'Connor (2001).

67. As reviewed in O'Connor (2001).
68. Mata (2010).
69. Solovey (2020).
70. Solovey (2020).
71. For a history, see Brown (2020).
72. Bardon (2019).
73. Jewett (2020), 2.
74. Brint (2019).
75. Javdani and Chang (2019).
76. Danziger (2010).
77. Mizruchi (2017).
78. These results are from a national 2014 YouGov survey, reported in Marietta and Barker (2019), Figure 12.2.
79. See Gross (2013) for an overview of what produces these distributions and Shields and Dunn (2016) for evidence that conservatives in academia limit their political interventions.
80. Norris (2020) includes a review of these data and original survey data on political scientists. Francoisa et al. (2016) provide data on French academics and the public, showing far more left-wing views among academics on social and economic concerns.
81. Van Bavel et al. (2020).
82. See Jeffrey Sachs, "The 'Campus Free Speech Crisis' Ended Last Year," 2019. Available at: https://www.niskanencenter.org/the-campus-free-speech-crisis-ended-last-year/.
83. Jewett (2020).
84. Jewett (2020).
85. Maloy (2019).
86. Quoted in Collini, Winch, and Burrow (1983), which offers a similar analysis.

Chapter 9

1. Chris Anderson, "The End of Theory," *WIRED*, 23 June 2008. Available at: https://www.wired.com/2008/06/pb-theory/.
2. Gamble, Gowlett, and Dunbar (2014).
3. "The Stockmarket Is Now Run by Computers, Algorithms and Passive Managers," *The Economist*, 5 October 2019. Available at: https://www.economist.com/briefing/2019/10/05/the-stockmarket-is-now-run-by-computers-algorithms-and-passive-managers.
4. See Zuckerman (2019) for the story of mathematician James Simons and Renaissance Technologies, including the wider context of changes in financial markets.
5. Andrea Jones-Rooy, "I'm a Data Scientist Who Is Skeptical about Data," *Quartz*, 24 July 2019. Available at: https://qz.com/1664575/is-data-science-legit/.
6. Spiegelhalter (2019).
7. Wu and Taneja (2020).
8. Deringer (2018), 4.
9. Mlodinow (2008), 153.
10. Wernimont (2018).
11. Strogatz (2019).
12. Porter, in Solovey, and Cravens, eds. (2012), xi.
13. Porter (1996).
14. Porter (1996).
15. Espeland and Stevens (2008).
16. Foucault (1970).
17. Bookstaber (2017).
18. Walters (1997).
19. Ross, in Walters (1997), 40.
20. Morris (2017).
21. Morris (2017).
22. Haskell (1977).
23. Furner (1975).

24. Haas (2017).
25. Clary (2008).
26. Bonjean, Schneider, and Lineberry, eds. (1976).
27. Cahalan (2019).
28. O'Connor (2001).
29. Appelbaum (2019).
30. Cowles (2020).
31. Benjafield (2019).
32. Danziger (2010).
33. Jasanoff (2018).
34. Staub (2011).
35. Baumberg (2018).
36. Baumberg (2018).
37. Patashnik, Gerber, and Dowling (2017).
38. Quammen (2018).
39. Godin (2017).
40. Godin (2017).
41. Jarvie and Zmora-Bonilla, eds. (2011).
42. Ridley (2020).
43. Smithsimon (2018).
44. Strathern (1997).
45. Levenson (2020).
46. Bardon (2019).
47. Oreskes (2019).
48. Kendi (2017).
49. Porter (2018).
50. Brown, in Walters (1997).
51. Wilson (2018).
52. Reich (2018).
53. Scott (2017).
54. Scott (2017).
55. Manzi (2012).
56. Epstein (2015), 2.
57. Cortada (2016).
58. Habermas (1981).
59. Johnston (2020).
60. Esmark (2020).
61. Marchand and Smith, in Walters (1997).
62. Arora et al. (2019).
63. Leahey (2008).
64. Godin (2017).
65. Brint (2019).
66. Brint (2019).
67. Brint (2019).
68. Page (2018).
69. Goldin and Katz (2020).
70. Stephan (2015).
71. Bookstaber (2017).
72. Gruber and Johnson (2019).
73. Frey (2019).
74. Neilson (2014).
75. Boyd and Crawford (2012).
76. Waldfogel (2018).
77. Davies (2019).
78. McAfee (2019).

79. See Stokes (2020) and Rabe (2018) for two great examples. Both Leah Stokes and Barry Rabe are active in political efforts to address climate change, but both took painstaking efforts to review efforts to decarbonize economies (across American electricity prices in Stokes's example and global carbon pricing in Rabe's book). Following the evidence does not lead either scholar to expect an easy transition or tout obvious and widely implementable answers. Instead, the practical focus leads to more attention to the policy process, including implementation and political blowback.
80. Allan (2018).
81. Ridley (2020).
82. Crease (2019).
83. Burawoy (2005).
84. Gavazzi and Gee (2018).
85. Owen-Smith (2018).

Chapter 10

1. Pinker (2011).
2. See Beauchamp (2015) for an overview of this debate. Contrast it with Bevir and Blakely (2018), who want to second-guess Pinker's definitions of violence (in order to oppose his conclusions) rather than debate real and important social trends.
3. Barash (2018).
4. Pinker (2018).
5. Deringer (2018).
6. Igo (2007).
7. King (2019).
8. Staub (2011).
9. Luigi (2019).
10. Hallett, Stapleton, and Sauder (2019), 545.
11. Ritchie (2019).
12. Baumberg (2018).
13. Baumberg (2018).
14. Lewenstein (1995).
15. Eyal and Buchholz (2010).
16. Posner (2003) and Jacoby (1987).
17. Rosenberg (2018).
18. Drezner (2017).
19. Kolbert (2014).
20. Renn (2020).
21. Derry, Schunn, and Gernsbacher (2005).
22. Adams et al. (2019).
23. Baumberg (2018).
24. Levitt and Dubner (2005).
25. Ritchie (2020).
26. Walter and Tukachinsky (2019).
27. Staub (2011).
28. Cahalan (2019).
29. Jones (2016).
30. Richardson (2017).
31. Derksen (2019).
32. Ke, Ahn, and Sugimoto (2017).
33. Bisbee, Larson, and Munger (2019).
34. Waldfogel (2018).
35. McLeish (2019).
36. Medvetz (2012).
37. Medvetz (2012).
38. Medvetz (2012).

39. Wilson (1998).
40. Longino (2013).
41. See Vollrath (2020) for an accounting of the many factors in declines in economic growth.
42. Original in Wilson (1995). His latest comments are reported in Tyson (2019).
43. Ross, in Jarvie and Zmora-Bonilla, eds. (2011).
44. McCullough (2020).
45. Laland et al. (2015).
46. Laland et al. (2015).
47. Gokcumen and Frachetti (2020).
48. Boyer (2018).
49. Christakis (2019).
50. Mitchell (2018).
51. Rosenberg (2008).
52. Peeters-Zwart (2020).
53. Herculano-Houzel (2016).
54. Wrangham (2019).
55. Jones (2016).
56. Laland (2017).
57. Laland and Seed (2021).
58. Heyes (2018).
59. Gamble, Gowlett, and Dunbar (2014).
60. Moffett (2019).
61. Safina (2020).
62. Proffitt and Baer (2020).
63. Henrich (2015).
64. Tomasello (2019).
65. Rutherford (2019).
66. Wolf (2015).
67. Reich (2018), 128.
68. Mills and Tropf (2020) offer a useful, though triumphalist, literature review.
69. Harden and Koellinger (2020).
70. Panofsky (2014).
71. Panofsky (2014), 64.
72. Harden (2021).
73. Frey (2019).
74. Panofsky (2014), 192.
75. Jasanoff (2018).
76. Dumit (2004).
77. See Justin Wolfers, "How Economists Came to Dominate the Conversation," *New York Times*, 24 January 2015. Available at: https://www.nytimes.com/2015/01/24/upshot/how-economists-came-to-dominate-the-conversation.html. Google Ngram viewer searches for the names of the disciplines and practitioners of the disciplines show similar results. Economists and psychologists trade off for the most coverage, based largely on economic cycles.

Chapter 11

1. See *New York Times* projects: "Economic Diversity and Student Outcomes at America's Colleges and Universities." Available at: https://www.nytimes.com/interactive/projects/college-mobility/; "Detailed Maps Show How Neighborhoods Shape Children for Life." Available at: https://www.nytimes.com/2018/10/01/upshot/maps-neighborhoods-shape-child-poverty.html; and "Extensive Data Shows Punishing Reach of Racism for Black Boys." Available at: https://www.nytimes.com/interactive/2018/03/19/upshot/race-class-white-and-black-men.html.
2. Page (2018).
3. Perry (2020), 16.

4. Currie (2018).
5. Known as the Flynn effect. Discussed in Epstein (2019).
6. Baumberg (2018).
7. Tierney and Baumeister (2019).
8. Patrick Collison and Tyler Cowen, "We Need a New Science of Progress," *The Atlantic*, 30 July 2019.
9. Zhou, Li, and Sim (2019).
10. Nisbet (1980).
11. Page (2018).
12. Firestein (2012).
13. Cortada (2016).
14. Cortada (2016).
15. Reich (2018).
16. Rutherford (2019).
17. Boyd and Crawford (2012).
18. Page (2018).
19. Grimmer (2015), 80.
20. Grimmer (2015), 82.
21. Sachs (2020).
22. Cortada (2016).
23. Baumberg (2018).
24. Fortunato et al. (2018).
25. Collins (1998).
26. See Sachs (2020) for one version of this history.
27. Neilson (2014).
28. Collins (1998).
29. Elster (2015).
30. Reich (2018).
31. Jewett (2020).
32. Bregman (2020).
33. Easterlin (2019).
34. Easterlin (2019).
35. Klinenberg (2018).
36. Page (2018).
37. Parkeer, in Cartwright and Montuschi (2014).
38. Currie (2018).
39. Gugerty and Karlan (2018).
40. Oliver and Wood (2018).
41. Martin and Yurukoglu (2017).
42. Patashnik, Gerber, and Dowling (2017).
43. Mercier (2020).
44. Stimson and Wager (2020).
45. Cohen and Zenko (2019).
46. Bardon (2019).
47. Baumberg (2018).
48. Firestein (2012).

REFERENCES

Acharya, Anurag, Alex Verstak, Helder Suzuki, et al. 2014. "Rise of the Rest: The Growing Impact of Non-Elite Journals." Available at: https://arxiv.org/abs/1410.2217.

Adams, Rachel C., Aimée Challenger, Luke Bratton, et al. 2019. "Claims of Causality in Health News: A Randomised Trial." *BMC Medicine* 17(91).

Addams, Jane. 1895. *Hull-House Maps and Papers.* New York: Thomas Crowell & Co.

Aktipis, Athena. 2020. *The Cheating Cell: How Evolution Helps Us Understand and Treat Cancer.* Princeton: Princeton University Press.

Allan, Bentley B. 2018. *Scientific Cosmology and International Orders.* New York: Cambridge University Press.

Ambrosino, Angela, Mario Cedrini, and John B. Davis. 2019. "The Unity of Science and the Disunity of Economics." European Society for the History of Economic Thought Conference; Lille, France.

Amrhein, Valentin, Sander Greenland, and Blake McShane. 2019. "Scientists Rise Up against Statistical Significance." *Nature* 567: 305–307.

Anderson, Chris. 2008. "The End of Theory: The Data Deluge Makes the Scientific Method Obsolete." *Wired*, 23 June 2008. https://www.wired.com/2008/06/pb-theory.

Anderson, Melissa S., Brian C. Martinson, and Raymond De Vries. 2007. "Normative Dissonance in Science: Results from a National Survey of U.S. Scientists." *Journal of Empirical Research on Human Research Ethics* 2(4): 3–14.

Angrist, Josh, Pierre Azoulay, Glenn Ellison, et al. 2017. "Inside Job or Deep Impact?: Using Extramural Citations to Assess Economic Scholarship." Working Paper.

Angrist, Joshua D., and Jorn-Steffen Pischke. 2009. *Mostly Harmless Econometrics: An Empiricist's Companion.* Princeton: Princeton University Press.

Angrist, Joshua D., and Jörn-Steffen Pischke. 2010. "The Credibility Revolution in Empirical Economics: How Better Research Design Is Taking the Con out of Econometrics." *Journal of Economic Perspectives* 24(2): 3–30.

Appelbaum, Binyamin. 2019. *The Economists' Hour: False Prophets, Free Markets, and the Fracture of Society.* New York: Hachette Book Group.

Arora, Ashish, Sharon Belenzon, Andrea Patacconi, and Jungkyu Suh. 2019. "The Changing Structure of American Innovation: Some Cautionary Remarks for Economic Growth." NBER working paper.

Backhouse, Roger, and Philippe Fontaine. 2010. *The History of the Social Sciences since 1945.* Cambridge: Cambridge University Press.

Bajwa, Nidaul Habib, and Cornelius J. König. 2019. "How Much Is Research in the Top Journals of Industrial/Organizational Psychology Dominated by Authors from the U.S.?" *Scientometrics* 120(3): 1147–1161.

Baldwin, Melinda. 2018. "Scientific Autonomy, Public Accountability, and the Rise of 'Peer Review' in the Cold War United States." *ISIS* 109(3): 538–558.

Banerjee, Abhijit, Esther Duflo, Amy Finkelstein, et al. "In Praise of Moderation: Suggestions for the Scope and Use of Pre-Analysis Plans for RCTs in Economics." NBER Working Paper No. 26993.

Barash, David B. 2018. *Through a Glass Brightly: Using Science to See Our Species as We Really Are.* New York: Oxford University Press.

Bardon, Adrian. 2010. *The Truth about Denial: Bias and Self-Deception in Science, Politics, and Religion.* New York: Oxford University Press.

Bateman, Ian, Daniel Kahneman, Alistair Munro, Chris Starmer, and Robert Sugden. 2005. "Testing Competing Models of Loss Aversion: An Adversarial Collaboration." *Journal of Public Economics* 89(8): 1561–1580.

Baumberg, Jeremy. 2018. *The Secret Life of Science.* Princeton: Princeton University Press.

Beauchamp, Zach. 2015. "This fascinating academic debate has huge implications for the future of world peace." *Vox.* Available at: https://www.vox.com/2015/5/21/8635369/pinker-taleb

Becker, Gary. 1976. *The Economic Approach to Human Behavior.* Chicago: University of Chicago Press.

Benjafield, John G. 2019. "Keyword Frequencies in Anglophone Psychology." *Scientometrics* 118(3): 1051–1064.

Benjafield, John G. 2020. "Vocabulary Sharing among Subjects Belonging to the Hierarchy of Sciences." *Scientometrics* 125: 1965–1982. doi.org/10.1007/s11192-020-03671-7

Bergstrom, Carl T., and Jevin D. West. 2020. *Calling Bullshit: The Art of Skepticism in a Data-Driven World.* New York: Random House.

Berman, Elizabeth Popp. 2011. *Creating the Market University: How Academic Science Became an Economic Engine.* Princeton: Princeton University Press.

Bernhard, Michael, and Daniel I. O'Neill. 2017. "Our Editorial Vision." *Perspectives on Politics* 15(4): 947–950.

Bertocco, Giancarlo. 2017. *Crisis and the Failure of Economic Theory: The Responsibility of Economists for the Great Recession.* Cheltenham: Edward Alger.

Best, Joel. 2012. *Damned Lies and Statistics.* Berkeley: University of California Press.

Bevir, Mark, and Jason Blakely. 2018. *Interpretive Social Science: An Anti-Naturalist Approach.* New York: Oxford University Press.

Bisbee, James, Jennifer M. Larson, and Kevin Munger. 2019. "#polisci Twitter: A Descriptive Analysis of How Political Scientists Use Twitter in 2019." Working Paper. Available at: https://osf.io/dvkwt/.

Bishop, Dorothy 2019. "Rein In the Four Horsemen of Irreproducibility." *Nature* 568: 435

Bishop, D. V. M. 2019. "The Psychology of Experimental Psychologists: Overcoming Cognitive Constraints to Improve Research." Working Paper.

Blakely, Jason. 2020. *We Built Reality: How Social Science Infiltrated Culture, Politics, and Power.* New York: Oxford University Press.

Blatt, Jessica. 2018. *Race and the Making of American Political Science.* Philadelphia: University of Pennsylvania Press.

Bloom, Alan.1987. *The Closing of the American Mind.* New York: Simon & Schuster.

Blum, Andrew. 2019. *The Weather Machine: A Journey inside the Forecast.* New York: Ecco.

Bonaccorsi, Andrea, Cinzia Daraio, Stefano Fantoni, et al. 2017. "Do Social Sciences and Humanities Behave Like Life and Hard Sciences?" *Scientometrics* 112(1): 607–653.

Bookstaber, Richard. 2017. *The End of Theory.* Princeton: Princeton University Press.

Bonjean, Charles, Louis Schneider, and Robert Lineberry, eds. 1976. *Social Science in America: The First 200 Years.* Austin: University of Texas Press.

Bourdieu, Pierre. 2004. *Science of Science and Reflexivity.* Richard Nice, translator. Chicago: University of Chicago Press.

Boyd, Danah and Kate Crawford. "Critical Questions for Big Data." *Information, Communication, and Society* 15(5): 662-679.

Boyer, Pascal. 2018. *Minds Make Societies: How Cognition Explains the Worlds Humans Create*. New Haven: Yale University Press.

Bozeman, Barry, and Jan Youtie. 2017. *The Strength in Numbers: The New Science of Team Science*. Princeton: Princeton University Press.

Brannigan, Augustine. 2004. *The Rise and Fall of Social Psychology: The Use and Misuse of the Experimental Method*. New York: Routledge.

Bregman, Roger. 2020. *Humankind: A Hopeful History*. New York: Little, Brown and Company.

Brennan, Jason, and Phillip Magness. 2019. *Cracks in the Ivory Tower: The Moral Mess of Higher Education*. New York: Oxford University Press.

Brice, Brandon D., and Hugo M. Montesinos-Yufa. 2019. "The Era of Empirical Evidence." Working Paper.

Brick, Cameron, Bruce Hood, Vebjørn Ekroll, and Lee de-Wit. 2021. "Illusory Essences: A Bias Holding Back Theorizing in Psychological Science." *Perspectives on Psychological Science*. In Press. Available at: https://psyarxiv.com/eqma4/.

Brint, Steven. 2019. *Two Cheers for Higher Education: Why American Universities Are Stronger Than Ever—and How to Meet the Challenges They Face*. Princeton: Princeton University Press.

Brodeur, Abel, Nikolai Cook, and Anthony Heyes. 2019. "Methods Matter: P-Hacking and Causal Inference in Economics and Finance." Working Paper. Available at: http://conference.iza.org/conference_files/JuniorSenior_2019/brodeur_a7631.pdf.

Brown, Michael J. 2020. *Hope and Scorn: Eggheads, Experts, and Elites in American Politics*. Chicago: University of Chicago Press.

Brown, Nadia E., and David Samuels. 2018. "Introduction to Gender in the Journals, Continued: Evidence from Five Political Science Journals." *PS: Political Science & Politics* 51(4): 847–848.

Bruner, Justin P., and Bennett Holman. 2019. "Self-Correction in Science: Meta-Analysis, Bias and Social Structure." *Studies in History and Philosophy of Science* 78(5): 93–97.

Burawoy, Michael. 2005. "Presidential Address for Public Sociology." *American Sociological Review* 70 (February): 4–28.

Burgin, Angus. 2012. *The Great Persuasion: Reinventing Free Markets since the Depression*. Cambridge, MA: Harvard University Press.

Buyalskaya, Anastasia, Marcos Gallo, and Colin F. Camerer. 2019. "The Golden Age of Social Science." Working Paper.

Byrne, David, and Gill Callaghan. 2014. *Complexity Theory and the Social Sciences*. New York: Taylor & Francis.

Cahalan, Susannah. 2019. *The Great Pretender: The Undercover Mission That Changed Our Understanding of Madness*. New York: Grand Central Publishing.

Calhoun, Craig. 2007. *Sociology in America: A History*. Chicago: University of Chicago Press.

Camic, Charles, Neil Gross, and Michèle Lamont. 2011 *Social Knowledge in the Making*. Chicago: University of Chicago Press.

Campbell, James. 2019. "The Trust Is Gone." *PS: Political Science & Politics* 52(4): 715–719.

Campbell, W. Joseph. 2020. *Lost in a Gallup: Polling Failure in U.S. Presidential Elections*. Berkeley: University of California Press.

Cartwright, Nancy. 2007. *Hunting Causes and Using Them: Approaches in Philosophy and Economics*. Cambridge: Cambridge University Press.

Cartwright, Nancy, and Angus Deaton. 2018. "Understanding and Misunderstanding Randomized Controlled Trials.'" *Social Science & Medicine* 210: 2–21.

Cartwright, Nancy, and Eleanora Montuschi. 2014. *Philosophy of Social Science*. New York: Oxford University Press.

Cerrato, Andrea, Federico Maria Ferrara, and Francesco Ruggieri. 2018. "Why Does Import Competition Favor Republicans?" SSRN. https://papers.ssrn.com/sol3/papers.cfm?abstract_id=3147169.

Chen, Ying. 2020. "COVID-19 Pandemic Imperils Weather Forecast." *Geophysical Research Letters* 47(15). Available at: https://agupubs.onlinelibrary.wiley.com/doi/full/10.1029/2020GL088613.

Chibnik, Michael. 2020. *Scholarship, Money and Prose: Behind the Scenes at an Academic Journal.* Philadelphia: University of Pennsylvania Press.

Christakis, Nicholas. 2019. *Blueprint: The Evolutionary Origins of a Good Society.* New York: Little, Brown and Company.

Christensen, Garret, Jeremy Freese, and Edward Miguel. 2019. *Transparent and Reproducible Social Science Research: How to Do Open Science.* Berkeley: University of California Press.

Christensen, Garret, Zenan Wang, Elizabeth Paluck, et al. 2019. "Open Science Practices Are on the Rise: The State of Social Science (3S) Survey." Working Paper. Available at: https://osf.io/preprints/metaarxiv/5rksu/.

Clary, Betsy Jane. 2008. "Evolution of Allied Social Science Associations." *American Journal of Economics and Sociology* 67(5): 985–1005.

Coccia, Mario, and Lili Wang. 2016. "Evolution and Convergence of the Patterns of International Scientific Collaboration." *PNAS* 113(8): 2057–2061.

Cohen, Michael A., and Micah Zenko. 2019. *Clear and Present Safety: The World Has Never Been Better and Why That Matters to Americans.* New Haven: Yale University Press.

Collier, David, and Robert Adcock. 1999. "Democracy and Dichotomies: A Pragmatic Approach to Choices about Concepts." *Annual Review of Political Science* 2: 537–565.

Collini, Stefan, Donald Winch, and John Burrow. 1983. *The Noble Science of Politics.* Cambridge: Cambridge University Press.

Collins, Harry. 1985. *Changing Order: Replication and Induction in Scientific Practice.* Chicago: University of Chicago Press.

Collins, Harry M., and Robert Evans. 2002. "The Third Wave of Science Studies: Studies of Expertise and Experience." *Social Studies of Science* 32(2): 235–296.

Collins, Randal. 1998. *Sociology of Philosophies.* Cambridge, MA: Harvard University Press.

Cortada, James. 2016. *All the Facts: A History of Information in the United States since 1870.* New York: Oxford University Press.

Cowen, Tyler, and Ben Southwood. 2019. "Is the Rate of Scientific Progress Slowing Down?" Working Paper.

Cowles, Henry. 2020. *The Scientific Method: An Evolution of Thinking from Darwin to Dewey.* Cambridge, MA: Harvard University Press.

Crawford, Jarret T., and Lee Jussim, eds. 2018. *The Politics of Social Psychology.* New York: Routledge.

Crease, Robert P. 2019. *The Workshop and the World: What Ten Thinkers Can Teach Us about Science and Authority.* New York: W. W. Norton & Company.

Crenshaw, Kimberle Williams, Luke Charles Harris, Daniel Martinez-HoSang, and Geeoge Lipsitz, eds. 2019. *Seeing Race Again: Countering Colorblindness across the Disciplines.* Oakland: University of California Press.

Crow, Michael M., and William B. Dabars. 2020. *The Fifth Wave: The Evolution of American Higher Education.* Baltimore: Johns Hopkins University Press.

Crowther-Heyck, Hunter. 2005. *Herbert A. Simon: The Bounds of Reason in Modern America.* Baltimore: Johns Hopkins University Press.

Crowther-Heyck, Hunter. 2006. "Patrons of the Revolution: Ideals and Institutions in Postwar Behavioral Science." *Isis* 97(3): 420–446.

Csiszar, Alex. 2018. *The Scientific Journal.* Chicago: University of Chicago Press.

Currie, Adrian. 2018. *Rock, Bone, and Ruin: An Optimist's Guide to the Historical Sciences.* Cambridge, MA: MIT Press.

Currie, Adrian. 2019. *Scientific Knowledge and the Deep Past: History Matters.* New York: Cambridge University Press.

Danziger, Kurt. 2010. "Problematic Encounter: Talks on Psychology and History." Available at: http://www.kurtdanziger.com/Problematic%20Encounter.pdf.

Davies, William. 2019. *Nervous States: Democracy and the Decline of Reason.* New York: W. W. Norton & Company.

Davis, Jack. 2017. *The Gulf: The Making of an American Sea.* New York: Liveright.

Working Paper.Dehaene, Stanislas. 2020. *How We Learn: Why Brains Learn Better Than Anya Machine . . . For Now*. New York: Viking.

DeJesus, Jasmine M., Maureen A. Callanan, Graciela Solis, and Susan A. Gelman. 2019. "Generic Language in Scientific Communication." *PNAS* 116 (37): 18370–18377.

Derex, Maxime and Robert Boyd. 2016. "Partial Connectivity Increases Cultural Accumulation Within Groups." *PNAS* 113(11): 2982-2987.

Deringer, William. 2018. *Calculated Values: Finance, Politics, and the Quantitative Age*. Cambridge, MA: Harvard University Press.

Derksen, Maarten. 2019. "Putting Popper to Work." *Theory & Psychology* 29(4): 449–465.

Derry, Sharon J., Christian D. Schunn, and Morton Ann Gernsbacher, eds. 2005. *Interdisciplinary Collaboration: An Emerging Cognitive Science*. New York: Psychology Press.

Desch, Michael C. 2019. "How Political Science Became Irrelevant." *Chronicle of Higher Education*. Available at: https://www.chronicle.com/article/How-Political-Science-Became/245777.

De Souza Leão, Luciana, and Gil Eyal. 2019. "The Rise of Randomized Controlled Trials (RCTs) in International Development in Historical Perspective." *Theory and Society* (48): 383–418.

Devezer, Berna, Luis G. Nardin, Bert Baumgaertner, and Erkan Ozge Buzbas. 2019. "Scientific Discovery in a Model-Centric Framework: Reproducibility, Innovation, and Epistemic Diversity." *PLOS One*. Available at: https://doi.org/10.1371/journal.pone.0216125.

Dingwall, Robert. 2018. "Interrogating Ethnography—and Coming Up with the Wrong Answers?" Network Blogger post. Available at: https://www.socialsciencespace.com/2018/02/interrogating-ethnography-coming-wrong-answers/.

Dominus, Susan. 2017. "When the Revolution Came for Amy Cuddy." *New York Times Magazine* 18 October 2017. https://www.nytimes.com/2017/10/18/magazine/when-the-revolution-came-for-amy-cuddy.html.

Donato, Katharine M., and Donna Gabaccia. 2015. *Gender and International Migration*. New York: Russell Sage Foundation.

Douglas, Heather. 2009. *Science, Policy, and the Value-Free Ideal*. Pittsburgh: University of Pittsburgh Press.

Douglas, Heather. 2014. "Values in Social Science." In *Philosophy of Social Science: A New Introduction*, edited by Nancy Cartwright and Eleonora Montuschi, 162–182. New York: Oxford University Press.

Drezner, Daniel. 2017. *The Ideas Industry: How Pessimists, Partisans, and Plutocrats Are Transforming the Marketplace of Ideas*. New York: Oxford University Press.

Du Bois, W. E. B. 1899. *The Philadelphia Negro: A Social Study*. Philadelphia: University of Pennsylvania Press.

Dumit, Joe. 2004. *Picturing Personhood: Brain Scans and Biomedical Identity*. Princeton: Princeton University Press.

Eagly, Alice H. 2018. "The Shaping of Science by Ideology: How Feminism Inspired, Led, and Constrained Scientific Understanding of Sex and Gender." *Journal of Social Issues* 74(4): 871–888.

Earp, Brian. 2016. "The Unbearable Asymmetry of Bullshit." *Quillete*. Available at: https://quillette.com/2016/02/15/the-unbearable-asymmetry-of-bullshit/.

Easterlin, Richard A. 2019. "Three Revolutions of the Modern Era." *Comparative Economic Studies* 61: 521–530.

Edwards, Marc A., and Siddhartha Roy. 2017. "Academic Research in the 21st Century: Maintaining Scientific Integrity in a Climate of Perverse Incentives and Hypercompetition." *Environmental Engineering Science* 34(1).

Einstein, Katherine, and Jennifer Hochschild. 2017. "Studying Contingency Systematically." In *Governing in a Polarized Age: Elections, Parties, and Political Representation in America*, edited by Alan Gerber and Eric Schickler, 304–327. New York: Cambridge University Press.

Ellenberg, Jordan. 2014. *How Not to Be Wrong: The Power of Mathematical Thinking*. New York: Penguin Books.

Elster, Jon. 2015. *Explaining Social Behavior: More Nuts and Bolts for the Social Sciences.* New York: Cambridge University Press.

Epstein, Brian. 2015. *The Ant Trap: Rebuilding the Foundations of the Social Sciences.* New York: Oxford University Press.

Epstein, David. 2019. *Range: Why Generalists Triumph in a Specialized World.* New York: Riverhead Books.

Epstein, Steven. 2007. *Inclusion: The Politics of Difference in Medical Research.* Chicago: University of Chicago Press.

Eriksen, Thomas Hylland, and Finn Sivert Nielsen. 2001. *A History of Anthropology.* London: Pluto Press.

Eriksson, Kimmo. 2012. "The Nonsense Math Effect." *Judgment and Decision Making* 7(6): 746–749.

Esmark, Anders. 2020. *The New Technocracy.* Bristol: Bristol University Press.

Espeland, Wendy Nelson, and Michael Sauder. 2007. "Rankings and Reactivity: How Public Measures Recreate Social Worlds." *American Journal of Sociology* 113(1): 1–40.

Espeland, Wendy Nelson, and Mitchell L. Stevens. 2008. "A Sociology of Quantification." *European Journal of Sociology* 49(3): 401–436.

Everett, Caleb. 2017. *Numbers and the Making of Us: Counting and the Course of Human Cultures.* Cambridge, MA: Harvard University Press.

Eyal, Gil, and Larissa Buchholz. 2010. "From the Sociology of Intellectuals to the Sociology of Interventions." *Annual Review of Sociology* 36: 117–137.

Fabrigar, Leandre R., Duane T. Wegener, and Richard E. Petty. 2020. "A Validity-Based Framework for Understanding Replication in Psychology." *Personality and Social Psychology Review* 24(4): 316–344.

Fanelli, Daniele. 2012. "Negative Results Are Disappearing from Most Disciplines and Countries." *Scientometrics* 90(3): 891–904.

Fanelli, Daniele. and Wolfgang Glanzel. 2013. "Bibliometric Evidence for a Hierarchy of the Sciences." *PLOS One.* https://journals.plos.org/plosone/article?id=10.1371/journal. pone.0066938.

Fanelli, Daniele. 2017. "Meta-Assessmentassessment of Bias in Science." *PNAS* 114(11): 3714–3719.

Fanelli, Daniele. 2018. "Opinion: Is Science Really Facing a Reproducibility Crisis, and Do We Need It To?" *PNAS* 115(11): 2628–2631.

Farrell, Henry, and Jack Knight. 2019. "How Political Science Can Be Most Useful." *Chronicle of Higher Education.* https://www.chronicle.com/article/How-Political-Science-Can-Be/ 245852.

Fay, Brian. 1996. *Contemporary Philosophy of Social Science: A Multicultural Approach.* Malden, MA: Wiley-Blackwell.

Fernández, Luis Morís, and Miguel A. Vadillo. 2020. "Retracted Papers Die Hard: Diederik Stapel and the Enduring Influence of Flawed Science." Working Paper. Available at: https:// psyarxiv.com/cszpy.

Feynman, Richard. 1974. "Cargo Cult Science." Commencement Address. California Institute of Technology.

Firestein, Stuart. 2012. *Ignorance: How It Drives Science.* New York: Oxford University Press.

Folbre, Nancy. 1993. "How Does She Know?: Feminist Theories of Gender Bias in Economics." *History of Political Economy* 25(1): 167–184.

Forsell, Eskil, Domenico Vigano, Thomas Pfeiffer, et al. "Predicting Replication Outcomes in the Many Labs 2 Study." *Journal of Economic Psychology* 75(A): 102–117.

Fortunato, Santo, Carl T. Bergstrom, Katy Börner, et al. 2018. "Science of Science." *Science* 359(6379).

Foster, Jacob G., Andrey Rzhetsky, and James A. Evans. 2015. "Tradition and Innovation in Scientists' Research Strategies." *American Sociological Review* 80(5): 875–908.

Foucault, Michel. 1969. *The Archeology of Knowledge.* Paris: Gallimard.

Foucault, Michel. 1970. *The Order of Things: An Archeology of the Human Sciences.* New York: Pantheon.

Foucault, Michel, and Gilles Deleuze. 1972. Transcript. "Intellectuals and Power." Available at: https://libcom.org/library/intellectuals-power-a-conversation-between-michel-foucault-and-gilles-deleuze.

Fourcade, Marion, Etienne Ollion, and Yann Algan. 2015. "The Superiority of Economists." *Journal of Economic Perspectives* 29(1): 89-114.

Frey, Carl Benedikt. 2019. *The Technology Trap: Capital, Labor, and Power in the Age of Automation.* Princeton: Princeton University Press.

Frickel, Scott, and Neil Gross. 2005. "A General Theory of Scientific/Intellectual Movements." *American Sociological Review* 70(2): 204–232.

Fricker, Miranda. 2009. *Epistemic Injustice: Power and the Ethics of Knowing.* New York: Oxford University Press.

Fuentes, Agustin. 2019. *Why We Believe: Evolution and the Human Way of Being.* New Haven: Yale University Press.

Furner, Mary O. 1975. *Advocacy & Objectivity: A Crisis in the Professionalization of American Social Science, 1865–1905.* Lexington: University Press of Kentucky.

Gamble, Clive, John Gowlett, and Robin Dunbar. 2014. *Thinking Big: How the Evolution of Social Life Shaped the Human Mind.* London: Thames & Hudson.

Gavazzi, Stephen M., and E. Gordon Gee. 2018. *Land-Grant Universities for the Future: Higher Education for the Public Good.* Baltimore: Johns Hopkins University Press.

.Geiger, Roger L. 2019. *American Higher Education since World War II: A History.* Princeton: Princeton University Press.

Gelman, Andrew. 2018. "Does 'Status Threat' Explain the 2016 Presidential Vote?" Blog post. https://statmodeling.stat.columbia.edu/2018/07/01/status-threat-explain-2016-presidential-vote-diana-mutz-replies-criticism/.

Gelman, Andrew, and Eric Lokenz. 2013. "The Garden of Forking Paths: Why Multiple Comparisons Can Be a Problem, Even When There Is No Fishing Expedition or p-Hacking and the Research Hypothesis Was Posited Ahead of Time." Working Paper.

.Gigerenzer, Gerd. 2015. *Calculated Risks: How to Know When Numbers Deceive You.* New York: Simon & Schuster.

Gilbert, Daniel T., Gary King, Stephen Pettigrew, and Timothy D. Wilson. 2016. "Comment on 'Estimating the Reproducibility of Psychological Science.'" *Science* 351(6277): 1037.

Ginsberg, Benjamin. 2013. *The Fall of the Faculty.* New York: Oxford University Press.

Godin, Benoit. 2017. *Models of Innovation: The History of an Idea.* Cambridge, MA: MIT Press.

Goff, Philip. 2019. *Galileo's Error: Foundations for a New Science of Consciousness.* New York: Pantheon.

Goffman, Alice. 2014. *On the Run: Fugitive Life in an American City.* Chicago: University of Chicago Press.

Gokcumen, Omer, and Michael Frachetti. 2020. "The Impact of Ancient Genome Studies in Archaeology." *Annual Review of Anthropology* 49(1).

Goldin, Claudia, and Lawrence F. Katz. 2020. "The Incubator of Human Capital: The NBER and the Rise of the Human Capital Paradigm." NBER Working Paper No. 26909.

Goldman, Steven L. 2014. Science Wars: What Scientists Need to Know. Course. The Teaching Company. The Great Courses Lectures. Available at: https://www.thegreatcourses.com/courses/science-wars-what-scientists-know-and-how-they-know-it.html.

Gowera, Graham, Lindsey E. Fenderson, Alexander T. Salis, et al. 2019. "Widespread Male Sex Bias in Mammal Fossil and Museum Collections." *PNAS* 116(38): 19019–19024.

Gray, Phillip W. 2019. "Diagnosis versus Ideological Diversity." *PS: Political Science & Politics* 52(4): 728–731.

Green, Jon, Sean McElwee, Meredith Conroy, and Colin McAuliffe. 2018. "(Not) Fake News?: Navigating Competing Claims Regarding Status Threat and Trump Support." Data for Progress Report. https://thewpsa.files.wordpress.com/2018/05/57cb3-mutz_morgan_adjudication.pdf.

Griffin, Robert, and Ruy Teixeira. 2017. "The Story of Trump's Appeal: A Portrait of Trump Voters." Voter Study Group Report. https://www.voterstudygroup.org/publication/story-of-trumps-appeal.

Grimmer, Justin. 2015. "We Are All Social Scientists Now: How Big Data, Machine Learning, and Causal Inference Work Together." *PS: Political Science & Politics* 48(1): 80–83.

Gross, Neal. 2013. *Why Are Professors Liberal and Why Do Conservatives Care?* Cambridge: Harvard University Press.

Grossmann, Matt. 2018. "Racial Attitudes and Political Correctness in the 2016 Presidential Election." Niskanen Center. Available at: https://www.niskanencenter.org/racial-attitudes-and-political-correctness-in-the-2016-presidential-election/.

Gruber, Jonathan, and Simon Johnson. 2019. *Jump-Starting America: How Breakthrough Science Can Revive Economic Growth and the American Dream.* New York: PublicAffairs.

Guetzkow, Joshua, Michèle Lamont, and Grégoire Mallard. 2004. "What Is Originality in the Humanities and the Social Sciences?" *American Sociological Review* 69(2): 190–212.

Gugerty, Mary Kay, and Dean Karlan. 2018. *The Goldilocks Challenge.* New York: Oxford University Press.

Gumport, Patricia J. 2019. *Academic Fault Lines: The Rise of Industry Logic in Public Higher Education.* Baltimore: Johns Hopkins University Press.

Haas, Michael. 2017. *Political Science Revitalized.* Lanham, MD: Lexington.

Habermas, Jürgen. 1981. *Theory of Communicative Action,* Volume 1. Boston, Beacon Press.

Hacking, Ian. 1990. *The Taming of Chance.* Cambridge: Cambridge University Press.

Hallett, Tim, Orla Stapleton, and Michael Sauder. 2019. "Public Ideas: Their Varieties and Careers." *American Sociological Review* 84(3): 545–576.

Hannerz, Ulf. 2010. *Anthropology's World: Life in a Twenty-First-Century Discipline.* London: Pluto Press.

Hannikainen, Ivar R. 2018. "Ideology between the Lines: Lay Inferences about Scientists' Values and Motives." *Social Psychological and Personality Science* 10(6): 832–841.

Harden, K. Paige. 2021. "'Reports of My Death Were Greatly Exaggerated': Behavior Genetics in the Postgenomic Era." *Annual Review of Psychology* 72.

Harden, K. Paige, and Philipp D. Koellinger. 2020. "Using Genetics for Social Science." *Nature Human Behaviour* 4: 567–576.

Harding, Sandra. 1992. "Rethinking Standpoint Epistemology." *The Centennial Review* 36(3): 437–470.

Harding, Sandra. 2015. *Science and Objectivity: Another Logic of Scientific Research.* Chicago: University of Chicago Press.

Harris, Annaka. 2019. *Conscious: A Brief Guide to the Fundamental Mystery of the Mind.* New York: Harper.

Haskell, Thomas I. 1977. *Emergence of Professional Social Science.* Urbana: University of Illinois Press.

Heaney, Michael T. 2007. "The Chicago School That Never Was." *PS: Political Science and Politics* 40(4): 753–758.

Hedstrom, Peter, and Petri Ylikowski. 2010. "Causal Mechanisms in the Social Sciences." *Annual Review of Sociology* 36: 49–67.

Heilbron, Johan, Nicolas Guilhot, and Laurent Jeanpierre. 2008. "Toward a Transnational History of the Social Sciences." *History of the Behavioral Sciences* 44(2): 146–160.

Henrich, Joseph. 2015. *The Secret of Our Success: How Culture Is Driving Human Evolution, Domesticating Our Species, and Making Us Smarter.* Princeton: Princeton University Press.

Henrich, Joseph. 2020. *The WEIRDest People in the World: How the West Became Psychologically Peculiar and Particularly Prosperous.* New York: Farrar, Straus and Giroux.

Herbst, Susan. 1993. *Numbered Voices.* Chicago: University of Chicago Press.

Herculano-Houzel, Suzana. 2016. *The Human Advantage.* Cambridge, MA: MIT Press.

Herrnstein, Richard, and Charles Murray. 1994. *The Bell Curve: Intelligence and Class Structure in American Life.* New York: Free Press.

Heyes, Cecilia. 2018. *Cognitive Gadgets: The Cultural Evolution of Thinking.* Cambridge, MA: Belknap Press.

Hill, P. C., Laney, E. K., and Edwards, K. 2015. "The Development and Validation of Self-Report Measures of Humility and Intellectual Humility." Paper at the American Psychological Association meeting, New York, NY.

Hofstra, Bas, Sebastian Muñoz-Najar Galvez, Bryan He, et al. 2019. "Diversity Breeds Innovation with Discounted Impact and Recognition." Working Paper. Available at: https://arxiv.org/abs/1909.02063.

Hoogeveen, Suzanne, Alexandra Sarafoglou, and Eric-Jan Wagenmakers. 2020. "Laypeople Can Predict Which Social-Science Studies Will Be Replicated Successfully." *Advances in Methods and Practices in Psychological Science* 3(3): 267–285.

Horowitz, Mark, William Yaworsky, and Kenneth Kickham. 2019. "Anthropology's Science Wars: Insights from a New Survey." *Current Anthropology* 60(5): 674–698.

Igo, Sarah E. 2007. *The Averaged American: Surveys, Citizens, and the Making of a Mass Public.* Cambridge, MA: Harvard University Press.

Imai, Kosuke, and Gary King. 2008. "Misunderstandings between Experimentalists and Observationalists about Causal Inference." *Journal of the Royal Statistical Society* A 171(2): 481–502.

Imbensy, Guido W. 2019. "Potential Outcome and Directed Acyclic Graph Approaches to Causality: Relevance for Empirical Practice in Economics." Working Paper.

Intemann, Kristen. 2009. "Why Diversity Matters: Understanding and Applying the Diversity Component of the National Science Foundation's Broader Impacts Criterion." *Social Epistemology* 23(3–4): 249–266.

Ioannidis, John P. A. 2005. "Why Most Published Research Findings Are False." *PLOS Medicine* 2(8): e124.

Isaac, Joel. 2017. *Working Knowledge.* Cambridge, MA: Harvard University Press.

Jacobs, Alan M., Tim Büthe, Ana Arjona, et al. 2021. "The Qualitative Transparency Deliberations: Insights and Implications." *Perspectives on Politics.* FirstView. doi:10.1017/S1537592720001164.

Jacobs, Jerry*In Defense of Disciplines.* Chicago: University of Chicago Press.

Jacobs, Jerry, and Scott Frickel. 2009. "Interdisciplinarity: A Critical Assessment." *Annual Review of Sociology* 35: 43–65.

Jacobs, Jerry A., and Nissim Mizrachi. 2020. "International Representation in US Social-Science Journals." *The American Sociologist* 51: 215–239.

Jacoby, Russell. 1987. *The Last Intellectuals: American Culture in the Age of Academe.* New York: Basic Books.

Jaffe, Klaus. 2014. "Social and Natural Sciences Differ in Their Research Strategies, Adapted to Work for Different Knowledge Landscapes." *PLOS One.* Available at: https://journals.plos.org/plosone/article?id=10.1371/journal.pone.0113901.

Jamison, Julian. 2019. "The Entry of Randomized Assignment into the Social Sciences." *Journal of Causal Inference* 7(1): 1.

Jarvie, Ian, and Zmora-Bonilla, eds. 2011. *Sage Handbook of Philosophy of Social Science.* London: Sage.

Jasanoff, Alan. 2018. *The Biological Mind: How Brain, Body, and Environment Collaborate to Make Us Who We Are.* New York: Basic Books.

Jasanoff, Sheila. 2012. *Science and Public Reason.* New York: Routledge.

Javdani, Mohsen, and Ha-Joon Chang. 2019. "Who Said or What Said?: Estimating Ideological Bias in Views among Economists." IZA DP No. 12738. IZA Institute of Labor Economics.

Jeon, June. 2019. "Invisibilizing Politics: Accepting and Legitimating Ignorance in Environmental Sciences." *Social Studies of Science* 49(6): 839–862.

Jewett, Andrew. 2020. *Science under Fire: Challenges to Scientific Authority in Modern America.* Cambridge, MA: Harvard University Press.

Jiang, Fan, and Nian Cai Liu. 2020. "New Wine in Old Bottles?: Examining Institutional Hierarchy in Laureate Mobility Networks, 1900–2017." *Scientometrics* 125: 1291–1304.

Johnston, Sean F. 2020. *Techno-Fixers: Origins and Implications of Technological Faith*. Montreal: McGill University Press.

Jones, Garett. 2016. *Hive Mind*. Stanford: Stanford University Press.

Kabaservice, Geoffrey. 2004. *The Guardians: Kingman Brewster, His Circle & the Rise of the Liberal Establishment*. New York: Henry Holt.

Kay, John, and Mervyn King. 2020. *Radical Uncertainty: Decision-Making beyond the Numbers*. New York: W. W. Norton & Company.

Ke, Qing, Yong-Yeol Ahn, and Cassidy R Sugimoto. 2017. "A Systematic Identification and Analysis of Scientists on Twitter." *PLOS One* 12(4).

Kendi, Ibram. 2017. *Stamped from the Beginning: The Definitive History of Racist Ideas in America*. New York: Bold Type.

Key, Ellen M., and Jane Lawrence Sumner. 2019. "You Research Like a Girl: Gendered Research Agendas and Their Implications." *PS: Political Science & Politics* 52(4): 663–668.

Kida, Thomas. 2006. *Don't Believe Everything You Think: The 6 Basic Mistakes We Make in Thinking*. Buffalo, NY: Prometheus Books.

King, Charles. 2019. *Gods of the Upper Air: How a Circle of Renegade Anthropologists Reinvented Race, Sex, and Gender in the Twentieth Century*. New York: Anchor Books.

King, Gary, Robert Keohane, and Sidney Verba. 1994. *Designing Social Inquiry: Scientific Inference in Qualitative Research*. Princeton: Princeton University Press.

Klinenberg, Eric. 2018. *Palaces for the People: How Social Infrastructure Can Help Fight Inequality, Polarization, and the Decline of Civic Life*. New York: Random House.

Knorr Cetina, Karin. 1999. *Epistemic Cultures: How the Sciences Make Knowledge*. Cambridge, MA: Harvard University Press.

Kolbert, Elizabeth. 2014. *The Sixth Extinction: An Unnatural History*. New York: Henry Holt.

Krcmaric, Daniel, Stephen C. Nelson, and Andrew Roberts. 2020. "Studying Leaders and Elites: The Personal Biography Approach." *Annual Review of Political Science* 23: 133–151.

Krugman, Paul. 1995. "The Fall and Rise of Development Economics." In *Development, Geography and Economic Theory*. Cambridge, MA: MIT Press.

Krugman, Paul. 2020. "Paul Krugman Teaches Economics and Society." MasterClass Online Course. Available at: https://www.masterclass.com/classes/paul-krugman-teaches-economics-and-society.

Krumrei-Mancuso, E. J., and S. V. Rouse. 2016. "The Development and Validation of the Comprehensive Intellectual Humility Scale." *Journal of Personality Assessment* 98: 209–221. Doi:10.1080/00223891.2015.1068174.

Kubinec, Robert. 2019. "Getting Off the Gold Standard for Causal Inference." Working Paper.

Kurzman, Charles. 2017. "Scholarly Attention and the Limited Internationalization of US Social Science." *International Sociology* 32(6): 775–795.

Kusch, Martin. 2002. *Knowledge by Agreement*. Oxford: Oxford University Press.

Labaree, David F. 2017. *A Perfect Mess: The Unlikely Ascendancy of American Higher Education*. Chicago: University of Chicago Press.

Ladd, Everett Carll, Jr., and Seymour Martin Lipset. 1975. *The Divided Academy: Professors and Politics*. New York: McGraw Hill.

Lagerspetz, Mikko. 2020. "'The Grievance Studies Affair' Project: Reconstructing and Assessing the Experimental Design." *Science, Technology, & Human Values* 46(2): 402–424.

Laland, Kevin. 2017. *Darwin's Unfinished Symphony*. Princeton: Princeton University Press, 2017.

Laland, Kevin, and Amanda Seed. 2021. "Understanding Human Cognitive Uniqueness." *Annual Review of Psychology* 72: 689–716.

Laland, Kevin, Tobias Uller, Marcus W. Feldman, Kim Sterelny, Gerd B. Müller, Armin Moczek, Eva Jablonka and John Odling-Smee. 2015. "The extended evolutionary synthesis: its structure, assumptions and predictions." *Royal Society Proceedings B* 282(1813).

Lamont, Michèle. 2009. *How Professors Think: Inside the Curious World of Academic Judgment*. Cambridge, MA: Harvard University Press.

Lamont, Michèle, and Virág Molnár. 2002. "The Study of Boundaries across the Social Sciences." *Annual Review of Sociology* 28: 167–95.

Land, Kenneth C., and Stephen H. Schneider. 1987. "Forecasting in the Social and Natural Sciences: An Overview and Analysis of Isomorphisms." *Climatic Change* 11(1–2): 7–31.

Latham, Michael. 2000. *Modernization as Ideology: American Social Science and "Nation Building" in the Kennedy Era*. Chapel Hill: University of North Carolina Press.

Latour, Bruno. 2004. "Why Has the Critique Run Out of Steam?" *Critical Inquiry* 30(4): 225–248.

Lazear, Edward P. 2000. "Economic Imperialism." *Quarterly Journal of Economics* 115(1): 99–146.

Leahey, Erin. 2005. "Alphas and Asterisks: The Development of Statistical Significance Testing Standards in Sociology." *Social Forces* 84(1): 1–24.

Leahey, Erin. 2006. "Gender Differences in Productivity." *Gender and Society* 20(6): 754–780.

Leahey, Erin. 2008. "Methodological Memes and Mores: Toward a Sociology of Social Research." *Annual Review of Sociology* 34: 33–53.

Leahey, Erin, Christine M. Beckman, and Taryn L. Stanko. 2016. "Prominent but Less Productive: The Impact of Interdisciplinarity on Scientists' Research." *Administrative Science Quarterly* 62(1): 105–139.

Leahey, Erin, and James Moody. 2014. "Sociological Innovation through Subfield Integration." *Social Currents* 1(3): 228–256.

LeDoux, Joseph. 2019. *The Deep History of Ourselves: The Four-Billion-Year Story of How We Got Conscious Brains*. New York: Viking.

Leifer, Matthew. 2018. "Against Fundamentalism." Available at: https://arxiv.org/abs/1810.05272.

Lents, Nathan H. 2018. *Human Errors: A Panorama of Our Glitches, from Pointless Bones to Broken Genes*. New York: Houghton Mifflin Harcourt.

Lepore, Jill. 2020. *If Then: How the Simulmatics Corporation Invented the Future*. New York: Liveright.

Levenson, Thomas. 2020. "How Eugenics Shaped Statistics." *Nautilus* 92. Available at: https://nautil.us/issue/92/frontiers/how-eugenics-shaped-statistics.

Levitsky, Steven, and Daniel Ziblatt. 2018. *How Democracies Die*. New York: Crown.

Levitt, Steven, and Stephen J. Dubner. 2005. *Freakonomics: A Rogue Economist Explores the Hidden Side of Everything*. New York: William Morrow.

Lewenstein, Bruce V. 1995. "From Fax to Facts: Communication in the Cold Fusion Saga." *Social Studies of Science* 25(3): 403–436.

Lewis, Michael. 2003. *Moneyball: The Art of Wining an Unfair Game*. New York: W. W. Norton & Company.

Leys, Ruth. 2017. *The Ascent of Affect: Genealogy and Critique*. Chicago: University of Chicago Press.

Lilla, Mark. 2017. *The Once and Future Liberal: After Identity Politics*. New York: Harper.

List, Christian, and Kai Spiekermann. 2013. "Methodological Individualism and Holism in Political Science: A Reconciliation." *American Political Science Review* 107(4): 629–643.

Little, Daniel. 2016. *New Directions in Philosophy of Social Science*. Lanham, MD: Rowman & Littlefield.

Lockhart, Jeffrey. Forthcoming. "Paradigms of Sex Research and Women in STEM." *Gender & Society*.

Lohse, Simon. 2016. "Pragmatism, Ontology and Philosophy of the Social Sciences in Practice." *Philosophy of the Social Sciences* 47(1): 3–27.

Longino, Helen. 2013. *Studying Human Behavior*. Chicago: University of Chicago Press.

Lubet, Steven. 2017. *Interrogating Ethnography: Why Evidence Matters*. New York: Oxford University Press.

Luigi, Guidi Marco Enrico. 2019. "How the Economists Gained (and Lost) Consensus. The Popularisation of Economics and the Social Construction of Reality, 19th–20th Century." European Society for the History of Economic Thought Conference, Lille, France.

Lynd, Robert S., and Helen Merrell Lynd. 1929. *Middletown: A Study in Modern American Culture*. San Diego: Harcourt Brace Jovanovich.

Maloy, J. S. 2019. "Political Realism as Anti-Scholastic Practice: Methodological Lessons from Muckraking Journalism." *Political Research Quarterly* 73(1): 27–39.

Mannheim, Karl. 1936. *Ideology and Utopia*. International Library of Psychology, Philosophy and Scientific Method.

Mantzavinos, C. 2020. "Institutions and Scientific Progress." *Philosophy of the Social Sciences*. Available at: https://journals.sagepub.com/doi/abs/10.1177/0048393120978453?journalCode=posa.

Mantzavinos, C., ed. 2009. *Philosophy of Social Science*. New York: Cambridge University Press.

Manzi, Jim. 2012. *Uncontrolled: The Surprising Payoff of Trial-and-Error for Business, Politics, and Society*. New York: Basic Books.

Marietta, Morgan, and David C. Barker. 2019. *One Nation, Two Realities: Dueling Facts in American Democracy*. New York: Oxford University Press.

Marks-Anglin, Arielle, and Yong Chen. 2020. "A Historical Review of Publication Bias." Working Paper. Available at: https://osf.io/preprints/metaarxiv/zmdpk/.

Martin, Gregory J., and Ali Yurukoglu. 2017. "Bias in Cable News: Persuasion and Polarization." *American Economic Review* 107(9): 2565–2599.

Mata, Tiago. 2010. "The Enemy Within: Academic Freedom in 1960s and 1970s American Social Sciences." *History of Political Economy* 41(1): 77–104.

Matthews, Dylan. 2019. "The Radical Plan to Change How Harvard Teaches Economics." *Vox*. Available at: https://www.vox.com/the-highlight/2019/5/14/18520783/harvard-economics-chetty.

Mayo, Deborah. 2018. *Statistical Inference as Severe Testing*. New York: Cambridge University Press.

McAfee, Andrew. 2019. *More from Less: The Surprising Story of How We Learned to Prosper Using Fewer Resources—and What Happens Next*. New York: Scribner.

McCarthy, E. Doyle. 1996. *Knowledge as Culture: The New Sociology of Knowledge*. New York: Routledge.

McCullough, Michael E. 2020. *The Kindness of Strangers: How a Selfish Ape Invented a New Moral Code*. New York: Hachette Book Group.

McIntyre, Lee. 2019. *The Scientific Attitude: Defending Science from Denial, Fraud, and Pseudoscience*. Cambridge, MA: MIT Press.

McIntyre, Lee, and Alex Rosenberg. 2017. *The Routledge Companion to Philosophy of Social Science*. New York: Routledge.

McLeish, Tom. 2019. *The Poetry and Music of Science*. New York: Oxford University Press.

McLevey, John, Alexander V. Graham, Reid McIlroy-Young, et al. 2018. "Interdisciplinarity and Insularity in the Diffusion of Knowledge: An Analysis of Disciplinary Boundaries between Philosophy of Science and the Sciences." *Scientometrics* 117(1): 331–349.

Medvetz, Thomas. 2012. *Think Tanks in America*. Chicago: University of Chicago Press.

Menand, Louis, Paul Reitter, and Chad Wellmon. 2017. *The Rise of the Research University: A Sourcebook*. Chicago: University of Chicago Press.

Mercier, Hugo. 2020. *Not Born Yesterday: The Science of Who We Trust and What We Believe*. Princeton: Princeton University Press.

Mercier, Hugo, and Dan Sperber. 2019. *The Enigma of Reason*. Cambridge, MA: Harvard University Press.

Merton, Robert K. 1979. *The Sociology of Science: Theoretical and Empirical Investigations*. Chicago: University of Chicago Press.

Michaels, David. 2020. *The Triumph of Doubt: Dark Money and the Science of Deception*. New York: Oxford University Press.

Miles, Rufus E. 1978. "The Origin and Meaning of Miles' Law." *Public Administration Review* 38(5): 399–403.

Mills, Melinda C., and Felix C. Tropf. 2020. "Sociology, Genetics, and the Coming of Age of Sociogenomics." *Annual Review of Sociology* 46.

Milojevic, Stasa. 2019. "The Changing Landscape of Knowledge Production." Working Paper. Available at: https://osf.io/fkds2/.

Mitchell, Kevin. 2018. *Innate: How the Wiring of Our Brains Shapes Who We Are*. Princeton: Princeton University Press.

Mizruchi, Mark S. 2017. "The Current Crisis in American Sociology." Michigan Sociological Association Annual Meeting Keynote Address, Lake Superior State University, Sault Ste. Marie, MI.

Mlodinow, Leonard. 2008. *The Drunkard's Walk: How Randomness Rules Our Lives*. New York: Vintage Books.

Moffett, Mark. 2019. *The Human Swarm: How Our Societies Arise, Thrive, and Fall*. New York: Basic Books.

Monroe, Burt L., Jennifer Pan, Margaret E. Roberts, et al. "No! Formal Theory, Causal Inference, and Big Data Are Not Contradictory Trends in Political Science." *PS: Political Science & Politics* 48(1): 71–74.

Moody, James. 2004. "The Structure of a Social Science: Collaboration Network: Disciplinary Cohesion from 1963 to 1999." *American Sociological Review* 69(2): 213–238.

Morgan, Steven 2018. "Status Threat, Material Interests, and the 2016 Presidential Vote." *Socius* 4(1).

Morgan, Steven. 2018. "Correct Interpretations of Fixed-effects Models, Specification Decisions, and Self-reports of Intended Votes: A Response to Mutz." *Socius* 4(4).

Morin, Karen M. 2011. *Civic Discipline: Geography in America, 1860–1890*. New York: Routledge.

Morris, Aldon. 2017. *The Scholar Denied: W. E. B. Du Bois and the Birth of Modern Sociology*. Berkeley: University of California Press.

Motyl, Matt, Alexander P. Demos, Timothy S. Carsel, et al. 2017. "The State of Social and Personality Science: Rotten to the Core, Not So Bad, Getting Better, or Getting Worse?" *Journal of Personality and Social Psychology* 113(3): 34–58.

Mulgan, Geoff. 2017. *Big Mind: How Collective Intelligence Can Change Our World*. Princeton: Princeton University Press.

Mulimani, Priti. 2019. "Publication Bias towards Western Populations Harms Humanity." *Nature Human Behaviour* 3: 1026–1027.

Munger, Kevin. 2019. "The Limited Value of Non-Replicable Field Experiments in Contexts with Low Temporal Validity." *Social Media + Society* 5(3).

Muthukrishna, Michael, Adrian V. Bell, Joseph Henrich, et al. "Beyond Western, Educated, Industrial, Rich, and Democratic (WEIRD) Psychology: Measuring and Mapping Scales of Cultural and Psychological Distance." *Psychological Science* 31(6): 678–701.

Muthukrishna, M., and J. Henrich. 2016. "Innovation in the Collective Brain." *Philosophical Transactions of the Royal Society* B 371: 0192.

Mutz, Diana C. 2018. "Status Threat, Not Economic Hardship, Explains the 2016 Presidential Vote." *PNAS* 115 (19): E4330-E4339.

Mutz, Diana C. 2018. "Response to Morgan: On the Role of Status Threat and Material Interests in the 2016 Election." *Socius* 4(1).

Nakamura, Emi, and Jon Steinsson. 2018. "Identification in Macroeconomics." Working Paper. Available at: http://www.columbia.edu/~js3204/papers/macroempirics.pdf.

Newitz, Annalee. 2020. "Cities Lost, Decline of Written Record but Perhaps Inequality Overthrow." *New York Times*. 11 May. Available at: https://www.nytimes.com/2020/05/11/opinion/coronavirus-inequality-history.html.

Nielsen, Michael. 2014. *Reinventing Discovery: The New Era of Networked Science*. Princeton: Princeton University Press.

Nightingale, Florence. 1859. *A Contribution to the Sanitary History of the British Army during the Late War with Russia*. London: John W. Parker and Son.

Nisbet, Robert. 1980. *A History of the Idea of Progress*. New York: Basic Books.

Norris, Pippa. 2019. "The World of Political Science: Internationalization and Its Consequences." World of Political Science Report: ECPR-IPSA Survey. https://www.dropbox.com/s/v6y4ns8415xs9mw/ECPR%4050%20Chapter%203%20Sgl%20spaced.pdf?dl=0.

Norris, Pippa. 2020. "Closed Minds?: Is a 'Cancel Culture' Stifling Academic Freedom and Intellectual Debate in Political Science?" HKS Working Paper No. RWP20-025. Available at: https://papers.ssrn.com/sol3/papers.cfm?abstract_id=3671026.

Núñez, Rafael, Michael Allen, Richard Gao, et al. 2019. "What Happened to Cognitive Science?" *Nature Human Behaviour* 3: 782–791.

O'Connor, Alice. 2001. *Poverty Knowledge: Social Science, Social Policy and the Poor in Twentieth-Century U.S. History.* Princeton: Princeton University Press.

Oliver, Eric, and Thomas Wood. 2018. *Enchanted America: How Intuition and Reason Divide Our Politics.* Chicago: University of Chicago Press.

Olson, Richard. 2008. *Science and Scientism in Nineteenth-Century Europe.* Urbana: University of Illinois Press.

Oreskes, Naomi. 2019. *Why Trust Science?* Princeton: Princeton University Press.

Owen-Smith, Jason. 2018. *Research Universities and the Public Good: Discovery for an Uncertain Future.* Stanford: Stanford University Press.

Page, Scott. 2017. *The Diversity Bonus: How Great Teams Pay Off in the Knowledge Economy.* Princeton: Princeton University Press.

Page, Scott E. 2018. *The Model Thinker: What You Need to Know to Make Data Work for You.* New York: Basic Books.

Pallesen, Jonatan. 2018. "Guess Along About Which Social Science Studies Will Replicate." *Medium.* Available at: https://medium.com/@jsmp/guess-along-about-which-social-science-studies-will-replicate-e35263a5d49e

Panofsky, Aaron. 2014. *Misbehaving Science: Controversy and the Development of Behavior Genetics.* Chicago: University of Chicago Press.

Patashnik, Eric M., Alan S. Gerber, and Conor M. Dowling. 2017. *Unhealthy Politics.* Princeton: Princeton University Press.

Patterson, Orlando. 1985. *Slavery and Social Death.* Cambridge, MA: Harvard University Press.

Pearl, Judea. 2018. *The Book of Why: The New Science of Cause and Effect.* New York: Basic Books.

Peeters, Susan, and Hub Zwart. 2020. "Neanderthals as Familiar Strangers and the Human Spark: How the 'Golden Years' of Neanderthal Research Reopen the Question of Human Uniqueness." *History and Philosophy of the Life Sciences* 42(33).

Pennock, Robert T. 2019. *An Instinct for Truth: Curiosity and the Moral Character of Science.* Cambridge, MA: MIT Press.

Perry, Andre M. 2020. *Know Your Price: Valuing Black Lives and Property in America's Black Cities.* Washington, DC: Brookings Institution Press.

Pielke, Roger A., Jr. 2007. *The Honest Broker: Making Sense of Science in Policy and Politics.* New York: Cambridge University Press.

Piketty, Thomas. 2014. *Capital in the Twenty-First Century.* Cambridge, MA: Harvard University Press.

Pinker, Steven. 2019. *Enlightenment Now: The Case for Reason, Science, Humanism, and Progress.* New York: Penguin.

Pinker, Steven. 2011. *The Better Angels of Our Nature: How Violence Has Declined.* New York: Penguin.

Piper, Kelsey. 2019. "Science Funding Is a Mess. Could Grant Lotteries Make It Better?" *Vox.* Available at: https://www.vox.com/future-perfect/2019/1/18/18183939/science-funding-grant-lotteries-research.

Piston, Spencer. 2018. *Class Attitudes in America.* New York: Cambridge University Press.

Pollan, Michael. 2018. *How to Change Your Mind: What the New Science of Psychedelics Teaches Use about Consciousness, Dying, Addiction, Depression and Transcendence.* New York: Penguin.

Porteous, Obie. 2020. "Research Deserts and Oases: Evidence from 27 Thousand Economics Journal Articles on Africa." Working Paper. Available at: https://drive.google.com/file/d/1vGpzi_yV-H78VtibvxrFS1ZScLjmvtWw/view.

Porter, Alan L., and Ismael Rafols. 2009. "Is Science Becoming More Interdisciplinary?" *Scientometrics* 81: 719.

Porter, Theodore. 1996. *Trust in Numbers: The Pursuit of Objectivity in Science and Public Life.* Princeton: Princeton University Press.

Porter, Theodore M. 2006. "Speaking Precision to Power: The Modern Political Role of Social Science." *Social Research* 73(4): 1273–1294.

Porter, Theodore M. 2018. *Genetics in the Madhouse: The Unknown History of Human Heredity.* Princeton: Princeton University Press.

Posner, Richard. 2003. *Public Intellectuals: A Study of Decline.* Cambridge, MA: Harvard University Press.

Potochnik, Angela. 2017. *Idealization and the Aims of Science.* Chicago: University of Chicago Press.

Poundstone, William. 2019. *The Doomsday Calculation: How an Equation That Predicts the Future Is Transforming Everything We Know about Life and the Universe.* New York: Little, Brown.

Pozzoni, Gianluca. 2020. "What, If Anything, Is the Philosophy of Political Science?" *Philosophy of the Social Sciences.* doi.org/10.1177/0048393120976829.

Pritchett, Lant, and Justin Sandefur. 2015. "Learning from Experiments When Context Matters." *American Economic Review* 105(5): 471–475.

Proffitt, Dennis, and Drake Baer. 2020. *Perception: How Our Bodies Shape Our Minds.* New York: St. Martin's Press.

Quammen, David. 2018. *The Tangled Tree: A Radical New History of Life.* New York: Simon & Schuster.

Quetelet, Adolphe. 1835. *A Treatise on Man and the Development of his Faculties.* Edinburgh: W. and R. Chambers.

Rabe, Barry. 2018. *Can We Price Carbon?* Cambridge, MA: MIT Press.

Reay, Mike. 2007. "Academic Knowledge and Expert Authority in American Economics." *Sociological Perspectives* 50(1): 101–129.

Reckhow, Sarah. 2012. *Follow the Money: How Foundation Dollars Change Public School Politics.* New York: Oxford University Press.

Reich, David. 2018. *Who We Are and How We Got Here.* New York: Pantheon.

Renn, Jürgen. 2020. *The Evolution of Knowledge: Rethinking Science for the Anthropocene.* Princeton: Princeton University Press.

Ribes, David. 2018. "STS, Meet Data Science, Once Again." *Science, Technology, and Human Values* 44(3): 514–539.

Richardson, Ken. 2017. *Genes, Brains, and Human Potential.* New York: Columbia University Press.

Ridley, Matt. 2020. *How Innovation Works: And Why It Flourishes in Freedom.* New York: HarperCollins.

Rios, Kimberly, and Zachary C. Roth. 2019. "Is 'Me-search' Necessarily Less Rigorous Research?: Social and Personality Psychologists' Stereotypes of the Psychology of Religion." *Self and Identity* 19(7): 825–840.

Ritchie, Stuart. 2020. *Science Fictions: How Fraud, Bias, Negligence, and Hype Undermine the Search for Truth.* New York: Macmillan.

Roberts, Robert C., and W. Jay Wood. 2007. *Intellectual Virtues: An Essay in Regulative Epistemology.* Oxford: Clarendon Press.

Roberts, Steven O., Carmelle Bareket-Shavit, Forrest A. Dollins, et al. 2020. "Racial Inequality in Psychological Research: Trends of the Past and Recommendations for the Future." *Perspectives on Psychological Science* 15(6): 1295–1309.

Rodrik, Dani. 2008. "The New Development Economics: We Shall Experiment, but How Shall We Learn." HKS Working Paper No. RWP08-055, Available at http://dx.doi.org/10.2139/ssrn.1296115.

Rohde, Joy. 2013. *Armed with Expertise: The Militarization of American Social Research during the Cold War.* Ithaca, NY: Cornell University Press.

Rojas, Fabio. 2007. *From Black Power to Black Studies.* Baltimore: Johns Hopkins University Press.

Rom, Mark Carl. 2019. "A Liberal Polity: Ideological Homogeneity in Political Science." *PS: Political Science & Politics* 52(4): 701–705.

Rosenberg, Alexander. 2008. *Philosophy of Social Science.* New York: Routledge.

Rosenberg, Alexander. 2018. *How History Gets Things Wrong*. Cambridge, MA: MIT Press.

Rosling, Hans. 2018. *Factfulness*. New York: Flatiron Books.

Ross, Dorothy. 1992. *The Origins of American Social Science*. New York: Cambridge University Press.

Rutherford, Adam. 2019. *Humanimal: How Homo Sapiens Became Nature's Most Paradoxical Creature*. New York: The Experiment.

Sachs, Jeffrey. 2020. *The Ages of Globalization: Geography, Technology, and Institutions*. New York: Columbia University Press.

Safina, Carl. 2020. *Becoming Wild: How Animal Cultures Raise Families, Create Beauty, and Achieve Peace*. New York: Henry Holt & Company.

Saini, Angela. 2017. *Inferior: How Science Got Woman Wrong—and the New Research That's Rewriting the Story*. Boston: Beacon Press.

Sapolsky, Robert M. 2017. *Behave: The Biology of Humans at Our Best and Worst*. New York: Penguin Press.

Sassenberg, Kai, and Lara Ditr. 2019. "Research in Social Psychology Changed between 2011 and 2016: Larger Sample Sizes, More Self-Report Measures, and More Online Studies." *Advances in Methods and Practices in Psychological Science* 2(2): 107–114.

Saugstad, Per. 2018. *A History of Modern Psychology*. Cambridge: Cambridge University Press.

Schabas, Margaret. 2002. "Coming Together: History of Economics as History of Science." *History of Political Economy* 34(1): 208–225.

Schabas, Margaret. 2006. *The Natural Origins of Economics*. Chicago: University of Chicago Press.

Scheel, Anne, Leonid Tiokhin, Peder Isager, and Daniel Lakens. 2020. "Why Hypothesis Testers Should Spend Less Time Testing Hypotheses." Working Paper. Available at: https://psyarxiv.com/vekpu/.

Scheidel, Walter. 2018. *The Great Leveler: Violence and the History of Inequality from the Stone Age to the Twenty-First Century*. Princeton: Princeton University Press.

Schrodt, Philip. 2014. "Seven Deadly Sins of Contemporary Quantitative Political Analysis." *Journal of Peace Research* 51(2): 287–300.

Schurz, Gerhard. 2019. *Hume's Problem Solved: The Optimality of Meta-Induction*. Cambridge, MA: MIT Press.

Schuster, Jack H., and Martin J. Finkelstein. 2006. *The Academic Faculty*. Baltimore: Johns Hopkins University Press.

Schuurman, Bart. 2020. "Research on Terrorism, 2007–2016: A Review of Data, Methods, and Authorship, Terrorism and Political Violence." *Terrorism and Political Violence* 32(5): 1011–112626.

Schwemmer, Carsten, and Oliver Wieczorek. 2019. "The Methodological Divide of Sociology: Evidence from Two Decades of Journal Publications." *Sociology* 54(1): 3–21.

Schwert, G. William. 2020. "The Remarkable Growth in Financial Economics, 1974–2020." NBER Working Paper #28198. Available at: https://www.nber.org/papers/w28198.

Scott, James C. 1998. *Seeing Like a State: How Certain Schemes to Improve the Human Condition Have Failed*. New Haven: Yale University Press.

Scott, James C. 2017. *Against the Grain: A Deep History of the Earliest States*. New Haven: Yale University Press.

Searle, John. 2010. *Making the Social World*. New York: Oxford University Press.

Segerstrale, Ullica. 2000. *Beyond the Science Wars: The Missing Discourse about Science and Society*. Albany: SUNY Press.

Sewell, William. 2005. *Logics of History: Social Theory & Social Transformation*. Chicago: University of Chicago Press.

Shapiro, Ian. 2002. "Problems, Methods, and Theories in the Study of Politics." *Political Theory* 30(4): 596–619.

Sharman, J. C. 2019. *Empires of the Weak: The Real Story of European Expansion and the Creation of the New World Order*. Princeton: Princeton University Press.

Shubin, Neil. 2020. *Some Assembly Required: Decoding Four Billion Years of Life, from Ancient Fossils to DNA*. New York: Pantheon.

Shwed, Uri, and Peter S. Bearman. 2010. "The Temporal Structure of Scientific Consensus Formation." *American Sociological Review* 75(6): 817–840.

Skidelsky, Robert. 2020. *What's Wrong with Economics?: A Primer for the Perplexed.* New Haven: Yale University Press.

Sides, John, Michael Tesler, and Lynn Vavreck. 2018. *Identity Crisis: The 2016 Presidential Campaign and the Battle for the Meaning of America.* Princeton: Princeton University Press.

Sigelman, Lee. 2006. "The Coevolution of American Political Science and the American Political Science Review." *American Political Science Review* 100(4): 463–478.

Silverberg, Helene, ed. 1998. *Gender and American Social Science: The Formative Years.* Princeton: Princeton University Press.

Simmons, Joseph P., Leif D. Nelson, and Uri Simonsohn. 2011. "False-Positive Psychology: Undisclosed Flexibility in Data Collection and Analysis Allows Presenting Anything as Significant." *Psychological Science* 22(11): 1359–1366.

Simonton, Dean Keith. 2015. "Psychology as a Science withinWithin Comte's Hypothesized Hierarchy: Empirical Investigations and Conceptual Implications." *Review of General Psychology* 19(3): 334–344.

Skidelsky, Robert. 2020. *What's Wrong with Economics?: A Primer for the Perplexed.* New Haven: Yale University Press.

Small, Mario. 2019. American Education Research Association Spencer Lecture. Available at: https://www.youtube.com/watch?v=z1Hje2syc1Y.

Smith, Neil. 1987. "Academic War over the Field of Geography: The Elimination of Geography at Harvard, 1947–1951." *Annals of the Association of American Geographers* 77(2): 155–172.

Smith, Roger. 1998. "The Big Picture: Writing Psychology into the History of the Human Sciences." *History of the Behavioral Sciences* 34(1): 1–13.

Smithsimon, Gregory. 2018. *Cause and How It Doesn't Always Equal Effect.* Brooklyn, NY: Melville House.

Soloman, Steven, and Philip Fernbach. 2017. *The Knowledge Illusion: Why We Never Think Alone.* New York: Macmillan.

Solovey, Mark. 2001. "Science and the State during the Cold War: Blurred Boundaries and a Contested Legacy." *Social Studies of Science* 31(2): 165–170.

Solovey, Mark. 2020. *Social Science for What?: Battles over Public Funding for the "Other Sciences" at the National Science Foundation.* Cambridge, MA: MIT Press.

Solovey, Mark, and Hamilton Cravens, eds. 2012. *Cold War Social Science: Knowledge Production, Liberal Democracy, and Human Nature.* New York: Palgrave.

Soss, Joe, and Vesla Weaver. 2017. "Police Are Our Government: Politics, Political Science, and the Policing of Race-Class Subjugated Communities." *Annual Review of Political Science* 20: 565–591.

Spanos, Aris. 2018. "The Replication Crises and the Trustworthiness of Empirical Evidence." Available at: https://editorialexpress.com/cgi-bin/conference/download.cgi?db_name=IAAE2019&paper_id=59.

Spiegelhalter, David. 2019. *The Art of Statistics: How to Learn from Data.* London: Pelican Books.

Stasavage, David. 2020. *The Decline and Rise of Democracy: A Global History from Antiquity to Today.* Princeton: Princeton University Press.

Staub, Michael. 2011. *Madness Is Civilization: When the Diagnosis Was Social, 1948–1980.* Chicago: University of Chicago Press.

Staub, Michael E. 2018. *The Mismeasure of Minds: Debating Race and Intelligence between Brown and "The Bell Curve."* Chapel Hill: University of North Carolina Press.

):Stehr, Nico, and Volker Meja, eds. 2005. *Society and Knowledge: Contemporary Perspectives in the Sociology of Knowledge and Science.* New York: Routledge.

Stephan, Paula. 2015. *How Economics Drives Science.* Cambridge, MA: Harvard University Press.

Stimson, James A., and Emily Wager. 2020. *Converging on Truth: A Dynamic Perspective on Factual Debates in American Public Opinion.* New York: Cambridge University Press.

Stoker, Laura, and M. Kent Jennings. 2013. "Life-Cycle Transitions and Political Participation: The Case of Marriage." *American Political Science Review* 89(2): 421–433.

Stokes, Leah. 2020. *Short-Circuiting Policy: Interest Groups and the Battle over Clean Energy and Climate Policy in the American States.* New York: Oxford University Press.

Strathern, Marilyn. 1997. "Improving Ratings: Audit in the British University System." *European Review* 5(3): 305–321.

Strogatz, Steven. 2019. *Infinite Powers: How Calculus Reveals the Secrets of the Universe.* New York: Houghton Mifflin Harcourt.

Sunstein, Cass. 2018. *The Cost-Benefit Revolution.* Cambridge, MA: MIT Press.

Swidler, Ann, and Jorge Arditi. 1994. "New Sociology of Knowledge." *Annual Review of Sociology* 20: 305–329.

Tetlock, Philip, and Dan Gardner. 2015. *Superforecasting: The Art and Science of Prediction.* New York: Random House.

Tetlock, Phillip E., and Gregory Mitchell. 2009. "A Renewed Plea for Adversarial Collaboration." In *Research in Organizational Behavior*, vol. 29, edited by B. M. Staw and A. Brief, 71–72. New York: Elsevier.

Thomas, Diana W., and Michael D. Thomas. 2020. "Behavioral Symmetry, Rent Seeking, and the Republic of Science." *Public Choice* 183: 443–459.

Thomas, George. 2014. *The Founders and the Idea of a National University.* New York: Cambridge University Press.

Tierney, John, and Roy F. Baumeister. 2019. *The Power of Bad: How the Negativity Effect Rules Us and How We Can Rule It.* New York: Penguin Press.

Tomasello, Michael. 2019. *Becoming Human: A Theory of Ontogeny.* Cambridge, MA: Belknap Press.

Tropo, Greg. 2019. "'Neuromyth' or Helpful Model?" Inside Higher Ed. Available at: https://www.insidehighered.com/news/2019/01/09/learning-styles-debate-its-instructors-vs-psychologists.

Tversky, Barbara. 2019. *Mind in Motion: How Action Shapes Thought.* New York: Basic Books.

Tyson, Charlie. 2019. "A Legendary Scientist Sounds Off on the Trouble with STEM." *Chronicle of Higher Education.* 7 May.

Urbanska, Karolina, Sylvie Huet, and Serge Guimond. 2019. "Does Increased Interdisciplinary Contact among Hard and Social Scientists Help or Hinder Interdisciplinary Research?" Working Paper. Available at: https://www.researchgate.net/publication/332078647_Does_increased_interdisciplinary_contact_among_hard_and_social_scientists_help_or_hinder_interdisciplinary_research.

Urquiola, Miguel. 2020. *Markets, Minds, and Money: Why America Leads the World in University Research.* Cambridge, MA: Harvard University Press.

Utych, Stephen M. 2020. "Powerless Conservatives or Powerless Findings?" *PS: Political Science and Politics* 53(4): 741–745.

Van Bavel, Jay, Diego A. Reinero, Elizabeth Harris, Claire E. Robertson, and Philip Pärnamets. 2020. "Breaking Groupthink: Why Scientific Identity and Norms Mitigate Ideological Epistemology." *Psychological Inquiry* 31(1): 66–72.

Verhulst, Brad, and Peter K. Hatemi. 2020. "Gray's False Accusations Necessitate Establishing Standards of Evidence for Making Claims of Misconduct." *PS: Political Science and Politics* 53(4): 746–750.

Vince, Gaia. 2020. *Transcendence: How Humans Evolved through Fire, Language, Beauty, and Time.* New York: Basic Books.

Vollrath, Dietrich. 2020. *Fully Grown: Why a Stagnant Economy Is a Sign of Success.* Chicago: University of Chicago Press.

Waldfogel, Joel. 2018. *Digital Renaissance: What Data and Economics Tell Us about the Future of Popular Culture.* Princeton: Princeton University Press.

Wallerstein, Immanuel. 2004. *The Uncertainties of Knowledge.* Philadelphia: Temple University Press.

Walter, Nathan, and Riva Tukachinsky. 2019. "A Meta-Analytic Examination of the Continued Influence of Misinformation in the Face of Correction: How Powerful Is It, Why Does It Happen, and How to Stop It?" *Communication Research* 47(2): 155–177.

Walters, Ronald G., ed. 1997. *Scientific Authority and 20th-Century America*. Baltimore: Johns Hopkins University Press.

Washburn, Anthony N., Brittany E. Hanson, Matt Motyl, et al. 2018. "Why Do Some Psychology Researchers Resist Adopting Proposed Reforms to Research Practices?: A Description of Researchers' Rationales." *Advances in Methods and Practices in Psychological Science* 1(2): 166–173.

Waya, Samuel F., Allison C. Morgana, Aaron Clauseta, and Daniel B. Larremore. "The Misleading Narrative of the Canonical Faculty Productivity Trajectory." 2017. *PNAS*. Available at: https://doi.org/10.1073/pnas.1702121114.

Watts, Duncan. 2011. *Everything is Obvious: How Common Sense Fails Us*. New York: Atlantic Books.

Weber, Max. 1946. "Science as Vocation." In *From Max Weber*, translated and edited by H. H. Gert and C. Wright Mills. New York: Free Press.

Wernimont, Jacqueline. 2018. *Numbered Lives: Life and Death in Quantum Media*. Cambridge, MA: MIT Press.

Wheelan, Charles. 2013. *Naked Statistics: Stripping the Dread from the Data*. New York: W. W. Norton.

Whitcomb, Dennis, Heather Battaly, Jason Baehr, and Daniel Howard-Snyder. 2015. "Intellectual Humility: Owning Our Limitations." *Philosophy and Phenomenological Research* 94(3): 509–539.

Whitcomb, Dennis, and Alvin I. Goldman, eds. 2011. *Social Epistemology: Essential Readings*. New York: Oxford University Press.

Whitley, Richard. 1984. *The Intellectual and Social Organization of the Sciences*. New York: Oxford University Press.

Wilson, Cristina G., Thomas F. Shipley, and Alexandra K. Davatzes. 2020. "Evidence of Vulnerability to Decision Bias in Expert Field Scientists." *Applied Cognitive Psychology* 34(5): 1217–122323.

Wilson, E. O. 1998. *Consilience: The Unity of Knowledge*. New York: Vantage.

Wilson, Matthew Charles, and Carl Henrik Knutsen. 2020. "Geographic Coverage in Political Science Research." *Perspectives on Politics*. FirstView. doi:10.1017/S1537592720002509.

Wilson, Robert A. 2018. *The Eugenic Mind Project*. Cambridge, MA: MIT Press.

Wlezien, Christopher. 1995. "The Public as Thermostat: Dynamics of Preferences for Spending." *American Journal of Political Science* 39(4): 981–1000.

Wolbrecht, Christina, and J. Kevin Corder. 2020. *A Century of Votes for Women: American Elections since Suffrage*. New York: Cambridge University Press.

Wolf, Andrea. 2015. *The Invention of Nature: Alexander von Humboldt's New World*. New York: Knopf Doubleday Publishing.

.Wrangham, Richard. 2019. *The Goodness Paradox: The Strange Relationship between Virtue and Violence in Human Evolution*. New York: Pantheon.

Wray, K. Brad. 2011. *Kuhn's Evolutionary Social Epistemology*. New York: Cambridge University Press.

Wright, John Paul, Ryan T. Motz, and Timothy S. Nixon. 2019. "Political Disparities in the Academy: It's More Than Self-Selection." *Academic Questions* 32: 402–411.

Wu, Angela Xiao, and Harsh Taneja. 2020. "Platform Enclosure of Human Behavior and Its Measurement: Using Behavioral Trace Data against Platform Episteme." *New Media & Society*. In press.

Yadon, Nicole, and Mara C. Ostfeld. 2020. "Shades of Privilege: The Relationship between Skin Color and Political Attitudes among White Americans." *Political Behavior* 42: 1369–1392.

Yanofsky, Noson S. 2013. *The Outer Limits of Reason: What Science, Mathematics, and Logic Cannot Tell Us*. Cambridge, MA: MIT Press.

Yarkoni, Tal. 2020. "The Generalizability Crisis." Working Paper. Available at: https://psyarxiv.
    com/jqw35.

Zhou, Haotian, Xilin Li, and Jessica Sim. 2019. "Conflating Temporal Advancement and Epistemic
    Advancement: The Progression Bias in Judgment and Decision Making." *Personality and
    Social Psychology Bulletin* 45(11): 1563–157979.

Zuckerman, Gregory. 2019. *The Man Who Solved the Market: How Jim Simons Launched the Quant
    Revolution.* New York: Portfolio.

INDEX